SAGE was founded in 1965 by Sara Miller McCune to support the dissemination of usable knowledge by publishing innovative and high-quality research and teaching content. Today, we publish more than 750 journals, including those of more than 300 learned societies, more than 800 new books per year, and a growing range of library products including archives, data, case studies, reports, conference highlights, and video. SAGE remains majority-owned by our founder, and on her passing will become owned by a charitable trust that secures our continued independence.

Los Angeles | London | Washington DC | New Delhi | Singapore

Becoming Minority

Becoming Minority

How Discourses and Policies Produce Minorities in Europe and India

Edited by
Jyotirmaya Tripathy
Sudarsan Padmanabhan

www.sagepublications.com
Los Angeles • London • New Delhi • Singapore • Washington DC

First published in 2014 by

 SAGE Publications India Pvt Ltd
B1/I-1 Mohan Cooperative Industrial Area
Mathura Road, New Delhi 110 044, India
www.sagepub.in

SAGE Publications Inc
2455 Teller Road
Thousand Oaks, California 91320, USA

SAGE Publications Ltd
1 Oliver's Yard, 55 City Road
London EC1Y 1SP, United Kingdom

SAGE Publications Asia-Pacific Pte Ltd
3 Church Street
#10-04 Samsung Hub
Singapore 049483

Published by Vivek Mehra for SAGE Publications India Pvt Ltd, typeset at 10/13 Berkeley by Diligent Typesetter, Delhi and printed at Saurabh Printers Pvt Ltd, New Delhi.

Library of Congress Cataloging-in-Publication Data

Becoming minority : how discourses and policies produce minorities in India and Europe / edited by Jyotirmaya Tripathy and Sudarsan Padmanabhan.
    pages cm
    Includes bibliographical references and index.
    1. Minorities—Government   policy—India—History. 2.   Minorities—Government   policy—Europe—History. 3.   Ethnicity—Political   aspects—India—History. 4. Ethnicity—Political aspects—Europe—History. 5. Discourse analysis,   Narrative—Political   aspects—India—History. 6.   Discourse analysis,   Narrative—Political   aspects—Europe—History. 7.   India—Ethnic relations—History. 8.   Europe—Ethnic relations—History. 9.   India—Social policy. 10. Europe—Social policy. I. Tripathy, Jyotirmaya. II. Padmanabhan, Sudarsan.
    DS430.B43   305.800954—dc23   2014   2014028110

ISBN: 978-93-515-0035-3 (HB)

The SAGE Team: Rudra Narayan, Neha Sharma, Rajib Chatterjee, and Dally Verghese

For

Uwe Skoda

Our *Indian* friend in Europe

Thank you for choosing a SAGE product! If you have any comment, observation or feedback, I would like to personally hear from you. Please write to me at contactceo@sagepub.in

—Vivek Mehra, Managing Director and CEO,
SAGE Publications India Pvt Ltd, New Delhi

Bulk Sales

SAGE India offers special discounts for purchase of books in bulk. We also make available special imprints and excerpts from our books on demand.

For orders and enquiries, write to us at

Marketing Department
SAGE Publications India Pvt Ltd
B1/I-1, Mohan Cooperative Industrial Area
Mathura Road, Post Bag 7
New Delhi 110044, India
E-mail us at marketing@sagepub.in

Get to know more about SAGE, be invited to SAGE events, get on our mailing list. Write today to marketing@sagepub.in

This book is also available as an e-book.

Contents

Preface

The term minority is very fecund. It is all at once already constructed, in the process of being constructed, and yet to be constructed. It is not merely a theory or praxis, but also a discourse. One could pose several questions as to what leads to the construction of minority. Is the conception of minority a revolt against the tyranny of the universal that perennially attempts to camouflage the interstices? Or is it a clash of social imaginaries? Is it a postcolonial conundrum or a malign genie created by the nation state, the pride of modernity? Is it a given essence or a Sisyphean quest for that essence? Is a conception of minority–majority anachronistic in the postmodern/postnational epoch?

This volume is an endeavor to address some of the questions that animate current scholarship on minority and minoritization. We had initiated such an intervention in our anthology titled *The Democratic Predicament: Cultural Diversity in Europe and India* (2013) which offered a critical rethinking of democracy and multiculturalism, and implicated the latter not just in the preservation, but also in the production, of cultural diversity. We had touched upon the minority subject formation in Europe and India as an interpellative exercise through which minority is minoritized. The present volume is intended to expand those ideas and trace the processes through which minorities perform as minorities—their discursive formation, narrativization, and representation. It is thus evident that the book moves away from an uncritical understanding of the term minority as a container of some unchanging core ideals, and leads to a framework where minority comes into existence in the very act of representation. Our engagement is less with minority culture and more with the congealing of that culture and the way culture becomes a carrier of group identity and politics. Minority here is not to be seen as a stable practice of timeless values that are ahistorical and acultural, but as a discursive product to articulate a different and resistant experience.

Most theorists on minority, ethnic, or religious identity treat the minority–majority categories as mere binary opposition, but rarely treat them as constructed and discursive formations. In countries such as India, there was a lot of contestation and negotiation of minority–majority identities even after the caste system became hypostatized. The colonial imposition of the nation-state framework severed traditional and historical links between communities that had given rise to schisms within and without communities hitherto existing together for centuries. Though it is simplistic to believe that there existed a utopian state of deliberative and participatory democracy in the modern sense of the term, one cannot presume eons of raging Hobbesian state of war in which savages were killing each other. In many postcolonial nations in the Third World and post-World War II divisions of Eastern European states, the binary opposition between various religious and ethnic communities deepened further due to the arbitrary imposition of the nation-state framework combined with an unproblematic understanding of multicultural democracy that will make a state inclusive. However, it would be foolhardy to believe that there was an originary moment in the formation of minority identity and difference, or that the making of such an identity is complete. While agreeing with the aforementioned historical periods in the production of minority difference, we would like to propose here that the process of becoming minority will continue, and that such becoming will not be autonomous of our political cultures and their expediencies.

Borrowing from Bhabha (discussed later in Chapter 1), we may say that more often than not, the minority–majority distinction in both popular and academic literature is more pedagogical than performative, which makes the entire discourse shaky and vulnerable. What Bhabha identifies as the vulnerability of a discourse is its inability to confront its own historical contingency. In a minority–majority discourse, there is a split narrative of identities. Such a split in the narratives of national identities is classified as the pedagogical and the performative. The pedagogical totalizes people whose social and political identities are defined in terms of a homogeneous and consensual community. On the other hand, the performative is specific and addresses unequal interests and identities within a population, and their ways of living preestablished categories. What is germane to the crux of the discussion in this volume is whether the concept of minority is self-imagined or externally imposed, or both. This is where an understanding of split narrative of national identities assumes tremendous importance. This volume attempts to show that there is an irresolvable tension between the pedagogical and the performative narratives which obscures a nuanced understanding of the concept of minority.

The title of the book may sound a little intriguing because of the term "becoming," used here as a verb rather than an adjective, which refers to the ways through which minorities are ascribed an identity and also identify themselves as minorities. This "becoming" nature of minorities and their performativity contest the conventional wisdom of understanding minority as a fixed essence that cannot be questioned or debated. Our thesis is apparently provocative, given that the present time of democracy, in varying degrees, has accepted the politics of recognition as a gateway to inclusive polity. One may dismiss our "becoming" thesis on the ground that minority right has not only been acknowledged by democracies, but also has been made the basis of affirmative policies that protect minority religion, culture, language, and so on. Why then this debate which has no future in terms of policy implications?

We would like to respond that policies are historical and are made on the basis of a particular type of analysis that interprets contemporary times in a certain way. If multiculturalism was the toast of many European states, now we see a visible backlash against such projects. Similarly, Indian democracy has witnessed a visible anxiety, if not outright rejection, of minority politics (often derided as minority appeasement) that has affected social cohesion. However, we are not here to make any value judgment on the propriety or suspicion of such projects, nor do we intend to propose the need for such a backlash vis-à-vis minority rights. Our intention is modest, and is confined to the need for some kind of academic honesty while debating minority culture and the rights based on it. We see our aim not as one of constructing rights on the basis of particular cultures, but of deconstructing the idea of culture itself which makes the debate on minority rights much more problematic.

It is because of this reason that we use a poststructuralist framework to address minority difference that challenges the existence of origin and core. The questions we are interested in are: How does one come to see oneself as minor?; how is he perceived as a minor?; how is the knowledge of minority produced?; what are the narrative techniques that are used to weave minority identity?; whether minority identity exists before its representation; and so on. The reader may well understand that here we are interested in the delivery of minority knowledge and the stylization of minority subjects in becoming a minority category.

Unfortunately, the academic community has not responded to the constructed nature of minority identity, though a large body of such literature already exists on race, ethnicity, and gender. Similar literature also exists on the invention of majority Hindu culture or majority "white" ways of life. But academic theorizing has not sufficiently addressed the possibility of construction of minority culture that can complicate the question of minority rights. When we look at the academic output on minority studies from a constructivist framework, it does not come as a surprise that there has not been any significant effort (barring a few stray attempts) to raise these issues which are routinely discussed and debated in cultural studies. We imagine this book to bring some freshness in the area of minority studies, or what we call critical minority studies, by moving away from predictable, repetitive, routinized academic enterprises which see minority redemption in democracy and multiculturalism.

The Design of the Book

The book draws upon European and Indian experiences of cultural diversities to address the issues raised above. Europe and India are two of the most culturally diverse regions in the world and engage with diversity from within a democratic framework. Though we acknowledge different historicities in terms of the minority question in Europe and India, our poststructuralist template is aimed at creating a common platform from where both Europe and India can articulate themselves vis-à-vis their minority practices. The first part of this book, "The Making of Minority," consists of chapters raising theoretical/conceptual questions relating to minority identity formation. The second part, "The European Experience," draws from specific historical realities or case studies pertaining to Europe, and the third part, "The Indian Experience," engages with material experiences of India. These parts, however, are not intended as watertight compartments, but as a convenient way of structuring the anthology. In varying degrees, all the chapters reinforce our central thesis of "becoming minority."

Chapter 1 by the present editors historicizes minority politics by locating the latter in post-Cold War Europe and post-independence India. It offers a framework which shifts the attention away from an essential notion of minority identity to the processes through which minorities recognize themselves as minority. Drawing from poststructuralist vocabulary, the authors argue that minority as a politically invested term makes sense in representation which interpellates and inserts minorities into the larger domain of democratic multicultural discourse, and it is during these moments that minorities perform themselves as minorities. Chapter 2 by Barbara Franz continues with the need for historicizing the minority desire for recognition and tells us how the politics of naming and labeling are crucial for membership of groups. This chapter focuses on the minorities in Central Europe, and emphasizes the importance of specific ethnic minorities within the processes that led to the creation of modern nation states. Chapter 3 by Lajwanti Chatani attempts to understand the trend of asserting minority identity by various identity groups. It explores the underlying conceptual framework of justice on which the rights of minorities rest, but argues that justice can be discursive, and so any attempt to freeze it as absolute would rid it of its empowering credo.

The second part opens with Chapter 4 by Abdoulaye Gueye, which seeks to explain the manufacturing of racial minority, with a particular emphasis upon blackness in contemporary France, and argues that blackness is less an essence than a sociological outcome. The formation of blackness operates at the intersection of three major realms of meanings: propaganda discourse, belief, and material production. In other words, to bring blackness into existence is to say that it is real, to make people believe so, and to display facts supporting and fueling this belief. Chapter 5 by Ulf Mörkenstam argues that the construction of indigenous peoples in the national discourse of the countries in which they live is of importance in the justification of a continued colonization.

To substantiate that argument, the author analyzes Swedish Sámi politics during the current century with a specific focus on how the indigenous Sámi people have been constructed in discourse.

Chapter 6 by Sherrill Stroschein highlights the role of discursive and symbolic resources in political attempts at secession. The chapter outlines how the 1997 devolution for Scotland has provided an institutional resource for the Scottish National Movement. However, the author believes that the institutions of devolution did not only serve as material and infrastructural resource; they also provided a symbolic and ideational context for rhetorical and discursive disputes with the Conservative–Liberal Democrat British government established in Westminster in 2010. Chapter 7 by Apostolos Agnantopoulos maps the rivalry between the Greek-Orthodox majority and a Turkish/Muslim minority in Western Thrace, a region on the northeast border of Greece. This chapter argues that this enduring tension can be attributed to two factors: the prevalence of an exclusionary nation-state identity which has prevented the full internalization of European norms on minority protection, and the fact that the application of multicultural principles can be problematic, when minority issues are intertwined with competing nationalist claims and acute security concerns.

Chapter 8 by Peter Hervik looks at the drastic shift in the construction of minority others that came with the emergence of neonationalism, neoracism, and radical right populism in the post-1989 world. Through an analysis of a political philosophy launched in Denmark in the 1990s called the "Cultural War of Values," it argues that the social construction of thick minority identities can only be understood in relation to the cultural war of value strategy aimed at domestic political opponents. Chapter 9 by Paul Mutsaers, Hans Siebers, and Arie de Ruijter seeks to comprehend how matters of ethnicity, politics, and economy interrelate in The Netherlands by looking at the direct impact of migrant-hostile politics on ethnic boundaries on the labor market and in educational settings. The authors show that migrant-hostile policies and dominant discourses are complicit in turning such spaces into fertile breeding grounds of what they call "ethno-manufacturing". Chapter 10 by Gëzim Alpion proposes that Enoch Powell's speeches in the late 1960s reflected a "traditional" stance toward immigrants as well as a concern about the demographic changes which were taking place in England from the mid-1950s. It contends that the emphasis that Powell put on communalism was a casus belli for his eugenic solution to the immigration problem, and approaches his castigation by the British elites as a "timely" intervention to curb the rise of "ethnic" nationalism in England. The chapter is intended as a critique of Powell's essentialist views on ethnicity.

We turn to the third part with Chapter 11 by Bishnu N. Mohapatra. The chapter gathers many themes, evokes many ideological contestations, and conjures up conflicting visions about the state and nation. It looks at the "minority question" from the vantage points of institutions, policies, and larger governmental technologies. It also analyzes the historical contexts through which discourses on "minorities" evolved in India. The larger argument in this chapter is that as entities of history and government policies, minority groups experience their identities and their existence as constantly changing, often slippery, and greatly subjected to past historical trajectories. Chapter 12 by Mohamed Mehdi discusses the concept of hurt religious feelings and the corresponding politics of outrage in relation to what it means to be Muslim in the Indian context. The chapter draws a connection between the legal category of hurt religious feelings, its use in particular cases, and its assumptions about the nature of religious feeling. It also examines the particular picture of the emotional subject that emerges, and its implications for an emancipatory politics. Chapter 13 by Malavika Menon takes us back in time and tells us how the members drafting the Indian Constitution, while giving Indian minorities certain rights, stopped short of addressing the crucial question as to who is a minority. She addresses this question through the discursive practices of select Supreme Court cases and analyzes how they have impacted the concern of established minority communities in India.

Chapter 14 by Shireen Mirza links urban space and *Waqf* properties to describe the creation of a segregated Shi'a Muslim quadrant in Hyderabad's old city. Through this, it describes the process of constructing homogeneous Muslim space as well as the epistemic emergence of religious minority as a category. It also argues that the category of the minority, while homogenizing identities, can also be enabling when seen in relation to community space and collective experience. Chapter 15 by Anjana Raghavan is an attempt to expand the scope of minority by locating the latter within oppositional narratives. She primarily deals with the ideological construction and production of minor-ness, both as a category and an identity marker vis-à-vis the mythologized and origin narratives of Tamil identity. Her aim is to create a space to articulate these issues through the selective exploration of Tamil identity narratives by both their creators as well as their dissenters.

Jyotirmaya Tripathy
Sudarsan Padmanabhan

Acknowledgments

An edited volume such as this is a collective and participatory exercise which makes an otherwise ritualistic acknowledgment more meaningful. As we write this part, we are filled with gratitude to the European Commission which provided financial assistance in 2009 to start the Centre for Comparative European Union Studies in the Department of Humanities and Social Sciences, IIT Madras. The Centre in turn created and sustained interest in us to engage with Europe and India from a comparative framework which continues till date. Our former Head of Department, V. R. Muraleedharan, had played a crucial role in planning the Centre by forming a core group which included the present editors. Our deepest gratitude goes to him.

This book was conceived during our stay in the guest house of Aarhus University, Denmark, when we were there as Visiting Fellows in 2010. Now that the book has become a reality, we are reminded of the warmth and care we received from Aarhus University friends, particularly Uwe Skoda and Niels Brimnes. As we visited various European universities, we received immense support from Jakub Zajaczkowski (Warsaw University), Rahul Rao (SOAS, London), Luciano Segreto (University of Florence), Riva Kastoryano (SciencesPo, Paris), Beate Zimpelmann (Hochschule Bremen, Germany), Gerard Delanty (University of Sussex), Jean-Philippe Imbert, Aileen Pearson-Evans, and Debbie Ging (Dublin City University), and many others. Without their encouragement, this book would have been poorer.

The debt incurred at home is equally great, particularly from our Institute colleagues and students who gave us the opportunity to respond critically to the minority question and its various implications. Though many discussions were informal in nature, they made us conscious of the contested terrain of minority discourse. We would like to thank Umakant Dash, R. Swarnalatha, S. Mohan, and other colleagues.

We are immensely grateful to all our contributors who were flexible enough to adapt to the timeline set by us. We cannot thank them enough for having given us the opportunity to learn from them and for helping us to create a critical mass in relation to critical minority studies. This book is a tribute to all of them.

We had the privilege of having wonderful families who always understood, and to some extent appreciated, our frequent absence from home. We thank Sanghamitra, Akankhya, and Hema for their constant support which, though non-academic, always made the difference.

Finally, and very importantly, we are thankful to Rudra Narayan Sharma of SAGE Publications for his commitment to the project in spite of frequent delays from our side.

Jyotirmaya Tripathy
Sudarsan Padmanabhan

PART 1
The Making of Minority

1

Becoming a Minority Category*

Jyotirmaya Tripathy and
Sudarsan Padmanabhan

Situating the Subject[1]

Let us start with a rhetorical question. When did minority emerge? Or to make it simple, how did minority become a category for political analysis, policy research, and later, popular discourses? Or simpler still, how did minority become minority?

Though minority as a numerical adjective may have existed all along, the kind of political investment we have made in this term is fairly recent, and so must be seen in its historicity. It was sometime after the freedom from the British in India and after the collapse of communism in Europe that minority stopped being a numerical (or even religious, linguistic/ethnic) marker and emerged as a signifier of contemporary politics that claimed to be free from narrow understandings of nationalism. Minority as we understand today is, thus, a historical product—and almost an invention—to legitimate a new way of looking at citizenship that relies

---

* The aim of this chapter is twofold. It creates a post-structuralist/constructivist framework to engage with the idea of minority that makes the latter a performative construct. It is also intended as a reference point for the following chapters while inviting the readers to challenge the givenness of minority.

on a classificatory logic of its own, a logic that will permeate all political and social knowledge. The production of minority in governmental
and intergovernmental discourses was so timely and potent that as an
ascriptive template, minority became a knowledge field, and later an
experiential and material category.

Europe's engagement with the minority question was conditioned
by the imperatives of the fall of communism, conflicts in the Balkans
and Caucasus, and mass migration from formerly communist states
of Europe. Though the end of World War II (WW II) followed by the
decolonization of Asian and African states brought a significant number of migrants to Europe, the latter had not approached these migrant
groups from within a legal multicultural framework. The large wave of
migrants to European countries, however, came some 40 years ago and
consisted mainly of guest workers, though in recent years many migrants
have often been represented as "refugees" or "asylum seekers." In the
beginning, Europe was not very responsive to the needs of its minorities
or minorities elsewhere; on the contrary, it had supplied arms to authoritarian regimes in Africa and Asia to suppress minority demands.

Kymlicka (2008) believes that minority rights were virtually unknown
in Europe and that the sudden interest in minority affairs was the result
of three reasons: humanitarianism, self-interest, and ideology, which
resulted in the internationalization of minority rights. Maybe there was
some genuine humanitarian concern among the Western powers to end
the suffering of minorities. But when the euphoria over the end of the
Cold War was soon replaced by the fear of endless ethnic strife and the
return of communism, there was an increasing realization that sustained
ethnic violence would result in the large-scale influx of refugees from
problem areas to Western Europe. Combined with this practical problem is the belief in Western Europe that postcommunist European states
should evolve to manage their diversity, and for that to happen, Western
Europe must provide an ideal working model. It was a test case for the
success of Europe's liberal democracy and a new idea of Europe which is
inclusive and egalitarian.

What is important to note here is the approach to the minority question in a particular post-Cold War vision of the world that required a
new kind of politics. It is this politics which gave us a concept, and produced the idea of minority as a site of rights to such an extent that minority

will not be discussed outside this politics hereafter. The 1990 Conference on Security and Cooperation in Europe in Copenhagen declared that "the participating States note the efforts undertaken to protect and create conditions for the promotion of the ethnic, cultural, linguistic, and religious identity of certain national minorities by establishing… appropriate local or autonomous administrations" (Kymlicka 2008, 18). It is at this juncture that organizations like the Council of Europe or the Organization for Security and Cooperation in Europe came into existence. By 1999, the European Council in its Millennium Declaration had proposed that "the Union's citizens are bound together by common values such as freedom, tolerance, equality, solidarity, and cultural diversity."

India's response to minority rights through a secular polity was the product of post-independence and post-partition conditions. Prime Minister Nehru had imagined an India which is progressive, modern, scientific, and secular by breaking away from an idea of India that is predicated on Hindu cultural nationalism, something which was not only propagated by Hindu revival groups but also by what Nehru believed to be Gandhi's revivalism. Against the wishes of other Congress leaders like K. M. Munshi and Sardar Patel, Nehru was determined to send a clear signal to India's minorities that their culture and religion would not only be protected, but also be promoted which would produce an idea of India different from the idea of a theocratic Pakistan. Similarly, the linguistic division of India into states created in its trail large chunks of linguistic minorities living in other language states. So, Article 29(1) of the Indian Constitution decreed that any group of people residing in the Indian territory having a distinct language or culture will have the right to conserve the same. Similarly, Article 30 guaranteed that linguistic and religious minorities have the right to establish and administer educational institutions of their choice. Chandhoke (1999) has painstakingly shown the way the Constituent Assembly debated and discussed minority rights and produced arguments and counter arguments as to what constitutes minority rights. We can argue that these rights were not legislated because of any universal understanding of minority and rights, but because of a particular type of analysis in a given context. Perhaps, it is because of this historical and discursive nature that minority rights are understood and formalized differently in different places.

It would not be proper to say that minority consciousness did not exist before the legislation of minority rights, or that it is pure fiction. However, the earlier minority consciousness was one of marginalization, ghettoization, or a kind of life lived on the edge. But the material conditions prevailing after 1947 in India and 1989 in Europe created a scenario where the minority problem generated a near consensus that it can be a label of solidarity and a site of rights and privileges. The narrative strategies of post-Cold War politics and Indian independence did articulate and construct an apparently stable consciousness out of multiple and contradictory ways of life. It is in the articulation of a different notion of citizenship which included religious, linguistic, and cultural differences that a new minority political consciousness was born. This consciousness not only prescribed majority understanding of minority, but also minority understanding of themselves. It is this politics that congealed, codified, and prescribed resistant ways of living outside the assimilative majority culture and also empowered the minority to say no to the former's homogenizing impulse.

This project sought to heal the wounds that minorities had suffered; at the same time, it promised to retain those scars that will not only be a source of common identity, but also a reminder to the majority of the latter's excesses. Being minor did not mean invisibility any longer; rather a celebration of diversity, something that can be made public, discussed, even flaunted. Now it was not minority which needed a responsive system for its protection; rather, it was the democratic state which needed minority for its legitimacy. It is this democratic multicultural narrative that produced minority as we know it today, not by providing an epistemic access to the so-called minority core, but in the very act of representation. In short, minority was minoritized.

We have introduced the beginning of institutionalization of minority rights in Europe and India. The rest of the chapter offers a critique of mainstream theorizing on minority rights and proposes a poststructuralist approach to minority difference. The first section, in two parts, critically engages with established theories of minority culture as a fact of nature and seeks to expose their simplistic assumptions. The second section, again in two parts, proposes a nuanced understanding of minority culture by drawing from poststructuralist/constructivist insights to understand minority identity formation. The concluding part reiterates the productive nature of such an attempt. We would like to add here that for the sake of focus and clarity we would be engaging with Muslim difference as an indicator of the larger minority question, and that the representation of the minority subject as masculine in the course of the chapter has been done for the sake of convenience.

Section I

The Authentic Minority

Fundamental to minority difference is the prior existence of a set of core values forming some sort of essence which has survived temporal and spatial changes, and which the minor subject should reflect or carry. Let us see how ingrained is this notion of an essential minority culture in the so-called progressive and egalitarian political theory. It would be appropriate to start with Taylor (1994) who has influenced a generation of political theorists and commentators, and whose writing has become the framework for minority rights in practice. Moving away from the age-old idea of the individual as a carrier of rights, Taylor fervently pleads for a kind of group identity that can reverse negative stereotypes associated with minorities. After seeing an intrinsic connection between identity and recognition, he argues that identities are often shaped by the way we are perceived by others. He also sees identity as "a person's understanding of who they are" and goes on to argue that one's identity is "partly shaped by recognition or its absence, often by the misrecognition of others" (ibid., 25). One assumes that the discussion will engage with the question of ascription, its temporality, and its generative capacity through representation. However, after establishing the centrality of recognition as constitutive of minority identity, Taylor sees identity as "fundamental defining characteristics as a human being" (ibid.), thereby freezing identity as an unchanging and timeless essence, though one would have imagined a discussion on the slippery notion of subjectivity that is often shaped by recognition or misrecognition.

One does not see any critical engagement with this "politics of recognition," particularly with the question "recognition of what?". Taylor's project of recognition which he calls "a vital human need" (ibid., 26) is only concerned with the idea of minority culture as a finished product and an ahistorical essence. Since Taylor is more concerned with a positive perception of minority culture, he claims that this is to be seen as a shift from the ancient notion of honor to the "modern notion of dignity" (Taylor 1994, 27) which had its origin in the 18th century, a "notion that human beings are endowed with a moral sense" (ibid., 28). Borrowing from Rousseau, he argues that morality is to follow "a voice of nature within us" (ibid., 29) which gives us "an intuitive feeling for what is right and wrong" (ibid., 28). What is clearly visible here is the idea of the individual as a moral agent who has to recognize his inner voice or authenticity and what Taylor believes (drawing from Herder) the "original way of being human" (ibid., 30).

From here, Taylor suddenly moves from individual authenticity—that relies on insulating the individual from the outside world of majority—to group identity—that can only be fulfilled by interacting with other group members. This somehow compromises Taylor's position on authenticity and leads to a sense of self that is communitarian. The individual core suddenly appears to be something which was actually an effect of one's group affiliation, and the ideal of authenticity turns out to be conformity with the group: "Just like individuals, a *Volk* should be true to itself, that is, its own culture" (ibid., 31). Taylor then moves to the dialogic nature of human life and adds that "discovering my own identity does not mean that I work it out in isolation, but that I negotiate it through dialogue" (ibid., 34). For Taylor, formal equality is not enough to protect the minority from the outside world of majority that tries to produce minorities in the majority's image. Along with a formal notion of equality, Taylor introduces a substantive notion of inclusiveness by offering a politics of difference where one may actively decide to stay different and yet demand equal respect.

It is this difference which becomes the basis of a new politics. Taylor believes that it is the politics of difference (distinguished from the politics of equal dignity where everybody is treated equally) which should be the basis for a differential treatment that will make minorities confident that their culture will survive the onslaught of majority culture. Here, Taylor argues that assimilation is "the cardinal sin against the ideal of authenticity" (ibid., 38). One of the effects of the politics of difference is not only differential treatment for the minority, but also a kind of reverse discrimination that can be practiced as a temporary measure so as to help create a level playing field. Earlier, Kymlicka (1989) had proposed more resources for the aboriginal people of Canada. But according to Taylor, Kymlicka fails to do justice to the very idea of difference that is instrumental for the aborigines' survival. So Taylor proposes "to maintain and cherish distinctness, not just now but for ever" (1994, 40).

Chandhoke, in her defense of minority rights, approaches minority rights from the vantage point of democracy rather than secularism (1999, 4). Pitching for the preservation of minority culture, Chandhoke favors multicultural policies to "safeguard minority identities through the grant of cultural rights" (ibid., 8) which are over and above universal rights which everybody enjoys. Rejecting the conflict between individual and group rights, she says that we should "think of group rights 'as a precondition for individual rights'" (ibid., 11, emphasis original). She defines minority as a group whose characteristics "differ from the majority group and more importantly, it wishes to preserve these characteristics" (ibid., 26). The questions that are left unanswered are: What are these characteristics that need to be preserved? Who decides what these characteristics are? What agentic notion does it provide to individuals? Chandhoke, in her persuasive style, claims that even though minorities have other identities, they come to mobilize around their minority status when they feel marginalized. This sense of marginalization propels them to privilege their minority experience over other experiences. In this solidarity building, difference from the majority must be maximized and the internal differences within them neutralized.

Defenders of group identity tell us that individuals are socially constituted and liberals remind us that commitment to shared values can be achieved through reflection and choice, acts that imply freedom. Kymlicka (2007) tries to balance the two saying that premises of liberals and communitarians cannot be applied in multicultural societies. Instead, he proposes that commitment to community should be tempered by a commitment to the values of liberal individualism. He believes that minority rights can be justified from within liberal democratic theory. Chandhoke (1999) similarly tries to approach minority rights from the framework of democracy rather than secularism. What is ignored is that minority rights are constant attempts at homogenization that ignores differences in class, region, gender, etc. Because of these differences, there is a very serious epistemological danger in the general claim made on behalf of disempowered groups like minority. We may say that such emancipatory claims are less about minority, and more about the group that represents minority as powerless. The minority subject, thus, is an effect of the dominant discourse of democracy and multiculturalism.

Narratives of Minority Consciousness

One of the foundations on which strong multiculturalism is based is the prior existence of minority essence which exists before the individual. The minor, by his own volition and free will, decides to subject himself to that essence to be a minority subject. de Certeau (1997) sees in multicultural states a kind of ethnographic impulse to make minority cultures objects of knowledge. Interestingly, such knowledge does not acknowledge the process of its formation. Referring to Bretons, de Certeau argues that the ethnic group does not exist outside this ethnographic knowledge, "for the a priori of the ethnological method 'surpasses' the 'act' by which Bretons become Bretons and speak" (ibid., 76, emphasis original). The totalizing knowledge of the democratic state produces minority authenticity, and assigns them the so-called distinct characteristics, but fails to acknowledge the process through which a group becomes an object of knowledge.

Here, a reference to Bilgrami's (1995) ideas may be rewarding which presents identity as subject position that is often ascribed to or which we create for ourselves. It is a situation which can provide certain limited options to an individual in terms of identification that may have nothing to do with the ideal of authenticity. Bilgrami says, "It is obvious of course that being born a Muslim is neither a necessary nor a sufficient condition for having a Muslim identity" (ibid., 199). In this connection, reference may be made to the constructivist insights of Benhabib (2002) who understood the need for an interlocutor to identify oneself. The presence of such an interlocutor creates a situation where one must identify oneself as one and not many: "To be and to become a self is to insert oneself into webs of interlocution; it is to know how to answer when one is addressed and to know how to address others" (ibid., 15). But these situations are often out of our control and we are never free to create such situations. In fact, these situations, in de Beauvoir's (1949) terms, are something which we confront as facticity, not having the freedom to choose them. It prompts Benhabib to argue that "we never really 'insert' ourselves, but rather are 'thrown' into these webs of interlocution" (2002, 15, emphasis original).

Agency in this context is not about some mythical free will operating outside community. One continues to live as minority as long as one imagines his story as part of the larger narrative of community. Benhabib recognizes that these master narratives may give some freedom to choose one's personal stories, but do not allow a story that can erode the truth claims of the master story. If one goes against the master story in casting oneself as a subject, "one may run the risk of becoming an outcast or a convert, a marginal figure or a deserter of the tribe" (Benhabib 2002). Benhabib's discomfort with such essentialist/multiculturalist understanding of culture is that it creates "an overly socialized vision of the self" (ibid., 16).

It can be said that what we call authenticity can be context-specific, which cannot and should not erase the argumentative nature of all religions/cultures. Here, we would like to propose that between "being minority" and "having a minority identity," it is the latter which often has a larger stake in looking for something authentic that can remove competing notions of culture. Parekh (2006) captures this difference in Europe historically when he says that "the Islam of the first generation of immigrants (in Europe) is heavily folkish, oral, tied up with local culture and traditional. That of their children and grandchildren is textual, learned in mosques and schools..." (ibid., 201). The second model creates an idea of culture which is political or what Hervieu-Leger calls "belonging without believing" (in Casanova 2007, 62), and so minorities remain "already in Europe but not of Europe" (ibid., 63). Nandy also distinguishes between religion as faith and religion as ideology and argues that "the modern state always prefers to deal with religious ideologies rather than with faiths" (1998, 322–23). Bilgrami too mourns that for some "Islam is nothing short of a monolithic commitment, overriding all other commitments, whenever history or personal encounter poses a conflict" (1995, 200).

If group association helps develop a positive image of the self and successfully challenges negative stereotypes, it is necessary to know what actually changes during this process of identification with other group members. How are negative images transformed into positive ones? How do the sites of negation become sites of assertion? The fact of the matter is that nothing happens except that the group member starts seeing himself through the lens of his group. This new mediated look at himself not only makes him feel worthy, but also gives him a sense of superiority. This mediation is provided by the group narrative of common origin, language, ethnicity, etc. It tells him who they are, where they came from, how there was a divine plan in their arrival, and also how they will continue to prosper against all odds. This narrative also provides them a clear cut sense of inside and outside where everything inside is morally right and everything outside is degenerate and inferior. On the authority of Anderson (1983), we may say that in these situations a particular notion of nation is born through narration.

This narrative also lures the democratic multicultural state and its intellectuals to produce minority epistemology. Intellectuals dismiss the majority for clinging to some mythical past, whereas minority is celebrated for having successfully retained that past/tradition. However, in the process of creating such monoliths out of varied minority experiences, democracy uses the concept of minority in a reductionist way without grappling with issues of power, conflict, and larger political contexts that shape minority's ability to resist marginalization. The historicity and the internal conflict involved in the making of that kernel are conveniently forgotten. The attempt to preserve culture is something that, according to Benhabib (2002), is endorsed by both conservatives and liberals. When conservatives believe that cultures should be preserved to keep them separate so that no contact (and also confusion out of that contact) is possible, progressives believe that culture should be preserved to correct the patterns of domination and oppression.

In this understanding, cultures are clearly defined wholes, bounded and having nothing in common with other such cultures, and so Benhabib believes that this is a kind of "reductionist sociology of culture" (ibid., 4). Such uncritical understanding keeps minority culture at a sufficient distance from a reasonable and viable criticism. This notion of culture "attempts to create forced unity out of diversity, coherence out of inconsistencies, and homogeneity out of narrative dissonance" (ibid., 8). It is through the narrative strategies of continuity, homogeneity, and common future that cultural identity performs itself. The contradictions of daily life and the conflicts within various groups within minority culture are presented as a unified narrative. Benhabib's attempt is to offer a constructivist alternative to normative theorizing that reifies cultures and makes them vulnerable to exploitation in their quest for recognition. Her constructivist impulse gets the best expression when she says that "culture presents itself through narratively contested accounts" (Benhabib 2002, 6).

Section II

Discourse and Interpellation

Both liberal and communitarian traditions approach the individual in different ways, one as autonomous and the other as rooted. The problem with these traditions is their inability to question the very concept of the individual which continues to remain the source of identity. A poststructuralist approach problematizes identity formation and argues that the individual is always in the process of becoming. The individual, thus, is not displaced entirely; what is displaced is the idea of a stable and secured notion of self. In this condition, we become aware of the constructive power of all languages, or as Derrida (1978) observed, "language invaded the universal problematic, the moment when ... everything became discourse" (ibid., 280). In this linguistic universe, there can be no real outside its linguistic representation. The individual we know becomes a very slippery site which is always contingent and under both assertion and erasure.

Before we proceed with the production of minorities in discourse, it will be productive to use some space to describe discourse. Foucault defined discourse as "the general domain of all statements, sometimes as an individualizable group of statements, and sometimes as a regulated practice that accounts for a number of statements" (1972, 80, emphasis added). Here, Foucault highlights the regulatory nature of utterances that give the latter some kind of meaning. This coherence and meaning can only be realized within certain rules and frameworks, and in this scheme of things, only certain kinds of things can be said with claims to truth. What is most interesting about discourse is not the reflective nature of utterances, but their productive nature. It does not simply translate reality into language; it structures the way we perceive reality and make sense of it. For example, in a patriarchal society, men and women go on expressing themselves and experience their bodies/sexuality within certain parameters to appear as gendered subjects. Similarly, minorities in a democratic multicultural secular polity behave and express themselves in particular ways to be called minor subjects.

Though not intended as a Marxist term, discourse has some resemblance with ideology. The problem with ideology is that it is too top-down and appears as a negative force which dupes individuals. Discourse, on the other hand, does not always betray any direct political agenda and instead offers a gateway to engage with hegemony. It is not top-down as it implicates individuals in their own oppression and shows how certain types of subject positions are created not by the force of state ideology but by the complicity of the individual that perpetuates hegemony. Even though one can be critical within/of discourse, there is a limit to such a position. Discourse not only creates lines of conformity, but also limits of dissent, the reason why nobody really feels that he is powerless within discourse. It also collapses the difference between what is statist and what is popular. Though minority alterity is institutionalized by the state, the latter's power is realized by the successful internalization of that alterity by minorities themselves.

In Althusserian terms (1971), subjects are hailed or interpellated to recognize themselves as particular types of minority subjects and take up positions within a hierarchized system of majority–minority syndrome which results in the maintenance of status quo. Challenging the belief that individuals are the origins of their ideas, Althusser proposes the role of ideological state apparatuses in shaping subjecthood. His famous statement in this connection is "ideology hails or interpellates individuals as subjects" (ibid., 164). What we believe to be an expression of our will is actually a choreographed practice that inserts us into predetermined positions.

> Ideology "acts" or "functions" in such a way that it "recruits" subjects... by that very precise operation which I have called "interpellation" or hailing, and which can be imagined along the lines of the most commonplace every day police (or other) hailing: "Hey, you there!". (ibid., 162–63, emphasis original)

When the police officer calls "hey, you there!", the subject responds, thus, subjecting himself to a predetermined subject position, and it is in that moment of encounter that the subject becomes a subject. To be a minor is to recognize oneself as the one who is hailed. When Indian Law Minister Salman Khurshid referred to the Batla House encounter in Delhi (where two Indian Mujahideen members were killed) and told the audience how this had brought tears to Sonia Gandhi's (President of Congress Party) eyes, he was actually interpellating Muslim listeners as Muslims. Or when the General Secretary of Congress Party Digvijay Singh visited the family of the Batla House terror accused in Azamgarh (in the Indian state of Uttar Pradesh), he was creating a narrative of Muslim identity that cannot manage without sympathizing with terrorism. Or when former cricketer Md. Azharuddin was taken to Uttar Pradesh to contest elections in a Muslim-dominated constituency, prospective voters were intepellated as Muslims.

The best example of interpellation is to be found in a speech by Salman Khurshid. While campaigning for his wife during assembly elections in Uttar Pradesh, he spoke about the impoverishment of Muslims under non-Congress governments in the state and promised that Congress Party, if voted to power in Uttar Pradesh, would implement 9 percent of reservation for backward Muslims. When he asked the audience "my brothers, tell me whether you want to progress or not" or "tell me whether you need reservation or not," the audience had actually no option to say "no." No Muslim could have said no to the proposal without compromising his commitment to the development of Muslims. The question is asked in such a way that it eliminates the possibility of being a Muslim in any way other than interpellating oneself to the discourse. Similarly, during the 2005 general elections in the UK, Labour Party Member of Parliament Mike O'Brien canvassed for support by telling Muslim immigrants the kind of steps his government had taken to accommodate Muslim demands. Referring to the demand made by the Muslim Council of Britain for a new law banning religious discrimination, he said that it is a major victory for the Muslims in Britain. In The Netherlands, when migrants were given the right to vote in local elections, Prime Minister Ruud Lubbers went to mosques, spoke Arabic and Turkish, and encouraged voters to exercise their right. When a politician goes to a mosque to seek the support of the priest so that Muslims can vote for him, it creates the same subject position for Muslims who are projected as nonrational beings and as carriers of their religion.

It is in the act of responding to these carefully crafted situations or in the act of subjection that minority becomes minority and reinvents himself as a resistant subject. When All India Muslim Personal Law Board mandates "to adopt suitable strategies for protection and continued applicability of 'Muslim Personal Law,' i.e., Shariat Application Act in India," it creates a particular notion of proper Muslims. The Muslim Manifesto published by the London-based Muslim Institute in 1990 proposed that loyalty to the state can be overridden in case of conflict with Ummah. Thus, in the attempt of preserving diversity, the state/community make minorities prisoners of history and train them to develop ethnic chauvinism: "they are put under house arrest in their skins, in their origins" (Bruckner 2010, 145).

This resistant identity gathers strength over a period of time so much so that the outside world is suspected to be the enemy. At the slightest opportunity, this identity manifests itself through mass mobilization and violence as we saw during the Salman Rushdie controversy or the Prophet Muhammad cartoon controversy. In response to Danish cartoons, Muslims demonstrated outside the Danish embassy in London with placards reading "Bomb, bomb Denmark," "Nuke, nuke Denmark," "Europe comes crawling when Mujahideen comes roaring," and included an overzealous demonstrator dressed as a suicide bomber. This often comes in conflict with the idea of a civic society as when Muslims came in large numbers in Mumbai to protest against the condition of Rohingya Muslims in Myanmar and vandalized national symbols like the Amar Jawan, or when Abu Hamza declared that Europe would follow sharia in the near future. This sense of rage combined with disposition toward violence creates stereotypes which then are used by right wing parties to cast Muslims as intolerant, antinational, and antimodern, as in films like *Fitna* or *Innocence of Muslims*, or popular books such as *Londonistan* or *Eurabia*.

Performative Subjectivities

We have already argued how the religious affiliation of minorities, often seen as thick identity, is actually an effect of both statist and popular discourses. The category of the minority subject as something self-evident is, thus, demythologized. Butler (1990) tries to interrogate the notion of a permanent identity and traces the process through which individuals become gendered (or minored) identities within existing social relations. In such an understanding, the individual always seeks to enter into the social world of representation through an endless process of becoming by reiterating and stylizing those social roles. But it is not the minority question that offers institutional or state support for preserving minority identity; on the contrary, these institutions, in their act of preserving minority culture, end up producing minority identity as an undiluted essence that has remained the same since its originary moment. It will not be far-fetched to say that the myth of origin is a creation/invention of the democratic/secular narratives. Like de Beauvoir who believed that "one is not born, but rather becomes, a woman" (1949, 281), we may say that a minor is not born a minor, but becomes one through stylization, and so is a performative construct.

Butler tells us that there is no individual existing prior to the performative act. The performative, for Butler, is the "reiterative power of discourse to produce the phenomena that it regulates and constrains" (1993, 12). However, for Butler, there is no preexisting performer who plays those parts, nor is there any performer behind the deed. The term performer is a misnomer because performance presupposes the existence of an agentic being. Echoing de Beauvoir, Butler says, "Even when gender seems to congeal into the reified forms, the 'congealing' is itself an insistent and insidious practice, sustained and regulated by various social means" (1990, 33). Unlike the reification of gender through societal norms, the minored identity comes into existence not always through state-ascribed roles, but also in the very act of affiliation. By repeated acts of minority performance, minority congeals itself and solidifies into an ontological being. Minority identity is not just a process; it is a particular type of process.

Cultures are effects of that stabilization produced by authority which comes through the exclusion of any threatening presence that can dilute the purity of culture. Reference may be made here to Bhabha who distinguishes between "the continuist, accumulative temporality of the pedagogical" and "the repetitious, recursive strategy of the performative" (1994, 145) in the narrative of the nation. The first impulse is about consistency, coherence, unity, certainties, and continuity with a specific historical origin. The performative impulse is about anxiety, alteration, disintegration, contingence, and even invention. Nation emerges between these two dimensions, as both fact and also becoming; but the self-evident factual nation must make itself manifest through the performative. In the former, the nation is imagined as a continuous unit and its people as one; the latter is the intervention and invention of intellectuals, historians, and their representational strategies through which the nation's origin is re-enacted. The official version of the minority nation highlights the pedagogical to the exclusion of the performative. Bhabha (1990) questions the illusion of continuity (as in sharia or polygamy or skull cap) that marks the distinctness of culture and casts it as frozen in time.

In this context, it would also be productive to expose what Butler calls the "metaphysics of substance" which is a pervasive belief that sex/body (here minority) is a self-evident materiality. Borrowing from Rich (2003) who debunked the myth of a natural heterosexuality by calling it "compulsory heterosexuality," we may call this attitude compulsory minority. Butler sees in the demand for recognition the failure (or at least relativization) of the communitarian self. In the struggle for recognition, there is a continuous transformation, because while seeking recognition, the subject posits himself in a relationship with the other. In doing so, he is not only changed by that relationship, but also begins to develop a sense of cultures as exclusive, and, thus, imagines those aspects of culture which challenge other cultures as the essence of his culture. Thus, when burqa is targeted, it becomes the essence of Islamic culture. What Butler is interested in knowing is the kind of self which emerges out of this intersubjective encounter, and asking for recognition: "To ask for recognition, or to offer it, is precisely not to ask for recognition for what one already is. It is to solicit a becoming, to instigate a transformation, to petition the future always in relation to the Other" (Butler 2003, 31).

Gilroy has argued that race "is a political rather than scientific invention" (2000, 69). In India, we have examples of particular groups (like Jats) of people demanding to be recognized as Scheduled Tribes or Other Backward Castes so that they can get reservation benefits. More often than not, demands for recognition blur the difference between identity groups and interest groups. This is something we may call "political economy of cultural difference" where clamor for recognition is seen as a passport to economic benefit (Tripathy and Padmanabhan 2013, 23). Phillips speaks about the production of cultures in response to government initiatives (2007, 49). According to her, there is no preexisting entity that constitutes race or religion or culture "for these entities are themselves defined and shaped in response to the wider political environment" (ibid., 61).

Both Europe and India have reposed their faith in the idea of the state as producer of minority difference. The UK allows minority groups to apply for state funding to finance denominational schools, and accommodates dress codes and diets in schools and colleges. In The Netherlands, minorities have the right to be taught in their mother tongues in primary schools, something like madrasa education in India. The Muslim Youth was founded in 1994 in Germany and receives funding from the Ministry of the Interior. In Spain, there is provision for the protection of mosques, tax relief for religious activities, prescription of halal food, separate areas within cemeteries, and religious education in public schools. Similarly, Article 30 of the Indian Constitution guarantees that all religious and linguistic minorities can establish educational institutions of their choice. The infamous Shah Bano case is an episode in Indian history which established the power of the state to decide/confer what constituted Islamic value.[2] What is common to all these is the fact that a minority is continuously produced and made to exist in state policy and public discourses.

The narrative of minority is the narrative of marginalization and victimhood where the real minority has to be an oppressed minority. The anger of the minority ends up reinforcing stereotypical images of Muslims as irrational and medieval. Adnan (2012) expresses frustration over this irrational Muslim response to Muslim problems. Giving the example of the Muslim mobilization over the plight of Muslims in Assam and Rohingya Muslims in Myanmar, he wonders why suddenly Muslims come out to protest in large numbers if it involves the so-called Muslim question: "It tells us a great deal about the emotions which the Indian Muslims seem to have in excess" (Adnan 2012, 14). Suraiya articulates his frustration over the boycotting of Taslima Nasreen and Salman Rushdie in Kolkata and Jaipur. He wondered if these "self-proclaimed liberals and secularists often display a tendency to 'appease' minorities" (2012). It creates an idea of a Muslim who cannot exist with other groups, one who is oversensitive and always ready to die for religion.

Such anger provides a justification for the right wing political parties to represent Muslims as too demanding and also for being incompatible with the idea of the modern secular state. Though we know that some demands are genuine and can be easily accommodated, there are other demands such as polygamy, female circumcision, or sharia divorce which come in conflict with the values of most liberal states. This is unfortunately rationalized in some academic circles as genuine frustration over specific policies of the government. Similarly, community organizations routinely send out fatwas to reinforce these stereotypes of Muslims. In one such fatwa, an Islamic cleric in Europe forbade Muslim women to touch bananas and cucumbers as these fruits may create sexual desire among women (as they resemble the male sexual organ).

Conclusion

The celebration of minority difference is typical of democracies where political and intellectual discourses tend to be supportive of minority demands for recognition. This makes Triandafyllidou et al. argue that Muslim claims expose the "taken-for-grantedness of secularism in most European countries" (2006, 3). Ironically, it is in this democratic space that the immigrant or minority become *ausländer* (foreigner), or *extracomunitari* (people from outside), or the politics based on minority rights becomes "minority appeasement" or "vote bank politics." Minority claims lead to "creating new solidarities and asserting a 'permanent difference' with reference to Islam" (Kastoryano 2006, 58). The democratic state, being the preserver of minority culture, often knows the minority better than minorities themselves. It is like saying "you are still the other, but you are the state's other and your redemption lies with the state." In the act of rescuing minority, the democratic state often reproduces them in its gaze as vulnerable, and in the very act of inclusion excludes them. Like any other category knowledge, minority difference cannot afford to see any contact zones among cultures, nor can it see any dissonance of opinion within itself.

In this imaginative rendering of the minority, the latter always appears as helpless and in need of rescue, which is always ably provided by the multicultural polity of the state. In the narrativization of such identities, the secular democrat always appears as the true subject of democracy and minorities as recipients of democracy's favors. It would not be wrong to argue that the minority as a secularist formation is elided as an individual of flesh and blood, and emerges as a phantasmatic construct loaded with the prospect of political dividends. The figure of a helpless minority easily dovetails into the victim narrative that offers a rationale for the rescue narrative of affirmative action and reservation. In this architecture, a model minority must appear in his tribal gear or skull cap. This already always constituted minority subject can exist only as a believing member of the group, and anybody who does not exhibit such helplessness cannot be theoretically a minority subject.

We can end by asking another question: Is there any unmediated/prediscursive minority? This question seems to be meaningless in the contemporary political and patronizing discourse that prefers to see minority as an unchanging mass. This becomes even more ominous when general elections are held in India and many European countries as they offer unique opportunities for politicians and intellectuals to indulge in the perpetuation of minority difference. As long as multicultural democracy, its institutions, and its discourses continue to preserve minority culture for one reason or the other, minority subjects will continue to perform as minorities.

Notes and Bibliography

Notes

1. This chapter has benefited immensely from the interventions of our colleague S. Mohan and also from the generous supply of critical material by Animesh Mohapatra.
2. The Shah Bano case is a controversial law suit in India's judicial history which had far-reaching implications for minority politics. A 62-year-old woman, Shah Bano, was divorced by her husband, but was denied alimony. The Supreme Court of India ordered the husband to pay alimony to Shah Bano, which infuriated Muslim leaders and led to massive protests. This made the Indian Prime Minister Rajiv Gandhi pass the Muslim Women Act of 1986, overturning the Supreme Court judgment. The episode tells us how minority difference is produced by the narratives of the state.

Bibliography

Adnan. 2012. "Our Heart Must Bleed for Everyone… Not Just for Muslims." *Hindu*, August 19. http://www.thehindu.com/opinion/open-page/our-heart-must-bleed-for-everyone-not-just-for-muslims/article3792355.ece

Althusser, Louis. 1971. *Lenin and Philosophy, and Other Essays*. Translated by B. Brewster. London: New Left Books.

Anderson, Benedict. 1983. *Imagined Communities: Reflections on the Origin and Spread of Nationalism*. London: Verso.

Benhabib, Seyla. 2002. *The Claims of Culture: Equality and Diversity in the Global Era*. Princeton: Princeton University Press.

Bhabha, Homi K. 1990. "Introduction: Narrating the Nation." In *Nation and Narration*, edited by Homi K. Bhabha, 1–7. London: Routledge.

———. 1994. *The Location of Culture*. London: Routledge.

Bilgrami, Akeel. 1995. "What is a Muslim? Fundamental Commitment and Cultural Identity." In *Identities*, edited by Kwame Anthony Appiah and Henry Louis Gates Jr., 198–219. Chicago: University of Chicago Press.

Bruckner, Pascal. 2010. *The Tyranny of Guilt: An Essay on Western Masochism*. Princeton: Princeton University Press.

Butler, Judith. 1990. *Gender Trouble: Feminism and the Subversion of Identity*. New York: Routledge.

———. 1993. *Bodies That Matter: On the Discursive Limits of Sex*. New York: Routledge.

———. 2003. "Violence, Mourning, Politics." *Studies in Gender and Sexuality* 4 (1): 9–37.

Casanova, Jose. 2007. "Immigration and the New Religious Pluralism: A European Union/United States Comparison." In *Democracy and the New Religious Pluralism*, edited by Thomas Bachoff, 59–84. Oxford: Oxford University Press.

Chandhoke, Neera. 1999. *Beyond Secularism: The Rights of Religious Minorities*. New Delhi: Oxford University Press.

de Beauvoir, Simone. 1949. *The Second Sex*. Translated by H. M. Parshley. London: Everyman.

de Certeau, Michel. 1997. *Culture in the Plural*. Minneapolis: University of Minnesota Press.

Derrida, Jaques. 1978. "Structure, Sign and Play in the Discourse of Human Sciences." Translated by Alan Bass. In *Writing and Difference*, edited by Jaques Derrida, 278–94. Chicago: University of Chicago Press.

Foucault, Michel. 1972. *The Archaeology of Knowledge*. Translated by Sheridan Smith. London: A. M. Tavistock.

Gilroy, Paul. 2000. *Against Race: Imagining Political Culture Beyond the Color Line*. Cambridge: Belknap Press.

Kastoryano, Riva. 2006. "French Secularism and Islam: France's Headscarf Affair." In *Multiculturalism, Muslims and Citizenship: A European Approach*, edited by Tariq Moddod et al., 57–69. London: Routledge.

Kymlicka, Will. 1989. *Liberalism, Community and Culture*. Oxford: Clarendon Press.
———. 2007. *Multicultural Odysseys: Navigating the New International Politics of Diversity*. Oxford: Oxford University Press.
———. 2008. "The Evolving Basis of European Norms of Minority Rights: Rights to Culture, Participation and Autonomy." In *The Protection of Minorities in the Wider Europe*, edited by Marc Weller et al., 11–41. New York: Palgrave Macmillan.
Nandy, Ashis. 1998. "The Politics of Secularism and the Recovery of Religious Tolerance." In *Secularism and its Critics*, edited by Rajeev Bhargava, 321–44. New Delhi: Oxford University Press.
Parekh, Bhikhu. 2006. "Europe, Liberalism and the 'Muslim Question'." In *Multiculturalism, Muslims and Citizenship: A European Approach*, edited by Tariq Modood et al., 179–203. London: Routledge.
Phillips, Anne. 2007. *Multiculturalism Without Culture*. Princeton: Princeton University Press.
Rich, Adrienne C. 2003. "Compulsory Heterosexuality and Lesbian Existence." *Journal of Women's History* 15 (3): 11–48.
Suraiya, Jug. 2012. "Double Standards." *The Times of India*, February 7. http://blogs.timesofindia.indiatimes.com/jugglebandhi/entry/double-standards
Taylor, Charles. 1994. "The Politics of Recognition." In *Multiculturalism: Examining the Politics of Recognition*, edited by Amy Gutmann, 25–73. Princeton: Princeton University Press.
Triandafyllidou, Anna et al. 2006. "European Challenges to Multicultural Citizenship: Muslims, Secularism and Beyond." In *Multiculturalism, Muslims and Citizenship: A European Approach*, edited by Tariq Modood et al., 1–22. London: Routledge.
Tripathy, J. and S. Padmanabhan. 2013. "Introduction: Democracy and the Production of Cultural Diversity." In *The Democratic Predicament: Cultural Diversity in Europe and India*, edited by J. Tripathy and S. Padmanabhan, 1–34. New Delhi: Routledge.

2

Contextualizing Minority: The Production of Difference and Sameness in Europe

Barbara Franz

The politics of naming is essential in contextualizing minority. Through the use of labels, for example, definitions and membership to groups are developed; the rhetoric of exclusion constructs ingroups and out-groups (as shown, for example, by Delanty et al. 2008) everyday, and these practices relate to tactics of positive and negative self- and other-presentation and strategies of justification and legitimization of exclusionary practices through arguments (ibid., 57). But the politics of naming is by no means a straightforward process. Instead, it is often marked by contradictions and ambiguity. For example, the use of the term *Mitbürger*, fellow citizen, in German, actually "performs the opposite symbolic task from what is intended" (Mandel 2008, 126). The term calls attention to, but at the same time separates, the person named a Mitbürger from the proper bürger-ness, though the prefix "Mit" wishes to include a person or group apparently not a natural citizen per se. It, thus, connotes the opposite; the good intention of inclusion points instead to their political disenfranchisement. As Mandel emphasizes: "For, ultimately, true Mitbürgers would be burgers minus the prefix"

(Mandel 2008, 127). While discourse is a quintessential element in the inclusion and exclusion of groups, ethnic groups and other minorities have also begun to define themselves vis-à-vis the majorities.

The idea that a group of people want to be recognized as a "minority" is neither new nor culturally universal. That such status could be desirable, however, might have seemed incomprehensible prior to the late 20th century (Berbrier 2002, 554). In America, the term "minority" was initially used in the early part of the 20th century to denote European immigrants. Over time, its use was transformed and expanded. Louis Wirth defined a minority as "a group of people who, because of their physical or cultural characteristics, are singled out ...for differential and unequal treatment, and who therefore regard themselves as objects of collective discrimination" (1945, 347). Authors have argued that the most lasting influence of Wirth's definition within the USA at least has been the inclusion of a sense of "victimhood" into the popular understanding of minority status (e.g., Gleason 1991, cited in Berbrier 2002). Gleason points out that it would, thus, seem "almost perverse for minorities to wish to perpetuate" that status (1991, 400). Nevertheless, many minority groups have done just that—sought minority status for, among other things, specific political and economic privileges that are linked to such a status. While this understanding of the term is assimilationist and defines a minority as something temporary and undesirable, it places at least part of the responsibility for the problems of minority groups upon the majority society (ibid., 403). Here lies one of the major differences between the USA and Central Europe in acknowledging minorities. In America, as Berbrier emphasizes, with the recognition of minority status comes a greater potential for the understanding of grievances as being legitimate. This process is either nonexistent or only in its infancy in many European regions.

No clear definition of the term minority exists, and the term minority is used in a number of ways in Europe. In the UK, the Anglo-American sense of minority prevails. Thus, the minority is often conceived as the outcome of an interaction between majority and an immigrant newcomer group, involving actors from both sides and engendering both immigrant minority and national majority in the process. Immigrant groups and other minorities always engage in a "boundary-making process" (Wimmer 2011, 26). In reference to ethnic minorities, Wimmer

(2008) expands the argument that boundaries are the outcome of the "classificatory struggles and negotiations" between actors situated in a social field whose three characteristics—the institutional order, the distribution of power, and political networks—determine which actors will adopt which strategy of ethnic boundary making. This chapter focuses on minorities in Central Europe, and it differentiates between two different groups of minorities and minority definitions: the older use of the term refers to recognized established ethnic minorities, such as the Basques in Spain, the Walloons in Belgium, or the Slovenes in Austria. The more recent use of the term refers to immigrant newcomer groups from outside Europe, mostly Turkey and Middle Eastern and North African countries, specifically denoting people who can be easily detected as foreigners through visual markers.

Ethnic identity and ethnicity ranks as a prominent minority marker on the Continent and elsewhere. However, there is no precise or universally accepted definition for terms such as "ethnic group" or "nationality." In the context of European ethnography in particular, the terms ethnic group, national minority, ethnic minority, linguistic community, linguistic group, and linguistic minority are used synonymously, although usage may vary with respect to the situations specific to the individual countries of Europe. European mainstream society is frequently defined in terms of collective identity, constructed through the very process of opposing migrants (specifically nonwhite newcomers originating in non-European states) who often are collectively seen as "threats" and "problems" (Franz 2012). Immigrants and minority groups thereby become an issue by being linked to a whole range of domestic problems, such as unemployment, financial challenges to the welfare system, drugs, and crime. I argue that, historically, European minorities and majorities have, thus, always contextualized each other. Majorities could not have been created without minorities or defined themselves vis-à-vis minorities; majorities have historically excluded minorities from membership in society, the economy, and politics. This is as true today in modern Europe as it was in the 19th and 20th centuries.

In the first part of this chapter, I focus on the significance of minorities for the rise of the modern nation state. Particular attention is paid to the politics of cultural homogenization of ethnic minorities into larger national majorities. The imagining of larger national communities is, thus,

only possible after the forgetting of one's particularities, be they ethnic or regional or defined through any other identity markers. This part
emphasizes the lasting importance of minorities for Europe throughout the 20th century. By analyzing the German-speaking majorities in
Europe, the second part of the chapter centers on problems with majority identities, focusing on the widespread popular understanding of
culture as being a fixed bridge between the individual and the society,
which can be contaminated when intermixed with the strange or foreign
cultures of exotic minorities. The third part of this chapter centers upon
the development of the welfare state in Europe in general, and the influence of neoliberalism—with its rejection of the traditional social welfare policies of the first half of the 20th century in favor of unregulated
markets—on minorities in particular. In the fourth part of the chapter, I
show that the modern concept of multiculturalism, while standing for de
jure inclusion and acceptance of minorities, de facto allows and validates
economic differences between ethnic minorities and majorities in modern Europe. Multiculturalism has contributed to a rising tide of "reverse
racism" which Europe's far right exploits through xenophobic and anti-
Muslim campaigns. Beyond this, however, a level of everyday racism
persists in Europe today based on the generalization of stereotypes. Only
when these substantial obstacles are recognized can they be overcome
by acknowledging that minorities contribute substantially to a vibrant
healthy society and economy.

The Significance of Minorities for the Rise of the Nation State

The nation state is a European invention that spread through imperialism
all over the globe and is today universally established. To create nation
states, minorities had to be turned into majorities. In Central Europe, the
nation state has frequently been constructed based on the perception of
the existence of a culturally and ethnically homogeneous national population. In reality, even nation states that are perceived as extremely homogeneous, such as France, were once very heterogeneous. France was Europe's
first modern republic and, in the 19th century, arguably the most powerful state in the West. Well into the 19th century, many French citizens

were minorities and regularly spoke languages other than French—Breton, Basque, Catalan, Flemish, Alsatian, and Corsican—instead of French, and even in French-speaking areas, provincial loyalties often transcended the putative bond of the nation. Successive French governments took active steps to promote the elimination of provincial loyalties (McDonald 2009) and cultural particularities. Urbanization and industrialization aided the process, dislocating traditionally agricultural rural communities and allowing a specifically Francophile modernity to arise. Book and magazine publishing, popular music, and the like also played an important role in making French trendy for non-Francophile young people. Weber (1976) emphasizes that public education and conscription into the army were the most important methods for Francophonization, even though these schooling schemes were less than successful in homogeneous non-Francophone peasant societies, of which Brittany is the most spectacular example. But in areas even minimally open to the French language, mandatory schooling distanced the children from the traditional norms of the peasant society and within one or two generations, assimilated the minorities into a majority society, engineering a homogeneous population of Frenchmen.

McDonald (2009) emphasizes that most European nation states that we today perceive as very homogeneous have turned various ethnic minorities living in their territory into cohorts of homogeneous citizens. Sweden, for example, is traditionally thought of as the epitome of homogeneity. Yet, throughout its history, Sweden has received immigrating Walloons, Germans, Finns, Balts, Dutch, and others. The country became a melting pot even prior to the 19th century when Swedish sovereigns finally managed to establish the nation's uncontested boundaries. The country's modern boundaries were only defined in 1815, with the cession of Finland to the Russian Empire (ibid.).

Citizens of countries such as Germany, Switzerland, Austria, and Italy, however, are often adamant about their exclusivist nationalist background. Although they might have only recently become immigration countries in the narrow sense of the word, these countries' histories have been punctuated with frequent arrivals originating from the countries' overseas colonies or imperial possessions. For example, in the K. & K. monarchy, the Austrian–Hungarian army provided young men from the empire's border provinces the chance of a career and encouraged the mixing of various ethnicities into perhaps the first attempt at a multicultural institution. Despite these historic experiences, until fairly recently, at least these countries have undergone a convenient memory lapse that might have been produced by the western traditions of sovereignty established by the Peace of Westphalia—assuming that their ethno-national origins can be traced back to the proverbial German, Swiss, Austrian, and Italian Adam and Eve, respectively.

The Other Ethnic Group

Some authors have argued that prior to the political act of engendering one's own group identity vis-à-vis the other, ethnicity already exists. Smith (2005, 25) argues that ethnic communities, or what he calls *ethnies*, are human populations distinguished by both members and outsiders as possessing the attributes of:

1. an identifying name or emblem;
2. a myth of common ancestry;
3. shared historical memories and traditions;
4. one or more elements of common culture;
5. a link with a historic territory or "homeland";
6. a measure of solidarity, at least among the elites.

Smith's well-known argument is that there are powerful links between modern nations and preexisting, sometimes premodern, ethnies. According to many nationalist myths, the nation arises from a painful rite of passage where the ethnic group has to fight its adversaries—the other or the enemy within (Erikson 2005, 139). Thus, one of the strongest allegiances is usually to ethnic identity and group membership.

Forgetting one's past as a small group and imagining being part of a larger community, however, was and is, thus, quintessential for the creation of the nation state. Anderson (1983) argues that nations are imagined communities because members do not know each other face-to-face, but perceive a bond of camaraderie and fraternity to each other independent of class and status. Nations, however, are also imagined as sovereign and limited because they have finite boundaries beyond which other nations exist. Anderson argues that the rise of national consciousness in Europe was dependent on the printing press and the "revolutionary vernacular-izing thrust of capitalism" (Anderson 1983, 53). It was supported by a change in the Latin language, the universal language of the Middle Ages, the Reformation, and the geographically uneven spread of particular ver-naculars as instruments of administrative centralization.

Thus, majorities are made. They are made of others who speak different dialects or languages, pray to other gods, and perhaps even have different myths of origin. Conceivably, prior to the spread of a vernacular or reli-gious conversion, majorities and minorities were not clearly distinguish-able; they had to be engineered through political means. We are instructed to belong to a particular national, racial, ethnic, and regional or local group with whose members we share certain identity traits.

Belonging to a group is by definition an exclusive process. Gilroy (2005, 155) argues that identity is always bounded and particular. Thus, for the invention of one's own identity, the Other has to be identified and categorized as different. Then the Other's identity, constructed frequently as the opposite of the majority, has often been construed as threatening the existence of one's own identity group itself. Through the pronoun "we," patterns of inclusion and exclusion emanate. Calculating the rela-tionship between identity and difference and sameness and otherness is an "intrinsically political operation" (ibid.). Max Weber maintained that ethnic groups were *künstlich* (artificial, a social construct) because they were based on a subjective belief in shared community or *Gemein-schaft* (Banton 2007). This belief in shared community, he insisted, did not create the group; the group created the belief. Contrary to the pre-vailing view of the time, which held that socio-cultural and behavioral differences between peoples stemmed from inherited traits and tenden-cies derived from common descent, Weber argued that group forma-tion resulted from the drive to monopolize power and status (ibid.). Smith (2005) and authors who adhere to a primordialist—as opposed to instrumentalist or modern—understanding of ethnicity and group membership have, thus, argued that the origins of the nation state can be found in the ethnic group. This might not be the case for nations such as the USA and France where state institutions and elites contributed substantially to the formation of the nation. However, for nations whose ethnic groups' most driving impetus was the desire for secession from larger multiethnic empires, such as the Austrian–Hungarian or Ottoman empires, the formation of independent nation states became the motto of the age. Thus, to paraphrase, the Italian nationalist Guiseppe Mazzini's call for "One state per nation and only one nation per state" became the dictum for other nationalists in 19th-century Europe.

The liberal commitment to the self-determination of nations stems from notions of national autonomy and ethnic self-rule. The American President Woodrow Wilson was instrumental in applying the principle of self-determination to the newly independent states of Southeastern Europe, such as Czechoslovakia and Yugoslavia (initially named the Kingdom of Serbs, Croats, and Slovenes). As *the* political principle of post-World War I (WW I) Europe, different standards, however, were applied to the quest of self-determination of non-European colonies. Winter (2006) points out that a paternalistic midpoint was constructed between colonial rule and self-government through which European powers were to administer territories on behalf of the international community with the creation of mandates (58–59). The Middle East and Africa were partitioned among the European winners of WW I based on the racist perception that those territories needed a period of apprenticeship in independence during which these populations would learn to govern themselves before they would be granted actual self-determination. This paternalism was also tinged with self-interest. Winter emphasizes that Wilson never lost sight of the racial limits to self-determination: "It was—at least for the foreseeable future—the white man's business" (64). Self-determination was a policy reserved for those populations that shared the values and traditions conceived of by "civilized" nations. Thus, the liberal concept of self-determination as applied in Europe and delayed in Africa and Asia during the early decades of the last century laid the political groundwork for what was to come during the remainder of the 20th century. Minorities—their inclusion and exclusion in various polities—as determined by the imperial powers of the age, thus, became the crux of the most central conflicts of 20th century Europe: the Armenian Genocide, the Holocaust, the expulsions and large migrations during the post-WW I and post-WW II periods, ethnic cleansing, and modern-day migration issues. Repressive elements of identity constructions are found in many of the policies leading to the major genocides of the 20th century.

Problems with Majority Identity

Torgovnick argues that the majority's identity construction is a call to have an imaginary brotherhood of mutual interest including a "repressive politics of inclusion, in which those who identify with it must surrender crucial aspects of themselves" (1992, 48, cited in Tripathy 2010). Members of both the majority and the minority, thus, lose their individuality under these conditions. Often, majority identities appear to be strong and secure, if not outright aggressive. This is how German-ness, for example, is perceived in many parts of Europe and the world. Forsythe (1989, 137, cited in Erikson 2005, 140) argues that this central and powerful identity, considered by many as the dominant national identity in the European Union (EU), is characterized by anomalies, fuzzy boundaries, and ambiguous criteria for belongingness. This chapter was written before the German unification; thus, the author argues that, first of all, it is unclear where Germany is. Although the inhabitants of both the Federal Republic and the German Democratic Republic were clearly German, not all west Germans would include the GDR as inland or domestic territory. Erikson elaborates that even after reunification, the distinction between Wessies and Ossies, referring to economic and cultural differences, is salient. Moreover, many Germans would include the areas lost to Poland and the former Soviet Union during WW II as German territory. Referring to the Nazi period (1933–45), Forsythe argues that "the German past is not one that lends itself comfortably to nostalgia, nor is it well suited to serve as a charter for nationalists' dreams for the future" (1989, 138). So the question "What is German?" is complicated, but so is the question "Who is German?".

The criterion for German-ness, as applied by ordinary Germans, can be either a language or "a mixture compounded of appearance, family background, country of residence and country of origin" (ibid., 143). Austrians and the majority of Swiss speak German, but are not German. On the other hand, millions of people of German descent, whose German language skills might or might not be intact, live in Central and Eastern Europe. Thus, German identity is not clear cut, solid, and well demarcated: it seems to have frontiers but no boundaries because it is possible to be "somewhat German" and "not really foreign" (Erikson 2005, 142).

These anomalies do not necessarily pose specific German problems. They are general and quite widespread. Indeed, German identity appears to me to be much more solid and well demarcated than, for example, Austrian identity, which is very much defined by an obscure affinity for the Habsburg K. & K. monarchy, the individual's birth, and residence in one of the nine *Länder* (provinces), all of which have distinct dialects, as well as a clear demarcation against each other and the immigrant Other. However, migrants from the former Habsburg monarchy are less foreign than Turkic or North African newcomers. Many Austrian citizens crowd together under the banner of reactionary nationalism and exclusivism (e.g., of immigrants from the benefits of the welfare state), opposing the perceived threat that these newcomers bring to Austria, its culture— frequently seen as a mélange of Habsburg K. & K. nostalgia, Austrian coziness with Wiener Schnitzel, Apfelstrudel, and Weisse Spritzer, café house and restaurant traditions—and a mythical understanding of the golden age of the Second Republic, when it was still considered the "Island of the Blessed," basically, a society seen as white, middle class, meritocratic, and static (Franz 2012).

Identity Issues of the Ausländer—Or the Ones Who belong Outside[1]

Within these regions, identity is seen as fixed, assuming the function of a bridge sometimes between the self and society, and in some regions connecting the present to the past. This attitude has dramatic consequences for immigrants and other minorities. A primordial understanding of oneself and one's in-group assumes that minorities and others in the outgroup possess a different essence. As Taylor (1994) emphasizes, minority culture, understood as a finished and unalterable product, perceives the individual as a moral agent who has to recognize his "authenticity" and whose individual core is part of one's group affiliation but will always remain different from the Austrian majority society's essence. Thus, in processes of integration, acculturation, or inclusion, the majority seeks to produce minorities in the majority's image, despite the dilemma, widely acknowledged in the majority society, that the immigrant group possesses an essential difference that cannot be altered and will never "fit into" the majority society.

Nevertheless, minorities tend to mobilize around their minority status (Chandhoke 1999). This is, in particular, true for Europe's old minorities, such as Austria's Slovenes who have fought many political battles in the 1970s and 1980s for their status recognition. Once recognized, their minority identity is assumed to be unified and frozen and all group-internal differences ought to be neutralized (ibid.). Such status anxiety might not be that clearly detectable for more recent newcomers, such as Turkish, Serbian, and Romanian migrants to Central European countries.

To be sure, the minority subject is an effect of the dominant discourse of democracy and multiculturalism. When national and ethnic identities are represented and projected as pure, exposure to the different Other threatens these identities with dilution and contamination (Gilroy 2005, 160). People then can become bearers of difference "that the rhetoric of the absolute identity invents" (ibid., 159). They are "obedient, silent passengers moving across a flattened moral landscape toward the fixed destinies to which their essential identities, their genes, and the closed cultures they create have consigned them once and for all" (ibid.). Much of what the proponents of this perspective perceive as essential is based on the view that one needs to defend what has been rightfully earned and given to oneself by the nation state and the government—be it culture and tradition or unemployment benefits, pensions, and health care. The European welfare state is, thus, directly or indirectly one of the core concerns for majority populations, causing anxiety and trepidation.

The Nation State and Social Welfare Policies

Beginning in the 19th century, Central European nations frequently built their states on an understanding of societies as cohesive units with a common language, history, and tradition. In certain regions, particularly those geographic areas that were latecomers to industrialization and modernization, belonging to a nation was linked to one religion and a perceived common ancestry. The core constituency of this modern nation was often, particularly in Central and Eastern Europe, a population that was constructed as *one* ethnic people—and, thus, one nation. The great Hobsbawm (1989) describes the rise of the term "nationalism" frequently engendering a political program with the objective of unifying or creating nation states:

> For the word "nationalism" itself first appeared at the end of the nineteenth century to describe groups of right-wing ideologists in France and Italy, keen to brandish the national flag against foreigners, liberals, and socialists, and in favour of that aggressive expansion of their own state which was to become so characteristic of such movements. This was also the period when the song "*Deutschland Über Alles*" (Germany above all others) replaced rival compositions to become the actual national anthem of Germany.... The basis of "nationalism" of all kinds was the same; the readiness of people to identify themselves emotionally with "their" nation and to be politically mobilized as Czechs, Germans, Italians or whatever a readiness which could be politically exploited. (Hobsbawm 1989, 142–43)

Despite these nationalist trends, however, liberal governments had to incorporate welfare programs, perhaps also to keep at bay and undermine the popularity of the rising socialist parties during the large democratization periods in 19th-century Europe. The man who united Germany, Otto von Bismarck, for example, "had already decided in the 1880s to cut the ground from under socialist agitation by an ambitious scheme of social insurance" (ibid., 103). Symbolizing the birth of the modern welfare state before 1914, Austria, Great Britain, and France all followed Germany's example and introduced old age pensions, public labor exchanges, and health and unemployment insurance for their citizens. Today's liberal nucleus, the United States, did not introduce similar social programs or any policies effectively limiting free enterprise until decades later, during the Great Depression in the 1930s. Nevertheless, American elites quickly learned how to mobilize and tranquilize the public through wars, such as the Spanish–American War in 1898, and American imperialism, such as the US occupation of the Philippines.

> Indeed the ruling elites of the USA, headed by Theodore Roosevelt (1858–1919, President during 1901–09), had just discovered the gun-toting cowboy as symbol of true Americanism, freedom, and native white tradition against the invading hordes of low-class immigrants and the uncontrollable big city. (ibid., 104)

The country has idealized that symbol ever since.

While America's social policy has traditionally been akin to the rise of liberalism, three different welfare regimes developed in Europe, each influencing states' stance vis-à-vis minorities and immigrants.[2] Esping-Andersen's (1996) broad tripartite division includes:

1. The Anglo liberal regime, found in not only Great Britain but also the post-Soviet Baltic states and large Eastern EU members such as Poland, focusing strongly on the market: a liberal work ethic that favors private welfare programs combined with a system of means-tested public welfare approaches targeted at temporary aid to low-income groups and based on a universalism of minimal needs.

2. The conservative Central and Southern European corporate regime, highly influenced by Christian values, which focuses on the conservation of the traditional family, a morally sanctioned social order, and which reproduces a particularistic and hierarchic edifice of citizenship.

3. The social democratic regime, most typical for Scandinavia, focusing on values of equality and individuality, and which is occupied with safeguarding a high degree of universalism in an extensive public welfare system, catering even to the differentiated needs of the middle class (Schierup et al. 2006, 84–85).

The Central and Northern EU countries, with their stronger unions and more regulated labor markets, tend to generate permanent, higher unemployment, which in combination with the relative robust welfare states can create welfare dependency. In the Northern European research discourse, immigration and ethnic minorities are routinely associated with high unemployment, inflated welfare dependency, and heavily burdened municipal budgets, urban unrest, and high criminality. This stands in contrast to the liberal welfare regimes, best seen in the USA, where an increasing polarization has developed between the high-salaried professional elites and the inner-city (black or immigrant) ghetto underclass. Nevertheless, scholars have observed a parallel development in German and American cities (e.g., Kasarda et al. 1992). In both states, the relocation of economic activity leaves behind islands of structural unemployment, which are composed of particular ethnic minority groups. Despite these similarities, most researchers emphasize that there are no easy comparisons which can be made between the nodes of high unemployment and the ethnic segregation in big European cities and the racial ghettos in the USA (e.g., Burgers and Kloosterman 1996). The existence of the institutions of the welfare state in Europe gives the high unemployment and welfare-dependent ethnic neighborhoods in the cities the character of "welfare refuges" that provide assistance, rather than of the US "ethno-racial prison" haunted by police and authoritarian "workfare" (Wacquant 2002, cited in Schierup et al. 2006, 101).

The Southern European states—the "new of immigration countries" of Greece, Italy, Spain, and Portugal—currently experience a severe economic depression. Characteristic of these countries' immigrant regimes are a high degree of informality and lack of regulation of employment and social welfare conditions (ibid., 103). In this socio-economic climate, immigration and minorities have come to be seen as a "social problem." Yet, some indicators point at the rising neoliberal trends that encroach upon not only the British but also increasingly the continental European labor market, and have begun to influence social welfare policies within the EU.

This is where the notion of minorities begins to clash with neoliberalism. The core idea of neoliberal ideology is the belief that open, competitive, and unregulated markets, liberated from all forms of state interference, such as unemployment benefits and health care, represent the optimal mechanism for economic development. This "utopia of unlimited exploitation" (Bourdieu 1998) first gained prominence during the late 1970s and early 1980s in response to declining profitability of traditional mass-production industries and the crisis of Keynesian welfare policies. It entailed, first and foremost, the dismantling of the basic institutional components of the post-WW II social policy settlement and the mobilization of a range of policies intended to extend market discipline, competition, and commodification throughout all sectors of society. Neoliberal doctrines justified the deregulation of state control over major industries, assaults on organized labor, the reduction of corporate taxes, the shrinking of public services, the dismantling of welfare programs, and the enhancement of international capital mobility (Brenner and Theodore 2002, 2–3).[3] The victims of these policies were both ethnic minorities and those economic minorities that could not adjust to the changing capitalist landscape fast enough. Either way, right wing neoliberal elites easily split this otherwise natural alliance between ethnic and economic minorities with often nationalist exclusivist rhetoric, based on fear-mongering and racism. While the radical right became more exclusivist and racist, the mainstream began to adhere to globalization and multiculturalism with its associated tolerance for minorities and immigrants alike.

Multiculturalism and Minority

Particularly in the British and Dutch context, multiculturalism emphasizes diversity across cultural border lines. It relates to communities containing multiple cultures. As a descriptive idiom, it usually refers to the demographic make up of a specific city, region, or state. As a normative term, multiculturalism refers to policies that promote diversity. It is often used in reference to immigration as one idealized outcome of the potential societal composition, whereas the other extreme often features the concept of assimilation, usually depicted as the almost forceful inclusion of colorful migrants' cultures into one large gray majority society. French *laicite* (secularity), expressed through integration and other social policies, is often seen as an example of the latter. Implying an essential difference between ethnic minority groups and the majority, Wimmer (2011, 30) explains multiculturalism's assumptions as follows:

> ...Each ethnic group is endowed with a unique universe of norms and cultural preferences and [...] these cultures remain largely unaffected by upward social mobility or spatial dispersion. Thus, such perduring ethnic cultures and communities need to be recognized publicly in order to allow minority individuals to live their lives in accordance with group-specific ideas about the good life and thus enjoy one of the basic human rights that a liberal, democratic state should guarantee.

In western liberal democracies such as the UK and the USA, multicultural policies usually include the clear recognition of ethnic and cultural differences while ignoring the economic implications. For example, Turkish immigrants living in New York city might be called "Turkish Americans" or "Kurdish Americans." A hyphenated vocabulary of ethnic groups is readily available, and usually individual immigrants identify with these concepts within years or decades after their arrival.

While the concept of multiculturalism supports struggles for the recognition of, for example, the LGBT rights (Lesbian, Gay, Bisexual, and Transgender people), it falls short of acknowledging and sustaining economic equality. Within the modern welfare state, specifically its liberal variant, the neoliberal concept of multiculturalism is part of the argument that everybody takes care of himself or herself (Stråth 2008; Máiz and Requejo 2005; Cooper 2004). Stråth emphasizes that everybody is encouraged to exercise his or her own cultural practices, rites, and customs, but there are no social ties beyond the border of each cultural enclave (2008, 31). The concept, thus, has proven to lack solidarity with the newcomers and minorities to be a useful tool with the various European policy approaches toward acculturation and integration. Thus, within the multicultural discourse, the majority society accepts and respects the minority's identity and understands its intrinsic worth, allowing and encouraging the group to follow its own norms and customs. The majority will make gestures of support and cultural recognition (Fisk 2005). However, these gestures will not challenge the source of economic inequality that keeps the minority relatively powerless. Instead, recognition is expressed through cultural gestures that indicate a hope of maintaining minority identities without acknowledging the existing economic differences.

In this sense, it is indeed the democratic multicultural narrative that produces minority, as Jyotirmaya Tripathy and Sudarsan Padmanabhan point out in the Introduction to this volume. However, the actual political and economic manifestation of this multiculturalism is perhaps more akin to the nationalities question in the K. & K. monarchy, where ethnic recognition was layered and some minorities, e.g., the Hungarians, were more Austrian and had more political rights than others, e.g., the Serbs. In neoliberal Europe today, just like in the Habsburg monarchy more than 100 years ago, the minority subjects represent the outcome of the dominant discourse of multiculturalism—including the production of minority consciousness. While the rhetoric of acknowledgment and recognition is clear, the policy implementation of such language is clearly absent in Europe and elsewhere. De facto, thus, the multicultural discourse has led to continuous production of minority as the (often Muslim) Other within the hierarchized system of majority–minority, which reproduces power structures through the partially layered exclusion of out-groups from the notion of national belonging, therewith maintaining the status quo.

The neoliberal perspective conflates the globalization discourse and the liberal understanding of the nation state, as an institution solely responsible for maintaining territorial sovereignty without any notion of social compact. Multiculturalism in the Central European nation states, such as Germany and Austria, is often seen as a cultural concept or policy that has established a particular form of reverse racism (by recognizing ethnic minorities and promoting their cultural particularities). This is often perceived as an activity directed against the established majority societies by an aloof, often leftist, elite, with limited practical implications for the general population whose adherence to the welfare state principles remains as strong as its exclusive stance on it—often expressed through racism and xenophobia.

In Vienna, Zurich, and Berlin, immigrants are considered *Ausländer*. Ausländer is a gloss for the "ethnic other." The term means more than merely foreigner; "it implies the unwanted foreigner who does not belong" (Mandel 2008, 80). It denotes the "unintegratable outsider" (ibid.). Mandel insists that the use of the term has served the agenda of the state in the sense that immigrants are entitled to rights while Ausländer are set apart from citizens and immigrants with residence rights (ibid.). The very act of naming reflects "the definitial dependence of hegemonic majorities vis-à-vis minorities they may well oppress and ghettoize" (Handler and Segal 1993, 5). As the ontological other, it is a short step to the generalized belief that Ausländer "lack the civilization or culture which is taken as the defining characteristic of the hegemonic nation" (ibid.).

Introducing a more tolerant approach toward other cultures—often reaching the extent that members of the majority society now also frequent the kebab take-out hut in addition to the obligatory *Würstelstand* (little sausage stand) visit—has been arguably multiculturalism's greatest achievement. While this might appear to be a cynic's statement, the economic implications for the small migrant business owners are not to be underestimated. Despite these changes, multiculturalism has been frequently seen as an assault against the majority culture and society of particular nation states, such as The Netherlands or Denmark, often resulting in draconian immigration and integration policies. In Norway, it took the expression of violent massacres, where on July 22, 2011, Andres Behring Breivik killed 77 people in Oslo and on Uytola Island.

Encompassing the extreme right's ideological xenophobia, Breivik described his worldview in a compendium of texts entitled *2083: A European Declaration of Independence* that he distributed electronically on the day of the attacks. According to these texts, he regards Islam and "cultural Marxism" as the enemy and argues for the violent anni-hilation of "Eurabia" and multiculturalism as well as the deportation of all Muslims from Europe. While Breivik expresses in these texts what only a very small percentage of Europeans feel, the far right of the political spectrum has consolidated its constituency through a clear antiforeigner, anti-Muslim minority message spiced with xenophobia and everyday racism. Racism and xenophobia are a common occur-rence in Europe today.

Europe and Xenophobia

Europe acquired distinction and salience when pitted against the Other, historically Jewish and, today, often Muslim minorities, who originated most frequently from North Africa and the Middle East. The EU is an interesting point of departure here. Its supposed objective is to overcome nationalist and exclusivist antagonisms and to ensure solidarity among its members. As in any construction of collective identity, a definition of the Other, the nonmember, the one who remains outside, is required. To draw clear lines implies the false assumption that identity is stable and unchangeable. Indeed, identity is always in the process of becoming. No stable and secure notion of the self can exist. However, this is irrelevant because for inclusion and exclusion policies, clear borders need to be drawn and maintained. As Stråth (2008, 34) points out, the inclusion of European "insiders" of course implies the exclusion of non-European or not-yet-European "outsiders," which frequently conflicts with humanis-tic ideals such as equality and freedom.

One important question in this regard is to what extent Europe defines itself in terms of what it is not. Brague (2002, cited in Stråth 2008, 35) argues that Europe is based on an Asian founding myth ("Europa and the Bull") and an Asian religion. Europe, thus, has emerged through the formation of an occidental distinction, which involves the invention of an Other, entailing the alienation from its Asian origins (Stråth 2008). Others have emphasized that essential to the success of the EU is a sense of a transnational European identity, based on common values, rooted in a common past, distinguishing the continent from the rest of the world while connecting nations with vastly different cultures (El-Tayeb 2008). The quest for this common European identity, however, has fallen far behind the process of creating a common legal and economic system.

Authors such as Wodak (2008) have pointed repeatedly at the discursive elements of the nature of racism that is linguistically based and proliferates in subtle ways throughout European society. In many ways, the non-European Other today is seen as possessing a distinctly different premoridal essence and constructed as the "racial opposite which threatens the existence of the self" (Tripathy 2010, 256). Often, in daily discourse, the Other is excluded as the unredeemable "they" from the imaginary brotherhood of the "we," as Torgovnick (1992) once put it, because the speaker must suspend particularities while affirming her similarity with the larger group. In this layered understanding of multiculturalism, differences take on a negative character to minority groups; it is not the difference itself or the existing political and social inequalities that produce exclusion and negative labeling of the minority groups, but the generalization of such differences into negative categories and their attribution to whole groups (Delanty et al. 2008, 4). One response to this labeling is ethnic chauvinism among second generation male youth of various ethnic backgrounds. Categorizing individuals into different groups—the labeling—is, thus, the first step of the discursive construction of minority groups. The second step unfolds as a generalization that includes individuals who appear to have these negative attributes as part of the same group. Each individual encounter with a Turkish migrant, for example, is seen as typical of the whole group of Turks living in the majority society. However, positive experiences are categorized as exceptions. This allows for the maintenance of stereotypical, often racist, assumptions in the majority society. Indeed, Delanty et al. (2008) show that the discursive construction of the "us" and "them" is the foundation of prejudiced and racist perceptions and discourses. To overcome these current racist perceptions, policy changes and broad social actions on the legal, educational, and social fronts will need to be implemented.

Conclusion

Minority in Central Europe is often bound with ethnic identity markers. Majority identities, however, are also often problematic. To be sure, the creation of majorities is only possible through the inclusion of certain minority groups at the expense of others. In France, the state created the nation—through policies that mended together various regional minorities; in Central Europe, nations molded states, sometimes out of the remnants of the multinational empires of the 18th and 19th centuries. Many Central Europeans today have a layered perception of minorities and foreigners—feeling an affinity to immigrants originating from the former territories of these empires, whereas discriminating against those who come from elsewhere because they are seen as essentially different peoples. For these Europeans, identities are still understood as fixed, and newcomer minorities, therefore, cannot help but dilute and contaminate majority identities. That much of these narratives are based on invented pasts and imagined communities is very well known. However, I have shown in this chapter that these national constructs are more complicated and often more ambiguous than they appear to be at first sight. There is no clear definition for what a Turkish or Serbian immigrant is. It is even more complicated if we include these immigrants' children, the so-called second and third generations, often born in Austria and Germany. They are neither Turkish or Serbian, nor Austrian or German, but perhaps something new altogether. Neither, however, is it clear who an Austrian or German is. Identity has much to do with nostalgia in some cases and also with the demarcating of the Other and the establishment of "us" versus "them."

This chapter has shown that nationalist policies and social welfare programs, albeit considered relatively successful in maintaining national coherence and social tranquility during the second part of the 20th century, have been replaced by multiculturalism and neoliberalism. The latter with its "free market über alles" assertiveness clearly began to limit the financial support for the needy, a key characteristic of the Keynesian system. Moreover, today immigrants and minorities are often associated with high welfare dependency, particularly in Northern European states, but also in Central European states. While these liberal policies of multiculturalism were designed to promote diversity (which, however, resulted often in resentments within the majority society), what they really encompassed was the inclusion of wealthy minorities, such as the LGBT groups, at the expense of minorities who would be in need of financial assistance.

Juxtaposing the xenophobia expressed in everyday racism in Europe today with the EU's supposed objective to overcome such nationalist and exclusivist trends makes us realize that the future might be bleak on the continent. This commentator fears that stereotypical and racist assumptions about minorities will stay with us in Europe in the foreseeable future.

However, a different future could also unfold. To usher us toward that better climate for minorities and the majorities, we need to perhaps first begin to articulate the existing reality—with its layered understanding of belonging and difference as well as the ever-changing constructs of identity, specifically clearly visible with second and third generation groups in Europe who are not what the majority expected them to be and often do not behave as the majority would like them to. Asking challenging questions and being willing to change stereotypical thinking will be one key in overcoming some of these problems. Minorities certainly play a role in creating and maintaining minority status. While the involvement of minorities in the currently unfolding processes of labeling and exclusion is clear, to categorize this as complicity in perpetuating the status quo is far-fetched and misleading. Agency does not imply collaboration.

Notes and Bibliography

Notes

1. The German term "Ausländer," loosely translated as foreigner, means literally the one who belongs outside.
2. Welfare regime is here understood as qualitatively different arrangements between state, market, and the household that different historically established modes of governance and class relationships have given birth to (see Schierup et al. 2006, 85).
3. One anonymous reviewer remarked here that there might have been problems within the social welfare systems even without the devastating influence of neoliberalism. Be that as it may, I contest that these are issues of redistribution and not economic reality, and, thus, they fall within the responsibility of the state, rather than shortcomings of Socialist or Marxist theories.

Bibliography

Anderson, Benedict. 1983. *Imagined Communities: Reflections on the Origin and Spread of Nationalism.* New York: Verso.

Banton, Michael. 2007. "Weber on Ethnic Communities: A Critique." *Nations and Nationalism* 13 (1): 19–35.

Berbrier, Mitch. 2002. "Making Minorities: Cultural Space, Stigma Transformation Frames, and the Categorical Status Claims of Deaf, Gay, and White Supremacist Activists in Late Twentieth Century America." *Sociological Forum* 17 (4): 553–91.

Bourdieu, Pierre. 1998. *Acts of Resistance: Against the Tyranny of the Market.* New York: Free Press.

Brenner, Neil and Nik Theodore. 2002. "Cities and Geographies of 'Actually Existing Neoliberalism'." In *Spaces of Neoliberalism: Urban Restructuring in North America and Western Europe*, edited by Neil Brenner and Nik Theodore. Oxford, UK: Blackwell.

Burgers, Jack and Robert Kloosterman. 1996. "Dutch Comfort: Postindustrial Transition and Social Exclusion in Spangen, Rotterdam." *Area* 28 (4): 1–13.

Chandhoke, Neera. 1999. *Beyond Secularism: The Rights of Religious Minorities.* New Delhi: Oxford University Press.

Cooper, Davina. 2004. *Challenging Diversity: Rethinking Equality and the Value of Difference.* Cambridge: Cambridge University Press.

Delanty, Gerard, Ruth Wodak, and Paul Jones (eds). 2008. *Identity, Belonging and Migration.* Liverpool: Liverpool University Press.

El-Tayeb, Fatima. 2008. "'The Birth of a European Public': Migration, Postnationality, and Race in the Uniting of Europe." *American Quarterly* 60 (3):649–70.

Erikson, Thomas. 2005. "Ethnicity and Nationalism." In *Nations and Nationalism: A Reader*, edited by Philip Spencer and Howard Wollman, 135–48. New Brunswick, NJ: Rutgers University Press.

Esping-Andersen, Gøsta (ed.). 1996. *Welfare States in Transition: National Adaptations in Global Economies.* London: SAGE.

Fisk, Milton. 2005. "Multiculturalism and Neoliberalism." *Praxis Filosofica* 21 (2005): 21–28. Accessed August 5, 2012. http://www.miltonfisk.org/writings/multiculturalism-and-neoliberalism/

Forsythe, Diana. 1989. "German Identity and the Problem of History." In *History and Ethnicity*, edited by E. Tonkin, M. McDonald, and M. Chapman, 137–56. London: Routledge.

Franz, Barbara. 2012. "Immigrant Youth, Hip Hop and Feminist Pedagogy: Outlines of an Alternative Integration Policy in Vienna, Austria." *International Studies Perspectives* 13 (3): 270–88.

Gilroy, Paul. 2005. "Between Camps." In *Nations and Nationalism: A Reader*, edited by Philip Spencer and Howard Wollman, 149–62. New Brunswick, NJ: Rutgers University Press.

Gleason, P. 1991. "Minorities (Almost) All: The Minority Concept in American Social Thought." *American Quarterly* 43 (3): 392–424.

Handler, Richard and Daniel Segal. 1993. "Introduction." *Social Analysis* 33: 3–8.

Hobsbawm, Eric. 1989. *The Age of Empire: 1875–1914*. New York: Vintage Books.

Kasarda, John, Jürgen Friedrichs, and Kay Ehlers. 1992. "Urban Industrial Restructuring and Minority Problems in the US and Germany." In *Ethnic Minorities and Industrial Change in Europe and North America*, edited by Malcolm Cross, 250–75. Cambridge: Cambridge University Press.

Mandel, Ruth. 2008. *Cosmopolitan Anxieties: Turkish Challenges to Citizenship and Belonging in Germany*. London: Duke University Press.

Máiz, Ramón and Feran Requejo (eds). 2005. *Democracy, Nationalism and Multiculturalism*. London: Frank Press.

McDonald, Randy. 2009. Review of *Peasants into Frenchmen*, by Eugene Weber. Accessed August 5, 2012. http://rfmcdpei.livejournal.com/1889178.html

Schierup, Carl-Ulrik, Peo Hansen, and Stephen Castles. 2006. *Migration, Citizenship, and the European Welfare State: A European Dilemma*. New York: Oxford University Press.

Smith, Anthony. 2005. "Ethno-Symbolism and the Study of Nationalism." In *Nations and Nationalism: A Reader*, edited by Philip Spencer and Howard Wollman, 23–31. New Brunswick, NJ: Rutgers University Press.

Stråth, Bo. 2008. "Belonging and European Identity." In *Identity, Belonging and Migration*, edited by Gerard Delanty, Ruth Wodak, and Paul Jones, 21–37. Liverpool: Liverpool University Press.

Taylor, Charles. 1994. "The Politics of Recognition." In *Multiculturalism: Examining the Politics of Recognition*, edited by Amy Gutmann, 25–73. Princeton: Princeton University Press.

Torgovnick, Marianna. 1992. "Politics of the 'We'." *The Southern Atlantic Quarterly* 91 (1): 43–63.

Tripathy, Jyotirmaya. 2010. "Democracy and its Others." *Journal of Third World Studies* 27 (1): 253–72.

Weber, Eugene. 1976. *Peasants into Frenchmen: The Modernization of Rural France 1870–1914*. Stanford, CA: Stanford University Press.

Wimmer, Andreas. 2008. "The Making and Unmaking of Ethnic Boundaries: A Multilevel Process Theory." *American Journal of Sociology* 113 (4): 970–1022.

———. 2011. "How to Study Ethnicities in Immigrant Societies." In *The Bosnian Diaspora: Integration in Transnational Communities*, edited by Marko Valenta and Sabrina Ramet, 25–61. UK: Ashgate.

Winter, Jay. 2006. *Dreams of Peace and Freedom: Utopian Moments in the Twentieth Century*. London: Yale University Press.

Wirth, Louis. 1945. "The Problem of Minority Groups." In *The Science of Man in the World Crisis*, edited by Ralph Linton, 347–72. New York: Columbia University Press.

Wodak, Ruth. 2008. *Critical Discourse Analysis: Theory and Interdisciplinarity*. London: Palgrave Macmillan.

3

Re-Turning the Idea of Minority: Going beyond the Politics of Recognition

Lajwanti Chatani

In recent times, India has witnessed several protests and movements by different groups demanding for their recognition as minorities and seeking the guarantee of minority rights. Everyday politics has been replete with political incidents and struggles for the acknowledgment and security of minority rights. A cursory glance at contemporary politics in the recent past would substantiate this position. In March 2012, the Jats, a supposedly upper-caste Hindu community, organized violent protests demanding their inclusion under the ambit of the policy of positive discrimination, more popularly known as the policy of reservation in government employment. In May 2012, women activists agitated against the government's apathy toward passing the Women's Reservation Bill. In October 2012, tens of thousands of India's poorest citizens marched to Delhi to demand that the government give them land on which to live and from which to earn a livelihood. In November 2012, hundreds of gay rights activists marched through Delhi to demand for recognition and respect to lead their lives with dignity in a society which has remained conservative on sexual considerations. A few days later, more than 500 Christian Dalits from across the country staged a rally in Delhi to protest against the deferment of a Supreme Court ruling on whether

Dalit converts to other faiths can avail of affirmative action policies of the government. Although these protests were organized and carried out by different groups of people, they all invoked the politics of identity and expressed their demands in the language of minority rights.

The policy of reservation remains among the more empowering and equalizing provisions guaranteed by the Indian Constitution. Under the provisions of this policy, seats are reserved in elected bodies, educational institutions, and government employment for members of the disadvantaged groups and minority communities. Initially, such groups and communities were identified as Scheduled Castes and Scheduled Tribes; however, with the passing of the Mandal Recommendations, the Other Backward Classes were included under the provisions of this policy. Through such reservations, the disadvantaged groups and communities in India have been able to slowly, yet meaningfully, access positions of power and equality. Looking at this success, there have been several demands by different groups for inclusion under the ambit of this legislation.

Such spates of the demands for the guarantee of minority rights have resulted in growing cynicism and skepticism about the recognition of minorities and the politics of identity. In fact, some suggest that the rise in demand for recognition as minorities undermines the spirit and value of India's democratic and secular edifice. The contention is often that groups and communities in India endeavor to become a minority in order to gain privileges and entitlements, which they justly do not deserve.

Some questions do emerge from the increase in demands for minority recognition. Why do certain groups desire the status of a minority? Why do social groups choose to become a minority? Does the recognition of a group as a minority substantially contribute to the promotion and strengthening of the claims to justice and equality of such a group? How should this politics of "becoming a minority" be read and managed by a constitutional democracy like India?

This chapter involves an attempt to look closely and critically at the ongoing discourse on minority rights and the politics of cultural recognition, in the context of such increasing demands for recognition. Its concern is to explore the underlying conceptual framework on which the rights of minorities rest. The language of and demand for minority rights and recognition is poised on the idea of justice. Justice, as a political value, is inherently open and discursive, and any attempt to lock it or render it absolute would rid it of its remedial and empowering ethos. Justice requires not only open and supple principles and guarantees, but also an open and discursive context from which to operate. By making the context rigid or impregnable, justice can only be denied. Similarly, the question of the minor and her rights is essentially and fundamentally a question of justice and equality, and, therefore, must depend and work through an open and supple understanding of politics, in terms of both, the principles and the context. Closing and fixing the idea and the politics of the minor would inevitably result in getting rid of the emancipatory and equalizing potential of the discourse, leaving it merely as a vacuous claim to equality and freedom. It is such an open understanding of the minority which remains essential for the politics of a postcolonial, democratic, and culturally plural society like India.

This chapter argues that even though minority rights have been guaranteed to certain groups in India, the context of the guarantee of such rights remains essentially rigid and unbending. This hinders and diminishes the potential of the guarantee and works against the ideal of justice. The chapter raises such questions as: When does a group count as a minority? Are minorities fixed entities, or do they evolve and get constituted within the context of a majoritarian politics? Can the language of rights, which is inherently the language of individual reason, be applied to groups? Since minority rights are inherently about justice, and justice is remedial and open, does this entail that the discourse on minority rights necessarily remains open and remedial? Can we have a fixed closed understanding of the minority, or does it necessarily have to remain an open account? The chapter seeks to respond to these questions by focusing on three aspects of the discourse on minorities, namely, the politics of recognition, the conception of the self, and the ideal of nationalism underlying the nation state. Its concern is to underscore the need for an open understanding of the minority and her context in order to address the injustices she experiences. The argument, put differently, is in favor of re-turning the idea and the context of a minority by rendering it open, and thereby going beyond the politics of recognition. In attempting to respond to some of these questions, the chapter looks mainly at the arguments of Charles Taylor and Jürgen Habermas, who have contributed significantly to the discourse on minority rights. In doing so, the chapter, while upholding the brilliance of their arguments, seeks to demonstrate the inherent open understanding of their ideas of recognition, rights, and the minority.

The question on and of minorities has come to occupy a position of significance and notable concern in our contemporary theoretical discourse as well as in our ongoing social political practice. The minority question in its main can be approached and understood in different ways; and then, how we understand and approach this question often guides our response to the question. To begin with, one can confront the minority question from two different and desirably distanced standpoints. The first is an understanding of the minority question from a utilitarian perspective, where the individual self is understood to be led by "interests" defined in terms of utility or preferences. To this extent, the minority and majority are groupings or aggregates of such interests and preferences. This understanding of minority is a procedural one, and its question is understood to be somewhat resolved, if not dismissed, through the procedures and structures of democratic representation as well as the guarantee of equal and similar rights.

The second is an understanding of the minority question from a constitutive or substantive perspective. Going beyond the procedural account, this idea of the minority questions the conception of the individual self, portraying the self and its other as communities which are constitutive of "identity." And this identity could be in terms of class, religion, gender, class, sexuality, language, or one's conception of the good. To this extent, the minority is not fashioned by enumeration, but instead by one's experience of disadvantage or one's position and location in an unjust unequal order of things. A minority, therefore, can be mapped out either, as Rawls would have us believe, through the unfair distribution of the benefits and burdens of social cooperation and conflict, or, as Taylor would argue, by practices of recognition or misrecognition of one's substantive self, or then, as Fraser would argue, by both maldistribution and misrecognition.[1]

With the gradual global encompassment of the idea and institutions of procedural democracy, the first understanding of minority, which is numerical minorities, figures as desirable as well as defensible. It is the second or substantive understanding of minority which has come to challenge, if not alter, much of the tradition of contemporary moral and political discourse, and understandably so. While it is imperative for us to respond to the minority question in its substantive understanding, this task is certainly complicated and thorny. An adequate response to this question would mean not only a reconceptualization of our dominant political discourse, but also going beyond the available guarantee of procedural democracy to a democracy poised on the guarantee of justice and recognition. In other words, the substantive understanding or question of minority hinges on a response which compels the working out of the justice of political arrangements rather than the order of such arrangements.

In response to the question of substantive minorities and in step with the shift in the concern of contemporary political discourse, much has been persuasively said about the valid claims to justice, justice defined both, and somewhat disjointedly, in terms of redistribution and recognition, of different minorities and the imperative to accommodate such claims within our history, narratives, and practices. Theorists like John Rawls, Charles Taylor, Jürgen Habermas, I. M. Young, Will Kymlicka, Amy Gutmann, and Nancy Fraser, among others,[2] have proffered thoughtful and critical arguments on the dominant theoretical discourse, underlining its exclusions and neglect toward the claims of others. Such arguments have convincingly questioned widely held assumptions about the inclusiveness of the mainstream, the candor of the canon, the neutrality of the state, the encompassment of the nation, and the representative possibilities of the universal individual self. The questioning of the singular uncontested individual self, and the uncovering of its limited and oppressive politics, opened up the possibility of an alternative mode of theorizing, a theorizing conscious of the ethical and authentic claims of the other, the minor and the margin.

A major contribution of these arguments has been to shift the agenda of contemporary political and social theorizing from an obsession with the concern of order and control to one with a focus on justice and equality. Not too long ago, much of social and political theory remained centered around concerns of order, sovereignty, and power, which understood politics to be principally about the self and the citizen. With the growing concern on minority rights and the politics of recognition, political theory is now focused on the politics of the other—her recognition, respect, and accommodation. And it is this new concern with justice that has resulted in the emergence of a wide and varied discourse on the other.

The theoretical engagement with the other in terms of class has been much easier to work with. As argued by Rawls, justice requires a more equitable distribution of collective goods for compensating the unequal conditions of life in capitalist societies; and such distribution is achievable and agreeable under conditions of our intuitive and political rationality. Also, Rawls positions his theory of justice in line with the theory of individual rights; because the primary goods (in Rawls' understanding) are either distributed among individuals (like money, free time, and services) or used by individuals (like the infrastructure of transportation, health care, and education), and can, thus, take the form of individual claims to benefits.

The tension emerges when rights are to be awarded to groups, that is, when groups or collectivities are to be recognized as minorities and guaranteed minority rights. This leads to two fundamental questions: first, can rights which are squarely worked out for individuals be applied to groups and collectivities?; second, when should a group be recognized as a minority? Interestingly, both these questions are poised on the perspective of justice, and ought to be responded to from such a perspective.

Let me begin with the first aspect, namely, the politics of recognition. Contemporary political debates have been characterized by a comprehensive and elegant theorization of the politics of identity and minority rights, and one political theorist who has contributed immensely to this debate is Charles Taylor. In his much celebrated paper titled "The Politics of Recognition" (1992), Taylor puts forth a rather convincing account of the politics of identity and the need for recognition. According to Taylor, the politics of recognition must be understood as a correction to the politics of nationalism: while the latter works out and depends on a false homogenization of cultural diverse peoples, the latter recognizes, respects, and accommodates such diversities. Taylor's underlying thesis is that

> ...our identity is partly shaped by recognition or its absence, often by the "misrecognition" of others, and so a person or group of people or society can suffer real damage, real distortion, if the people or society around them

mirror back to them a confining or demeaning or contemptible picture of themselves. (Taylor 1992, 25)

For Taylor then, identities are formed not in a monological manner, but rather in a dialogical process. In his words, one of the "crucial features of human life is its fundamentally dialogical character. We become full agents, capable of understanding ourselves, and, hence, of defining our identity, through our acquisition of rich human languages of expression" (ibid., 32). He uses language in a broad sense to cover not only the words we speak, but also other modes of expression whereby we define ourselves, and which we learn through our exchanges with others. Since the construction of one's identity is a dialogical process, it remains essentially political and, therefore, potentially violent. In his words,

> Nonrecognition or misrecognition can inflict harm, can be a form of oppression, imprisoning someone in a false, distorted, and reduced mode of being.... Within these perspectives, misrecognition shows not just a lack of due respect. It can inflict a grievous wound, saddling its victims with a crippling self-hatred. Due recognition is not just a courtesy we owe people. It is a vital human need. (ibid., 25–26)

This dialogical relationship, for Taylor, is not a fixed or finite moment in the formation of our identities. For him, the formation of our identity is not limited to the origins, but rather remains a permanent feature, of a person's life.[3] As Taylor argues,

> ...this is not just a fact about genesis, which can be ignored later on. We don't just learn the languages in dialogue and then go on to use them for our own purposes.... We define our identity always in dialogue with, sometimes in struggle against, the things our significant others want to see in us. Even after we outgrow some of these others... and they disappear from our lives, the conversation with them continues within us as long as we live. (ibid., 32–33)

In this way, Taylor leaves the process of identity formation open and supple, so that one can shift between the political positions of dominant and minor, without having to entirely disrupt or negate who she is.

More importantly, Taylor identifies two changes that together have made the modern preoccupation with identity and recognition inevitable. The first, according to him, "is the collapse of social hierarchies, which used to be the basis of honor" (ibid., 26–27). Honor, as he rightly suggests, is not democratically distributed; rather, it is essential that not everyone have it: "Honor is intrinsically a matter of preferences" (Taylor 1992, 27). Against the notion of honor, modernity brings in the notion of dignity, which is more universalist and egalitarian. "The underlying premise here, as Taylor states, is "that everyone shares in it" (ibid.). Obviously, it is this concept of dignity which is compatible with a truly democratic society. However, for Taylor, "democracy has ushered in a politics of equal recognition, which has taken various forms of demands for the equal status of cultures and genders" (ibid.). Intrinsically related to this notion of dignity is the second change brought forward by modernity, which Taylor labels as "the ideal of authenticity." In accordance with this ideal, each one of us is free to discover our own original way of being. Also, this way of being cannot be socially derived, but must be inwardly generated, albeit in a dialogical manner. It understands human beings to be endowed with a moral sense, an intuitive feeling for what is right and wrong. For Taylor, "the original point of this doctrine was to combat a rival view, that knowing right and wrong was a matter of calculating consequences, in particular those concerned with divine reward and punishment" (ibid., 28).

For Taylor, then, identity comes to each of us through a political process and in relation to our significant others, a process which is permanent and open. It is such openness and impermanence which underlies his arguments in terms of the politics of recognition and the demand for minority rights. A fixed and permanent account of the minority would only close the potential of the politics of recognition, rendering it inherently unjust. In fact, as rightly suggested by de Certeau (1997), it would result in a negative approach to politics and an understanding of the self which is poised on denial. As de Certeau points out,

> ...the difficulty that a certain number of minority movements are facing is one of being located negatively. A cultural, social or ethnic autonomy always draws attention to itself by saying no: No, says the black, I am not American. No says the Breton, I am not French. (ibid., 69)

And to continue, "No," says the Dalit, "I am not Hindu," and then, "No," says the Hindu, "you are not Indian enough." Even though denial and negation constitutes the philosophical basis for the validity of minority claims, it must be left open and susceptible to change for it to be just and egalitarian.

In the Indian situation, we have come to understand the minority in terms of a closed, fixed, and permanent category. Rather than one's identity being determined by significant others, the other has become the permanent other, thereby leaving no room and no possibility for an emancipatory and equalizing politics. A Dalit is permanently a Dalit; a woman permanently so. This not only closes the process of emancipation by locking the identity of the other, it also fails to question the deeply hierarchical nature of the society, thereby diminishing the claims of equal dignity for all. Here, one who becomes a minority does so permanently. As rightly pointed out by Bilgrami, is it sufficient for the sake of justice to realize and recognize the identity of the other, or does this realization in itself result in the other of justice? In other words, is the realization and recognition of identity and difference the remedy, the symptom of a deeper pathology, or the pathology itself? As noted by Bilgrami, "One might think that our obsession with questions such as what is a Muslim? (and thereby what is an Indian, what is a woman, what is a minor) is irrational... and that that realization should by itself be the basis of cure" (1992, 823).

I now move on to the second aspect which is about the conception of the self. There has been a long standing debate in contemporary political theory over the morally and politically valid conception of the self—the self which engages in politics and authors the law for herself. On one side of this debate are the liberal individualists who understand the self to be an individual, standing at a distance from all her identities, ends, and conceptions of the good, and thereby free to choose among such ends and goods; on the other side are the communitarians who criticize this individualist conception as flawed and false, and who see us to be constituted by our identities and ends. Even though the communitarians question the language of the individual, they do not fail to employ the language of rights which, many would argue, remain located in the politics of individualism. While it is possible to at once question the possibility of collective rights, that is, rights awarded to a group, a closer and more careful look would demonstrate that the two are not so entirely incompatible. In fact, it is only when both the individual and collective rights are placed beside each other that the openness of the politics of the minority can be assured.

According to Habermas, "modern constitutions owe their existence to a conception found in modern natural law according to which citizens come together voluntarily to form of a legal community of free and equal consociates" (1994, 107). Consequently, he asks whether a theory of rights that is so individualistically constructed can deal adequately with struggles for recognition in which it is the articulation and assertion of collective identities that seem to be at stake. At first glance, he claims, they would seem to be incompatible. For Habermas, however,

> ...this interpretation of the system of rights is paternalistic in that it ignores half of the concept of autonomy. It does not take into consideration that those to whom the law is addressed can acquire autonomy only to the extent that they can understand themselves to be the authors of the laws to which they are subject as private legal persons. (ibid., 112)

According to him, private and public autonomy are equiprimordial. In his words, "it is not a matter of public autonomy supplementing and remaining external to private autonomy, but rather of an internal, that is, conceptually necessary connection between them" (ibid., 113). He continues by arguing that

> ...once we take the internal connection between democracy and the constitutional state seriously, it becomes clear that the system of rights is blind neither to unequal social conditions nor to cultural differences. The color-blindness of the selective reading vanishes once we assume that we ascribe to the bearers of individual rights an identity that is conceived intersubjectively. Persons and legal persons as well, become individualized only through a process of socialization. A correctly understood theory of rights requires a politics of recognition that protects the integrity of the individual in the life contexts in which his or her identity is formed. (ibid.)

In a similar vein, Kymlicka sees a complementary, rather than conflictual, relationship between individual rights and community membership when he argues in favor of internal freedoms and external equalities as against internal restrictions and external protections.[4] For both Habermas and Kymlicka, then, it is both possible and desirable to view individual freedoms and community rights as interrelated and interdependent. Since communities and collectivities are not voluntarily chosen in the first place, they would have to be interlaced with individual freedom and rights. Only when such interlacing takes place would the politics of recognition be rendered open and thereby just.

In India, once again, we seem to have moved very little in relating and interlacing the value of community membership with the guarantee of individual rights. As legal persons, we are either individuals or members of the collective, and never both at the same time. This vehemently opposes the emancipatory potential of minority rights as it fails to guarantee freedom and the right to author the law to members of the collective. Rather, such members are left imprisoned within the boundaries of the collective. As rightly maintained by Gutmann,

> ...full public recognition as equal citizens may require two forms of respect: (1) respect for the unique identities of each individual, regardless of gender, race or ethnicity, and (2) respect for those activities, practices, and ways of viewing the world that are particularly valued by, or associated with, members of disadvantaged groups. (1994, 8)

Suggesting a neat relationship between the two, Gutmann argues that we need to look at the identity of the group as an interest. A dominant perception of contemporary political theorizing is the split between the politics of interest from the politics of identity, so that those who focus on one can, and often do, manage to ignore the other. Consequently, theories of minorities are often, in the main, theories about the politics of identity and only attend partly, if at all, to the politics of interest. Is the politics of interest entirely alienated or alienable from the politics of identity? Or does the self have an interest in identity? To quote Gutmann:

> ...were it not for the mutual identification of individuals with one another, there would be no identity groups. Although mutual identification is basic to human existence, it has been neglected in democratic theory, where the language of "interest" and "interest groups" rather than "identity" and "identity groups," is far more common. Yet no one should doubt that identification with others makes a difference in how individuals perceive their own interests. (2003, 2)

It is thereby imperative for the promise of justice to integrate in essence the interest of the individual and the identity of the collective, the politics of interest and the politics of identity, and not simply to place them beside each other.

I now move to the third aspect, namely, the nationalism of the nation state. The world as we have come to understand and accept is divided into separate sovereign nation states. Underlying the conception of the nation state is the idea of a single political entity ruling legitimately over a single common brotherhood—a truly unitary self inhabiting a perfectly homogenized, if not sanitized, space. The borders dividing such nation states not only define and thereby close the territorial space, but, more importantly, mark out the identity of the insider from the outsider. The presence of an Other, an outsider, or what some constitutions would label an alien, either within the space of the nation or of the state—in most cases, the minority, is meant to be marked, normalized, included, or permanently excluded. Citizenship rights then are guaranteed only to those who fit into this straightjacket of the nation state. And it is this straightjacketing which sets apart or sets outside the gypsy, the refugee, and even the abnormal from the language of rights.

The inside, the nation state, is in this way often understood or rather misunderstood as the desire for or presence of a neat, uncomplex, and homogenized space of identification. In this way, the borders of the nation state, as Balibar argues, function in terms of a "Hobbesian reduction of complexity" or "supplement of simplicity" (2002, 77), although it is this very reduction of complexity that in the first place creates the complexity. In the words of Balibar,

> ...the state as nation state is among other things, a formidable reducer of complexity, though its very existence is a permanent cause of complexity, which then falls to it to reduce.... In utter disregard of certain borders, or in some cases under cover of such borders, indefinable and impossible identities emerge in various places, identities which are regarded, as a consequence as non-identities. And the existence of such non-identities inside the border is a life-and-death question for large numbers of human beings. (ibid.)

But then, in terms of human life, what differentiates the sovereign insider from the minority outsider? What defines the borders that divide the minority and majority inside the national border? Are these borders constituted by difference, or are they constitutive of difference? And more importantly, who defines, controls, and patrols this border?

All minorities pit themselves against the nation state, and, more specifically, the hegemonic and homogenizing project of nation building. Multicultural theorists have fittingly and insightfully underscored the bias toward the majority underlying the assumed neutrality of the modern nation state, a bias which expresses itself in apparently benign forms, such as the national language, national symbols, and national holidays. According to Kymlicka, for instance, the modern nation state with its guarantee of equal rights is incapable of a just inclusion of all cultural communities, as it inevitably, though not necessarily innocently, promotes, privileges, or protects the culture of the majority as the culture of the public, the nation. This not only compels the minority to accept and appropriate the culture of the majority as "their" national culture, it also systematically encourages and allows for the disappearance or disrespect of the culture of the minority. It is to correct this inherent bias of the apparently neutral nation state that Kymlicka argues in favor of different rights for the minority.

Within our ongoing discourse, there seems to be a developing consensus over this argument. The issue at stake, however, is that in questioning the justness and inclusiveness of the nation state, or even in identifying the nation state as unjust, minorities make a "return" to an identity which has been, or should have been, washed away, othered, and made foreign by the homogenizing and hegemonic nation state project. In the words of de Certeau, "there is a brutal return to local tradition, a local language, but it is a return to something that has already become foreign. We return to something that inhabits us (a means of identification) but it has already become other or altered" (de Certeau 1997, 71). And it is in its return to that which is othered and made alien that the minority must necessarily engage with the state in a somewhat tense oppositional politics. How do we respond to this tension? How can the state, or for that matter any dominant discourse, accommodate that which it has rendered alien, without denying itself? Within the selfhood of the state, how can the other be accommodated and respected as other? Can we explain this "return" in terms of a nonviolent consensual politics?

In a brilliant argument on the crisis of secular nationalism in India, Nigam (2006) examines how the project of modernity is ridden with at least two interrelated problems. In his words,

> [F]irst, the emancipatory project is fundamentally tied to the agency of the enlightened elite, which is seen as the carrier of Reason and Progress. This idea is based on the assumption of inertia and backwardness of the masses who have to be delivered from darkness and brought to light. The second, related problem is that this vision is virtually innocent of any understanding of power. (ibid., 3)

When we read the idea of nationalism from a political perspective and inject it with the concept of power, it no longer appears as singular or wholesome as it claims to be. Rather, it appears as a totalizing logic which attempts to erase all others and homogenize them into a unitary Self. As Nigam suggests,

> ...can we really assume that the "national societies" which came to acquire their specific form and structure through entirely contingent factors, are really governed by some singular logic? On the other hand, if we reject the idea of a social totality... are we left with just so many "little selves," continuously at odds with each other? (Nigam 2006, 19)

Employing the metaphor of time and memory, Nigam identifies the dominant discourse on nationalism with the logic of a homogeneous empty time, which in his words "does not merely 'offer accommodation' to other cultures..., it does so by inserting them into a larger totality where they represent mere survivals of the past" (ibid., 25). Recognizing minority rights and being just to other cultures would then inevitably depend on the questioning and possible disintegration of the dominant culture of nationalism. It would require a rethinking of the conditions for living together and a respect for the different cultural entities that inhabit the social space.

Earlier in this chapter, I somewhat simplistically distinguished between the understanding of a minority as a procedural category of enumeration and the understanding of a minority as a substantive category of denial. Simplistic, as I seemed to compel myself to believe that these two categories of understanding are altogether unrelated. In fact, one of the major sites of contestation for the minor has been the collapsing of these categories. Peoples today are, for the most part, reduced to populations, with the identity of people being condensed into data. Within the forces of our existing democratic institutions and procedures, a minority is a group which not only experiences discrimination, domination, and denial, but one which, in terms of numbers, must be a force to reckon with. On the other hand, a numerical majority is one which reserves the democratic right to rule and define. To what extent does the democratic framework of numerical majorities and minorities influence or intrude upon the substantive categories of majorities and minorities?

The world we inhabit is a world characterized by the move of people and cultures across, and sometimes against, nation state boundaries; and it is this move that further weakens the minority question as well as strengthens it. Unlike before, when humans were divided culturally into nations, today, human societies are characterized by diversity and difference, and thereby minorities.

Such questions and many more dominate the theoretical discourse on minorities today. On one hand, they enrich the available discourse in terms of the claims of minorities; on the other, they question its utility and effectiveness in responding to the question on/of the minority. Our contemporary discourse, both in terms of theoretical understanding and practical politics, and unlike ever before, is confronted at once with the futility and unfeasibility of evading such questions and with the ethical and political challenge of responding to them.

We in India, inhabiting and making up what could be the most diverse and different of human societies, with our uncompromising promise to democratic procedures and institutions coupled with the fate of our postcolonial histories, ought to sit up to this challenge put forward by the minority question. To respond to this question in a somewhat just mood would be to reshape the history of our future in an open inclusive manner, by re-turning the idea of a minority and going beyond the politics of recognition; to evade and leave this question unaddressed would be to provide the basis for our violent future.

Notes and Bibliography

Notes

1. See Rawls (1971), Taylor (1992), and Fraser (1997).
2. See Rawls (1971), Taylor (1992), Young (1990), Kymlicka (1995), Gutmann (2003), Habermas (1998), and Fraser (1997).
3. The idea of a continuous dialogue has been put forward also by Bakhtin. See Bakhtin (1984).
4. See Will Kymlicka (1995, 35–44), *Multicultural Citizenship*, pp. 35–44.

Bibliography

Bakhtin, M. M. 1984. *Problems of Dostoyevsky's Poetics*. Minneapolis: University of Minnesota Press.

Balibar, Etienne. 2002. *Politics and the Other Scene*. London: Verso.

Bilgrami, Akeel. 1992 "'What is a Muslim': Fundamental Commitment and Cultural Identity." *Critical Inquiry*, 18 (4): 821–42.

de Certeau, Michel. 1997. *Culture in the Plural*. Minneapolis: University of Minnesota Press.

Fraser, Nancy. 1997. *Justice Interruptus: Critical Reflections on the "Postsocialist" Condition*. New York: Routledge.

Gutmann, Amy. 2003. *Identity in Democracy*. Princeton: Princeton University Press.

Habermas, Jürgen. 1994. "'Struggles for Recognition in the Democratic Constitutional State'." in Amy Gutmann (ed.), In *Multiculturalism: Examining the Politics of Recognition*, edited by Amy Gutmann. Princeton: Princeton University Press.

———. 1998. *The Inclusion of the Other: Studies in Political Theory*. Cambridge, MA: MIT Press.

Kymlicka, Will. 1995. *Multicultural Citizenship: A Liberal Theory of Minority Rights*. Oxford: Clarendon Press.

Nigam, Aditya. 2006. *The Insurrection of Little Selves: The Crisis of Secular-Nationalism in India*. New Delhi: Oxford University Press.

Rawls, John. 1971. *A Theory of Justice*. London: Oxford University Press.

Taylor, Charles. 1992. "The Politics of Recognition." in Amy Gutmann (ed.), In *Multiculturalism and the Politics of Recognition*, edited by Amy Gutmann, 25–73. Princeton: Princeton University Press.

Young, I. M. 1990. *Justice and the Politics of Difference*. Princeton: Princeton University Press.

PART 2
The European Experience

4

Manufacturing Blackness at the Turn of 20th-century France

Abdoulaye Gueye

This chapter is focused upon two arguments binding together the concepts of minority and propaganda.[1] First, the existence of a minority implies the public claim for both difference and inclusion. This claim does not spring up ex nihilo. It results from the awareness of a regime of summoning discourses and practices that conceals a division of the nation between a homogenized and dominant category of entitled subjects often referred to as majoritarian society, and a (diverse) category of subservient subjects kept at the margin.[2] This conception departs from any essentialization of minority. Nevertheless, it corresponds with many studies that stress the relational dimension of identity. Althusser (1971) highlights this dimension through his analysis of the act of interpellation. By reacting positively to an interpellation, he posits, the individual on the street becomes a knowing subject. In Weedon's interpretation (2004), the individual thereby becomes both the product of this process and its producer. Had s/he not responded positively, the individual would have broken the majority's regime of intimating discourses and practices in which the act of interpellation partakes.

Anti-essentialist by definition, this conception inscribes power relations at the heart of the production of minority. In doing so, it also converges with notable theories including those of Hall (1990, 2000), Butler (1990, 1993), or de Certeau (1997). Acknowledging that identities are always constructed "through relation to the Other," Hall argues that "they emerge within the play of specific modalities of power, and thus are more the product of the marking of difference and exclusion" (2000, 17). Similarly, Butler's theory of performativity (1990) points out that the power to produce the Other is not effective as long as the subject summoned to an identity (or position) refuses to respond to these summons. This idea was already traceable in Foucault's thesis that the social existence of homosexuality was effective only at the moment when, in response to the medical institution, it manifests in "the formation of a 'reverse' discourse [through which] homosexuality began to speak on its own behalf, to demand that its legitimacy or 'naturality' be acknowledged" (Foucault 1978, 101). De Certeau localizes minorities' production in the same nexus of power relations, often translated in oppression/exploitation of said group by a "majoritarian society." Hence, his statement: "the feeling of being different is tied to the designation of this difference by other, and to a situation that... continued to diminish lived autonomy" (de Certeau, 1997, 71). Reflecting on the eruption of the Negritude, de Certeau elaborates further by positing that Negritude is nonexistent "insofar as it is a collection of cultural objects created through ethnological analysis," but exists "only as of the moment when there is a new subject of history, that is when people opt for the defiance of existing" (ibid., 75–76). In short, the determining role of the "colonial library,"[3] namely the regime of purported scientific discourses, practices, and representations weaved at the request of, or by, the state apparatus to manufacture a black collective subject, is debatable. As long as there is not a collective subject investing in this narrative and standing up to express its existence, these discourses are doomed.

The etymological root of the concept of minority constitutes opportune ground to elaborate further on the aforementioned theories. The Latin root of minority, that is, *minuere*, means: "to lessen." This etymology confirms the dynamics of power relations at the heart of minorityness. Minority evokes, in this regard, the division of the nation, and alludes to the condition of disadvantage or prejudice of one group naturalized through an ideological mechanism invoking characteristics such as race, sex, skin color, or religion, as perceived by de Certeau, Butler, and other recent studies (Fassin and Fassin 2006; Skrentny 2002; Wieviorka 2008). Taylor suggests convincingly that the sense of minority-ness evolves as members of a society, often considering themselves to be the "'old stock' population," continue to function politically and deliberate amongst themselves concerning the future of the nation without listening to the subgroup(s) of the nation (2011, chap. 7).

This condition is worth highlighting to warn against the tendency implicit in many studies of equating majority and minority with demographic size, which the expression "women and minorities" conveys by the extrusion of women from the minority category on the sole basis of their numbers.[4] Louw's study (2004), although it saves the cost of theorizing the concept of minority/majority, offers grounds to contend that minority-ness is not to be assessed through a demographic lens: fearing the emergence of a black power in 1948, the Afrikaans seized the opportunity to gain control of the central state from the British during exclusively white democratic elections, and to turn the resources and infrastructures consubstantial with the state into instruments of domination. Apartheid would, thus, propel them to a de facto majoritarian society.

My second argument is that becoming minority hinges upon a responsive propaganda machine devised by an elite. A premise of this argument is to equate the making of a minority with that of a nation. The designation of minority groups as nations in academic studies and political addresses offers the justification of such a premise. French Jews were also viewed as a nation in the discourse of the revolutionary politician Clermont-Tonnerre (Birnbaum 2000, 19; Rosanvallon 2004). In Du Bois' writings (2000) and President Johnson's address to the Howard University community (Curry 1996), American Negroes were a nation. In a recent examination of the roots of religion-based political unrest in India, Gupta posits that the dynamic of minority-ness is founded on the majoritarian representation of themselves as the "people," namely the true nation, and of minorities as the "'natural' enemies of the nation-state," that is, as communities whose "origins, heritages, and loyalties are rooted in other countries" (2007, 31).

Through Gellner's (1983) and Anderson's (2006) studies, modernist approaches of the nation, beyond their varieties, all contend that the making of the nation fundamentally requires communication, that is, a means by which nation builders reach out to potential members of the nation (Eley and Suny 1996). Yet, communication is also a component of propaganda. It is mainly an act of sharing knowledge, of bringing to individuals information about their environment. Propaganda goes further though. It is a direct intervention in one's autonomy of decision and thought. Although Trotsky defends propagandists, including himself, of "creating mass opinion" by arguing that "we are only attempting to formulate it" (cited by Domenech 1951, 268), Bourdieu (2001, 2002) reveals that the position of delegate or spokesperson, resulting from one's capacity to persuasively frame or formulate ideas, is always conducive to the monopolizing of power to define the world, and imposing this worldview on the masses. Althusser convincingly connects propaganda and identification to a model demonstrating how the "communications apparatus" injecting individual subjects with doses of oriented discourses leads to the internalization of "peculiar meanings and values conveyed to said subjects through said discourses and take up the identity offered to them by the institution in question" (quoted by Weedon 2004, 12). Propaganda is, therefore, the use of the communication tool to generate in the Other an attitude in conformity with Ego's goal. Timasheff, thus, defines propaganda as "a series of actions whose purpose is to induce an indeterminate mass of people to accept definite principles of actions" (1943, 10). For Domenech, propaganda is a "political revelation" concerned with impacting both the mind and emotions of its targeted subjects (1951). In light of this discussion, the ultimate rationale of propaganda is to inform—*informare*—that is, to shape the attitudes, beliefs, and even narratives of a population. In many respects, the emergence of a black minority in contemporary France conforms to this conception. Black organizations seize the various communication networks to articulate a narrative of difference and a claim for recognition. Groups of influence, institutions, and intellectual agents are, thus, turned into means for the construction of blackness. This goal does not materialize solely by way of simple discourses. Blackness is lived through narratives, images, and actions. Taking stock of both the volition for equality and recognition and the development of a propaganda mechanism, I aim to demonstrate that blackness, as a minority, is less of an essence than it is a sociological outcome. Its formation operates at the intersection of three realms of meanings: discourse, belief, and material production. In other words, to bring blackness into existence is to say that it is real, to make people believe so, and to play it out through (f)acts quick to support and fuel this belief. Both the majoritarian society and the black population are engaged actively in this process.

The Paths Black French Walk On

The existence of a black minority stems basically from a triangular nexus of discourses and representations linking actors separately positioned at the different ends of this frame. First is an aggregate of opinion makers speaking in the name of France, and claiming to embody, if not express, the will and vision of the nation. Mostly politicians, intellectuals, artists, or media contributors, they alternately refer to the majority's right to rule, in accordance with democratic principles, advocate the preservation of the spirit of the French Constitution, and deem unrepresentative of the nation authors of any divergent discourse or attitude, thereby conducting a segmentation of the nation between "Frenchmen" and "enemies within" that (accidentally) coincides with racial/ethnic, or sexual boundaries. The second aggregate incorporates various activists articulating a divergent discourse that promotes difference and claims the recognition of the French-ness of groups excluded from the deliberation on the collective identity and future of the nation. The *paritaires* and the *beur* activists who strive to publicize the desire of French women and French of Arab descent to break into the national decision-making spheres constitute prominent examples of this set.[5] A final set of actors is composed of black activists who aim, through a dialectical process, to naturalize both their existence as a distinctive group in France and the French-ness of this community. These black activists coalesce around five major organizations. *Collectif Égalité* was founded by writer Calixthe Beyala with the assistance of comedian Dieudonné, actor Martial, and playwright and actor Saint-Eloy, in December 1998, and in the wake of the celebration of the 150th anniversary of the French abolition of slavery. That same year, black entrepreneurs under the leadership of Dogad Dogoui created *Africagora*. In 2002, Carole Da Silva founded the Association pour Favoriserl'Intégration Professionnelle (AFIP). In 2004, a small

group of politicians, civil society activists, and academics launched the
Cercle d'Action pour la Promotion de la Diversité (*CAPDIV*). In the fall of
2005, Conseil Représentatif des Associations Noires de France (*CRAN*—
Representative Council of France's Black Associations) was born as the
result of the efforts of *CAPDIV*'s leadership to merge the atomized black
organizational initiatives.[6] Despite their ideological divergences, these
partnering organizations seek the advancement of the black population
in the state's various decision-making spheres.

Before elaborating farther on the aforementioned triangular nexus, it
is worth underlining that the conception of minority construction presented here departs clearly from traditional theorizations of this sociological process, including that argued by de Certeau. I suspect the latter
to be ensconced in a binary conception of the heterogeneous nation in
which a dominant group in control of the levers of power ("Us") influences the course of a minority groups' existence ("Them"). However,
in recognition of the complexity of contemporary multiracial societies,
it is worth emancipating our intellects from the framework of a two-
way street dialogue consisting of a majority with a soon-to-be minority,
and introducing at least the plurality of minority. If, for the dominant
group, there is often no difference between those excluded from the
"true nation" and labeled "Them," the same logic does not hold in the
perspective of the latter. My conceptual framework suggests that minority today often emerges by positioning itself vis-à-vis a dominant group,
obviously, but also a set of diverse minorities. This process is different
from the one conceptualized by Hall, who, positing that "identity is also
the relationship of the Other to oneself," still circumscribes the "dialogic
relationship" to a conversation between two parties (1996, 345).

Whitening French-ness

The French Constitution, and its motto "Liberty, Equality, Fraternity,"
does not advocate for any stratification of the nation based on particular
characteristics. Rather, in accordance with the spirit of the Revolution,
these pillars of the French state infrastructure hint at the erasure of birth
privileges that structured the political orientation of the previous regime.
While these guiding principles remain as cultural values, French society is fractured by race, ethnicity, religion, and even gender. This frac-
ture has several sources. One probably lies in the time lag that manifests

between ideals, or values, and their materialization. The materialization of Republican values has been envisioned through various ways, including assimilation, later renamed integration. First, integration reflects to a certain extent the ideal of equality in that it considers one as worthy of partaking in the community. Provided that one is not, objectively speaking, so worthy, integration then also appears as an act of generosity, which is implied in any relation of fraternity, since fraternity supposes a gift and even a degree of sacrifice. But, following Taylor's (2011, 135) conceptual rendition of the Jacobin understanding of national cohesion, which "forbids any other ways of living modern citizenship" and "castigates as unpatriotic a way of living which would not subordinate other facets of identity to citizenship," integration collides also with the ideal of liberty. It is a collision with liberty as integration also suggests the exercise of either power or authority upon people who are not given a choice about the form of their participation in society. Second, the notion of integration suggests a covert division of the French society. On the one hand, it designates an entitled majoritarian group, which is explicitly alluded to as being the quintessence of the nation, the repository of the culture around which society must cohere. On the other, it isolates minorities to put under the directorship of the majoritarian entity. Through the very notion of integration itself, the French nation constructs the former as different, marginal, and, therefore, distinct from the referential group. The enactment of the integration principle through facts such as policies, bylaws, and everyday interactions accounts for a racialization of the boundaries between the majoritarian and minorities. One of the national policies most explicitly intended for the preservation of social cohesion is that of diversity in public housings (Simon 2003). Yet, as performed on the ground, this policy contradicts the French nation's claim of color-blindness and, more importantly, reveals the entitlement of white French to the position of referential unit and this group's culture as *the* French culture. A white Frenchman, including a Corsican, is never refused access to a public housing on the basis of his/her skin color or culture, whereas limitation of the population of colored people to a certain threshold in public housing is a fact. French in their own right, Antilleans are faced with this limitation that only their race and cultural background could justify. Beriss provides evidences of this unequal treatment: "the public housing authorities… stigmatized

[Antilleans] and applied quotas limiting their numbers," and "[Antillean] clubs and teams were not permitted to use the town's public facilities—including the meeting hall and the soccer fields—as often as other groups"; a restriction thusly justified by the mayor during a 1998 meeting in the Saint-Denis department: "as a group, you [Antilleans] do cause specific problems with your habit of noisy parties and loud music in public housing, you are fun loving and boisterous" (Chapman and Frader 2004, 4–17). The extrusion of the Antillean group from Frenchness is conspicuous through those policies and discourses, although its historical presence in the nation is well documented. The exposure of black Africans to the same treatment is largely evidenced. In the 1980s, the Communist Party-administered city of Montreuil put itself under the limelight. After having sent bulldozers to tear down buildings housing African immigrants (many of whom were in fact naturalized French citizens), the mayor of Montreuil defended this action as a preventative measure against the rise of racism that the concentration of such a population might generate among his constituencies. He further stressed the need to distribute this black population as equally as possible amongst the various cities of the *Ile de France* region (see Gueye 2006). In 2001, a legal case unveiled the application of a similar policy in the 92nd department. Having denied the application for an apartment of a black French of African descent, the representative of the community housing management firm confessed that the firm felt the need to enforce a racial/ethnic selection policy, "specifically in this high rise housing, [where] there are already many tenants of African and Antillean families," adding "it is not discrimination, but social diversity" (Gilles Wallon, *Libération*, August 2, 2005).[7] These cases demonstrate that the extrusion of blacks (Africans and Antilleans) from the majoritarian society is not founded on their citizenship status, but their race and culture.

This extrusion is again more conspicuous in light of the way the French nation, through mediation of the concept of integration, is "figured," represented. Integration, let us remember, implies one's real or supposed strangeness from the nation, and identifies immigrants as candidates for integration. But interestingly, on the visual level, the subject of integration, as portrayed in cartoons, photographs, or television, is clearly racialized. Rosello (1998) showed that the African has come to embody the figure of the immigrant in French media. One can go further by arguing that more than an ethnic characterization, the media actually offers a racial characterization of the immigrant since the blackness of the represented body begs the question as to whether the subject is French, born and bred, African, or rather a subject hailing freshly from Guadeloupe. The pervasiveness of this visual representation sets blacks apart from the nation regardless of their citizenship status, and designates any black as a de facto outsider to the nation. In this regard, we could agree with Butler by arguing that integration in France is a discursive production of subjects confined to the margin in relation to a referential entity vested with the status of majority (Butler 1993). Upon this "regime of representation" (Hall 1996) is built the very first forerunner of the current black identity, of which the call was launched in 1999 by philosopher Dia for people of African descent to put an end to the "dispersal of their energies, stand up, organize, and start speaking on their behalf" (Gueye 2001).

As suggested earlier, the discourse of the French majority does not itself bring into existence a black minority. Instead of a two-party dialogue, the making of a black minority unfolds in at least a three-party interaction. Indeed, black identity entrepreneurs create their identity as minority in relation and response to parallel minorities, including mostly women, beurs, and gays.

Engaging with Non-Black Minorities

The 1980s and 1990s could undeniably be referred to as the era of minority rights revolution on French soil, after Skrentny (2002). Blackness surges in this favorable context of minorities' mobilization. In the main, three specific groups have blazed the trail: the beur, feminist, and gay activists. Beur activism is a socio-political protest movement steered by young French-born Arabs, and which reached its apogee in 1983 (Wihtol de Wenden and Leveau 2007, 41). It articulated a claim of "the 'double-ness' of similarity and difference" analyzed by Hall (2000, 227): on the one hand, the equality of rights with French of other origins; on the other, the right to be different expressed through the term beur, which is meant to evidence both the acknowledgment of their Arab heritage and the recognition of their French-ness so as to escape a reduction to the exclusive figure of the Arab immigrant (Wihtol de Wenden and Leveau 2007; Geisser 1997). Beur activism constitutes one of the main minority movements in whose mirror the making of blackness is conceived. Some of the outcomes of this movement can be seen in the controversial institutionalization of a Muslim minority through the efforts of the then-interior minister, Sarkozy, to organize a French Muslim community as shown by the establishment of the Union of Islamic Organizations of France, his New Year's wishes to the country's Muslim community, and his well-publicized appointment of a "Muslim prefect" on January 14, 2004. References are made to the Arab minority by black French organizers in either a competitive or an emulating fashion, with the gains of this minority inspiring strategies by and demands from other groups. Taking stock of the accomplishments of these marginalized French citizens in asserting their religious identity in the public sphere, black French progressively increased their own efforts to pronounce their own, equally banned, racial identity in said space. For instance, having been informed of Sarkozy's appointment of Dermouche as the first prefect of Arab descent, the founders of CRAN and Africagora warned the government against the reduction of minority-ness to Arabness. Eventually, Sarkozy nominated NGahane—an academic born in Congo—subprefect in January 2007, then prefect in 2008, and prided himself on being the first statesman to acknowledge recognition of black French existence.

Blacks' claims for difference also owe a debt to the parité movement, a feminist activism that specifically aimed to ensure women equal representation in the political sphere (Wallach-Scott 2005). Disparaged by politicians and intellectuals in the name of the preservation of abstract individualism, the parité movement culminated in an historical success: on June 6, 2000, the French Parliament passed a law demanding that political parties have equal numbers of women and men on their electoral lists or face financial penalties in the case of violation of the new legislation (ibid.). Cognizant of, and inspired by, the successes of the parité movement, black organizations mirrored the feminists' determination and paralleled their own condition in society with that of French women. References to the parité movement become conspicuous in their activity. For instance, to fight the marginalization of blacks within the major political parties during regional elections in 2004, Dogoui, inspired by the parité approach, created Diversité, an electoral list comprising an equal number of white and nonwhite candidates.

Benefiting from the visibility of the international mobilization against AIDS,[8] and having secured the de-penalization of homosexuality, French gay activists challenged the conservative notion of family by demanding the extension of the right to a legal union for people of the same sex (Martel 2000). Through an intense activism, the homosexual population achieved a landmark victory through the ratification in 1999 of the law known as the *Pacte de Solidarité Civile* (Pact of Civil Solidarity).[9]

This movement provided the black movement with a key member whose activism experience had become instrumental in reshaping this struggle: the organizer of the International Day Against Homophobia, academic L. G. Tin, who advised black activists to follow gays' strategy by claiming openly the true identity of their organization, in this case blackness (Tin 2008). As a result, the word black that was shorn in many black organizations became explicitly appropriated. The most conspicuous example is its use in the naming of *CRAN*, which subscribed thereby to Tin's invitation to "call things by their name," and, therefore, to call a black a black (Kaufmann 2005). Blackness would come to blossom and thrive within *CRAN*, which spearheaded propaganda efforts for the recognition of a black minority in France.

Propaganda for a Black Minority

Propaganda is clearly a relational activity. It implies the existence of both speaker and audience, whom the former strives to convert to her/his own view. Since propagandists seek to influence the largest audience possible, they need to secure specific tools and engage with targeted groups. The aim of ensuring the visibility of their cause, the objective, and the ethical principles thereof often determines the choice of these tools and interlocutors.

Courting and Coaxing Opinion Makers

As argued in the previous sections, the division of the French nation between an entitled majoritarian group and a purported monolithic minority of which blacks is conveyed mostly in representation. By figuring the (illegal) immigrant as black, by showcasing (in French films) a French nation in which no black actor appears in the cast, television, as an "ideological state apparatus," to quote Althusser (1971), "speak[s], to [blacks] or hail [them] into place as the social subjects of particular discourses" (Hall 2000, 19), and even as a distinct identity group. The power of this representation, and of the instrument of representation in the making of blackness, is indicated by the primary effort of black activists to engage with this instrument and the representations it generates. The very first organization advocating for the compatibility of French-ness and blackness challenged, and strove to use, the television, to perform its own definition of blackness; indeed, the primary action undertaken by which *Collectif Egalité* was to demand revision of television content. In 1999, Beyala, the founder of *Collectif Égalité*, wrote an open letter to Culture and Communication Minister Trautmann in which she denounced the "deficit of representation of blacks [on TV]" and threatened to sue the state. In 2001, the organization hijacked the *Cérémonie des Césars*, France's annual, and widely watched, celebration of national cinematographic production. In the middle of the ceremony, broadcasted nationwide on Canal+, Saint-Eloy and Beyala left their seats in the rear rows of the balcony of the *Théâtre des Champs Élysées* and made their way to the podium. Interrupting the live televised program, they read aloud a manifesto denouncing the exclusion of blacks from the film industry, thereby informing several million viewers of the black cause. Moreover, the issue of blacks' presence on-screen was related to the broader demand for representation of black social life by, or with, black media professionals. This claim is based on the assumption that the lives-world, history, and experiences of black French are distinct from that of mainstream French. This assumption seems to be confirmed by black movie directors who represent blackness in their works as the condition of victims of, or resistors of, white supremacy, as shown through such characters as an anticolonialist taken down by the white establishment, black musicians condemned to convert to European musical styles as the result of the disparagement of blacks in their environment, and slaves submitted to cruelty for the financial advancement of their white master, respectively, in films such as *Alikes, Biguine, Passage du milieu* and *Tropiques amers*.

Following in the footsteps of *Collectif Egalité*, CAPDIV and CRAN accomplished the most surprising feat with respect to the acknowledgment of blackness in France. The latter convinced TF1, France's leading television channel, to broadcast a powerful 28-second advertisement meant to represent the life course of black French. The ad consisted of a rotating black hand as the words "birth," "kindergarten," "high school," "high school diploma," and "high education" appeared successively on the screen. The image was accompanied with a voice-over: "To land your first job is never simple. Worse when you are black. For the sake of equal opportunities, *CRAN* sponsors black youth's access to the job market. Help us to help them." Through this ad, *CRAN*, pulling TF1 in its wake, fueled the representation of blackness as a distinct identity.

Investing in the media is in line with the common goal of bringing blackness into existence, as justified by a cofounder of *CRAN*:

> We understood from the beginning that to win this battle we have to win over the media and political spaces. This is why we prioritized spreading the word in the small circle of media professionals, convince them of the relevance of our fight instead of organizing street marches.

The question of why investing, or even hijacking, the media is deemed to be a sound strategy stems naturally from the preceding elements of analysis. By definition, society is a constructed entity to which agents of unequal influence and power contribute. Media—and more specifically television outlets—characterized as the fourth power, are among said social agents (Bourdieu 1996; Thompson 2002; Chomsky 2002). The celerity of coups d'état perpetrators to control national television and radio, the determination of authoritarian regimes to muzzle the free (foreign) media, and the willingness of even neoliberal governments to maintain state-funded media outlets all illustrate the strategic role of media in propaganda arrangements. Writing at a time when the press was the most efficient tool of propaganda, Lenin (1961) urged revolutionaries to multiply the number of publications addressed to the working class and their sympathizers. Anderson (2006) theorized the media's role in the making of a "community of history and destiny" as large as the nation, to quote Smith (1991, 97). But what Anderson failed to mention is that citizens are predisposed to believe that the media describes reality and delivers truth. It is in this claimed capacity to render reality or administer the truth to the audience that the media's power to make or influence opinion resides (Lodziak 1986; Chomsky 2002). Bourdieu explicated this notion by stressing that the function of television is to inform, in the etymological sense of the word informare, i.e., to shape opinion (Bourdieu 1996, 17).

Black organizations also strive to invest in the political and intellectual spheres. Compared to the media, the political space is recognized as the principal space of power in contemporary societies (Bourdieu 2002). Although arguably credited with the expression of truth, political actors, as lawmakers, still hold the power to turn idea(l)s into facts. Thereby, politicians impose upon citizens a specific worldview. The intellectual sphere wields considerable influence in France, which obliges both political actors and interest groups to pay close attention to the opinions framed therein. Debray lists intellectuals among the power holders in France (1979), and Hourmant and Leclerc (2012), in the same logic, credit them with the "tutorage of the public opinion," an influential service by which the intellectual function blurs the boundaries of propaganda in the sense underlined earlier.

Aware of the influence of the political and intellectual spheres, black activists displayed ingenious strategies to bring into existence the black minority. They associated with significant figures of these spheres. In 2002, *Africagora* held its first *Assises des Populations Noires de France* (Conference of Black Populations of France) at the French Senate. They secured the patronage of the event by the president of the Senate, Christian Poncelet, and convinced every major political party to send delegates. *CRAN* officially announced its existence in a conference room at the French Parliament that they got access to thanks to Green Party MP Noël Mamère, whom Tin met at Bègles as the deputy celebrated the first (then unconstitutional) gay marriage (Gabizon 2005).

This strategy of association is unarguably sound. Association implies commensality. This implies a reciprocal acknowledgment that Ego shares with Other a certain worldview. By association, Ego and Other come together into a shared framework of narratives or goals. Thereby, Other's existence and goals are legitimized, and Ego's responsibility engaged in Other's discourses and actions. By hosting these black events, the Senate and the National Assembly, two dominant law-making institutions, produce the black minority.

Black identity entrepreneurs strove to impose the issue of blackness onto the national political agenda, as well as the terms and timelines of this inclusion, conceding to politicians solely the option to accredit the existence of a black minority. A good illustration thereof can be found in *CRAN*'s propaganda plan. In the winter of 2007, as the presidential campaign kicked off, *CRAN* conducted a survey of the various candidates to collect their opinions regarding blacks' expectations and predicament. The survey is worth mentioning for two reasons. *Primo* (first), it is the first in the genre to be carried out publicly in France. Presidential candidates are not compelled to respond to the survey of religious, ethnic, and racial groups, although events such as the annual gala of the *CRIF* (Representative Council of the Jewish Institutions of France) are often turned into a campaign platform and a venue for political grievances by Jewish activists.[10] *Deuxio* (second), the survey was a relevant option with regard to the making of a black minority, given its supposed effect as a communication tool. Bourdieu suggests that survey opinion has the power to create, if not impose, a worldview that may not be initially that of the surveyed people. This power is different from the one Austin (1962) detects in certain types of discourses. It resides rather in the "effect of imposition of a problematic" that is inherent to a survey opinion (Bourdieu 2002, 230). In *CRAN*'s opinion survey, the existence of blackness was integrated as a taken-for-granted fact, by way of an affirmative form illustrated in this question: "If elected, would you implement affirmative action?" Thus, *CRAN* inhibits respondents' potential act of expressing their doubts about the reality of minority-ness. Respondents are subtly diverted from contesting it and simply prompted to (dis)agree with an Affirmative Action program. The findings of the survey reflect the adequacy of this discursive strategy. With the exception of Segolène Royal, all candidates approved the implementation of an Affirmative Action policy.

In this specific case, the making of blackness is indisputably the "production of a representation of the world." Yet, as Bourdieu contends, this operation "is the quasi monopoly of intellectuals" (ibid., 62). Unlike in other spheres, the intellectual arena is host to "the struggle to impose an appropriate, just and legitimate way of discussing the social world" (ibid.). Protagonists of the intellectual sphere are vested with an "authorized language," which, by that token, is "a language of authority" (ibid., 65). They are sure "to be not only listened [to], but heard" (ibid., 96) all the more so that this language relies on scientific protocol and evidences. It is small wonder then why black organizations deem it necessary to promote their own intellectuals and break into the intellectual sphere. Conferences and colloquia are, thus, being multiplied. Two aspects of these events must be highlighted, for they elicit the way in which these events are consistent with the prospect of making a black minority in France: the systematic association with these events of external intellectuals with relative authority in their own discipline, and the selection of reputed scholarly institutions as venues for those activities. On February 19, 2005, *CAPDIV* convened a conference titled "*Les Noirs de France: Anatomie d'un Groupe Invisible*" (France's Blacks: The Anatomy of an Invisible Group), with conferees including prominent political figures as well as academics. In October 2007, *CRAN* organized at the National Institute of the Audiovisual a conference titled "*Les Statistiques de la Diversité*" (Diversity Statistics)[11] that brought together renowned social scientists. By agreeing to discuss this issue, these scholars inscribed and gave visibility to blackness in an authorized space of discussion, even if their position could conflict with that of black organic intellectuals. As holders of a "language of authority," they made black intellectuals' discourse a legitimate framework able to produce meanings of French social organization.

According to Domenech (1951), the success of propagandists in turning discourse into belief and converting audiences to their cause requires the production of facts. Black organic intellectuals seem well aware that the administration of the proofs of existence of blackness is not a cost to be saved. As a result, they initiated several actions. Perhaps the most compelling is *CRAN*'s unprecedented initiative to take the census of the black population. This survey would become a powerful propaganda instrument, both for its findings and its symbolic meaning. First, it provides a scientifically sound estimate of the black minority (only those aged 18 years and over represented 3.86 percent of the French population) and establishes the level of race consciousness in France (only 3 percent of the surveyed population refused to indicate their race). Second, it mapped the contours of a black (sub) nation within the French nation, and provided the condition of the reification of this group, an outcome that Anderson (2006) convincingly evidenced by demonstrating how census-making contributes to the imagining of nations and minority groups. Third, the survey shatters the consensus on race neutrality upon which the indivisibility of the nation supposedly depends.

The public reactions to this survey evidence the impact of this instrument. On January 31, 2007, the survey hit the front page of the *Parisian*, France's daily newspaper with the largest readership (http://www.senat. fr/rap/r07-013/r07-0133.html). Over the following days, other newspapers, television and radio programs reviewed the survey. A debate followed among high-profile intellectuals, politicians, and journalists, thus, giving visibility to the issue of blackness.

Adding a Zest of Violence

In many studies, mostly of Marxist inspiration, violence is reduced to a cathartic means, an instrument of emancipation. Fanon (2005) saw violence as a vehicle to restore oneself, turning it, thus, as comments Mbembe, into a "key phase in the becoming subject of the colonized" (2012, 21). Sartre vested violence with the power of 'reconstruction' of self (Sartre 2005, lv). If Arendt' s critical review fell short of positing any specific function of violence, due to her concern with examining its nature and causes, she discusses a series of works equating violence with a "technique of social control and persuasion" or a vehicle of "power of man over man" (1970, 19, 37). Despite the relevance of the previous analysis, we need to go further and follow Formwalt's suggestion of violence as a propaganda instrument (1987). Violence has the capacity to ensure visibility to a cause, although it could alienate the potential sympathizers to the cause, especially in civility-driven societies which promote pacifism and argument to solve conflicts (Elias 1969). Albeit marginal, violence (either symbolic or physical) participates in the propaganda for blackness. The actions of Dieudonné, and those of the Tribu Ka, a marginal radical organization, offer opportunities for this articulation. These activists build their propaganda on a common strategy: attacking the Jewish community. Dieudonné used various public appearances to charge Jews for an alleged responsibility in the slave trade. The Tribu Ka undertook street expeditions in the heart of the Parisian Jewish quarter against the Jewish League of Defense, which they accused of attacking blacks. This instrumentalization of the Jewish figure is worth dwelling upon. First, it is in keeping with the purpose of propaganda. The preliminary measure/indicator of propaganda's efficiency is securing visibility to a cause, which violence against Jews happens to generate. The guilt of the French state due its documented responsibility in the holocaust (Marrus and Paxton

1981) has generated a high sensitivity to any public action or discourse deemed anti-Semitic in France. The visibility of violence against Jews is all the more probable considering that organizations, including the *CRIF*, restlessly monitor and publicize any progression of anti-Semitic acts, and that Jews are credited by one out of three French citizens with a greater influence in the media than any other group, according to a survey conducted by the French Jewish Students' Association (http:// uejf.org/blog/2012/04/29/luejf-attaque-google-en-justice-pour-la-prop- osition-juif-de-son-moteur-de-recherche). Evidences of the efficiency of such a propaganda action are the prompt and severe reactions of the French government against authors of this violence. For example, on February 18, 2005, the justice minister ordered an investigation into comments made by Dieudonné during a press conference in Algiers (*Le Monde* 2005). On July 28, 2006, the Tribu Ka was dissolved by Presidential Decree on the basis that: "Tribu Ka propagates theories and ideas that tend to justify and encourage discrimination, hatred and violence against people due to their ethnic origin and their reli- gion…. Their anti-Semitism is no longer to be documented, and the Republic cannot tolerate such schemes and behaviors" (Blecher 2006). In response, the Tribu Ka's leader rejoiced: "We are honored to see a country with so much of our people's blood on its hands talk about us during Cabinet meeting [Conseil des ministres]; as a result we are now more visible on the net, for everybody is talking about us" (ibid.). This comment clearly points to the propagandist dimension of violence, especially when directed against a group capable of giving public echo to its own worries and claims.

The second important point worth noting with respect to the instru- mentalization of the Jewish figure is that the violence against Jews points to the complex process of minority construction. This falls within the theoretical framework displayed here, according to which the making of minority is not confined to a two-party relationship but rather unfolds in a triangular nexus. Blacks do not attempt to bring blackness into exis- tence in sole response to the majoritarian white French discourse and representations, but also by relating to the experience of other minority groups. The minority-ness of Jews is perceived by both mainstream black organizations and blacks who instrumentalize Jews. In condemnation of Dieudonné's attacks against Jews, his former companion of struggle,

Beyala characterizes French Jews as a minority and points at their epidermal invisibility as their main difference from blacks. In Dieudonné's rhetoric, the expression "elected people" (*peuple élu*) needs to be read beyond its theological meaning. The Jews are represented as the minority chosen among many other minorities by the dominant group, and given a distinctive treatment of a model minority. In the sketch "My excuses to the chosen people," Dieudonné subtly underscores the reactions of Prime Minister Raffarin, President Chirac, and Justice Minister Perben to his controversial televised sketch to suggest the supposed unequal treatment of Jews comparatively to other minorities by the dominant group.

Conclusion

A minority consciousness is clearly expressed within the contemporary public sphere. The terms "visible minorities" and "diversity" are frequently used in both ordinary and cultivated languages. The state entrusted a prominent sociologist with a research mission on diversity (Wieviorka 2008). Moreover, since the surge of claims of minority-ness, the successive governments have systematically appointed a nonwhite minister, and taken public pride in this decision. President Sarkozy arrived at his first visit to the White House accompanied by two female ministers, Dati and Yade, who are Arab and black, respectively, thus, pairing race and gender revolutions (Simons 2007). This symbolic showcasing of diversity can be seen as evidence of the recognition of blackness and Arab-ness as French minorities. CRAN's success in securing the label of "association of public interest" (*association d'intérêt public*)—delivered only by the interior minister as testament to the state's gratefulness to an organization for its public contribution to the national welfare—is also of paramount significance. In light of CRAN's active propaganda for blackness, the French administration's designation of this organization as being in the public interest is an overt acknowledgment of a black minority in France. However, black organizations' reactions to the treatment and achievements of other minority groups, as they respond in parallel to the representation of blacks by the majority group, open a new window in the conceptualization of minority-ness, at odds with the classical theory that inscribes minority-ness in a relational framework involving at least three parties.

Notes and Bibliography

Notes

1. I am grateful to my colleague Barry Riddell, Shawn Jackson, and the anonymous reviewers for their insightful comments and criticisms.
2. The simple expression of this will is an explicit criticism of democratic societies, for it casts doubts on these countries' compliances with the principle of equality. The minority issue calls into question France's declaration of having enacted equality since the 1789 revolution (Rosanvallon 2004; Chapman and Frader 2004).
3. See Mudimbe (1988).
4. Although, in the case under study here, the minority group is in fact also a demographic minority, I consider this precision worth making.
5. *Paritaires* designates a group of citizens, mostly feminists, who fought for the implementation of a policy that would result in a fair representation of women in the national parliament (Wallach-Scott 2005). *Beur* is an inversion of the word Arab crafted according to the rule of verlan, a suburbanite working class's way of speaking.
6. For a detailed presentation of all these organizations, see Gueye 2006, 2010, and 2012.
7. According to *Le Parisien*, LOGIREP, one of the most important of its category in the *Ile de France* region, had files with racial and ethnic coding of the information provided by applicants.
8. A disease associated with homosexuality since the publication of Schilts' controversial book (1987).
9. This law forbids discrimination on the basis of sex, and therefore enables same-sex couples to secure nearly equal rights as married heterosexuals with a few notable exceptions, including child adoption and medically assisted procreation.
10. During a February 3, 2005 radio program following the president of *CRIF*'s admonition of the envoy of the French government to this dinner for the insufficient struggle against anti-Semitism in France, philosopher Alain Finkielkraut qualified this annual meeting as "a kind of trial dinner [*tribunal dînatoire*] where the head of the French government is summoned by a Jewish community that tells him what's on their mind" (Vidal 2011).
11. *CRAN* strategically uses this expression instead of ethnics/race statistics so as to curb any accusation to promote racial division in France.

Bibliography

Althusser, L. 1971. *Lenin and Philosophy and Other Essays*. New York: Monthly Review Press.

Arendt, H. 1970. *On Violence*. New York: A Harvest Book Hartcourt Inc.

Anderson, B. 2006. *Imagined Communities*. London: Verso.

Austin, J. L. 1962. *How to Do Things with Words*. Oxford: Clarendon.

Blecher, L. 2006. "La Tribu Ka Dissoute." *Libération*, July 26.

Birnbaum, P. 2000. *Jewish Destinies: Citizenship, State, and Community in Modern France*. New York: Hill and Wang.

Bourdieu, P. 1996. *Sur la Television*. Paris: Raisons d'agir.

———. 2001. *Langage et pouvoir Symbolique*. Paris: Seuil.

———. 2002. *Questions de Sociologie*. Paris: Minuit.

Butler, J. 1990. *Gender Trouble*. New York City: Routledge.

———. 1993. *Bodies That Matter*. London: Routledge.

Chapman, H. and L. Frader (eds). 2004. "Introduction: Race in France." In *Race in France: Interdisciplinary Perspectives on the Politics of Difference*, 1–19. New York: Berghahn Books.

Chomsky, N. 2002. *Media Control: The Spectacular Achievement of Propaganda*. New York: Seven Stories Press.

Curry, G. E. (ed.). 1996. "Introduction." In *The Affirmative Action Debate*, xiii–xv. Reading, MA: Addison-Wesley.

Debray, R. 1979. *Le pouvoir intellectuel en France*. Paris: Ramsay.

de Certeau, M. 1997. *Culture in the Plural*. Minneapolis: University of Minnesota Press.

Domenech, J.-M. 1951. "Leninist Propaganda." *Public Opinion Quarterly* 15 (2): 265–73.

Du Bois, W. E. B. 2000. "The Conservation of Races." In *Race and Racism*, edited by L. Back and J. Salomos, 79–86. London: Routledge.

Eley, G. and R. G. Suny (eds). 1996. "Introduction: From the Moment of Social History to the Work of Cultural Representation." In *Becoming National*, 1–37. New York: Oxford University Press.

Elias, N. 1969. *The Civilizing Process, Vol. 1: The History of Manners*. Oxford: Blackwell.

Fanon, F. 2005. *The Wretched of the Earth*. New York: Grove Press

Fassin D. and E. Fassin (eds). 2006. "Conclusion: éloge de la complexité." In *De la question sociale à la question raciale: représenter la société française*, 249–59. Paris: La Découverte.

Formwalt, L. W. 1987. "The Camilla Massacre of 1868: Racial Violence as Political Propaganda." *Georgia Historical Society* 71 (3): 399–426.

Foucault, M. 1978. *The History of Sexuality: An Introduction, Vol. 1*. New York: Pantheon Books.

Gabizon, C. 2005. "*Les Noirs de France se regroupent en fédération*." *Le Figaro*, November 28.

Geisser, V. 1997. *Ethnicité républicaine: les élites d'origine maghrébine dans le système politique français*. Paris: Presses de Science Po.

Gellner, E. 1983. *Nations and Nationalism*. Ithaca NY: Cornell University Press.

Gueye, A. 2001. *Les intellectuels africains en France*. Paris: L'Harmattan.

———. 2006. "The Colony Strikes Back: African Protest Movements in Postcolonial France." *Comparative Studies of South Asia, Africa and the Middle East* 26 (2): 226–42.

Gueye, A. 2010. *Aux Nègres de France la patrie non reconnaissante*. Paris: Dagan.

————. 2013. "The Labyrinth to Blackness: On Naming and Leadership in the Black Associative Space in French." *French Cultural Studies* 24 (2): 196–207.

Gupta, D. 2007. "Citizens Versus People: the Politics of Majoritarianism and Marginalization in Democratic India." *Sociology of Religion* 68 (1): 27–44.

Hall, S. 1990. "Cultural Identity and Diaspora." In *Identity, Community, Culture, Difference*, edited by J. Rutherford, 222–37. London: Lawrence and Wishart.

————. 1996. "Ethnicity: Identity and Difference." In *Becoming National*, edited by G. Eley and R. G. Suny, 339–49. New York: Oxford University Press.

————. 2000. "Who Needs 'Identity'?." In *Identity: A Reader*, edited by P. Du Gay, J. Evans, and P. Redman, 15–30. London: SAGE.

Haski, P. 2007. "Au Congres US, Sarkozy dit 'I love You'". *Rue89*, November 7.

Hourmant, F. and A. Leclerc. 2012. *Les intellectuels et le pouvoir: déclinaisons et mutations*. Rennes: Presses universitaires de Rennes.

Kaufmann, S. 2005. "Patrick Lozès: Noir, tout simplement," *Le Monde*, December 7.

Kesteloot, L. 1991. *Black Writers in French: A Literary History of Negritude*. Washington D.C.: Howard University Press.

Le Monde. 2005. "L'humoriste Dieudonné, à nouveau accusé d'antisémitisme, tente de se justifier." February 19.

————. 2009. "Calixthe Beyala: 'Il n'y a pas de Navarro ou de Julie Lescaut noirs.'" October 11.

Lenin, V. I. 1961. *Collected Works, Volume 1*, 347–530. Moscow: Foreign Languages Publishing House.

Lodziak, C. 1986. *The Power of Television*. London: Frances Pinter.

Louw, P. E. 2004. "Political Power, National Identity, and Language: The Case of Afrikaans." *International Journal of the Sociology of Language* (170): 43–58.

Marrus, M. R. and R. O. Paxton. 1981. *Vichy France and the Jews*. New York: Basic Books.

Martel, F. 2000. *Le rose et le noir: les homosexuels en France depuis 1968*. Paris: Seuil.

Mbembe, A. 2012. "Metamorphic Thought: The Work of Frantz Fanon." *African Studies* 71 (1): 19–28.

Mudimbe, V. Y. 1988. *The Invention of Africa: Gnosis, Philosophy, and the Order of Knowledge*. Bloomington: Indiana University Press.

Rosanvallon, P. 2004. *Le modèle politique français: la société civile contre le jacobinisme de 1789 à nos jours*. Paris: Seuil.

Sartre, J. P. 2005. "Preface." In *The Wretched of the Earth*, edited by F. Fanon, xliii–lxii. New York: Grove Press.

Schilts, R. 1987. *And the Band Played On: Politics, People and the AIDS Epidemic*. New York: St Martin's Press.

Simon, P. 2003. "*Le logement social en France et la gestion des 'populations à risqué'.*" *Hommes et Migrations* (1246): 76–91.

Simons, S. 2007. "Sarkozy's Gender Revolution." *Der Spiegel*, June 29.

Skrentny, J. D. 2002. *The Minority Rights Revolution*. Cambridge: Harvard University Press.

Smith, A. D. 1991. *National Identity*. London: Penguin.

Taylor, C. 2011. *Dilemmas and Connections*. Cambridge: Harvard University Press.

Thompson, J. B. 2002. *The Media and Modernity*. Stanford: Stanford University Press.

Timasheff, N. S. 1943. "On Propaganda." *The American Catholic Sociological Review* 4 (1): 10–15.

Tin, L.-G. 2008. "Who is Afraid of Blacks in France? The Black Question: The Name Taboo, the Number Taboo." *French Politics, Culture, and Society* 26 (1): 32–44.

Vidal, D. 2011. *"Ceux qui parlent au nom des Juifs de France,"* *Le Monde Diplomatique*, July.

Wallach-Scott, J. 2005. *Parité! Sexual Equality and the Crisis of French Universalism*. Chicago: Chicago University Press.

Weedon, C. 2004. *Identity and Culture: Narratives of Difference and Belonging*. London: Open University Press.

Wieviorka, M. 2008. *La Diversité*. Paris: Robert Laffont.

Wihtol de Wenden, C. and R. Leveau. 2007. *La Bourgeoisie*. Paris: CNRS.

5

The Constitution of the Swedish Sámi People: Swedish Sámi Policy and the Justification of the Inner Colonization of Sweden[*]

Ulf Mörkenstam

Introduction

Indigenous rights have been in the forefront of the international debate on human rights for the past decade. In many ways, this is an effect of an international ethno-political mobilization of indigenous peoples (see, e.g., Daes 2011; Xanthaki 2007). The United Nations Declaration on the Rights of Indigenous Peoples (UNDRIP), adopted by the UN General Assembly in 2007, was also a confirmation of this indigenous struggle and recognition of their rights as peoples. The declaration states, among other things, that "[i]ndigenous peoples have the right to

* This chapter has originally been written within the project *Globalisation and New Political Rights. The Challenges of the Rights to Inclusion, Self-Determination and Secession* (financed by the Swedish Research Council).

self-determination," to "practise and revitalize their cultural traditions and customs," and "to lands, territories and resources which they have traditionally owned, occupied or otherwise used or acquired" (Articles 3, 11, 26).

The fact of being "indigenous" ("native" or "aboriginal") has in a historical perspective justified a completely different political order, as is well known. In the European context, for instance, indigenousness played a crucial role in justifying a continuous European colonization overseas ever since the discovery of the Americas in the late 15th century. As Tully (1993, 139) claims in his analysis of John Locke's political philosophy, it justified both a denial of the indigenous peoples' right to self-determination, as "Amerindian government" did not "qualify as a legitimate form of political society," and a denial of their right to land, as the "customary land use" was not considered "a legitimate type of property." The legitimacy of the new states was, thus, founded on an idea of *terra nullius*, that is, the "discovered" land was seen as "unoccupied or uninhabited" (Pateman 2007, 36).

The adoption of the UNDRIP can be seen as an institutionalization of rules and norms in radical opposition to the worldview of the era of colonization; indigenousness now justifies self-determination. The meaning of the right to self-determination is, however, still under negotiation, and "there is little if any guidance" in international law as to what it "means in actual practice" (Quane 2011, 269). Moreover, the recognition of the rights of indigenous peoples has not put an end to the process of colonization, and the dominant national narratives rarely include acknowledgments of a history of violent conquest and systematic oppression of indigenous peoples. In this chapter, I will argue that the construction of indigenous peoples in the national discourse of the countries in which they live is of immense importance in the justification of a continued oppression and domination. To substantiate my argument, I will analyze the Swedish Sámi policy with a specific focus on how the Sámi people have been constructed in discourse.

The Sámi are an indigenous people living in northwestern Europe, divided in the course of history by four nation states: Finland, Norway, Russia, and Sweden. Estimates of the number of Sámi differ depending on the sources used; however, the figures most often seen vary between 80,000 and 100,000, of which 50,000–65,000 reside in Norway, around 20,000 in Sweden, 8,000 in Finland, and 2,000 in Russia. Despite this partitioning, the Sámi people are in contemporary politics considered to be "one people residing across national borders" with "its own culture, its own society, its own history, its own traditions, its own language, its own livelihoods, and its own vision of the future" (Draft Nordic Saami Convention 2007).

Sweden signed the UNDRIP in 2007, and the special status of the Sámi people was recognized constitutionally for the first time in 2010. The overarching research question, then, is how a denial of the Sámi people's right to self-determination is possible in contemporary Swedish politics, and how a continued exploitation of the natural resources within the traditional Sámi settlement area can be justified. Part of the answer is to be found in how the Sámi people have been constructed historically in Swedish politics. In the following, I analyze the use and meaning of the concept Sámi (or "Lapps" as the Sámi in Sweden were officially referred to up until the 1960s) in Swedish politics for more than a century.[1]

What is the meaning of the concept Sámi in Swedish politics? What has become associated with the concept (for instance, being uncivilized)? And, what political institutions are explained and justified by this concept?

A Brief Methodological Remark

In Tully's (1995, 41) historical analysis of "the language of contemporary constitutionalism" in an age of cultural diversity, he claims that this language is so interrelated to the public institutions of modern societies that it is almost impossible for an indigenous people "to challenge the prevailing forms of constitutional recognition." Without a historical perspective that opposes the bias of the modern language of constitutionalism, the debate today runs the risk of perpetuating historical oppression rather than challenging it. What is needed is to conduct "a survey which brings to critical light the unexamined conventions that govern the language games in which both the problem and the range of solutions arise" (ibid., 35).

The methodological approach in this chapter is quite similar to Tully's, where his ambition highlights the need to study ideas in context: how the Sámi as a people have been constructed in Swedish politics, i.e., how the concept Sámi (or "Lapp") is used, what it cognates, and what other concepts it is associated with. To understand the meaning of a concept, it is necessary to analyze its role in a "conceptual scheme," or "belief system," by the way it is used in a specific historical and rhetorical context. In the words of Skinner (1989, 13),

> when a word changes its meaning, it also changes its relationship to an entire vocabulary. What this tells us about such changes is that we must be prepared to focus not on the "internal structure" of particular words but rather on their role in upholding complete social philosophies.

In this analysis of public policy in Sweden, the empirical analysis proceeds with two types of inquiry. The first is a synchronic analysis, in which the concept Sámi (or "Lapp") is analyzed in relation to other concepts used at the same time. The concept is, thus, situated within its rhetorical context. The second type of inquiry is a diachronic analysis, which entails a historical comparison of the meaning of a concept in different periods of time in order to grasp if and how the concept has changed.

It is important to note that my focus on Swedish politics and the analysis of the debate within the dominant society marginalize the political mobilization and resistance of the Sámi. The importance of the Sámi struggle for political change is, thus, partly neglected, although previous research provides clear evidence of the fact that almost "all major changes in Swedish Sámi policy have been the result of collective actions by the Sámi movement, i.e., by its ethno-political mobilization" (Lantto and Mörkenstam, forthcoming). However, I believe that the analysis in itself will clarify how this marginalization has been explained and justified in the public debate by the constitution of a specific Sámi identity.

The Formative Moment of Contemporary Swedish Sámi Policy

The Sámi people have played an important part in the narrative of Sweden for centuries (see, e.g., von Linné 1732). The situation of the Sámi has historically been regulated in relation to the Swedish population, primarily in and through the colonization of northern Sweden, "Lapland,"

and the expansion of farming.[2] The colonization process was, until the mid-1800s, considered to be relatively free from conflicts, and the dominant idea, the so-called "parallel theory," was that domiciled (Swedish) farmers and nomadic (Sámi) reindeer herders could coexist side by side as long as simple rules existed. This idea was further strengthened by the volition of the Swedish State to steer the farmers and their settlements toward areas of fertile land. The land considered unfit for farming was to be recognized as land to be used exclusively by the Sámi, where they should have an "absolute right to pasture for their reindeer" (SFS 1850:81, §1).[3]

The Sámi reindeer herding was also the main reason that more comprehensive legislation came to be considered necessary toward the end of the 19th century. Practical measures were needed, it was argued, as the farmers were "complaining about the reindeer owners' increasing encroachment on their grounds and about a wanting care of the reindeers" (Farup's individual statement, in KMB 1883, 127).[4] Legislation could further "a peaceful cohabitation" between the two livelihoods competing on the same land: farming and reindeer herding. The customary rights for the Sámi to herd reindeer were, thus, to be replaced by special legislation. The question of what Sámi rights actually entailed was, however, only a hazy background to the discussions. Rather, the main problem was formulated in terms of how to avoid damage to private property caused by the reindeer. The debate was, thus, focused on proper reindeer herding, not the potential rights of the Sámi. And proper reindeer herding could "not with success be conducted," it was argued, "if the reindeer's herder does not follow him on his wanderings" (KMB 1909, 18). Thus, a nomadic way of life was claimed to be a prerequisite for proper reindeer herding (see, e.g., Mörkenstam 1999, 103–07).

In this debate, the Sámi were described as a nomadic people, a "tribe," or "race," in need of protection by the Swedish State. Reindeer herding was the only way for them to survive. A common idea was that "too close contact with a superior race is the main reason for the misfortunes of the Lapp" (Statement by the King's representative in Jämtlands län, in Prop. 1886:2, 30).[5] The relation between the Sámi, on the one hand, and the Swedes, on the other, was often described in terms of "the old battle between the lower and the higher civilisations [....]" (Olivecrona, Justice of the Supreme Court, in Prop. 1886:2, 10). The "natural" explanation for the "underdevelopment" of the Sámi culture was, it was claimed, that it was impossible to combine civilization and reindeer herding. With this focus on reindeer herding, a "real," "authentic," and homogeneous Sámi identity was constructed—distinctly different from the "Swedish"—in spite of the well-known fact at the time that the majority of Sámi were not nomadic reindeer herders.

In this formative moment, the effects of making a nomadic way of life the normative foundation of Swedish Sámi policy was, in many ways, decisive. First, the Sámi were not recognized as owners of the land, although they were recognized as the original inhabitants of northern Sweden. On the one hand, it was considered "indisputable that the Lapps were the first to make use of Swedish Lapland," and it could not be "denied that they have been pushed aside by culture" (Prop. 1886:2, 14). There could, thus, be no infringements on the rights "they have had since time immemorial" (Prop. 1883:36, 91). On the other hand, "use or custom on the part of the Lapps" alone could not constitute the foundation of "a legal relationship between this native tribe" and the "individual land owner," with the consequence of "transferring" the right to private property to the former (Glimstedt, Justice of the Supreme Court, in Prop. 1886:2, 2–3). The conclusion of this discussion on ownership was considered to be obvious: the land was either the property of the Swedish State ("Crown land") or of private land owners (who had received the land from the State generations ago). The traditional theories of property since the days of John Locke were in this way reaffirmed and used to justify a denial of Sámi property rights. Following this debate, the nomadic Sámi reindeer herders were granted a usufructuary right, but not ownership rights. In the first Act on Reindeer Herding in 1886 (SFS 1886:38), the Sámi were granted a specific right to herd reindeer, i.e., a monopoly on reindeer herding as being "*the* Lappish occupation," which included a right to hunt, to fish, and to forestry on "Crown land."

This worldview both explained and justified a continued colonization of "Lapland." I can mention one example: the development of the hydropower industry in the early 20th century. The exploitation of lakes and rivers in the north was regulated in the Water Act of 1918 (SFS 1918:523), and although the legislation was enacted in order to facilitate exploitation, the Act also regulated the scope of the exploitation: it was not to harm the "public interest." The public interest was considered to be harmed if the exploitation deprived "a substantial number of residents" of their homes, or if it seriously damaged the conditions for other important industries, or if it changed the nature in a way "that considerably reduced the comfort for nearby inhabitants" (Össbo and Lantto 2011, 338). With the construction of the Sámi as nomads lacking ownership rights, the regulations in the Water Act did not apply to them, according to the authorities: as nomads, they were not settled and, thus, not deprived of their homes; they were supposed to move to another district if changes in the natural conditions were too devastating, and Sámi reindeer herding did not have the same status as other industries (such as fishing and agriculture).

Second, this homogeneous Sámi identity excluded the majority of the Sámi from the system of Sámi rights: the Sámi not engaged in reindeer herding. The exclusive character of the legislation was reinforced even further during the 1920s, when Sámi land rights were explicitly transformed into a "Lapp privilege" in order to reduce the number of reindeer in certain areas that were considered to be "overcrowded," by reducing the number of Sámi with a right to herd reindeer (Mörkenstam 1999, 135–45). The right to herd reindeer was a right granted to the Sámi by the Swedish State, it was argued, and all persons of Sámi origin could not have this right; that would be to "define the Lapp capacity in conflict with the public opinion" (SOU 1927:25, 45). Therefore, the right to herd reindeer should only apply to someone of "Lappish origin" if the father, mother, or grandparents had had reindeer herding as a permanent occupation, as stipulated in the Reindeer Herding Act of 1928 (SFS 1928:309, §1). Two categories of Sámi were, thus, constructed in discourse: reindeer herders (with rights) and non-reindeer herders (without rights). This forced "category-split" had severe effects on the Sámi as a people; it pitted different Sámi groups against each other and created a foundational cleavage within the Sámi community (Ruong 1982, 187–88). Moreover, when the Sámi right to land was conceived of as a "privilege" defined through legislation, this right could always be withdrawn in full or gradually restricted through political or administrative decisions. Sámi ownership of the lands was, thus, definitively ruled out, and the inner colonization was henceforth both explained and justified by reference to prevailing legislation (the "Lapp privilege").

Third, the constructed Sámi identity contributed to and reinforced a social and political order in which the Sámi people's relation to the dominant Swedish society was defined in terms of the former's lesser value. This valuation was explicit when the Sámi identity was closely related to "objective" and "neutral" "facts," such as their "nature," "race," or "culture," something thought of as naturally given and, therefore, immutable. This hierarchical way of apprehending the relation between the Sámi and the Swedes also justified a paternalistic policy, excluding the Sámi themselves from the decision-making process. For instance, in a parliamentary debate in 1917, it was claimed that

> ...the Lapp in many ways is a child. It is not so easy for him to obtain a broader picture of the future; he often looks more towards the comforts of the day. That is why we, who may think of ourselves as somewhat more intelligent, should [...] make a wise and reasonable decision. (von Sydow, in Debatt AK 1917:70, 46)[6]

Fourth, the concept Sámi made claims from the Sámi movement easy to reject within discourse. For instance, all demands that were made in the name of the Sámi as a people with ownership rights or a right to self-determination were excluded beforehand. However, even when Sámi leaders adapted their claims to Swedish policy and made demands or rights claims based on the needs of the reindeer herders, they met fierce opposition. In this context, the constructed identity worked in two ways: the leaders were either perceived of as reindeer herders—and as such did not know their own best interests, according to the dominant conception of a Sámi—or they were too estranged from reindeer herding, according to the authorities, to be considered as their legitimate representatives. They did not conform to the dominant conception of an "authentic" Sámi (Lantto and Mörkenstam, forthcoming). The debate in Sweden was in no way unique in an international perspective. On the contrary, indigenous peoples were marginalized as actors on their own behalf all over the world; they lacked value in a historical–political context created by the majority societies (see, e.g., Tuhiwai Smith 1999, 68–72).

Sámi Rights in the Emerging Democratic Welfare State

With this dominant conception of the Sámi people—based on an alleged racial and cultural superiority of the Swedes—the spatial colonization of the traditional Sámi areas had found a firm normative foundation, and all forms of Sámi self-government were rendered illegitimate in discourse. Moreover, Sámi rights as a "Lapp privilege" became even more important in justifying the Swedish policy after WW II, when individual human rights and decolonization became a contemporary concern on the international political agenda. Given that Sweden defended all kinds of groups in foreign countries "without regard to race or other circumstances," it was now stated to be "an obvious duty" of the Swedish State to protect the rights of "the small minority" of Sámi and, through legislation, "safeguard the rights they have had since time immemorial" (The Parliamentary Ombudsman, in SOU 1968:16, 37). In general, equality had become an increasingly important normative value in Swedish politics, manifested in an active foreign policy characterized by antiracism and democratic arguments, and in the social and economic equality characteristic of the expanding Swedish welfare state (see, e.g., Sainsbury 2012, 214–28). The values of equality and democracy made Sámi actors important in the debate, and with the establishment of the National Union of the Swedish Sámi (*Svenska Samernas Riksförbund, SSR*) in 1950, the Sámi had for the first time obtained a national organization to represent them in their contacts with the Swedish State (see, e.g., Lantto 2003). Societal developments after WW II, it was claimed, necessitated a new Sámi policy fully in line with a modern democratic society.

The postwar "era" was, however, also considered to affect reindeer herding in a new way, with major consequences for the traditional Sámi way of life, i.e., the nomadic lifestyle.

> A growth in railway traffic and road traffic as well as timber cutting and silvicultural measures within the winter grazing areas, a growth in tourism and leisure life, hunting and fishing, the construction of power plants and the regulations of lakes [...] put an ever growing set of demands on reindeer management to adjust to new circumstances. (SOU 1966:12, 196)

One industry was an obstacle to the other, it was argued, and it was obviously the reindeer herders that were not in pace with the broader societal developments; they had to catch up. The unavoidable process of rationalization and modernization was, however, hindered by a "certain conservatism" on the part of the reindeer herders and "the traditionalism that a peculiar occupation and way of life tend to bring," something that called for "society" to intervene (SOU 1968:16, 51). A precondition for rationalization to occur was, thus, for the reindeer herders to break with their traditional way of life and to adopt a rational, economic way of thinking. The former distinction between the Sámi way of life and the Swedish one was, thus, no longer pronounced in terms of degrees of civilization but rather in terms of the Sámi having an underdeveloped industry that was not viable in a modern society. Adjustments to the expanding Swedish welfare state and integration in Swedish society called for assimilation; how could the Sámi otherwise rise to a socioeconomic position equal to that of the Swedes?

In this debate, the meaning of the concept Sámi had, thus, changed. The previously dominant conception of the nomad had been replaced by the Sámi as an effective, rational, and profitable reindeer herder. The Sámi policy, however, did not change in any significant way, and the new legislation—the Reindeer Farming Act of 1971 (SFS 1971:437)—was almost identical to the former acts. Likewise, the system of Sámi rights continued to be explained and justified by reference to reindeer herding, although "proper reindeer herding" through "a nomadic way of life" was replaced as a justificatory foundation. Reindeer herding did not need any support per se; it was the Sámi culture that was in need of protection. And the strongest support for Sámi culture was still supposed to be found among the reindeer herders. They were the hub around which Sámi culture, Swedish politics, and Sámi claims were to be construed. "It is," it was claimed, "a public interest [...] that the profitability of the reindeer industry is improved. The reindeer industry is a prerequisite for the preservation of Sámi culture" (Prop. 1971:51, 112). In this way, the concept Sámi was transformed from being closely attached to a nomadic way of life to denoting the bearer of Sámi culture.

Sámi culture as the new foundation of Swedish Sámi policy, thus, did not challenge the institutionalized system of Sámi rights. On the contrary, economic and political support for the reindeer industry became even more important. An alternative and more inclusive policy, put forward by other Sámi groups, for instance, "that the fishing Sámi" belonged "to the indigenous population in the mountain world" and that "they have the same right to the reindeer grazing areas as the reindeer herding Sámi" (Prop. 1976/77:80, 62), was excluded from discourse. Fishing Sámi were not part of the concept Sámi that served to explain and justify the existing system of Sámi rights; they were not reindeer herders. The concept Sámi was, thus, still as exclusive as before, despite the justification of Swedish Sámi policy as a means for protecting Sámi culture.

The reconstruction of the Sámi identity in an egalitarian and democratic postwar context, thus, reified the former worldview, rather than challenge it. First, as we have seen above, the system of rights established in the late 1900s was still as exclusive and delimited (to rights connected to reindeer herding) as before. Second, the rationalization policy of the 1960s was decisive for the continued colonization of Sámi land, as the detraction of the grazing lands could be justified by referring to more effective methods and management of the reindeer industry, something that in turn could allow for "other interests" to exploit the natural resources in the traditional reindeer grazing areas. However, the increasing exploitation after WW II brought the question of the ownership of land even more to the forefront than previously, and the Sámi challenged the State in the important Taxed Mountain Case (*Skattefjällsmålet*), initiated by *SSR* in 1966. The Sámi sued the Swedish State and claimed "full ownership rights to the property in dispute [...] located in taxed mountains." The Swedish State responded in a way so as to reaffirm the established view that Sámi rights were a "privilege" granted to them by the State and claimed its ownership "of the properties in dispute, and that only the special rights stated in the Reindeer Farming Act now belong to the Sámi and the Sámi villages" (Supreme Court Decision No. DT2. Case No. 324/76, edited by Jahreskog 1982, 148–51). In the final decision in 1981, the Supreme Court—not surprisingly—ruled in favor of the State, and with the reaffirmation of the State's ownership rights, the "usufructuary right" of the Sámi had to be balanced against the legitimate interests of "other" users of the land. The legal process, thus, opened up for a continued exploitation and colonization of Sámi lands.

Third, with the focus still on reindeer herding, the cultural hierarchy between the Swedish and the Sámi was upheld. In the postwar context, however, the valuation—the hierarchy—was implicit, and based on norms and rules of behavior, traditions, and social routines. A traditional Sámi way of life was obsolete, and the reindeer industry had to be rationalized through modern technology and methods, i.e., a new

(Swedish) way of life. The boundary between groups was, thus, upheld by not explicitly mentioning it, something that was obvious in the paradox characterizing Swedish politics during this period: on the one hand, the system of Sámi rights was justified in terms of a protection of Sámi culture, with the reindeer herders as bearers of this particular culture in their day-to-day lives; on the other, the reindeer industry had to be rationalized in order to break with the same cultural traditions it was supposed to be a prerequisite for.

Fourth, although the concept Sámi still justified an exclusion of the Sámi from political decision making, the work of SSR created a platform for Sámi participation in the political debate. SSR challenged Swedish policy primarily by raising arguments on Sámi rights to land and water, as we saw in the Taxed Mountain Case, rejecting the dominant State view that Sámi use of the land was a "privilege" (Lantto and Mörkenstam 2008, 36). However, with the firm focus on rationalization after WW II—and with the concept Sámi still evolving around the reindeer herder as the bearer of Sámi culture—Swedish Sámi policy may best be described as a transformation into an "agricultural policy" on reindeer herding. Instead of seeing the SSR as an organization representative of a heterogeneous people, the State treated the organization as one interest group among others with expertise in reindeer husbandry.

Contemporary Sámi Policy: International Law and the Right to Self-Determination

Although the postwar Swedish Sámi policy did not change noticeably, the discourse was opened up when Sámi culture became its justificatory foundation. As we saw earlier on, the policy was gradually transformed into a means for protecting Sámi culture: "The aim of the Reindeer Farming Act is ultimately to protect the Sámi population's possibilities to maintain and develop their own cultural life." It was, thus, not "only an economic policy," but a "minority protection" (SOU 1983:67, 135). This political change was well in accordance with the multicultural turn in Swedish politics in general, manifested in a new policy on immigrants adopted by a unanimous Swedish Parliament in 1975. The explicit ambition of this policy was formulated in three catchwords: equality, freedom of choice, and cooperation, with a focus on the right of immigrants to protect and develop their own distinct cultures and languages (see, e.g., Mörkenstam 2010).

In this perspective—and with a policy to protect a minority group and an indigenous people—the non-reindeer herders gradually became part of the concept Sámi; their way of life could also be included in Sámi culture. It was no longer "meaningful," it was claimed, to try to find out "what element of culture [it was] that had to exist and be active for anyone to define themselves as belonging to a Sámi cultural sphere" (Ds 1989:38, 19).[7] The changing view on Sámi culture and identity was primarily expressed in the increasing importance attached to language as a people's most significant cultural feature, and the concept Sámi was, thereby, seriously challenged. In the Sámi Parliament Act of 1992 (SFS 1992:1433, Ch. 1 § 2), the legal definition of a Sámi was made more inclusive for the first time: "A Sámi in this Act is regarded as anyone [...] who considers himself/herself to be Sámi" and has made plausible the fact that he/she has spoken Sámi in his/her home, or had grandparents that have spoken Sámi in their homes.

In the 1980s, the recognition of the Sámi as a minority group and an indigenous people called for a Sámi policy in conformity with the international debate of the day, as Sweden attaches great weight "to their global reputation" and to upholding "international law and conventions" (Minnerup and Solberg 2011, 14). The starting point in this discussion was the first Article in the two UN conventions from 1966, on civil and political rights and on economic, social, and cultural rights, i.e., the principle of all peoples' right to self-determination. The prevailing apprehension was, however, that the principle would not apply to the Sámi. This interpretation was based on the fact that the right to self-determination in international law only applied to colonized peoples, it was argued, and "it is our opinion that it is impossible to equal the Swedish influence over the traditional Sámi settlement areas with what is usually called colonialism" (SOU 1986:36, 164). A clear distinction was made between colonization overseas and inner colonization, an interpretation supported by contemporary international law (see, e.g., Anaya 2004, 54). Sweden recognized the Sámi as a people, but not as a people in the international legal sense.

Other forms of minority protection were put forward as well, such as Article 27 in the 1966 UN International Convention on Civil and Political Rights. This Article states that in

> ...those states in which ethnic, religious or linguistic minorities exist, persons belonging to such minorities should not be denied the right, in community with other members of the group, to enjoy their own culture, to profess and practise their religion, or to use their own language (UN 1966, Art. 27).

In the Swedish debate, the Article was conceived of as a strong protection of Sámi culture—including reindeer herding—and language. Although formulated in individual terms, it was in Swedish politics interpreted as a justification for collective rights, i.e., as a right to cultural autonomy. Moreover, it was not only a right establishing the "principle of equality between cultures," but also an acknowledgment of the fact that "real equality demands equality in resources, i.e., the group lagging behind have to be the object of affirmative action" (Ds 1989:38, 29).

The right to cultural autonomy both explained and justified the establishment of a Sámi Parliament in 1993. A parliament would establish an institutional prerequisite for the Sámi "to independently develop its culture on its own terms" through a "decision making body representative for the entire minority and elected by it" (SOU 1989:41, 147). It was, however, made absolutely clear that the parliament was not to be "a body for self-government, [acting] in place of the parliament or municipal councils or in competition with those bodies" (Prop. 1992/93:32, 35). Instead, the Sámi Parliament was given the status of a government agency under the Swedish Government—although popularly elected by the Sámi constituency—with the general mission to work for a living Sámi culture. The parliament was, thus, assigned dual roles: as a government agency with tasks strictly regulated by law (an administrative role) and as a popularly elected body to represent the Sámi people (a political role).

The Swedish interpretation of the rights of indigenous peoples in terms of a rather limited right to cultural autonomy was, however, in the early 2000s, transformed in accordance with the debate in international law into a full-fledged right to self-determination: "the Sámi people is [...] a 'people' in the international legal sense, that have rights, including the right to self-determination" (Prop. 2005/06:86, 38). The Swedish interpretation of what the Sámi right to self-determination actually means seems, however, to confirm the traditional policy of the last century. Sweden's statement in the General Assembly in conjunction with the signing of the UNDRIP in 2007 could, for instance, be interpreted as an affirmation of status quo. The Swedish representative claimed "that a large part of the realization of the right to self-determination could be ensured through [...] a consultative process between institutions representing indigenous peoples and Governments, and through participation in democratic systems, such as the current Swedish system." Moreover, it "did not entail a collective right of veto," and the references "to ownership and control of land" would be interpreted as "the traditional rights of the Sami people," which in Sweden "were called reindeer herding rights" (United Nations General Assembly 2007). Once again, then, the State reaffirmed the conception of Sámi rights as a "privilege."

In spite of the recognition of the Sámi as an indigenous people, there has been little discernible change so far in terms of changes in the well-established system of Sámi rights and in terms of increased autonomy. The Sámi Parliament is, for instance, still only accorded administrative duties, and the parliament has no political decision-making power. Moreover, the institutional design of the Sámi Parliament clearly involves an inherent clash of interests between the two roles. As a government agency, on the one hand, the Sámi Parliament should implement the policy of the Swedish Government; as a parliament elected by the Sámi people, on the other, it should represent the will of its constituency (Lawrence and Mörkenstam 2012, 43–45). The inherent conflict between the interests of the Sámi people and of the Swedish Government has also been brought to the fore by the Sámi. If Sweden "is a country founded on the territory of two peoples," as the Sámi Parliament declared, it implies that "these peoples have to exercise their right to self-determination side by side" and that "none of the two people's right to self-determination have priority over the other people's" (Sametinget 2004, Ch. 7.1). This is, however, a perspective that has been excluded in discourse so far, mainly due to how the Sámi people have been constructed as a people not capable of handling its own affairs.

This worldview seems to be reproduced in contemporary politics, particularly in the debate on the work and performance of the Sámi Parliament. In a report from the Swedish Agency for Public Management in

2010 (Statskontoret 2010, 15, 43–45), for instance, the Sámi Parliament was criticized for wanting follow-up of its work, for a lack of systematic planning of its activities, for unclear internal hierarchies, and for breaching its budget on several occasions. The conclusion following this critique was that the Sámi Parliament should be kept closer to the Swedish Government, thus, reducing the parliament's autonomy rather than strengthening it. Furthermore, the Swedish media representation of the Sámi Parliament conveys a similar viewpoint in the frequent descriptions of the performance of the parliament as weak or poor. In the media, the blame for this weak performance is most often put on the Sámi themselves (and not on the design of the parliament, i.e., the Swedish State), as a result of "individual incompetence of the members of parliament or the functionaries, immature behavior, or a not fully developed organization" (Mörkenstam et al. 2012, 20). In spite of having a popularly elected parliament, the Sámi, thus, still seem to be subject to a lingering hierarchic worldview denying them the right to self-determination.

Moreover, the spatial colonization may continue as well. A report from the Sámi Parliament in 2012, for instance, indicated a continuing exploitation of traditional Sámi land used for reindeer herding, with severe consequences for the Sámi. Forestry in particular, but also other industries, such as hydropower, mining, windpower, and tourism have devastating effects (Sametinget 2012, 36). Without ownership rights, "other interests" may lay legitimate claims to use the same land as the Sámi. In this perspective, the main function of the State is to strike a balance between different "interests" competing over the same land. Following the pattern of colonization during the past 100 years, the interests of the reindeer herding industry tend to be depreciated when competing with "other interests," as those of the windpower or mining industry. This hierarchical order is explicitly made in statements both by local authorities—"windpower interests should take precedence in those cases where coexistence [with reindeer herding] is not considered possible in the use of water or land areas" (County Administrative Board in Norrbotten, quoted in Lawrence 2009, 26)—and by the Swedish Government. In a decision in 2013, when the Government overruled appeals from two Sámi villages concerning the right for a mining company to start processing within their traditional reindeer grazing area, the Government claimed that "the national interest for valuable substances and material" was to be given priority, in spite of the fact that "the conditions for reindeer herding within the areas of interest" ceased to exist. It was considered "undisputable" that the national economic revenues from the mining industry would be larger, just as "the possibilities for an increase in social welfare," than what the ongoing reindeer herding generated (*Näringsdepartementet* 2013, 10).[8]

Concluding Remarks: Challenging the "Discursive Colonization"

In this chapter, I have analyzed how the concept "Lapp" or Sámi has been a node in the justification of Swedish Sámi policy. It has been decisive in how the political problems of the day have been formulated, just as it has delimited the range of possible solutions. The dominant concept "Lapp" or Sámi has in that way provided a logical field of possible political options—they prescribe how to act, think, and express oneself—and it has, thereby, set normative limits on legitimate action. The normative discussion in Swedish Sámi policy has, thus, been dependent on the different dominant conceptions of the Sámi people. The values put forward, such as culture, race, and nation during the first half of the 20th century, or the contemporary values of democracy, equality, and multiculturalism, have derived their meaning in relation to the question of what a Sámi is. To be conceived of as legitimate participants in discourse, the Sámi themselves have been forced to adapt to the dominant concept Sámi. In this perspective, the concept Sámi has upheld a conceptual scheme or belief system that is very difficult for an indigenous people like the Sámi to seriously challenge. Moreover, the normative vocabulary of modern constitutionalism in itself reinforces the social relations of power in contemporary societies and functions as a constraint on indigenous peoples' struggle for their rights. They are, to use the words of Tully (1995, 39), forced to use the constitutional language available within discourse—terms like people, nation, and self-determination—"even though these terms may distort or misdescribe the claim they would wish to make if it were expressed in their own language."

The arduousness in challenging this "discursive colonization" can be illustrated by the way indigenous peoples' political struggle for recognition challenges the dominant norms permeating contemporary political theory and practice. In this concluding section, I will briefly mention two. The first concerns democracy, where the conception of the Sámi as a people obviously challenges the traditional nation-state-centered understanding of democracy, an understanding that in a historical perspective effectively excluded the recognition of indigenous peoples' right to self-determination. However, if there are two peoples with a right to self-determination sharing a territory—something recognized by the Swedish State today—this fact must set limits on "the rights of existing nation states and setting these into more cooperatively regulated relationships" (Young 2005, 52). This, in turn, calls for a reinterpretation of the classical model of self-determination. Instead of equating self-determination with independence and state sovereignty, in which the State has the central and final authority within a bounded territory, self-determination has to be defined in relational terms, and we have to discuss different forms of shared sovereignty.

The second concerns the discussion on Sámi land rights, which is permeated by the classical view on property rights denying indigenous peoples ownership, as we have seen. Recognition of indigenous land rights would challenge prevailing policy and the claim that the State or private land owners are the only rightful owners of the land. The "fact that indigenous peoples were defrauded and expropriated" and lost their right to land and natural resources in vast territories brings with it, as Margaret Moore argues, "some responsibility on the part of the nonindigenous population to take steps to rectify this injustice" (Moore 2003, 12). Rectification, however, must be preceded by an acceptance on the part of the colonial nation states that they are founded on a history of violence, injustice, and oppression—something still denied in the national narratives of most countries—and an acceptance of the fact that indigenous peoples may have more than a right to use the land; they may have ownership rights.

In our case, it is obvious that an acceptance of Sweden's colonial past seems very distant in contemporary politics. The logical field of possible political options—upheld by the historical construction of the Sámi people—has hitherto excluded a reformulation of Swedish Sámi policy and the ongoing exploitation of natural resources in terms of a continuation of the colonization process that started more than 150 years ago. The continuing spatial colonization of northern Sweden, as well as the ongoing colonization in other parts of the world, is paralleled and supported by a "discursive colonization" much more difficult to refute than the ideology of colonization itself. This is not least because indigenous peoples have been denied the power to define their own societal structure, politics, economy, and culture, i.e., the right to self-determination, something emphasized in the 2007 UNDRIP.

The Sámi (and indigenous peoples all over the world) continue, however, to challenge this "discursive colonization" when they put an equal sign between contemporary politics and the colonial past. In the opening speech at the Sámi Parliament Plenary, for instance, the Chairperson of the Parliament, Stefan Mikaelsson (2013) stated:

> The mining plague that today spreads over Europe [...] is the result of more than hundred years of colonialism. The European colonialism, based on racism, seems to envisage the Sámi people as inferior and unable to understand our own good, and even less able to administer our own culture and heritage to the future generations. This [view] is as strong today as it was 1919, when Sweden started its forced relocation of reindeer herding Sámi and their families [...].

Without an understanding of how this "discursive colonization" has been institutionalized in national politics, it is difficult to seriously challenge the contemporary domination and oppression of indigenous peoples. And this is decisive today when the exploitation of natural resources are more effective and expansive than ever before, and when the right to self-determination is to be negotiated and transformed into political practice on a nation-state level.

Notes and Bibliography

Notes

1. "Lapp" is originally a Finnish term that the Sámi themselves perceived as derogatory, and, primarily as a consequence of their political struggle, the

term used in the public debate changed to "Sámi." The term Sámi will be used consistently throughout the chapter, except for in quotations and expressions in which the term "Lapp" occurs.

2. In the contemporary debate, this region is most often referred to by the Sámi as the Swedish part of Sápmi, with the whole of Sápmi covering northern Finland, Norway, and Russia as well.

3. SFS is an abbreviation for *Svensk författningssamling*, the Swedish Code of Statutes.

4. KMB is an abbreviation for *Kunglig Majestäts betänkanden*, His Majesty's Official Reports.

5. Prop. is an abbreviation for Proposition, Government Bill.

6. Debatt AK is an abbreviation for *Debatt i Andra Kammaren*, Debate in the Second Chamber.

7. Ds is an abbreviation for *Departementsserien*, Ministerial Reports.

8. *Näringsdepartementet* is the Ministry of Enterprise, Energy, and Communications.

Bibliography

Anaya, S. J. 2004. *Indigenous Peoples in International Law*, 2nd edn. Oxford: Oxford University Press.

Daes, E-I. 2011. "The UN Declaration on the Rights of Indigenous Peoples: Background and Appraisal." In *Reflections on the UN Declaration on the Rights of Indigenous Peoples*, edited by S. Allen and A. Xanthaki, 11–40. Oxford: Hart Publishing.

Draft Nordic Saami Convention. 2007. Accessed June 18, 2014 http://www.regjeringen.no/upload/BLD/Nordic%20Sami%20Convention.pdf

Jahreskog, Birgitta (ed.). 1982. Supreme Court Decision No. DT2. Case No. 324/76. In *The Sami National Minority in Sweden*, 146–248. Stockholm: Almqvist and Wiksell International.

Lantto, P. 2003. *Att göra sin stämma hörd: Svenska Samernas Riksförbund, samerörelsen och svensk samepolitik 1950–1962*. Umeå: Kulturgräns norr.

Lantto, P. and U. Mörkenstam. 2008. "Sami Rights and Sami Challenges: The Modernization Process and the Swedish Sami Movement, 1886–2006." *Scandinavian Journal of History* 33 (1): 26–51.

———. forthcoming. "Action, Organization and Confrontation: Strategies of the Sámi movement in Sweden During the 20th Century." In *Indigenous Politics: Institutions, Representation, Mobilisation*, edited by M. Berg-Nordlie, J. Saglie, and A. Sullivan. Colchester: ECPR Press.

Lawrence, R. 2009. "The Last Frontier? Windpower Developments on Traditional Saami Lands." In *Shifting Responsibilities and Shifting Terrains: State Responsibility, Corporate Social Responsibility, and Indigenous Claims*. PhD Thesis, Stockholm Studies in Sociology Series 37, Stockholm University, Stockholm.

108   Ulf Mörkenstam

Lawrence, R. and U. Mörkenstam. 2012. "Självbestämmande genom myndighet-sutövning? Sametingets dubbla roller." *Statsvetenskaplig Tidskrift* 115 (2): 207–39.

Mikaelsson, S. 2013. "Opening-speech at the Sámi Parliament Plenary February 19–21 2013." Accessed March 27, 2013. http://www.svtplay.se/klipp/1040670/inledningstal-vid-sametingets-plenum

Minnerup, G. and P. Solberg (eds). 2011. "Introduction." In *First World, First Nation*, 1–21. Brighton: Sussex Academic Press.

Moore, M. 2003. "The Right of Indigenous Peoples to Collective Self-Determination." In *Self-Determination and Secession, NOMOS* XLV, edited by S. Macedo and A. Buchanan, 89–118. New York: New York University Press.

Mörkenstam, U. 1999. Om *"Lapparnes privilegier": Föreställningar om samiskhet i svensk samepolitik 1883–1997*, Stockholm Studies in Politics Vol. 67. Stockholm: Stockholm Studies in Politics 67.

————. 2010. "Ekonomi, kultur och jämlikhet: teman i svensk politik i invandrarfrågor decennierna efter det andra världskriget." *Historisk tidskrift för Finland* 95 (4): 572–607.

Mörkenstam, U., A. Gottardis, and H-I. Roth. 2012. The Sámi Parliament: A Challenged Recognition? *ACCEPT PLURALISM*. Florens: EUI.

Näringsdepartementet. 2013. "*Regeringsbeslut 2013-08-22*." Accessed November 5, 2013. http://sverigesradio.se/diverse/appdata/isidor/files/2327/13751.pdf

Össbo, Å. and P. Lantto. 2011. "Colonial Tutelage and Industrial Colonialism: Reindeer Husbandry and the Early 20th-Century Hydroelectric Development in Sweden." *Scandinavian Journal of History* 36 (3): 324–48.

Pateman, C. 2007. "The Settler Contract." In *Contract & Domination*, edited by C. Pateman and C. Mills, 35–78. Cambridge: Polity Press.

Quane, H. 2011. "New Directions for Self-Determination and Participatory Rights?" In *Reflections on the UN Declaration on the Rights of Indigenous Peoples*, edited by S. Allen and A. Xanthaki, 259–87. Oxford: Hart Publishing.

Ruong, I. 1982. *Samerna i historien och nutiden*. Stockholm: Bonnier fakta.

Sainsbury, D. 2012. *Welfare States and Immigrant Rights. The Politics of Inclusion and Exclusion*. Oxford: Oxford University Press.

Sametinget. 2004. "Betänkande av det svenska Sametingets kommitté med uppgift att ta fram ett förslag till strategi för en implementering av det samiska folkets rätt till självbestämmande på den svenska sidan av Sápmi." Accessed March 25, 2013. http://www.sametinget.se/1328

————. 2012. "Rapport. Regeringsuppdrag: 'Utformningen av ett förvaltningsverktyg för förekomst av stora rovdjur baserat på en toleransnivå för rennäringen.' JO 2010/2752." Accessed December 5, 2012. http://www.sametinget.se/40201

Skinner, Q. 1989. "Language and Political Change." In *Political Innovation and Conceptual Change*, edited by T. Ball, J. Farr, and R. Hanson, 6–23. Cambridge: Cambridge University Press.

Tuhiwai Smith, L. 1999. *Decolonizing Methodologies: Research and Indigenous Peoples*. London: Zed Books.

Tully, J. 1993. *An Approach to Political Philosophy: Locke in Contexts*. Cambridge: Cambridge University Press.

————. 1995. *Strange Multiplicity. Constitutionalism in an Age of Diversity*. Cambridge: Cambridge University Press.

United Nations General Assembly. 2007 (September 13). "GA/10612: General Assembly Adopts Declaration on Rights of Indigenous Peoples." Accessed August 28, 2011. http://www.un.org/News/Press/docs/2007/ga10612.doc.htm.

United Nations International Covenant on Civil and Political Rights. Accessed June 18, 2014. http://www.ohchr.org/en/professionalinterest/pages/ccpr.aspx

von Linné, C. 1975 (1732). *Lapplandsresa. År 1732*. Stockholm: Wahlström & Widstrand.

Xanthaki, A. 2007. *Indigenous Rights and United Nations Standards. Self-Determination, Culture and Land*. Cambridge: Cambridge University Press.

Young, I. M. 2005. *Global Challenges. War, Self-Determination and Responsibility for Justice*. Cambridge: Polity Press.

Public Documents

Debatt AK 1917:70. *angående ändringar i lagen om de svenska lapparnas rätt till renbete i Sverige*.

Ds 1989:38. *Saemien kultuvre—Sáme kultuvra—Samisk kultur*.

KMB 1883. *Förslag till förordning angående de svenska Lapparne och de bofaste i Sverige samt till förordning angående renmärken*.

KMB 1909. *Förslag till omorganisation af lappskolväsendet*.

Proposition 1883:36. *Kungl. Maj:ts nådiga proposition till riksdagen med förslag till förordning rörande de Lappar, som med renar flytta emellan de förenade konungarikena Sverige och Norge*.

Proposition 1886:2. *Kungl. Maj:ts nådiga proposition till riksdagen med förslag till lag angående de svenska Lapparnes rätt till renbete i Sverige och till lag angående renmärken*.

Proposition 1971:51. *Kungl. Maj:ts proposition till riksdagen med förslag till rennäringslag, m.m.*

Proposition 1976/77:80. *Regeringens proposition om insatser för samerna*.

Proposition 1992/93:32. *Regeringens proposition Om samerna och samisk kultur m.m.*

Proposition 2005/06:86. *Ett ökat samiskt inflytande*.

SFS 1850:81. *Kungl. Maj:ts nådiga stadga för afwittring och skattläggning i Luleå lappmark*.

SFS 1886:38. *Lag angående de svenska Lapparnes rätt till renbete i Sverige*.

SFS 1918:523. *Vattenlag*.

SFS 1928:309. *Lag om de svenska lapparnas rätt till renbete i Sverige*.

SFS 1971:437. *Rennäringslag.*

SFS 1992:1433. *Sametingslag.*

SOU 1927:25. *Förslag angående de svenska lapparnas rätt till renbete i Sverige m. m. avgivet av särskild tillkallad sakkunnig.*

SOU 1966:12. *Renbetesmarkerna.*

SOU 1968:16. *Rennäringen i Sverige.*

SOU 1983:67. *Rennäringens ekonomi.*

SOU 1986:36. *Samernas folkrättsliga ställning.*

SOU 1989:41. *Samerätt och sameting. Huvudbetänkande av samerättsutredningen.*

Statskontoret 2010:15. *Myndighetsanalys av Sametinget.*

6

Institutional Change and Identity Shift: The Case of Contemporary Scotland

Sherrill Stroschein

Abstract

Many studies of state fragmentation and secession emphasize the importance of institutions in these dynamics. Devolved or federal institutions may be intended to placate national sentiments at the regional level, but they often provide a foundation for attempts at secession or independence. Much of the literature on these dynamics emphasizes the material and network resources and infrastructure that sub-state institutions can provide for independence movements. Their discursive and symbolic resources have been less examined. This contribution outlines how the 1997 devolution for Scotland has provided an institutional resource for the Scottish National Movement. However, the institutions of devolution did not only serve as material and infrastructural resource. They also provided a symbolic and ideational context for rhetorical and discursive disputes with the Conservative–Liberal Democrat British government established in Westminster in 2010. The Scottish case is particularly useful for illustrating both the possibilities and limits of these discursive contestations. The Scottish example shows how identities are solidified in the process of contention (Tilly 2008); thus, whatever the referendum outcome in 2014, Scottish-ness is strengthened by these events.

Introduction

When the UK government of Tony Blair moved to create devolved government for Scotland in 1997, it did not expect that years later this institutional platform might produce a challenge to the existence of the UK itself. Devolution was intended by Blair's Labour government as part of a move to placate the Scottish Nationalists (Curtice 2009, 55). In September of 1997, a successful referendum confirmed the foundation of a Scottish parliament, now an active institution at Holyrood in Edinburgh. In the 15 years since, the Scottish National Party (SNP) has increased its power and support, partly due to its platform within the new Scottish Parliament (Mitchell 2009, 31). Following the Scottish elections in 2007, and then codified in 2011, it even began to wrest votes and seats away from the Labour Party in Scotland. With most of Scottish voters registering preferences for leftward-leaning policies, Scottish relations with the British central government in Westminster began to decay following the establishment of a Conservative–Liberal Democrat coalition government in London in 2010. In the years of budget cuts and a program of austerity that followed, the SNP's view that Scotland might be better off without the rest of Britain gained increasing support among the population. By 2012, a settlement was negotiated between Westminster and Edinburgh that a referendum on Scottish independence was to be held in late 2014.

This chapter examines the dynamics leading up to the decision on the referendum, to illustrate how identities are both constructed and constitutive parts of political change. The elites, British Prime Minister David Cameron and Scotland First Minister Alex Salmond, have been negotiating the specifics of the referendum, but public responses to these discussions become part of the story. Much of the literature on separatist dynamics argues that regional institutions such as the Scottish parliament can provide the resources and infrastructure for further independence (Bunce 1999; Gorenburg 2003; Roeder 2007). In this chapter, I argue that in addition to material, infrastructure, and network resources, the institutions of the Scottish Parliament have also provided a symbolic and ideational basis to legitimize Scottish-ness as a political position. In addition, Scottish identity has been strengthened in the course of disputes between Scotland and Westminster since a Conservative–Liberal Democratic government took power in the British government in 2010. As noted by Tilly (2008), identities are strengthened and solidified in the course of contentious action and discourse, and the Scottish case demonstrates the dynamics of this process. In this contentious discourse, Scottish identity has been clarified in terms of what it is *not*, in its rejection of the rightward-leaning policies of the post-2010 Westminster government.

In the discussion that follows, I first outline the content of the 1997 reforms and give an overview of the literature on institutions as producing potential secession. I then outline how the discourse of identities in opposition is legitimized by and provides content for these institutions. I illustrate these dynamics using some of the examples from the Scotland–Westminster disputes since 2010, which show an entrenchment of identity over time that is constituted by an intensifying discourse of difference on what it means to be Scottish or English.

An Outline of the Devolved Scottish Institutions

Scotland has been subject to English (and then British) rule since the middle ages, and was then codified with the Acts of Union of 1707. However, Scottish identity retained many independent elements, which prompted the recognition of a broader need for autonomy by the Labour government during the 1990s. The government embarked on a process of increased devolution throughout Britain, also granting additional powers to Wales and northern Ireland. As part of this process, a referendum was held among Scottish voters in September 1997.

The referendum put two questions to Scottish voters. The first question, regarding whether a Scottish Parliament should be established, received an overwhelming yes vote of 73.4 percent. An additional question, regarding whether the Scottish government should have the powers to adjust the rate of taxes (tax-varying powers), received a yes vote of 63.5 percent (McFadden and Lazarowicz 2000, 4). With these results, the Labour government in Westminster passed the Scotland Act in November 1998. The Scotland Act primarily focused on the creation of the Scottish Parliament of 129 members and the Scottish Executive, comprised of the First Minister and Cabinet Secretaries. While Westminster members are referred to as MPs, members of the Scottish Parliament are referred to as MSPs.

The law-making powers of these bodies remain subordinate to the authority of the British Government and Parliament in Westminster, with just some powers transferred from Westminster to Scottish authority. The Scotland Act outlines these powers in reverse, specifying which powers *cannot* be performed by the Scottish institutions—with those not specified being those that Scotland *can* perform (McFadden and Lazarowicz 2000, 5–6). In essence, the Scottish Parliament can only pass laws that pertain to matters within the Scottish territorial boundaries and must adhere to European legislation. A number of powers such as foreign relations and security, immigration, and many economic powers are reserved for the UK government, as well as regulatory authority over several areas. The British Parliament can also override any of the Scottish laws with which it disagrees. With these limitations, matters that are devolved include the National Health Service in Scotland, education, local government, and social programs such as housing, local economic development and transport. In addition, some matters of criminal and civil law (including the keeping of public records) are devolved to Scotland, and there are some environmental, agricultural, and cultural powers (ibid., 9–11, 17–20).

In sharp contrast to the First-Past-the-Post or Single Member District majoritarian election system that is used to elect the UK parliament, the Scottish parliament uses a Mixed Member Proportional system. In this system, 73 MSPs are elected from districts (constituencies) and 56 are chosen via proportional lists. Observers of Scottish politics have described the creation of this system as "an electoral lifeline" for the SNP (Curtice 2009, 59). As noted by Curtice, the SNP has tended to draw a broad base of support that was spread over several districts, but never in a majority. The addition of the proportional element to the electoral system allowed the SNP to begin to reflect these votes in seats in the parliament, rather than having them wasted in majoritarian district elections (ibid., 56–60). In addition, the creation of the Scottish Parliament has meant that the SNP could become more than a party in constant opposition to Westminster—now they could also achieve constructive goals (Mitchell 2009, 33; Mackay 2009, 79–80).

While the first two Scottish Parliament elections in 1999 and 2003 produced Labour majorities, the SNP dominated the 2007 and 2011 elections, demonstrating its upward trend in popularity. Interestingly, those considering themselves as "Scottish not British" began to demonstrate increasing support for the SNP during this time, showing an increase of those who linked the party with a Scottish identity. Of those with a primary Scottish identity, 43 percent voted for the SNP in 1999—but by 2007, 58 percent voted for the SNP. In addition, among those voting for the SNP in 2007, 78 percent supported an agenda of Scottish independence, an increase from 62 percent in 1999 and 58 percent in 2003 (Curtice 2009, 63, 64). These figures demonstrate both an increase in support for the SNP party over time, and a simultaneous increase among its supporters for its agenda of independence.[1] Several theorists of secession and independence movements would attribute this increase in support for the party and its program to the new institutional base, as providing resources and institutional support, as outlined below.

Devolved Institutions, Material and Network Resources, and Infrastructure

Devolved institutions of government for specific national groups are intended to provide these groups with institutions of self-government, or an ability to regulate some of their own affairs. This reasoning is that this type of inclusion should make them more involved in the workings of the general state, and, thus, should placate potential desires for independence or secession (Heintze 1998; Rothchild and Hartzell 1999). While this reasonable position has achieved a great deal of support within the theoretical as well as the policy community, many have observed that in practice, such institutions can serve as a platform for additional separatism (Mozaffar and Scarritt 1999; Cornell 2002; Jenne 2006).

There are a few reasons that devolved institutions might provide a platform for further separatism. First, institutions can serve as material resources and infrastructure for further claims of independence from the state. As outlined by Bunce, the federations of the Soviet Union,

Yugoslavia, and Czechoslovakia all fragmented along the lines of their devolved institutions, because the local units were able to collect and hold the resources that "leaked" out of the center to these regional units (Bunce 1999, 39). Second, institutions can serve as network resources that guide the type of networks and the communication that can be fostered for mobilizations (Gorenburg 2003, 3). This type of institutional infrastructure also concentrated mobilization activities within the local unit rather than across the broader state (Bunce 1999, 39). Devolved institutions, thus, create the material, network, and infrastructural platform for both elites and masses to mobilize behind a national identity.

These accounts provide a solid understanding of the structural conditions that can foster mobilizations. But how do the dynamics of identity mobilizations emerge? Is it possible to trace changes in the content of these ideas? As outlined by Roeder in his "segmental institutions thesis," in addition to these structural conditions, there must be identities, grievances, and a willingness of masses to engage in mobilization. Each of these components must be present and "mutually reinforcing." In his view, it is institutions that achieve the alignment of these components, providing a structure to channel identities, grievances, and the will to mobilize together behind the focus of a national goal (Roeder 2007, 9–10). He notes that devolved units, or "segment-states," thus, "create a nurturing environment for nationalist machines to emerge before independence" (ibid., 84).

Have Scotland's devolved institutions been able to channel identities, grievances, and the will to mobilize? An answer to this question would require some attention to the "content of what is being said" about Scotland, and about its relationship with the rest of Britain. Some theoretical background for an examination of this discourse is outlined below.

Discourses of Opposition and Support for Independence

During the run-up to the 2007 elections, the SNP and its leader Alex Salmond began to present a positive, optimistic image. Taking an "unfailingly positive" stance regarding Scotland's future became part of the party's campaign strategy, assisted by some adept public relations and campaign consultants (Mackay 2009, 85). It is no accident that the party won the most seats in the Scottish Parliament in the 2007 elections, as this optimistic image gained ground with voters. While the ideational nature of political support is under-studied in Political Science (often upstaged by materialist or rationalist approaches), the power of ideas, images, and symbols is well-understood in the hands-on world of political campaigns. A positive image is a good place to start to garner support.

However, for a campaign to be successful, it also needs a clear identity and set of goals. And in order for its identity and goals to resonate clearly among a voting population, its characteristics must be clearly visible and resonate with prior understandings and grievances (Motyl 1999). The SNP benefited from its new positive image in the 2007 campaign, but in order to sustain momentum through the next elections, it needed a foil. It found its villain in the Conservative–Liberal Democrat government that took power at Westminster in mid-2010. The SNP had difficulty carving out a true niche, while the Labour government that had produced devolution remained in power in Westminster, particularly due to the left-leaning viewpoints shared between Labour and the SNP. With the advent of the Conservative–Liberal Democratic government and its policies of cuts and austerity, the SNP was able to ground its pro-Scottish rhetoric solidly on what it was *not*, establishing its clear differences from the new Westminster government. These differences go beyond the material issue of the cuts and austerity themselves. They have become part of a rhetoric of identity about a northern "country" emulating the model of the Nordic states—one that pursues a social democratic agenda funded by North Sea Oil. Grievances against Westminster include an anti-austerity and anti-Conservative rhetoric that supports this clear stance (SNP Interview 2011).

In theoretical terms, the clarification of an identity requires the establishment and preservation of a boundary between categories of "us" and "them" (Abbott 2001). Identities, thus, emerge in a relational manner, and in opposition—it is hard to envision a category of Scots without an understanding of "not-Scots." An understanding of identity from a relational perspective requires that instead of starting with an identity essence, we first approach the interactions of opposition that create and preserve that identity as an essence, or a bounded category (Tilly 2005, 61; Tilly 2008). Corporate identities exist as a function of the boundaries between them, and the mechanisms of creation and maintenance of those boundaries. Group-ness requires an identity of distinction, sustained by the maintenance of a boundary between individuals or groups as paired categories (Abbott 2001; Tilly 2005, 2008). For example, states can be best understood as projects that emerge relationally, with some being more successful state projects than others (Jackson and Nexon 1999). Similarly, national groups as bounded categories with certain goals can be understood as successful or less successful projects in terms of their boundary creation and maintenance over time. These dynamics are the essence of identity construction—construction is not an abstract phenomenon, but emerges through relational interactions.

These relational insights help to demonstrate how it is that identities can increase or decrease in salience over time, with the unfolding of interactions that increase or decrease the strength of the boundary. In the course of public discussion and debate, some rhetorical focal points recur and become anchors for these identity boundaries. The concept of "rhetorical commonplaces" (Jackson 2006) is used to denote these stable focal points, which can be used to legitimize desired political goals. For example, the notion of Scotland as emulating a Nordic model is one such rhetorical commonplace, deployed by the SNP but also resonating among many ordinary Scots. As outlined by Jackson, the effort to establish and anchor rhetorical commonplaces becomes the nature of political struggle—"legitimation contests" for public support between those deploying different goals (ibid., 253).

A quite successful rhetorical commonplace among many Scots is the notion that the UK government in Westminster (and the English) take a patronizing attitude toward Scotland. As noted by Condor and Abell following their repeat interviews with 60 Scottish participants, a recurrent theme in discussions with Scots was resentment of what they perceive as an unjustified "superior" attitude of the English (2006, 61–62). This perspective regarding a patronizing English attitude experienced by Scots from the "South" also emerged quickly in conversations with the author while in Edinburgh.[2] This rhetorical commonplace is expertly navigated by Scottish First Minister Alex Salmond in his dealings with the Westminster government, in deploying language that refers to resentment about London telling Scotland what it should do. The author's interactions with a few London-based academics on the Scotland issue have revealed that Scottish perceptions of a patronizing attitude are actually evident in much of the London-based discourse.[3] It could perhaps be the case that among the "English" or the London-based policy community, a rhetorical commonplace of Scotland needing a hand in governance has been established. But such an idea does not ring well with Scots.

The arena in which these focal points for identity are presented is that of the media. Interactions between the Scottish First Minister Alex Salmond and the Westminster government made headlines throughout 2010–12, with most media discussions adding to a boundary between Scottish and English/British identity. The media portrayal of most of the exchanges as acrimonious has conveyed to the public that a "side" is to be chosen in these discussions, and that opinions must be formed. But individuals are constrained in formulating these choices and opinions, illustrating that persuasion has its limits (Tilly 2008). A person in Scotland with a Scottish accent cannot suddenly become English any more than someone born in London or Bristol to English parents could suddenly become a strong Scottish nationalist. In putting forth boundary-solidifying positions, elites on both sides of the discussion have some limits to the breadth of potential audiences that they might mobilize. Therefore, a strategy of emphasizing difference in their discussions, or the depth and salience of these identities, is more evident.

Scottish leader Alex Salmond's attempts to present Scotland as a unique identity deserving of independence is countered by a Westminster rhetoric of Britain as a heroic, historical, unitary territory. Each side is attempting to create a hegemony with their own particular narrative—and such discursive hegemonic projects constitute the nature of politics (Finlayson 2012, 752–54; Bacon 2012). As noted by Finlayson, the role of argument in politics is often overlooked by theorists eager to attribute rationality and material incentives to what political actors do. But politicians themselves are quite aware of the crucial role of argument and persuasion in moving toward their political goals (Finlayson 2012, 752, 758).

These theoretical foundations illustrate how rhetoric and discourse can be traced to illustrate the rise and decline of the Scottish boundary-creation project. The post-2010 rhetoric between the Scottish government and Westminster provides a useful demonstration of these dynamics at work. The evidence in the section that follows reveals that identity salience increases when Westminster and Edinburgh are in opposition, and weakens somewhat when Westminster gives in to or supports Scottish claims.

Post-2010 Examples of Oppositional Discourse: Scotland and the Conservatives

The post-2010 discussions between Scotland and the British government have been organized around a few primary themes. Each of these themes has become a set of talking points for both the Scottish and the British positions—allowing each side to deploy and reference its own rhetorical commonplaces. To illustrate these dynamics in action, this section sketches how rhetoric and discourse constitute the debate. The themes that follow sketch some of the key motifs of the different narrative accounts (Bacon 2012) that constitute the boundary between Scottish-ness and British-ness or English-ness. Interactions that are fraught with disagreement tend to solidify Scottish-ness in relation to British-ness, clarifying the boundary between these identity categories for those absorbing the media discourse. The identity boundary is more blurred in interactions that demonstrate agreement between the two sides. The discussion that follows will explore the following themes: the independence referendum, economic prospects for Scotland, Scottish distinctiveness from Britain, and Scotland and the European Union (EU).

The Independence Referendum

The SNP has pursued independence for Scotland as a longstanding goal. After two sessions of a Labour Party majority in the Scottish Parliament (following the 1999 and 2003 Scottish elections), the SNP gained a one-seat victory over Labour in the Scottish Parliament elections in 2007. After a rather successful period of governance between 2007 and 2011 with just this slim majority, the party won a decisive victory of 69 of the 129 parliamentary seats in the May 2011 elections. The SNP then perceived a mandate to openly pursue its independence agenda, and talk of a referendum on independence soon followed (SNP Interview 2011).

A debate between the Scottish and UK governments over the conduct of the referendum became especially visible in the media by early 2012. UK Prime Minister David Cameron put forth statements that if Scotland was indeed serious about holding a referendum on independence, it should do so quickly within the next 18 months (by mid-2013). The Scottish government's response included an accusation that Westminster was "trying to dictate the future for the Scottish people" (Curtis 2012), a reference to the rhetorical commonplace for Scots about British pretentions of superiority toward them. Scottish First Minister Salmond expertly used this moment, making a statement in the Scottish Parliament that: "The terms of the referendum are for the Scottish Parliament and the people of Scotland to decide," proposing that Scotland and England should be viewed as "equal partners" (Burns and Cowell 2012). Poll results at that time (and into 2013) showed that a referendum would not pass, perhaps one of the main reasons behind Prime Minister Cameron's push for a quicker process. For the Scottish side, a slow upward trend in support for independence in opinion polls was one likely reason for wishing to delay the referendum (Curtis 2012). There was also a clear symbolic aspect. Early in these discussions, Salmond proposed that the referendum should be held in late 2014 to coincide with the 700-year anniversary of a battle for Scottish independence—the Battle of Bannockburn (Watt 2012).[4]

Settling the question for the referendum was a complex affair. Initially, Salmond proposed that there might be two potential questions—one on full Scottish independence, and one on increased powers for Scotland within the framework of Britain. This second question on maximum devolution, or "devo-max," was understood by most analysts to be a kind of insurance policy for the SNP if they could not attain a majority "yes" vote on a question for full independence. British Prime Minister Cameron diligently pushed the position that only one question on full independence should be allowed. Indeed, on this aspect, Cameron found the SNP's weak flank, as the two-question position revealed the SNP's worries about not being able to achieve enough support for actual independence. In the end, the "devo-max" question did not survive the referendum negotiations. By the autumn of 2012, one question was decided upon, referring simply to independence: "Do you agree that Scotland should be an independent country?" (Carrell 2012a, 2012d;

Ascherson 2012; Mitchell 2012; Watt and Carrell 2012). The date set for the referendum is September 18, 2014, reflecting the wishes of the SNP with regard to its timing.

Scotland's Economic and Social Prospects

The Westminster government has been keen to argue that an independent Scotland would no longer benefit from subsidies that it receives from the distribution of tax revenues. This rhetorical commonplace references the UK's prosperous Southeast region, including London's financial center, as providing the support for Scottish social programs—support that would be lost in the event of independence (Carrell 2012c). The SNP response frequently invokes revenues from North Sea Oil, arguing that if Scotland were able to use all of these oil revenues, it could sustain a social democracy in the style of Norway (SNP Interview 2011; Burns and Cowell 2012; Salmond 2012; McFadyen 2012). Comparisons of Scotland to other small, independent countries are frequent in this line of discussion (Finlay 2009, 28).

Before the EU's economic crisis, the notion that Scotland might use the Euro as its currency was a more attractive idea than it began to be around 2011 and 2012. Discussions over the independence referendum, thus, also began to invoke the currency question—if Scotland were to leave the British union, what currency would it use? The Scottish rhetoric on the currency issue began to reflect the notion that Scottish independence would not require a change of currency, and that the pound could still be used (Salmond 2012). The Westminster government quickly attacked this position, stating that independence would indeed require a separate currency, and that the British government would not allow the pound to be used by a newly-independent Scotland (Wright 2012). Such discussions were especially notable in light of the existence of Scottish pound banknotes, as outlined in the section on Scottish distinctiveness below.

One of the most distinct social differences between Scotland and the rest of the UK is the fact that Scottish students do not pay tuition fees to attend Scottish universities. However, English students attending universities in Scotland must pay such fees. Scotland's relationship with the EU has translated into a policy that EU students receive the same educational benefits as Scottish students. As a result, English or other UK students must pay increasingly high university tuition fees for universities in Scotland, while Scottish and EU students do not pay such fees.[5] Resentment over this issue by English students has produced an ongoing dispute and court case—and has raised questions regarding the cost of sustaining this policy. In spite of the justice and financial aspects involved, the prevalence of this issue in Scottish rhetoric illustrates it as linked to an oppositional identity with Westminster. One of the most visible moves of the post-2010 Conservative–Liberal Democrat government was to triple the amount of tuition fees that undergraduates must pay per year. Scottish resistance to implementing this policy is made possible by the Scottish Parliament's powers over education—and the will to resist fees for Scottish students is related to an identity stance that resists the free-market emphasis of the post-2010 UK government (Benn 2012).

Scottish Distinctiveness from Britain

One of the first things a visitor to Scotland will notice is the use of Scottish pound banknotes. Such banknotes are for all practical purposes are the same as those used in London, but they include Scottish iconography that is intended to reflect a distinct Scottish identity (Penrose and Cumming 2011). Separate pound banknotes are not exclusive to Scotland—Northern Ireland also has its own pound notes with local iconography. While both sets of banknotes are officially legal tender in the rest of the UK, in practice, an attempt to spend them in London may result in the payer being asked to produce "less dodgy" notes, or those without these local iconographies.

Other symbols of a distinct Scottish identity have become prevalent in everyday life throughout the UK in an increasing fashion since 1997. The British Broadcasting Company (BBC) includes in its programming a broadcast of proceedings from the Scottish Parliament. Any UK resident who is skipping through the television listings is, thus, passively reminded of Scotland's distinct political identity. The Scottish government also wholeheartedly embraced the release of the Disney film *Brave* in 2012. The film, which depicts a Scottish-accented heroine in the context of medieval Scotland, was described as a "showcase for Scotland" that would add to Scottish tourism (Scottish Government on *Brave* 2012). In addition to these examples of a symbolic media presence, interviews, speeches, and conversations reveal persistent references to

Scotland's similarity with the Nordic countries—in terms of national character, culture, and support for left-leaning economic and social policies (SNP Interview 2011; Salmond 2012).

Cultural resources, however, are not the exclusive property of Scotland. The successful Olympic Games in London during the summer of 2012 have also been deployed in the struggle for Scottish identity. Arguing against Scottish independence, former (Labour) Prime Minister Gordon Brown invoked the Olympics as an example of what the countries could achieve together with a pooling of resources and effort (Higgins and Carrell 2012). The seemingly inane nature of these discussions in the media demonstrates how the independence debate is grounded in everyday discourse, with attempts made regularly by both sides to push their rhetorical arguments.

Scotland and the EU

One of Scotland's longstanding rhetorical commonplaces has been its close relationship to EU institutions. Given the persistent voices of anti-EU forces within other parts of the UK, Scotland's identity along these lines was reasonably easy to establish as a rhetorical commonplace. Its role as an EU-friendly country was supported in practice by the Scottish government's maintenance of its agreement to treat EU students in a manner similar to Scottish students in terms of free tuition at Scottish universities. In addition, Scotland maintained a favorable position toward the Euro as a potential currency long after the crisis began to turn this support into a potential liability.

In light of its support for the EU as a rhetorical device, Scotland had envisioned that with potential independence it would be granted automatic membership within the EU. It, thus, came as a strong blow to its position that the president of the European Commission (EC) called this potential membership into question in September 2012. Declaring that new states would not be granted automatic membership but would have to apply, EC President Barroso (from Portugal) appeared to discredit the SNP position that there would be few risks resulting from independence. This statement was later backed by a Spanish official and by other officials in Brussels, codifying this blow to Scottish aspirations (Carrell 2012b; Tremlett and Carrell 2012; Maddox 2012). The fact that Spain is dealing with its own simultaneous separatist movement in Catalonia might be one reason behind its adamant stance on this matter. In taking a hard line toward Scottish aspirations, the Spanish government can send a rhetorical message to quell the aspirations of the Catalan movement within its own borders.

Conclusions: Rhetorical Commonplaces and Competition via Discourse

The four areas sketched above illustrate how competing rhetorical commonplaces constitute the battle for hearts and minds on the issue of Scottish independence. The 2014 referendum may push the boundaries of these dynamics, because as of this writing, polls of Scottish voters do not show majority support for a yes vote on independence. At the same time, the increasing power of the SNP in terms of vote share and its successful deployment of rhetorical arguments is an indicator that the issue of Scottish independence will not easily disappear—even in light of a negative referendum result. The example of Quebec illustrates the longevity of separatist goals, even after two failed independence referenda.

Scotland, Quebec, and Catalonia all received ample media attention for their separatist movements in 2012. Each of these movements has an institutional foundation. But because institutions are relatively stable, the source of "change" over the past few years must be identified elsewhere. In the Scottish example, the SNP was able to increase its support especially after the advent of a Conservative–Liberal Democrat government in Westminster in 2010. Since that time, interactions between Scotland and Westminster have taken on an acrimonious character that has solidified Scottish identity in opposition to that of the UK central government. Are similar dynamics at play in Quebec or in Catalonia, with these regional identities being entrenched in opposition to their central governments? Might such oppositions easily emerge during economic downturns, when it might be easier to convince publics to believe in local solutions? Or might the answer lie in a more general discursive shift that favors decentralized government or federal structures? An examination of the discursive identities that comprise these discussions provides a promising avenue for future research.

Notes and Bibliography

Notes

1. However, it is of note that not only SNP supporters would vote in an independence referendum, and general polls as of this writing in late 2013 do not show support for a yes vote for independence.
2. The author's American accent perhaps marks this as "safe" conversational territory.
3. Statements have included language such as: "They [Scots] really have no idea what they are asking" or "They really need to realize that...."
4. He was generally successful in this effort, with the referendum scheduled for September 18, 2014.
5. While attractive from a social perspective, staff at Scottish universities has noted that this policy has produced ever-reduced funding for universities there.

Bibliography

Abbott, A. (ed.). 2001. "Things of Boundaries." In *Time Matters*, 37–63. Chicago: University of Chicago Press.

Ascherson, N. 2012. "Will Scotland Go Its Own Way?" *The New York Times*, February 26. http://www.nytimes.com/2012/02/27/opinion/independence-for-scotland.html?pagewanted=1&_r=0&emc=eta1

Bacon, E. 2012. "Public Political Narratives: Developing a Neglected Source Through the Exploratory Case of Russia in the Putin–Medvedev Era." *Political Studies* 60 (4): 768–86.

Beissinger, Mark. 2002. *Nationalist Mobilization and the Collapse of the Soviet State*. New York: Cambridge University Press.

Benn, M. 2012. "Why Scotland's Approach to Publicly Funded Education Works." *The Guardian*, August 27. http://www.guardian.co.uk/education/2012/aug/27/scotland-supports-publicly-funded-education

Brown, A. 2000. "Scottish Politics After the Election: Towards a Scottish Political System?" In *Scotland: The Challenge of Devolution*, edited by A. Wright, 32–48. Aldershot: Ashgate.

Bunce, V. 1999. *Subversive Institutions: The Design and the Destruction of Socialism and the State*. New York: Cambridge University Press.

Burns, J. and C. Cowell. 2012. "Scots Begin Bid for Vote on Independence." *The New York Times*, January 25. http://www.nytimes.com/2012/01/26/world/europe/scots-launch-bid-for-vote-on-independence.html?emc=eta1

Carrell, S. 2012a. "Alex Salmond Targets May 2016 for Independent Scottish Parliament." *The Guardian*, January 26. http://www.guardian.co.uk/politics/2012/jan/25/alex-salmond-may-2016-independent

Carrell, S. 2012b. "Barroso Casts Doubt on Independent Scotland's EU Membership Rights." *The Guardian*, September 12. http://www.guardian.co.uk/politics/2012/sep/12/barroso-doubt-scotland-eu-membership

———. 2012c. "IDS Accused of Scaremongering over Scottish Independence Remarks." *The Guardian*, September 19. http://www.guardian.co.uk/politics/2012/sep/19/iain-duncan-smith-scottish-independence-welfare

———. 2012d. "Election Watchdog Begins 12-Week Review of Scottish Referendum Question." *The Guardian*, November 9. http://www.guardian.co.uk/politics/2012/nov/09/watchdog-review-scottish-referendum-question

Condor, S. and J. Abell. 2006. "Vernacular Constructions of 'National Identity' in Post-Devolution Scotland and England." In *Devolution and Identity*, edited by J. Wilson and K. Stapleton, 51–75. Aldershot: Ashgate.

Cornell, S. 2002. "Autonomy as a Source of Conflict: Caucasian Conflicts in Theoretical Perspective." *World Politics* 54 (2): 245–76.

Curtice, J. 2009. "Devolution, the SNP and the Electorate." In *The Modern SNP: From Protest to Power*, edited by G. Hassan, 55–67. Edinburgh: Edinburgh University Press.

Curtis, P. 2012. "Does David Cameron Have the Power to Dictate When Scotland Votes on Independence?" *The Guardian*, January 9. http://www.guardian.co.uk/politics/reality-check-with-polly-curtis/2012/jan/09/scottish-independence-legality

Fairclough, N. 1995. *Critical Discourse Analysis: The Critical Study of Language*, 2010 edn. Harlow, UK: Pearson Longman.

Finlay, R. 2009. "The Early Years: From the Inter-War Period to the Mid-1960s." In *The Modern SNP: From Protest to Power*, edited by G. Hassan, 19–30. Edinburgh: Edinburgh University Press.

Finlayson, A. 2007. "From Beliefs to Arguments: Interpretive Methodology and Rhetorical Political Analysis." *British Journal of Politics and International Relations* 9 (4): 545–63.

———. 2012. "Rhetoric and the Political Theory of Ideologies." *Political Studies* 60 (4): 751–67.

Goffman, E. 1974. *Frame Analysis: An Essay on the Organization of Experience*, 1986 edn. Boston: Northeastern University Press.

Gorenburg, D. 2003. *Minority Ethnic Mobilization in the Russian Federation*. New York: Cambridge University Press.

Hassan, G. (ed.). 2009. *The Modern SNP: From Protest to Power*. Edinburgh: Edinburgh University Press.

Heintze, H. J. 1998. "On the Legal Understanding of Autonomy." In *Autonomy: Applications and Implications*, edited by M. Suksi. Cambridge: Kluwer Law International.

Higgins, C. and S. Carrell. 2012. "Gordon Brown Cites Olympic Success as Reason to Oppose Scottish Independence." *The Guardian*, August 13. http://www.guardian.co.uk/politics/2012/aug/13/gordon-brown-olympic-success-scottish-independence

Jackson, P. T. 2006. *Civilizing the Enemy: German Reconstruction and the Invention of the West*. Ann Arbor: University of Michigan Press.

Jackson, P. T. and D. Nexon. 1999. "Relations Before States: Substance, Process, and the Study of World Politics." *European Journal of International Relations* 5 (3): 294–314.

Jenne, E. 2006. *Ethnic Bargaining: The Paradox of Minority Empowerment*. Ithaca: Cornell University Press.

Johnstone, B. 2008. *Discourse Analysis*. Oxford: Blackwell.

Laclau, E. and C. Mouffe. 1985. *Hegemony and Socialist Strategy: Towards a Radical Democratic Politics*. London: Verso.

Mackay, C. 2009. "The SNP and the Scottish Parliament: The Start of a New Sang?" In *The Modern SNP: From Protest to Power*, edited by G. Hassan, 79–92. Edinburgh: Edinburgh University Press.

Maddox, D. 2012. "Scottish Independence: Separate Scotland Must Apply to Join EU, Warns Brussels." *The Scotsman*, December 6. http://www.scotsman. com/the-scotsman/scotland/scottish-independence-separate-scotland-must-apply-to-join-eu-warns-brussels-1-2677200

McFadden, J. and M. Lazarowicz. 2000. *The Scottish Parliament: An Introduction*. Edinburgh: T. & T. Clark.

McFadyen, A. 2012. "Scottish Independence: Who'll Pay the Price?" *Aljazeera*, April 17. http://www.aljazeera.com/indepth/features/2012/04/2012415131621369702.html#.T5qy8SAjtpI.facebook

Millar, S. 2006. "Marketing Identities in Devolved Regions: The Role of Global Corporate Culture in Scotland and Wallonia." In *Devolution and Identity*, edited by J. Wilson and K. Stapleton, 157–71. Aldershot: Ashgate.

Mitchell, J. 2009. "From Breakthrough to Mainstream: The Politics of Potential and Blackmail." In *The Modern SNP: From Protest to Power*, edited by G. Hassan, 31–41. Edinburgh: Edinburgh University Press.

———. 2012. "The Scottish Independence Referendum Will Not Offer What Most Scots Want." *The Guardian*, October 15. http://www.guardian.co.uk/politics/2012/oct/15/scottish-independence-referendum-offer-scots

Mitchell, J., R. Johns, and L. Bennie. 2009. "Who are the SNP Members?" In *The Modern SNP: From Protest to Power*, edited by G. Hassan, 68–78. Edinburgh: Edinburgh University Press.

Mole, R. (ed.). 2007. *Discursive Constructions of Identity in European Politics*. Basingstoke: Palgrave.

Motyl, A. 1999. "Inventing Invention: The Limits of National Identity Formation." In *Intellectuals and the Articulation of the Nation*, edited by R. Suny and M. Kennedy, 57–75. Ann Arbor: University of Michigan Press.

Mozaffar, S. and J. Scarritt. 1999. "Why Territorial Autonomy is Not a Viable Option for Managing Ethnic Conflict in African Plural Societies." *Nationalism and Ethnic Politics* 5 (3–4): 230–53.

Penrose, J. and C. Cumming. 2011. "Money Talks: Banknote Iconography and Symbolic Constructions of Scotland." *Nations and Nationalism* 17 (4): 821–42.

Powel, B. 2012. "(Re)Locating the International: Discourse Theory and the Dismantling of the UK." Paper presented at the Central and East European Studies Association Conference, Krakow, Poland, September 21.

Roeder, P. 2007. *Where Nation-States Come From: Institutional Change in the Age of Nationalism.* Princeton: Princeton University Press.

Rothchild, D. and C. Hartzell. 1999. "Security in Deeply Divided Societies: The Role of Territorial Autonomy." *Nationalism and Ethnic Politics* 5 (3–4): 254–71.

Salmond, A. 2012. "Independence and Responsibility: The Future of Scotland." Lecture at the London School of Economics and Political Science, February 15. http://www2.lse.ac.uk/assets/richmedia/channels/publicLecturesAndEvents/transcripts/20120215_1830_independenceAndResponsibility_tr.pdf

Scottish Government. 2012. "*Brave* World Premiere." 29 June. http://www.scotland.gov.uk/News/Releases/2012/06/bravepremiere19062012.

Scottish National Party. 2011. Interview by author with party official, SNP Party office, Edinburgh, August. Source anonymized; further information and precise date available from author.

Tilly, C. 2005. *Identities, Boundaries, and Social Ties.* Boulder: Paradigm.

———. 2008. *Contentious Performances.* New York: Cambridge University Press.

Tremlett, G. and S. Carrell. 2012. "'Join the Queue' for EU Membership, Spain Tells Alex Salmond." *The Guardian*, October 24. http://www.guardian.co.uk/politics/2012/oct/24/scotland-eu-membership-spain

Watt, N. 2012. "Scottish Referendum: PM's Tough Stance Startles Lib Dems and Labour." *The Guardian*, January 9. http://www.guardian.co.uk/politics/2012/jan/09/scottish-referendum-labour-lib-dems

Watt, N. and S. Carrell. 2012. "Scottish Referendum Countdown Begins with Cameron Visit to Salmond." *The Guardian*, October 15. http://www.guardian.co.uk/politics/2012/oct/15/scottish-referendum-countdown-begins-cameron-salmond

Wilson, J. and K. Stapleton (eds). 2006. "Introduction." In *Devolution and Identity*, 1–10. Aldershot: Ashgate.

Winetrobe, B. and R. Hazell. 2005. "What Has the Scottish Parliament Achieved, and What Can It Teach Westminster?" In *Anglo–Scottish Relations from 1900 to Devolution and Beyond*, edited by W. L. Miller, 63–77. Oxford: Oxford University Press, for the British Academy.

Wright, A. (ed.). 2000. "Introduction." In *Scotland: The Challenge of Devolution*, 3–13. Aldershot: Ashgate.

Wright, O. 2012. "Osborne: Independent Scots Could Lose Pound." *The Independent*, September 7.

7

The European Minority Rights Regime and the Turkish/Muslim Minority of Western Thrace

Apostolos Agnantopoulos

Introduction

Western Thrace is a region in the northeast of Greece, bordering Bulgaria and Turkey. The region hosts a Muslim community, which was exempted, in tandem with the Christian-Orthodox populations who resided in Istanbul and the islands of Imvros and Tenedos, from the compulsory population exchange agreed between Greece and Turkey in 1923, under the so-called Lausanne Treaty. Comprising around 120,000 individuals of Turkish origin, Slav-speaking Pomaks, and Roma/Gypsies, but who largely identify themselves as "ethnic Turks," this community has experienced a paradoxical condition: On the one hand, the Lausanne framework guaranteed political and legal equality with the rest of the population and conferred upon this community a special status which acknowledged the right to establish and manage autonomous charitable, religious, and social institutions (known as *Waqfs*), maintain a separate bilingual system of primary education, freely practice its religion, and preserve its customs in personal and family matters.[1] On the other hand, its members were often treated by Greek authorities as "second-class" citizens and endured wide-ranged discrimination, political repression, and economic marginalization. The advent of a densely institutionalized minority rights regime in Europe, following the end of the Cold War, has challenged this constellation, not only because the underlying ideology of multiculturalism, which emphasized tolerance, acceptance, respect, and recognition, was incompatible with the enactment of discriminatory policies, but also because it internationalized an issue which was hitherto dealt with exclusively as part of the enduring Greek–Turkish rivalry. In response, Greek minority policy went through a process of gradual liberalization, which included, inter alia, the abolition of the most overt discriminatory measures, a favorable revision of the Citizenship Code, and the initiation of targeted development strategies and affirmative action. Despite a substantial improvement in the minority's living condition, however, certain practices that create grievances and strain in its relation with the Christian-Orthodox majority have been remarkably resilient to change.

The chapter explores the sources of the enduring tension in majority–minority relations in Western Thrace. It argues that this can be attributed to two factors. The first relates with the failure to address the root cause of anti-minority policies: the dominance of an ethnocentric nationalism, which negates linguistic, religious, or ethnic difference and constructs minorities as alien and potentially threatening entities. The interplay of this exclusionary nation-state identity with a widespread representation of Turkey as inherently aggressive has prevented the full internalization of European norms on minority protection. Instead, the Greek state has tried to accommodate the pressure by adopting minimal reforms when necessary and resisting change in areas that were perceived to serve core national security interest. The second factor relates with the very content of European norms. More precisely, I argue that the application of multicultural principles can be problematic, in particular when minority issues are intertwined with competing nationalist claims and acute security concerns.

The chapter is structured as follows. The first section provides an overview of the discriminatory measures applied until the late 1980s and of the grievances that these created for the minority. The second section discusses the formation of the Greek nation-state identity and elucidates how this has informed notions of Greek-ness, citizenship, and minority rights. The third section presents the European human rights regime, as it pertains to minorities, and how this diverged from the Greek legal framework and policy practice. The fourth section outlines the reforms introduced in response to this European challenge and the areas that have been resilient to change. The fifth section examines the process of reform and shows that this was driven by instrumental calculations. The sixth section focuses on the area of education, where the Greek policy presents the most marked affinity with multicultural ideology, in order to showcase its limits.

The Period of Overt Discrimination

As mentioned above, despite the protective bilateral treaty framework between Greece and Turkey, the Turkish/Muslim minority of Western Thrace was subjected to systematic repression and discrimination. Anti-minority policies were systematically introduced in the mid-1950s as a result of the deterioration of Greek–Turkish relations over Cyprus, climaxed with the imposition of the military regime in 1967, and have persisted despite the return of democratic rule in 1974.

Arguably, the most common discriminatory practice used against the minority was the informal enactment of "administrative restrictive measures" that hindered a host of everyday activities such as the selling and acquisition of property, the setting up of business, the reception of bank loans, the acquisition of tractor licenses, and the building or reparation of schools and mosques. In addition, the Greek authorities undertook large-scale expropriations of Muslim-owned land and imposed strict controls on the movement of persons to and from the mountainous border area, which had been declared "restricted military zone." Most controversially, the extensive and arbitrary use of Article 19 of the Greek Citizenship Code, which opened the possibility to revoke Greek citizenship from "a person of non-Greek ethnic origin, who left Greece with no intention to return," had resulted in the loss of citizenship for between 45,000 and 50,000 minority Turks/Muslims, some of whom had only been away for a short period, to study or seek temporary work, and who were subsequently confined to live in a precarious status of statelessness (Sitaropoulos 2004).

Minority Turks/Muslims also complained that the Greek state attempted to restrict the administrative and financial autonomy of their *Waqfs* by substituting their elected commissions with state-appointed officials and imposing strict controls over their budgets. Another significant problem related to the repudiation of a 1920 law that provided for the direct elections of the muftis—the minority's religious leaders who are also responsible to adjudicate on certain civil and family matters according to Sharia law. The situation deteriorated in the mid-1980s, when the Greek government overrode the tacit consensus to appoint persons who had been approved by minority representatives. This prompted the minority to elect alternative muftis, who were subsequently prosecuted and imprisoned for "usurping of authority" (see Human Rights Watch 1999, 19–20).

Minority rights were also curtailed in the field of education, despite the fact that the Lausanne Treaty requirement for a bilingual primary education was nominally met. A first problem concerned the banning of imported textbooks from Turkey, which forced minority students to use outdated material, usually in photocopied form. A second problem related to the gradual replacement of minority teachers trained in Turkey with graduates of the Special Pedagogical Academy of Thessaloniki, recruited mainly from the Pomak community, who were considered by ethnic Turks to be "poorly equipped" and "disconnected" from the local society (ibid., 26). A third problem concerned the limited availability of secondary education—two minority high schools and two religious schools (*medreses*) with a capacity of 400 and 200, respectively—which resulted in high drop-out rates (ibid.). A fourth problem concerned the role of teachers from the majority (responsible for the Greek part of the curriculum) who were not adequately prepared to address the peculiarities of teaching in a minority environment and were mistrusted by the minority community.

At the political level, the members of the minority were practically excluded from Greek political life and suffered from severe restrictions in the freedom of expression, which were manifested through obstacles in setting up new media and the prosecutions of journalists and political activists (Aarbakke 2000). Of particular significance in that respect has been the insistence of successive Greek governments that the minority is merely "religious" as specified in the Lausanne Treaty and the concomitant rejection of the demand of a large segment of the minority to be recognized as "ethnic Turks." This denial of self-identification was also enacted by the Greek courts through the banning of minority associations that were using the name Turk/Turkish as well as the prosecution of minority representatives, who were referring to the minority as Turkish, for engaging in "propaganda dissemination" or "disturbance of public order" (Aarbakke 2000).

Political repression and administrative discrimination went hand-in-hand with economic deprivation and marginalization. Although the whole of western Thrace was economically disadvantaged vis-à-vis the rest of Greece, minority Turks/Muslims were on average significantly worse off than the Christians, and the Muslim neighborhoods and villages poorer and with worse infrastructure than Christian ones (Asimakopoulou and Christidou-Lionaraki 2002, 242). While this gap may be explained by structural factors, such as the concentration of the vast majority of Muslims in the low-paid/productivity agricultural sector, the Greek state contributed in exacerbating it by targeting national development policies in areas that benefited primarily the Christian majority, and tacitly excluding minority members from jobs in the public sector (Anagnostou 2001, 105–06).

The Drivers of Discrimination

The restrictive way in which minority rights were conceptualized and practiced in the Greek polity was underpinned by an ethnocentric organic representation of the nation. More precisely, although early Greek nationalism was nurtured by the spirit of Enlightenment, the French Revolution, and the liberal ideas that they espoused, the Greek nation-state identity has eventually been built on ethno-cultural foundations. As a result, Greek-ness is not associated with shared political institutions and territory, but instead, it is defined primarily by reference to religious convictions (Orthodox Christianity), with language, descent, and consciousness playing an auxiliary role (Roudometof 1998; Koliopoulos and Veremis 2002).

This construction of the Greek nation as a timeless and immutable entity, which is irreducible to its individual components, has generated suspicion, if not outright hostility, toward those who are perceived to challenge the idealized homogeneous "national corps." This aversion toward diversity became particularly pronounced after the defeat of the Greek army in Asia Minor in 1922, which put an end to the century-old irredentist aspiration (the so-called "Great Idea") of liberating the unredeemed Christian-Orthodox brethren who lived under the Ottoman rule, and re-establishing the Greek dominion to its ancient glory. Thus, while during the period of expansionist fever the ethnic, linguistic, and cultural pluralism among the Christian-Orthodox populations was tolerated, with the logic that the supremacy of the Greek civilization would eventually lead to their amalgamation into the Greek nation, in the post-irredentist period, the emphasis shifted to the rapid homogenization of the population through forceful assimilation, expulsion, and marginalization (Tsitselikis and Christopoulos 2008, 35–39). This more introvert and restrictive construction of Greek-ness was substantiated in the legal category of *allogenis* (Greek citizen of alien descent), which effectively relegated those who were deemed unable of integrating into the Greek phenotype to a status of "second-class" citizens with circumscribed rights (Christopoulos and Tsitselikis 2003).

To be sure, the Thracian minority, by virtue of the protection offered to it by the Lausanne framework, has been spared from the devastating fate of the Albanian-speaking Muslims of Epirus (*Tsams*) and the Slav-speaking inhabitants of Macedonia who were violently expelled in the aftermath of WW II. However, minority Turks/Muslims were not seen as an integral part of the Greek nation, because they did not speak Greek as the first language and worshiped a different religion than the Christian-Orthodox majority. Most importantly, the fact that several of those identified themselves as ethnic Turks was interpreted as evidence that they lacked Greek national consciousness. It is characteristic in that respect that when the first independent minority MPs were elected in the late 1980s, they were immediately marginalized by their colleagues and were on repeated occasions reprimanded for unpatriotic and undignified behavior that was not akin to a member of the Greek Parliament (see, for example, Greek Parliament 1990, 77–79; 1991, 5875–77).

The mutual exclusiveness of Greek-ness and Turkish-ness was also buttressed by the juxtaposition of negative representations of Turkey as backward, inferior, and uncivilized to the dominant representation of Greece as the cradle of civilization (see Heraclides 2001). Cast in this way, the minority Turks/Muslims were not just "random foreigners." Instead, they represented an essential element in the constitution of the Greek nation-state identity; a negative and threatening "internal other" against which Greek-ness was constituted, and which helped consolidate Greek nationalism in the post-irredentist era (Triandafyllidou and Paraskevopoulou 2002, 85; Borou 2009).

In addition to the symbolic challenge that the religious, linguistic, and ethnic diversity of minority Turks/Muslims presented to the essence of the Greek nation, the articulation of the minority as an alien entity rendered meaningful the argument that it was being manipulated by Greece's external enemies, most notably Turkey.[2] A key concern expressed by Greek politicians and public opinion was that the high fertility rates among minority Turks/Muslims coupled with the decline of the Christian population may alter the demographic composition of Western Thrace to an extent that would tempt the minority to openly seek autonomy or even independence. The so-called "demographic problem" was intertwined with fears about Turkey's ever-increasing interventionism into minority affairs, in particular through the Turkish Consulate of Komotini, with the ulterior aim of fueling an internal upheaval that would provide the pretext for military intervention following the Cyprus model.[3] In this context, Turkey was accused of endeavoring to cultivate a Turkish national consciousness in minority students (Asimakopoulou and Christidou-Lionaraki 2002, 338), supporting ultranationalist politicians who "spread the seeds of discord" and "torpedo national coexistence" (Greek Parliament 1991, 5875), and sponsoring massive acquisitions of Greek-owned land and business (Greek Parliament 1993, 3251).

A related discursive pattern was the contrast of Turkey's pro-minority stance in Thrace with its problematic human rights record at home. This was perceived in Greece as both hypocritical and invested with revisionist aspirations (Tsouderou 1990, 281). In this context, the so-called "reciprocity" principle of the Lausanne Treaty[4] was evoked in order to frame the discriminatory and repressive measures against the minority as a legitimate response to the prior systematic violation of the

Lausanne framework by Turkey, which had led to the depletion of the Greek communities in Istanbul, Imvros, and Tenedos. In other words, the perceived failure of Turkey to fulfill its obligations under the Lausanne Treaty has been interpreted through a legalistic prism as entailing an exoneration of the other contracting party from meeting its commitments and, therefore, depriving the Turkish/Muslim minority from the protection that was conferred upon it (Grigoriadis 2005). In fact, it was not uncommon for Greek officials to turn accusations of minority rights violations on their head by depicting the poor condition of the minority as part of a deliberate Turkish attempt to destabilize the region. As a local MP eloquently put it, when he was interrogated on the poor status of minority education: "Who has left uneducated the "innocent" and "pure" Muslims? It is of course the [Turkish] consulate and the plant exploiters, who sponsor Turkish irredentism by closing down the schools" (Greek Parliament 1990, 94, emphasis added).

This is not the place to assess whether these allegations were true. What is important is that the presupposition of a well-orchestrated Turkish plan aiming at the revision of the territorial "status quo" and the concomitant relegation of the minority to the position of a "Trojan horse" and "fifth column" had created a discursive space where it made sense to reject calls for a radical revision of antiminority policies on a national security platform.

The European Challenge to the Greek Minority Policy

It is well documented that, in contrast with the interwar efforts of the League of Nations to establish a special regime for the protection of ethnic, religious, and linguistic minorities, minority rights did not feature high in the agenda of the United Nations. As a result, minority protection was confined to the articulation of general human rights standards that connected with essential concerns of individuals belonging to minority groups. These included the principle of nondiscrimination, the freedom of expression and association, religious freedom, the right to education, and the right to vote and political participation (Nasic 2007). However, since the end of the Cold War, the protection of minorities has re-emerged as an issue in its own right. Under the influence of the ideology of multiculturalism, international organizations and governments have codified a set of minority-specific rights pertaining to four concerns: the survival and existence of minorities, including their protection from genocide and crimes against humanity; the promotion and protection of their national, ethnic, cultural, religious, and linguistic identity and prevention of forced assimilation; the prevention of direct and indirect discrimination; and the effective and meaningful participation of persons belonging to minorities in public affairs and in all aspects of political, economic, social, and cultural life.[5] In addition to extending and clarifying existing norms, particularly in terms of education, language, contact, association, and participatory rights, this minority-specific dimension of the international human rights regime has introduced an explicit requirement for states to undertake positive measures in order to achieve substantive (as opposed to formal) equality (Henrard 2000).

The European minority rights regime builds on this normative basis, but has buttressed it with a thick institutional structure, which is based on three pillars: the Council of Europe (CoE), the European Union (EU), and the Organization for Security and Cooperation in Europe (OSCE). The CoE has initiated and provided a forum for the negotiation for the Framework Convention for the Protection of National Minorities—the most comprehensive multilateral treaty devoted to minority rights—and the European Charter for Regional and Minority Languages. The CoE also hosts the European Court of Human Rights (ECtHR), which constitutes the most authoritative international enforcement mechanism on human rights, by virtue of its compulsory jurisdiction and the opportunity provided to individuals to lodge applications against their respective governments for violating the European Convention for the Protection of Human Rights and Fundamental Freedoms. Finally, the European Commission Against Racism and Intolerance (ECRI) and the Commissioner for Human Rights have the potential to exercise normative pressure by reporting on the situation of minorities within the CoE member states and disseminating best practices.

With regards to the EU, minority protection constitutes one the political criteria that prospective member states have to meet before beginning accession negotiations, and has also been inscribed in its primary law as one of the founding principles of the Union.[6] Despite the absence of a legally binding mechanism to monitor and enforce minority protection in EU member states, the fact that human and minority rights constitute such an important aspect of the EU's international identity entails a de facto binding quality. EU institutions also support a number of specialized organizations such as the European Bureau for Lesser Used Languages, the European Union Agency for Fundamental Rights, and the EU Network of Independent Experts on Fundamental Rights Mechanism. Furthermore, the EU has developed competence in several policy areas that, although not exclusively concerned with minorities, have a significant impact on their condition.[7]

The OSCE has played a pioneering role in promoting the idea that minority rights affect international security, and concomitantly persuading national governments to accept international scrutiny of their minority policies (Nasic 2007). It was also within the OSCE that the outline of a specifically tailored set of norms for minorities was initially formulated, through a series of declarations that were then incorporated in the legally binding instruments of the CoE.[8] Although its influence in the articulation, promotion, and upholding of normative standards has subsequently receded, the OSCE continues to play a key role in preventing minority disputes from escalating into violent conflicts through the "quiet diplomacy" of its High Commissioner on National Minorities. Moreover, the Review Meetings of the Human Dimension provides a forum for states to deliberate on their minority rights practices.

From the above overview, it is obvious that the policies pursued by the Greek state toward the Turkish/Muslim minority were incompatible with European and international normative standards. For instance, the administrative restrictions and the arbitrary application of Article 19 of the Citizenship Code constituted a blunt violation of the principle of nondiscrimination, and were also hampering the effective and meaningful participation of the minority in the political, economic, and social life of Greece. With regard to Article 19, one could also argue that its excessive use constituted a nonviolent form of ethnic cleansing that threatened the very survival and existence of the minority. In the same vein, the inadequacies observed in minority education and the interventionism of the Greek authorities in the administration of the *Waqfs* and the selection of the muftis could be seen as violating both the individual religious and education rights of minority Turks/Muslims as well as the collective right of the minority to develop its cultural and religious identity. Moreover, although existing treaties shy away from establishing a clear and incontestable collective "right of self-identification," the imposition of prohibitions on specific individuals to use the word "Turk" and "Turkish," either as a self-definition or as denomination for civic associations, violated their rights of free expression, association, and assembly (Papastylianos 2008). At a more general level, the appeals to the principle of reciprocity and the concomitant assertion that the respect of the rights of the Turkish/Muslim minority was conditional upon the fulfillment by the Turkish state of its treaty obligations vis-à-vis the Greek minority in Turkey contravened the notion of unalienable human rights (Pollis 1992). These incompatibilities became very pronounced when members of the minority started filing complaints with the ECtHR. The piling of cases, together with the critical reporting on the inadequacies of Greek minority policies by the ECRI, the CoE Human Rights Commissioner, and the OSCE's human dimension created an intense pressure for change.

Gradual Liberalization

The relations between the Greek state and the Turkish/Muslim minority entered a different course in 1991 following a seminal visit of the Greek Prime Minister Konstantinos Mitsotakis in Western Thrace. During this visit, Mitsotakis admitted that the Greek state had often made "mistakes" in its treatment of the minority and announced a new approach based on the principles of "legal equality and equal citizenship" (*isonomia–isopolitia*) (Aarbakke 2000, 141). The immediate implication of the new approach was the tacit abolition of most administrative discriminatory practices and the introduction of measures aimed at achieving the economic revitalization of the region and combating the economic disparities between Christians and Muslims.

A second, more ambitious wave of reform was launched following the coming into power of Costas Simitis in 1996. In addition to completing the lifting of petty discrimination, the Greek government stepped up its efforts to improve the living conditions of the minority through the initiation of specifically tailored development programs (Anagnostou 2001;

Chorianopoulos 2009). Significant initiatives were also undertaken in the field of education through the introduction of a quota for minority students in order to facilitate their entry into Greek universities and the commencement of a large-scale interdisciplinary Project for Reform in the Education of Muslim Children (PEM) whose aim was to enhance the teaching of Greek as a second language, develop new educational materials, and improve teacher training. Finally, the Greek government's decision to abrogate the infamous Article 19 of the Citizenship Code constituted a gesture with great practical and symbolic connotations, even though the relevant legislative provision did not establish a retroactive effect.

The minority's condition continued to improve incrementally during the next decade. Notable new measures included a Greek–Turkish cultural agreement (signed in 2000), which, inter alia, paved the way for the introduction of new textbooks after almost a century; a legal amendment that limited the vested power of the local Christian-Orthodox clergy to block the construction and repair of mosques (Akgönül 2005, 211); and the extension of affirmative action to state exams for public sector posts (ECRI 2009, 9).

Despite these positive developments, however, majority–minority relations have remained tense. It has been documented, for instance, that local entrenched interests have undermined the administrative and economic reforms introduced during the 1990s (see Aarbakke 2000), and that educational initiatives have been hampered by mutual mistrust and sometimes outright opposition of local actors (see below). Greece has also done very little to address the grievances of the minority regarding the encroachments in the *Waqfs'* autonomy and the appointment of the mufti (Onar and Özgüneş 2010, 127; Bousiakou 2008, 9). A more significant problem has been the persistent effort of the Greek state to exercise political control over the minority. It is characteristic in that regard that the first wave of liberalization coincided with the imposition of a 3 percent minimum threshold for representation in the Greek Parliament, which intended to undermine the emancipatory political movement that had emerged under the leadership of Ahmet Sadik in the 1980s, by making it impossible for minority candidates to get elected on an independent ticket. In the same vein, a 1994 administrative reform, which instituted the position of elected prefect instead of the hitherto state-appointed one, was accompanied by the amalgamation of the largely Muslim prefectures of Xanthi and Rhodope in two predominantly Christian "enlarged prefectures," in order to prevent the election of minority candidates.

Most importantly, the right of self-identification continues to be curtailed. The boldest step that Greece has undertaken in that respect has been the acknowledgment of an "individual right" for the members of the minority to identify themselves as ethnic Turks. However, even this narrow interpretation of self-identification has been problematic. In fact, when George Papandreou firstly alluded to such a right in his capacity as Foreign Minister, he was immediately chastised for complaisance and naivety not only by the nationalists but also by relatively moderate and centrist circles.[9] What is more, despite the fact that the notion of individual self-identification has now been endorsed as an official government position, in practice, the Greek state continues to proscribe the use of the term Turkish by minority civic associations, and although criminal prosecutions are now less common, public references to the ethnic character of the minority elicit fierce reactions (see Skoulariki 2009).

Weak Socialization and Instrumental Adaptation

A key factor that has prevented bolder policy reforms in Greek minority policy is the fact that the principles and norms underpinning the European minority rights regime have not been fully internalized in the Greek context. Despite the alleviation of negative stereotypes, the idea that someone can be a loyal Greek citizen while being an ethnic Turk is still "meaningless" for most Greeks since it flies in the face of the concept of a mono-ethnic unitary nation.[10] A High Court's ruling against the use of the term Turkish by minority associations has articulated this incompatibility in no ambiguous terms: the word 'Turkish' refers to *citizens of Turkey* and could not be used to describe citizens of Greece" (quoted in Human Rights Watch 1999, 12, emphasis added). The view that the minority is an "alien" entity is also consistently expressed in public opinion studies (see Asimakopoulou and Lionaraki 2002, 248–49; Figgou and Conor 2012) and is implied in the continued distrust toward minority political representatives. For example, the nomination, in 2006, of Gulbeyaz Karahasan as a candidate of the Panhellenic Socialist Movement (PASOK) for the "enlarged prefecture" of Drama-Kavala-Xanthi generated a vigorous debate during which the Macedonia–Thrace Minister openly questioned Karahasan's patriotic ethos by wondering if she would dare to attend the festivities for the 1821 revolution against the Ottoman Empire, while the Prefect of Thessaloniki went as far as "challenging" the candidate to deliver the celebratory speech of the day (Skoulariki 2009, 83).

It is, therefore, not surprising that, despite the existence of a few principled activists who advocate the abolition of discriminatory measures on moral grounds, the bulk of the debate on the minority has followed an instrumental logic. This is evident in a leaked policy paper from a meeting of the leaders of the three biggest political parties (PASOK, New Democracy, and Coalition of the Left), which took place in January 1990, a few days after rising intercommunal tensions had culminated in violent incidents in the city of Komotini. In addition to proposing the abolishment of "administrative annoyances" [sic] which were depicted as ineffective and internationally embarrassing, the paper proposed a set of measures that had a clear antiminority character, including the settlement of Greek-Orthodox Pontic Greeks from the Soviet Union, as a means to redress the negative demographic trend and the systematic purchase of Muslim farmland. Most significantly, even seemingly positive measures, such as the improvement of the living and educational standards of the minority or the encouragement of urbanization and social mobility, were framed as means to reduce the minority's dependence on Turkey, not as a moral obligation.[11]

A similar line of reasoning can also be spotted in public speeches. For example, the Deputy Foreign Minister Virginia Tsouderou explained that the review of Greece's minority policy was dictated by the requirement of "consistency with the country's dynamic presence as protagonist in the defence of human rights" (Tsouderou 1992, 48). Another characteristic example is provided by the proceedings of an interparliamentary committee that examined the development prospects of Western Thrace and other border regions of Greece. Despite the seemingly technocratic character of the issue at hand, the committee's report and the subsequent plenary discussion evolved primarily around security issues, with the economic development of Western Thrace being depicted as "a national prerogative" and a "precondition for national survival" (Greek Parliament 1992, 6580–607). In another parliamentary session conducted a few months later, the majority of speakers converged on the view that targeted economic development policies were necessary in order to "fortify the region," while a local MP compared Thrace to "a covered fire which would burn everything if left unchecked" (Greek Parliament 1993, 3255).

An instrumental logic was also predominant in the case of the abrogation of Article 19. While the idea of abolishing the Article floated for several years, the actual process kicked off at the end of 1997, when the Monitoring Committee of the CoE set up a meeting to discuss a report that contested the legality of Article 19 and raised the prospect of proceeding with a monitoring process (Anagnostou 2005, 348). In the ensuing debate, the government and the main opposition party both supported the abolition on the very "pragmatic" argument that Article 19 had fulfilled its role and that Greece now had the "luxury" to repeal it in order to deprive those who were attempting to use it as a tool to unjustifiably criticize the country and cast doubt on its European credentials. At the same time, both parties converged to the view that establishing a retroactive effect was unacceptable, not only because of the negative demographic impact that massive restitution of citizenship would entail but also because it would imply an "acceptance of wrongdoing" on the part of Greece. The "principled" argument that the abolition was an ethical obligation of Greece was only advanced by two small left-wing parties and minority MPs, who also criticized the government for its refusal to restore citizenship to those who had unjustifiably lost it over the years. Finally, it is important to note that a small fraction of MPs from all parties accused the government for "giving-in to international pressures" and "failing to defend the national interest" (see Greek Parliament 1998a, 266–301; 1998b, 369–95).

The Limits of Multiculturalism

As mentioned above, the enduring tension in majority–minority relations in Western Thrace also reveals the limits of multiculturalism when minority issues are intertwined with competing nationalist claims—in this case, the nationalizing nationalism of the Greek authorities and the homeland nationalism of a significant part of the minority who perceive Turkey as their kin state (Yağcıoğlu 2004).

These limits are amply demonstrated by the difficulties encountered in the field of educational reform. The main policies pursued by the Greek state in that area—positive discrimination and the multiannual PEM—can be said to represent the epitome of a modern multicultural strategy of inclusion. The declared objective of the PEM was "the harmonious integration through school of the Muslim minority children into the Greek society and their being accepted by the majority as equal citizens."[12] This was to be pursued through five main lines of action aiming at confronting the chronic underachievement and high drop-out rates among minority pupils. The first line of action was the collection of primary data on the minority's educational condition, including, inter alia, language use and linguistic competence, drop-out rates from compulsory education, and cultural and identity representations. The second line of action was the production of new textbooks and educational materials for the Greek language program of minority schools that conformed to the linguistic and cultural needs of minority students. The third line of action was the extension of the teaching program with additional hours. The fourth line of action was the provision of teacher training with the organization of seminars for primary and secondary school teachers from both the majority and the minority. The fifth line of action was the setting up of Community Centers, staffed equally by majority and minority personnel, which operate a lending library and also offer compensatory afternoon classes, summer courses, creative workshops, educational and psychological counseling, Greek language courses for parents of minority pupils, and Turkish language courses to teachers from the majority.

The program, which has gone through five different phases, had recorded some notable successes. For example, school attendance increased significantly, with 3,950 pupils completing the nine-year compulsory education (up from 1,500 in 1997 and less than 1,000 in the 1980s). In a similar vein, the number of Minority students entering tertiary education rose from 62 in 1997 to 482 in 2011.[13]

However, the program has also faced serious limitations, created controversies, and encountered opposition from local actors. As Anna

Frangoudaki (Program Director) and Thalia Dragonas (Scientific Advisor) have pointed out in an interim evaluation,

> ...the presence of [the PEM's] team in the field stirred up a lot of emotions: suspicion from the local educational authorities; ambivalence at best, anger and hostility more often, on the part of the nationalists of the majority; hesitation and timid hope in the minority; caution among its elite. (Dragonas and Frangoudaki 2006, 34)

Such problems were very pronounced in the exploratory first stage of the project, with PEM field researchers facing resistance not only from local educational administrators but also minority representatives, both of whom used the same line of argument: that outside intervention was pointless because the "information was already known and could be provided by them personally" (ibid.). Of particular relevance in that respect is the controversy created over a survey that investigated the language used by pupils at home, which was seen by minority leaders as an attempt to repudiate the Turkish identity of Pomaks and Roma/Gypsies (Askouni 2004). Establishing channels of communication with minority teachers and parents was also a difficult task because of the mistrust that they displayed toward Greek educational authorities (Androussou et al. 2011, 232).

Concerns about the erosion of the minority's Turkish character have also been compounded by the significant increase of minority students enrolling in the mainstream primary schools. This choice seems eloquent, given that the acquisition of proficiency in Greek language increases significantly the prospects of social mobility. However, it also creates acute interpersonal conflicts for parents given that the preservation of a segregated education system is considered by minority elites as essential in order to preserve the Turkish character of the minority (Dragonas and Frangoudaki 2006, 33).

This conflict over identity is also eloquent in another inherent limitation of the PEM: its focus exclusively on the Greek side of the curriculum. This one-sided approach has led to accusations that despite its rhetorical commitment to multiculturalism, the underlying goal of the program was the subtle assimilation of the minority. Although there is little doubt that the prospect of gradual assimilation is seen positively by many within the majority, it is important to note that any attempt to intervene on the Turkish curriculum would, in most likelihood, have met strong resistance from the minority.[14] Thus, a persuasive argument can be made that the one-sided nature of the program has been an unwanted side effect of the desire of those who designed it to avoid what they perceived as "mistakes of the past" (Dragonas and Frangoudaki 2006, 35).

According to Mantouvalou, the aforementioned controversies and debates indicate the double domination to which the minority population has been subjected: The external domination by the state which attempts to impose an essentialist reading of its identity—as a "religious community" composed of "different ethnic groups" who had been unjustifiably marginalized "in the past" but now have the opportunity to fully integrate in Greek society while preserving their distinct culture, and the internal domination by powerful Turkish elites who repress their internal diversity (2009, 489–90). Mantouvalou's remark accords well and extends the argument advanced by Tripathy and Padmanabhan (this volume) regarding the way in which democratic states tend to construct a uniform and undiluted minority essence, articulating narratives of helplessness and victimhood with a rescue narrative of affirmative action and reservation, that end up unwittingly reproducing exclusion and marginalization. Such concerns are particularly relevant for the Pomak community. Caught between an ideological struggle between Greek and Turkish nationalisms, both of which tried to claim the Pomaks as their brethren, and the everyday reality of discrimination, geographical isolation, and economic marginalization, the Pomak population has sought a more secure identity by pursuing two competing strategies. While a large segment has developed a Turkish national consciousness, even abandoning the Pomak language in favor of Turkish, others have continued to seek recognition from and integration into the Greek state by accepting the idealized construction of their identity as "indigenous Greeks" and opting to study in Greek mainstream schools (Demetriou 2004; Troumpeta 2001).

As opposed to these hierarchized majority–minority relations, Mantouvalou proposes a democratic pluralist model that fosters minority participation under conditions of nondomination in common institutions and in decisions about how minority identity is represented (2009, 480). Although she does not propose the abandonment of separate education systems (to the extent that minority members so desire), she argues that the boundaries between them should become less rigid in order to enable majority–minority contact and that vulnerable minority members should be given a voice (Mantouvalou 2009, 494). The Community Centers can be said to represent a good example of such a policy not only because of the various services they provide but also because they have given the opportunity to members of the majority and the minority to work side by side on equal terms and with constantly alternating language, thus, fostering mutual understanding and helping overcome negative stereotypes, division, and segregation (Dragonas 2008). The pilot introduction of Turkish as an optional course in mainstream secondary schools could also be seen as an attempt to indirectly address some of these concerns, since it alleviates the dilemmas faced by minority parents. However, both the majority and the minority have been reluctant to explore bolder reforms, following models that have been tested in other bilingual environments (Dragonas and Frangoudaki 2006, 33).

Conclusion

This chapter sought to explore the sources of the enduring tension in majority–minority relations in Western Thrace. Adopting a constructivist approach, which acknowledges the mutual constitutive relationship between identity and policy, I have argued that the antiminority policies pursued by the Greek state were premised on and reproduced an ethnocentric exclusionary nation-state identity discourse, which constructed the Greek nation as a homogeneous organic community united by religion (Christian-Orthodox), language (Greek-speaking), descent, and consciousness. In this context, the religious and linguistic distinctiveness of Turkish-speaking Muslims and, above all, the fact that many of them portrayed an ethnic Turk self-identification substantiated a representation of the minority as an alien and potentially threatening entity. The interfacing of this negative representation of the minority with a national security discourse that depicted Turkey as a major threat to Greek territorial integrity provided a solid basis for the enactment of discriminatory and repressive measures inasmuch as these were serving the "national interest."

I have also argued that the advent of a densely institutionalized European minority rights regime has sparked a gradual liberalization of Greek minority policy which, however, falls short of representing a transformational change. The Greek political system has been remarkably resistant to internalizing multicultural norms. Instead, the main driver for the observed changes has been the realization that certain measures were counterproductive (e.g., administrative restrictions) or had fulfilled their role (e.g., Article 19). On the contrary, policies and practices which are perceived to serve core national security interest (e.g., encroachments in *Waqfs'* independence, political neutralization of the mufti, gerrymandering, imposition of electoral limits, denial of Turkish identity) have persisted, and in some cases have also been reinforced. By showcasing the interplay between international norms and domestic setting and the importance of instrumental strategic calculations in the process of state adaptation, this chapter, thus, contributes to the extensive literature of international socialization, siding with those who question the capacity of international institutions to shape national interests.

This chapter also sides with those who have criticized multicultural democratic theory and practice for its failure to take into account the fact that minority is a nuanced and slippery category which cannot exist outside representation. Following the framework presented by Tripathy and Padmanabhan in this volume, I have closely scrutinized an area where the Greek policy seems to follow closely multicultural norms, in order to destabilize their foundational assumptions and reveal the underlying constitutive processes and hierarchical relationships. In doing so, I aim to expose the way in which the policies currently pursued by the Greek government in Western Thrace have constituted the problem that they are supposed to address, and opening up a space for alternative conceptualizations of the minority issue that would enable the members of the minority to be free of the double domination to which they are subjected.

Notes and Bibliography

Notes

1. The text of the Lausanne Treaty can be found in http://www.hri.org/docs/lausanne/part1.html
2. Interestingly, until the revival of the Greek–Turkish rivalry in the mid-1950s, concerns about the minority's negative role were articulated mainly with reference to the so-called communist threat from the North. In this

context, the main threatening entity was the population of Slav-speaking Pomaks, and the Greek state actively pursued a policy of turkification of the minority and even requested the replacement of names and signs.

3. A common "warning" by nationalist circles is that in Cyprus, 18 percent of the Turkish Cypriot population was sufficient to warrant an invasion.

4. The sentence that Greek officials allude to in order to establish the reciprocity principle stated that "the rights conferred... on the non-Moslem minorities of Turkey will be similarly conferred by Greece on the Moslem minority in her territory." http://www.hri.org/docs/lausanne/part1.html

5. See 1992 Declaration on the Rights of Persons Belonging to National or Ethnic, Religious, and Linguistic Minorities.

6. Until recently, this was inferred from general references to human rights protection as well as more specific provisions contained in The Charter of Fundamental Rights of the EU with regard to nondiscrimination (Article 21) and the preservation of cultural, religious, and linguistic diversity (Article 22). However, Article 1A of the Lisbon Treaty explicitly recognizes that the rights of persons belonging to minorities constitute an integral part of human rights.

7. For example, as part of its antidiscrimination policy, the EU has passed the so-called "Race Directive" which requires member states to take measures against direct and indirect discrimination with regard to access to employment, education, and public services, and has also established a Community action program to combat discrimination.

8. These ideas were incorporated in the 1989 Vienna Document, the 1990 Copenhagen Document, and the 1991 Paris Charter.

9. The exact phrase that Papandreou used was:

   No one doubts that there are many Muslims of Turkish origin. Of course, the Treaties [of Lausanne] mention only Muslims. If no one contests the present borders, I could not care less if one calls himself a Muslim or a Turk, a Bulgarian or a Pomak.

   For reactions to this statement see http://www.greekhelsinki.gr/greek/press-release/national-minorities-gr.html#Reactions

10. It is characteristic that in Greek common parlance there is no distinction between the terms nationality and ethnicity, which are both captured by the term *ethnikotita*.

11. Text reproduced in Aarbakke (2000, 766).

12. For details regarding the structure and evolution of the program, see http://museduc.gr/en/

13. For statistics on minority education, see http://museduc.gr/en/%CE%B7-%CE%B5%CE%BA%CF%80%CE%B1%CE%B9%CE%B4%CE%B5%CF%85%CF%83%CE%B7-%CF%83%CE%B5-%CE%B1%CF%81%CE%B9%CE%B8%CE%BC%CE%BF%CF%85%CF%83

14. An attempt in 1992 to introduce a new Turkish language textbook had met fierce resistance from the minority with parents refusing to send their children to school and minority teachers refusing to use them arguing that this constituted an unacceptable intrusion in the minority's autonomy.

Bibliography

Aarbakke, V. 2000. *The Muslim Minority of Greek Thrace*. PhD Thesis, University of Bergen, Bergen, Norway.

Akgönül, S. 2005. "Towards Minority Policies Beyond Reciprocity? The EU, Greece, and Turkey." In *In the long shadow of Europe Greeks and Turks in the Era of Postnationalism*, edited by O. Anastasakis, C. Nicolaides, and Ö Kerem. Boston: Martinus Nijhoff.

Anagnostou, D. 2001. "Breaking the Cycle of Nationalism: The EU, Regional Policy and the Minority of Western Thrace, Greece." *South European Society and Politics* 6 (1): 37–41.

———. 2005. "Deepening Democracy or Defending the Nation? The Europeanization of Minority Rights and Greek Citizenship." *West European Politics* 28 (2): 335–57.

Androussou, A., N. Askouni, T. Dragonas, A. Frangoudaki, and E. Plexousaki. 2011. "Educational and Political Challenges in Reforming the Education of the Muslim Minority in Thrace, Greece." *The International Journal of Learning* 17 (11): 227–39.

Asimakopoulou, F. and S. Christidou-Lionaraki. 2002. *The Muslim Minority of Thrace and Greek–Turkish Relations*. Athens: Livanis (in Greek).

Askouni, N. 2004. "Minority Education in Thrace as a Research Field: The Political Parameters in Field Research." In *Proceedings of the Conference on Minorities in Greece*. Athens: Etairia Spoudon Neohellinikou Politismou kai Genikis Paideias (in Greek).

Borou, C. 2009. "The Muslim Minority of Western Thrace in Greece: An Internal Positive or an Internal Negative 'Other'?" *Journal of Muslim Minority Affairs* 29 (1): 37–41.

Boussiakou, I. 2008. "Religious Freedom and Minority Rights in Greece: The Case of the Muslim Minority in Western Thrace." Paper 21, Hellenic Observatory Papers on Greece and Southeast Europe.

Chorianopoulos, I. 2009. "Tackling social exclusion in Greece: Citizenship and participatory governance." *Environment and Planning* C, 27(3): 527–545.

Christopoulos, D. and K. Tsitselikis. 2003. "Treatment of Minorities and Homogeneis in Greece: Relics and Challenges." *History and Culture of South Eastern Europe—An Annual Journal* 5: 81–93.

Demetriou, O. 2004. "Prioritizing 'Ethnicities': The Uncertainty of Pomak-ness in the Urban Greek Rhodoppe." *Ethnic and Racial Studies* 27 (1): 95–119.

Dragonas, T. 2008. "From Isolation to Communicative Collaboration; From Mistrust to Acceptance: The Case of the Community Centers." In *Addition not*

152   Apostolos Agnantopoulos

Subtraction, Multiplication not Division: Reforming the Education of the Minority in Thrace, edited by T. Dragonas and A. Frangoudaki. Athens: Metaihmio (in Greek).

Dragonas, T. and A. Frangoudaki. 2006. "Educating the Muslim Minority in Western Thrace." *Islam and Christian–Muslim Relations* 17 (1): 21–41.

European Commission Against Racism and Intolerance. 2009. Fourth Report on Greece. http://www.coe.int/t/dghl/monitoring/ecri/country-by-country/greece/GRC-CbC-IV-2009-031-GRC.pdf

Figgou, L. and S. Condor. 2012. "Categorising Category Labels in Interview Accounts About the 'Muslim Minority' in Greece." *Journal of Ethnic and Migration Studies* 33 (3): 439–59.

Greek Parliament. 1990. Minutes of Proceedings, April 26.

———. 1991. Minutes of Proceedings, February 8.

———. 1992. Minutes of Proceedings, May 22.

———. 1993. Minutes of Proceedings, January 22.

———. 1998a. Minutes of Proceedings, June 9.

———. 1998b. Minutes of Proceedings, June 11.

Grigoriadis, I. N. 2005. "Reciprocity as Race to the Bottom in Religious Freedom." In *In the Long Shadow of Europe Greeks and Turks in the Era of Postnationalism*, edited by O. Anastasakis, C. Nicolaides, and Ö Kerem. Boston: Martinus Nijhoff.

Henrard, K. 2000. *Devising an Adequate System of Minority Protection: Individual Human Rights, Minority Rights, and the Right to Self-Determination*. The Hague: Martinus Nijhoff.

Heraclides, A. 2001. *Greece and the Threat from the East*. Athens: Polis (in Greek).

Human Rights Watch. 1999. Report on The Turks of Western Thrace.

Koliopoulos, J. and T. Veremis. 2002. *Greece: The Modern Sequel*. London: Hurst.

Mantouvalou, K. 2009. "Equal Recognition, Consolidation or Familiarization? The Language Rights Debate in the Context of the Minority of Western Thrace in Greece." *Ethnicities* 9 (4): 477–506.

Nasic, H. 2007. "Human and Minority Rights in the Life Cycle of Ethnic Conflicts." *MIRICO Project*, European Academy of Bozen, Bozen, Italy.

Onar, N. F. and M. Özgüneş. 2010. "How Deep a Transformation? Europeanization of Greek and Turkish Minority Policies." *International Journal on Minority and Group Rights* 17 (1): 1111–36.

Papastylianos, C. 2008. "Diversity and Public Order: The Freedom of Association and the Jurisprudence of European Court of Human Rights and Greek Courts." In *The Un-Confessable Issue of Minorities in Greek Legal Order*, edited by D. Christopoulos. Athens: Kritiki (in Greek).

Pollis, A. 1992. "Greek National Identity: Religious Minorities, Rights, and European Norms." *Journal of Modern Greek Studies* 10 (2): 171–96.

Roudometof, V. 1998. "From Rum Millet to Greek Nation: Enlightenment, Secularization, and National Identity in Ottoman Balkan Society, 1453–1821." *Journal of Modern Greek Studies* 16 (1): 11–47.

Sitaropoulos, N. 2004. "Freedom of Movement and the Right to a Nationality v. Ethnic Minorities: The Case of ex Article 19 of the Greek Nationality Code." *European Journal of Migration and Law* 6 (3): 205–23.

Skoulariki, A. 2009. "Declarations of National Consciousness: Political Discourse and Public Debates in Greece in Relation to the Right of Self-Determination and the Candidature of Giulbeyaz Karahasan." In *Immigrants and Minorities*, edited by M. Pavlou and A. Skoulariki. Athens: Vivliorama (in Greek).

Triandafyllidou, A. and A. Paraskevopoulou. 2002. "When is the Greek Nation? The Role of Enemies and Minorities." *Geopolitics* 7 (2): 75–98.

Troumpeta, S. 2001. *Constructing Identities for the Muslims of Thrace*. Athens: Kritiki (in Greek).

Tsitselikis, C. and D. Christopoulos. 2008. "From the Multicultural Great Dream of Hellenism of the Early 20th Century to the Multicultural Reality of the Early 21st Century." In *The Unconfessable Issue of Minorities in Greek Legal Order*, edited by D. Christopoulos. Athens: Kritiki (in Greek).

Tsouderou, V. 1990. "Stopping Pan-Turkism in Thrace." In *Eliamep Yearbook of Foreign and Defence Policy*, edited by I. Valinakis. Athens: Eliamep.

———. 1992. *Foreign Policy: The Great Patient*. Athens: Papazisis (in Greek).

Yağcıoğlu, D. 2004. From Deterioration to Improvement in Western Thrace, Greece: A Political System Analysis. Unpublished PhD Thesis, George Mason University, Fairfax, VA, USA.

8

Cultural War of Values: The Proliferation of Moral Identities in the Danish Public Sphere

Peter Hervik

The spread of antimigrant sentiments and policies at the level of governmental policies, media representations, and mainstream popular consciousness in Western Europe has had devastating consequences for ethnic and religious minorities. Moreover, as the Muhammad Cartoon Crisis—which originated in Denmark in 2005 as a moralizing issue with the publication of 12 cartoons of Prophet Muhammad—showed with the death of at least 150 people in Pakistan and Nigeria and elsewhere, the gravity of the issue of morality goes far beyond the Danish and European borders.

Add to this the tragic events in Oslo and Utøya on July 22, 2011 with 77 people killed, more people wounded, a bleeding nation, and neighboring countries in shock. In his compendium, copied and pasted from radical right websites, terrorist and mass murderer Anders Behring Breivik likewise reveals his anti-Muslim sentiment but adds to it an enemy image of multiculturalists, Marxists, and feminists. The radical right has detached itself from Breivik by encapsulating his attacks as the actions of an individual, deviant, criminal, crazy person and lone wolf (Hervik and Boisen 2013). However, though Breivik's acts may be unique, but his ideas are shared by many.

The Danish Muhammad cartoon conflict can be seen as a predictable outcome of the government's and mainstream media's cultural war of values strategy, which along with Breivik's predatory identities reflects the core moral ideas of neoconservatism, not least the two moral logics: Firstly, "there can be no moral equivalency" between "our" Western democracy and "their" different forms of governance and, secondly, approaching one's adversary as either friend or foe. The social construction of such moral logics can be defined as abstract, relatively context-free types of arguments for performing the intellectual tasks involved in distinguishing right from wrong (Kavolis 1977), and can, therefore, be found at various junctures in society. Like Samuel Huntington's narrative of clash of civilizations and its micro-level equivalent in neoracism, this construction relies on a monolithic and even enemy image that allows no space for socio-cultural variation.

My working theory in this chapter is that in the last 20 years, morality has become the basis for looking at minority difference in the Danish public sphere and private homes. The construction of minority others has shifted drastically with the emergence of neonationalism, neoracism, and radical right populism in the post-1989 world. In fact, these isms have used othering as their device to create new national cohesion (Hervik 2011). With this focus, not least on the idea of incompatible culture—rather on the materialist, political, social, cultural, and economic circumstances of production of difference—we may be better equipped to understand the gradual development of a radical environment that produced two dire events: the Muhammad Cartoon Crisis and the killings in Norway. In addition to a Danish nation state versus unwanted nonwestern minorities, the outcome is antagonism against multiculturalism, political correctness, feminism, and Communism.

The two cataclysmic events can now be seen as end products in a social constructionist approach, where minorities and other adversaries are marked as potential, future victims, and collectively pushed into a social symbolic corner prepared for elimination (Balibar 2005). In a recent research project on perceptions of the Muhammad Cartoon Crisis, focus group sessions confirmed our anticipation of how looking at difference has entered everyday lives. Participants said things like: "Danes consider xenophobia as acceptable" and "It is ok to be xenophobic" (Hervik 2012a).

Following this, bodies are marked in Balibar's terms. As I have argued earlier, such a development is the result of a process best described as radical right-wing populism, where populism, neonationalism, and neoracism go hand-in-hand producing "we-groups" of the nation kind, while excluding those who are not part of the imagined community of Danish people. One of the founding pillars of this "anti-elite," "for the people," and "against the migrants" triangle is the notion of cultural incompatibility, which is also a key part of new nationalism (Banks and Gingrich 2006). This nationalism is not isolated from older nationalism and its creation of "minorities," but encompasses the dramatic increase in upholding eternal values and defending timeless aspirations that re-emerge in the post-1989 world at a time when the nation state is well established (Gingrich 2006). With the idea of incompatibility, neonationalists use rhetoric of war and resistance (Boe and Hervik 2008); economic and cultural chauvinism (Gingrich and Banks 2006); emphasize descent, home, belonging, kinship, and primordialism (Gullestad 2006); and claim to be speaking the "plain truth," such as "there are too many immigrants" and "Muslims are dangerous people." Depicting immigrant minority culture as dangerous can pave the way for offering security—a firm control of migrants and immigration. Neonationalism generates out-groups of these "incompatibly different," who prefer to live among their own kind because it is most "natural" for them, claims to not be racist since everyone is equal, but argues that since migrants are not living where they "naturally belong," their presence in the wrong place will create xenophobic reactions as conflicts appear at the fault lines between cultures or civilizations. In other words, this neoracism is intimately tied to neonationalism as it refers to the same simultaneous process of inclusion and exclusion (Miles 1993, 55). Completing the triangle is criticism of the elite (arbiters of taste) as traitors and cowards who did not stop immigration, who stand up for freedom of speech, and who protect themselves behind a shield of political correctness. They are, in short, political adversaries and others in disagreement. Boe and Hervik argue that the attacks on traitors and cowards show that there is no simple bipolar Islam versus the West narrative in play; also, the politically correct, multiculturalists, feminists, and others converge at this time (2008).

This chapter addresses the emergence of ethnically marked moral minority identities of the cultural war strategy in public debate, specifically in Denmark but observable in other European countries as well.[1]

This construction of minorities in the news media, I argue, does not take place in a negotiation of meaning with minorities, but is the outcome of a cultural war strategy aimed at domestic political adversaries. This further underscores the constructedness of the minority; a constructedness that has little to do with the attributes of these groups, but nevertheless constitutes a significant condition for immigrants and ethnic minorities in Denmark. In fact, as Cora Alexa Døving rightly pointed out, Muslim minorities in Norway (and relevant for Denmark) do not form an organized "group" headed by a representative and carrying a shared message, but form a "category" of people with one or more shared features (Døving 2007). I will situate the cultural war strategy within a 15-year period to show the emerging moral logic and ultimate character of the above-mentioned populist triad: antimigration, neonationalism, and neoracism. I show that immigrants of non-European origin are talked about in increasingly crass and uncompromising ways as a consequence of the proliferation of moral identities in Danish news media and politics. My main ambition is to infer and discuss some of the salient features of the strategy, which produces a strained, polarized relation particularly to the country's Muslim minority.

First, I will present a slice of Danish history to situate the strategy against a larger historical dynamic within the historical emergence of the "minority" as an idea in the mid-19th century with blossoming European nationalisms. I will then briefly describe the comprehensive transformation of Danish society from having one of the most lenient integration policies to allegedly one of the strictest ones (Hervik and Rytter 2004). I will then go into the structural foundation of the cultural war, which did not appear out of the blue with its creation of the minority as a group, which forms a crucial context for the minorities as a category of people who have in common the quality that they are visibly different, "non-Danish" or "non-Westerners" by origin.

Denmark becomes Unified and the Minority Emerges

The historical emergence of Danish nationalism coincided with the loss of a multilingual, multicultural empire. The wars of 1848, 1864, the unification of southern Jutland with the rest of Denmark in 1920 after

WW I and WW II are significant in the production of minorities in Europe, unlike in India where de-colonization in the 1940s forms the most significant background for the new creation of majorities. The Danish constitution (Grundloven) was passed in 1849, institutionalizing the end of absolute monarchical rule. A few years later, in 1864, when Denmark was defeated in a war with Germany, the Danish empire had lost Norway, Sleswig, Holstein, and Lauenborg. For the first time, (almost) only Danish speakers lived within the borders, leaving a group of 170,000 Danish speakers right outside its territory. In 1920, most of these Danish speakers became Danes when the lost territory in southern Jutland, located on the German side of the border, was voted back in a referendum. This referendum came as part of the negotiations of borders following Germany's defeat in WW I, and ended up moving the national border further south, reflecting the linguistic border as closely as possible.

During the last third of the 19th century, nation-building efforts spread from the elite to peasants, workers, and small holders. This shift in the balance of power was the outcome of the varying success of three competing political programs that are crucial for understanding competing political forces in Denmark even today (Linde-Laursen 2007). The elitist National Liberals promoted a political type of nationalism, which promoted a popular sovereignty based on citizens who were "deemed cultured and educated enough to exercise democratic rights" (Hansen 2002, 57). Hansen notes that the National Liberals did not hold any romantic visions of an authentic peasantry, but maintained general discontent with everything that took place outside of Copenhagen. In their view, the Danish state could be extended beyond the Danish nation (ibid., 57–58).

A second line of thinking emerged from Nikolai Frederik Severin Grundtvig,[2] whose work resembled Herder's idea of the "Kulturnation" and sought to put "the people" and their rights to self-determination at the core of its nationalism. Accordingly, a linguistic criterion was the proper division in southern Jutland separating Danish and German speakers (ibid., 58–59). To counter the National Liberals' grip on power through education, Grundtvig sought to give uneducated peasants a chance to exchange ideas and organize politically. During the winter, peasants would come to "folk high schools," whose informal settings and absence of rigid teaching methods appealed to the Danish populace through a strong sense of community, public speakers, singing, dancing, gymnastics, and so on. With emphasis on "the living word," entertaining yet instructive exchanges contributed further to educating the peasants, building a national consciousness, and training them for political office.

A third line of political thought had journalist and politician Viggo Hørup as its spokesperson. People of this persuasion championed antipower politics. Denmark should pursue a pragmatic friendship with Germany in order to gain the most influence and should even be willing to settle for a state smaller than the linguistic boundaries (ibid.).

The Danish popular movement of peasants and workers created a separate public sphere and a civic society independent of the state, which came out of the nation's failure to establish norms for all citizens (Linde-Laursen 2007). At the time, Danish nationalists were motivated by the hostile relationship to Germany and using it within the country to gain social and political power.

To more fully capture the peculiar Danish popular relation to the state, it is helpful to contrast it with the strikingly different historical situation in neighboring Sweden. In 19th- and 20th-century Sweden, Social Democrats pursued nation building through a modernist, utopian ideal by uniting popular movement with an alliance of peasants and workers with the state. In the origin myth of Swedish nationalism, the free Swedish yeoman peasant and the King build an intimate alliance fighting against foreign powers and domestic nobility. Eventually, the success of the alliance grew into a strong idea: "the state and the people were joined in a common endeavor to safeguard the two freedoms, that of the nation and that of the individual" (Trägårdh 2002, 133–34). The Swedish state and people are inseparable, embedding an alliance of the friendly, strong, egalitarian state to which enlightened autonomous people willingly give up individual liberty and free choice (ibid., 142–43). The Danish tension between the responsible, educated, cultivated elite of the capital and the Grundtvigian view of the superior position of "the people" (Folket), whether it is comprised of peasants or workers (but not both at the same time), is indeed present in the debate about the use of free speech in the Muhammad cartoon coverage. Thus, the Aarhus-based Jyllands-Posten was scolded for its uneducated use of free speech by competing with the government-friendly Berlingske Tidende in Copenhagen.

Historically, the two powerful neighbors have influenced Danish nation building heavily: Sweden and Germany are the dominant others in this nationalism.

Cultural Minority Others of Danish Neonationalism

Like other European countries, Denmark received thousands of Bosnian refugees in the early 1990s. The 17,000 refugees were placed in temporary camps and kept more or less isolated from Danish society as they were expected to return to Bosnia when the war ended. The news media and Parliament (*Folketinget*) discussed to what extent Bosnian presence could influence Danish cultural identity. Bosnian minorities were considered real war refugees, but still the cultural minority other in the Danish imagination and construction of a national "we" feeling.

In 1997, Somali refugees from enormous camps in Kenya and elsewhere took over this role. They became the target of domestic Danish media coverage in late 1996 and early 1997, when the tabloid newspaper *Ekstra Bladet* and the newly formed radical right-wing populist party, the Danish People's Party, teamed up in an antimigrant endeavor. The Somalis were represented as too different to be integrated. In this approach, although unsaid, their cultural differences were naturalized and spoken of in ways that made it clear that "culture" had replaced "race" but the idea of incompatible difference remained. It was as if they were culturally as different as their dark skin complexion, which made Danes discover their own whiteness (Hervik 1999). In this process, Somalis took over the role of the others of Danish neonationalism from the Bosnian refugees. Scholars demonstrated that the Somalis were the group in Denmark that experienced most discrimination in everyday encounters (Møller and Togeby 1999).

In May 2001, a small group of individuals particularly critical of Islam and Muslims around ethnic politicians Naser Khader and Waillit Khan and their radical right-wing Danish friends went public with a story that young Danish-born Muslims of Pakistani ethnic background were foreign infiltrators, in favor of death penalty, and basically the same kind of people as the Taliban, whom they supported. The producers of the untrue stories were later instrumental in the networks and strategy of the cultural value war and confrontational, negative dialogue approach to Muslim minorities.[3] With this huge media story, "Muslims" took over the savage slot of neonationalism. Somalis were already considered incompatible with Danish values, but, subsequently, their difference was ascribed to them being Muslims as well as deprived, dark-skinned Africans. Being Muslim played no significant role in 1997 and never meant much in connection to the Bosnian refugees. Again, it should be pointed out that constructing these minority groups as incompatible is a point of view, not a feature of intergroup relations.

The unfolding of these different cultural others of neonationalism suggests a society that is undergoing drastic changes. A domestic transformation of the public service sector can be summarized as new public management, while the actual cultural war of values, discussed in this chapter, starts with the Danish activist foreign policy.

A couple of months after the news story, 9/11 occurred, and shortly after, the Danish national election resulted in a landslide victory to a new right-wing government consisting of the Liberals and the Conservatives. The Danish People's Party, which had a radical right-wing view on immigration, further supported the new government.

Intensified New Public Management and Enhanced Activist Foreign Policy

New Public Management

The change of government is crucial for understanding the scope of the new transformations and initiatives, not least the cultural war of values as a focal point of the government strategy. However, it must be emphasized that the previous government of Social Democrats and Social Liberals, led by Prime Minister Poul Nyrup Rasmussen, started several of those transformations. Common to other western European countries is a series of reform changes under the heading New Public Management. The changes started in the 1980s with Conservative Prime Minister Poul Schlüter (a lawyer), continued in the 1990s with Social Democratic Prime Minister Poul Nyrup Rasmussen (an economist), and peaked in the 2000s under

Liberal Prime Minister Anders Fogh Rasmussen[4] (also an economist). The premise of the changes is that the public service sector is not different from the private sector and should be approached as such. The reform agenda, therefore, includes: "performance management, responsiveness to uses of public services, regulation, marketization, and human resource management" (Hansen 2005). Contracting has been one important tool of control, for instance, to manage unemployed and migrants at the individual level. Universities were struck when rent of buildings and offices in inner cities rose to market prices. Academic staff has been subjected to the new idea of "bibliometrics," which basically divides publishers and journals into a crude hierarchy separated by points according to "qualitative" expert assessments and produces a system where individual academic staff members have to perform. Failure to perform results in a warning and possibly dismissal.

Poul Nyrup Rasmussen's government passed a new Integration Act in 1999, which had many good aspects but also stands out as the historically first legitimation of differential treatment of native Danes and newly arriving migrants. Refugees and others accepted into Denmark would receive less welfare money than Danes on welfare. This provision was new and controversial. Kirsten Hvenegård-Lassen identified the lower payment established by the Integration Act as the first historical legitimization of unequal treatment of certain people in Denmark after WW II (Hvenegård-Lassen 2002).

Although this discriminatory practice was illegal and abandoned 13 months later, it was only slightly altered and reappeared under new names ("startydelse," "introduktionsydelse") and, equally important, extended to other minority groups in vulnerable situations, the poor and the unemployed.

Activist Foreign Policy

On the foreign scene, the cultural war focus has become the constitutive element in the so-called new activist foreign policy, which follows the US foreign policy closely. The activist foreign policy began slowly in 1999, when Denmark sent troops to Kosovo without the proper UN mandate and later a navy vessel to Kuwait in the first Gulf War. The new policy was crucial for the new right-wing government of 2001. According to the new defense policy, the Danish military's primary objective was transformed from defending the country's sovereignty to international operations outside NATO's area and the idea that Denmark should play an active visible role in international politics (Klausen 2009). According to the opening text of the Danish military's website: "By being capable of fighting and winning, the military's soldiers promote a peaceful and democratic development in the world and a safe society in Denmark" (Forsvaret, n.d.). In this manner, so-called Danish values can be promoted far away from NATO's own nation states, while some communication strategies emphasized that Denmark was merely protecting itself preemptively by attacking training grounds for future terrorists.

In the process of joining Britain and the US in the invasion of Iraq, the Danish government also subscribed to the idea of not only defending our values, but also spreading them to Iraq which, according to Tony Blair, is "in our own national interest." Blair went on to conflate moral values of interest by saying: "The spread of our values makes the world safer" (Blair, quoted in Fairclough 2006, 153).

The foreign activist policy is closely connected to the cultural war of values in 2001 and both are characterized by their morality and moralizing. On the domestic scene, the "external threat" within Denmark was confronted by core Danish values and is still emphasized as a tool to solve the problem of incompatible values (Lykkeberg 2008, 253).

Foundation of Cultural War of Values

When Anders Fogh Rasmussen articulated the cultural war of value strategy in 2003, he strategically tapped into a preexisting schism on the left wing. Politicians in the Social Democratic party, authors, and other opinion makers had been criticizing left-wing intellectuals who saw the working class as suffering from false consciousness in need of conscientization, which they wanted to provide. The general class ambition was to use democracy (and the state) to control the free market and to fight privatism and excessive consumerism (Lykkeberg 2008). In another version of the schism, the state and capitalism were to be fought theoretically, giving way to a classless society of proletarians. The academic elite had begun to see itself as a vehicle for this process, which, for a start, had the goal of mobilizing the working class in its own interest but, according to a wide range of critics, created a gap between the "theoretical reflections" among academics and various forms and aspects of everyday, intuitive, common-sense and ordinary folks "in the street" (Lykkeberg 2008). This gap bore the features of a classic populist slot for others to capitalize on.

Already in 1986, in a Constitution day speech, Fogh Rasmussen alluded to the idea of a cultural war, when he asserted that the socialists were controlling ordinary people's perception of right and wrong: "If we do not get a hold on Danish cultural life, we cannot aspire to seriously change Danish society. The long-term influence on development does not come from economic life. It comes from cultural life" (A. F. Rasmussen in Lykkeberg 2008, 268). Even in his book *Fra socialstat til minimalstat* of 1993, he wrote:

> Indeed there is a need for a cultural war. In Danish ears the word "culture war" (*kulturkamp*) may sound a little harsh. And I do not think of armed rebellion. But I use the term "culture war" to underscore the all-encompassing character of that change of attitudes there is a need for. We must as a start do away with collectivist norms we, so to speak, have received from mother's milk. It will be a fight against inherited routine ways of thinking and discredit, alleged truths. (Rasmussen, in Lykkeberg 2008)

To short-circuit the left-wing cultural elite (of the political correct and so on), Rasmussen seeks to create a new triangular alliance: "The right-wing government wants to liberate the lower and middle class from the cultural upper class and pedagogical dominance" (ibid., 70–71).

Fogh Rasmussen became Prime Minister in 2001. He gave the populist slot a strong moral and ideological twist and phrased the cultural war of value as a war against those regimes of morally shady people, the politically correct arbiters of taste.

> In recent years a budding process has generated a true wilderness of state sponsored committees and boards and institutions everywhere. Many of them have evolved into state authorized arbiters of taste who define what is good and right in different areas. There are tendencies of a tyranny of experts, who risk suppressing the free popular debate. The people should not accept raised fingers from so-called experts who think they know best. Experts can be good enough for conveying factual knowledge. But when it comes to making personal choices, we are all experts. The government will abolish unnecessary committees and boards and institutions. This will be a very comprehensive clearance... we believe that humans are best suited to

choose for themselves. We don't need experts and arbiters of taste to decide for us (Nævnet for Etnisk Ligestilling n.d., 123).

When a populist slot is clear, for example, between Danish politicians and the Danish votes in the referendum on the Maastricht Treaty in 1992 to give a new political dimension to the European Union (Hervik 2011), or between the left-wing elite and the working class, which it seeks to instruct and educate, a populist manual would—if it existed—suggest three steps: First, emphasize the role of "the people" and their central position for your political aspirations. The people are at the center of the vision of the world and of the political institutions that organize the community. Second, state widely and clearly that those in charge have betrayed the people. Accuse the elites of abusing their position of power instead of acting in conformity with the interests of the people as a whole. Finally, the first priority is to restore the primacy of the role of the people. The elites have to be ousted and replaced by leaders capable of acting for the good of the community.

Cultural Civil War of Values Breaks Out

Shortly after winning the parliamentary election in November 2001, Anders Fogh Rasmussen launched what was afterwards coined a "culture war" (kulturkamp) or debate about the cultural values of Danish society.

In early January 2002, Danes saw how far the new government would go when it struck an agreement with the Danish People's Party to close the independent Danish Centre for Human Rights, the Board for Ethnic Equality, and the Documentation and Advisory Centre on Racial Discrimination. The Danish People's Party was particularly critical of the two chairpersons, Morten Kjærum of the Centre for Human Rights and Kjeld Holm of the Board for Ethnic Equality, whom they accused of being politically correct because of their criticism of the party's politics. After intense discussion and foreign pressure, a new deal was struck. The Board for Ethnic Equality was closed, the Centre for Human Rights was closed as an independent institution, and state support for the Advisory Centre was discontinued. Instead, the Danish Centre for International Studies and Human Rights, consisting of five previously separate institutions, was established as a single institute under the Danish Foreign Office. One of these was the Centre for Human Rights, which in the new version changed its name to Institute for Human Rights. The new director would be appointed based on applications, but much to the dismay of the Danish People's Party, Morten Kjærum was re-elected as director.

Although Fogh Rasmussen acted in the name of cultural war and spoke about it indirectly, it was not until January 2003 that he fully articulated the ideology of "culture wars" (kulturkamp):

> It is actually my opinion that setting the agenda in the debate of values changes society much more than legislative changes. I speak broadly about culture: It is the outcome of the culture war that decides Denmark's future. Not economic policies. Not technocratic changes to the judicial system. What is decisive is who has the fortune of setting the agenda in the debate about values. (Hardis and Mortensen 2003)

At this time, his ideas were already being enacted and the opposition was still paralyzed by its electoral defeat and the momentum of the new government. "Values," as in the cultural war of values, should be understood from the conventional attribute of the term in a sociological sense, namely "ultimate" value. There is no reason to compromise or go into a sustained, hermeneutical discussion cycle to develop a higher meaning and understanding. Intellectual forms of argument are shot down with metaphors, which appeals directly to the intuitive sense of injustice: The elite has betrayed you, the people; you need to take the power back and, in the process, don't listen to their seductive arguments.

The so-called betrayal concerned primarily the allegedly weak policies on immigrants. Within a few years, the policies for refugees, asylum seekers, and family reunification were tightened so much that Fogh Rasmussen proudly declared that Denmark now had the strictest immigration law in the world. For example, Danes could not marry foreigners younger than 24 and stay in Denmark, and only with some difficulty foreigners younger than 28. Particularly non-westerners, a majority of whom were Muslims, were targeted. In the drafting of some of these laws, it was directly stated that their forms of living were incongruent with Danish values (Hervik 2011). This declaration on difference and incompatibility are core ingredients in neonationalism and neoracism (ibid.), or radical right-wing politics (Mudde 2007). The new radical right-wing parties in other Western European countries are also radical in the language they employ to confront their political opponents and the political project they promote and defend. Consequently, they were far ahead of the political opposition and enjoyed overwhelming popular support.

Arming for the Information Warfare

In 1998, the Parliamentary election was won narrowly and surprisingly by the Social Democrats. After the election loss, Anders Fogh Rasmussen took over as chairman of his party, the Liberals. For the next three years, he prepared for the eventual takeover of power in the next election (which ended up being November 2001). A key effort in this preparation was to hire professional media relations people and to learn the background and ropes of President Bill Clinton's and Prime Minister Tony Blair's news management, not least their use of strategic spin communication represented by the work of Gould (1998) and Giddens (1998). Although Fogh Rasmussen never stated this, he seemed keenly aware that no war could be won without winning the media.

At the same time, it was clear that a revolution in political communication had started with heavy reliance on spin doctors and political commentators. This type of political communication uses sports journalism and court journalism as models: Who wins, who advances, who is wounded, and who capitulates short of completing their goals, counting the losses in terms of numbers.

Today, it is clear that Fogh Rasmussen's heavy investment in the knowledge of political communication, armament of spin personnel, and communications specialists in general can best be seen as a preparation for the cultural war of values. While the cultural war of values started in practice, Fogh Rasmussen's new government hired spin doctors, one for each cabinet member, and devised new news rules for the government's relationship with the press. Media training of politicians exploded and most ministers would not deliver sound bites for the news until their spin doctors had handed them their usual three metaphors or punch lines.

Most of the so-called spin doctors and communication experts were former journalists, male and from the blue segment of the political spectrum.

Spin is the act of formulating rhetoric through a certain angle on the truth in the media by someone with a certain political interest to further (Press 2002), or more generally to present your case, your position, your company, or your party in the most favorable light. Spin strategists are always aware of opposing views as they try to set the agenda. One of the more famous and long-lasting spins is the idea that "Either you are with us, or you are with the terrorists," an example that also shows how moralizing successful spin is (for fuller analysis, see Hervik 2011).

Stig Hjarvard has argued that value-based politics have evolved so much and become so salient that news media and politics have become so integrated that they can no longer be understood separately. This process, which he calls "mediatization" (Hjarvard 2008), started in the late 1990s and reached its first peak with the Muhammad Cartoons in 2005.

Cultural War of Values and the Muhammad Cartoon Publications

Since the late 1990s, online advertisement had sent printed newspapers into a downward spiral in sold copies and money earned. In Denmark, two new free newspapers *MetroExpress* and *Urban* made their début in 2001. By 2006, free dailies had captured close to 60 percent of the market, adding to the damage already done by the electronic news media. In response to this challenge, the largest established newspapers turned to values and opinions as a way to sell papers. Offering an often morality-based opinion in editorials, front-page stories, and invited opinion pieces, these newspapers echoed the political parties with some nuances and variation (Hjarvard 2008).

A few months after the government of Prime Minister Anders Fogh Rasmussen verbally declared a war of values in the weekly *Weekendavisen* in 2003, the largest Danish daily newspaper *Morgenavisen Jyllands-Posten* decided to join the strategy. With the new emphasis on values and "culture war," *Jyllands-Posten* decided, in the summer of 2003, to widen the concept of culture from high culture to include "habits, ways of thinking, and ways of life" and to debate culture (Elkjær and Bertelsen 2006). According to journalistic chief editor Jørn Mikkelsen, they based their priorities on the same focal points as the government:

"Danish Broadcasting Corporation (public service station), Islam, and ex-communists" (Elkjær and Bertelsen 2006).

To carry out the shift from traditional coverage of high culture to value-based cultural journalism, *Jyllands-Posten* brought home its correspondent in Moscow, Flemming Rose, in April 2004, to serve as cultural editor. Under his leadership, Islam received more articulated critical attention than it had during the Mona Sheikh story of 2001, although Rose had already written powerful editorials as part of the "culture war" against left-wingers.[5] Rose's promotion was an extra step to the right, noted in an internal survey made by *Jyllands-Posten* in 2004.

Conclusion

The cultural war of values incorporates a neonationalist defense of Danish "cultural values" such as democracy and freedom of speech, which are actually not specific to Denmark. The solutions offered to problems related to immigration, migrant presence, poverty, unemployment, and feminist demands for gender equality often center on restoring authority based on family values, national values, and (to some extent) male power (Hervik 2012b). The emphasis on values, cultural difference, and incompatibility can be seen as a new moral logic of exclusion and inclusion: one that constructs a national, or "Western," community pitted against a minority of non-western mostly Muslim minorities. In Balibar's words, the logic behind the use of these categories in the mediated political debates is that a "we-group" emerges by promoting itself through its opposite, which it negates. This group does its identity work by opposing the "cultural other," or establishing "itself as the other's other" (Balibar 2005). On their part, these Muslim minority others make up a category of people (not a group), who do not identify with this image (Harvik 2002). One expression of this is the eager military engagement in Iraq and Afghanistan. Such activist foreign policy rests on the neoconservative premise that there can be no moral equivalency. The example makes clear that the logic that embraces the neocolonial idea of Western superiority is revived (Huntington 1993, 1996), this time in terms of "cultural superiority" (Blaut 1992, Hannerz 1999).

Yet, building the nation's psychological bonding through aggressive policy making, confrontational media coverage, military presence in Muslim countries, and framed within a classic populist scenario of elite pitted against ordinary folks is not exclusively a neoracist matter, even though it builds on a hierarchization or inferiorization of Muslim others, which is used to control and deny their presence. Instead, the moral identities proliferating in the Danish public sphere are fundamentally anti-politically correct, antimulticulturalist, and anti-Marxist as confrontation is also directed at political adversaries using the same fighting spirit rhetoric as used when talking about Muslim minorities. The social construction of thick minority identities can only be understood in relation to the cultural war of value strategy aimed at domestic political opponents.

Notes and Bibliography

Notes

1. Parts of this chapter were previously presented at "Closing off the Folkhem? Right-Wing Populism and the Politics of Xenophobia in the North" organized by Peter A. Kraus (University of Helsinki) and Pasi Saukkonen (University of Helsinki) at Helsinki University, December 14, 2011 as a CEREN workshop (The Centre for Research on Ethnic Relations and Nationalism at the Swedish School of Social Science at the University of Helsinki). The authors are thankful for all the questions and comments from the different audiences.
2. N. F. S. Grundtvig (1783–1872) is one of the most influential and important figures in formulating Danish cultural nationalism in the second half of the 19th century. Grundtvig was, among other things, a politician, pastor, poet, historian, and author.
3. This cohort later joined forces with members of the Danish People's Party and other radical, if not extremist, right populists, the *Jyllands-Posten* foundation and the controversial Saxo Bank to form the Danish Free Speech Society (*Trykkefrihedsselskabet*, Free Speech Society) in 2004. This anti-Islamic association, which has popularly been coined the Danish Tea Party Movement, played a dominant role in the Danish media coverage of the Muhammad Cartoon Conflict of 2005 and 2006. In a study, Berg and Hervik concluded that this debate was far more confrontational and crass, and, hence, devastating, than the actual act of publishing the cartoons on September 30, 2005 (2007). Methodologically and epistemologically, this underscores the importance of

separating the actual events from the stories of these events (Hervik 2011, 2012a, 2012b).

4. When Anders Fogh Rasmussen became NATO's secretary general, Lars Løkke Rasmussen took over as Prime Minister. Løkke Rasmussen, thus, became the third Prime Minister with the surname Rasmussen. This name is fairly common in Denmark and the three individuals are unrelated family-wise, even in the extended meaning of the term family.

5. Rose had been a left-winger like many other neoconservatives (Hervik 2008).

Bibliography

Balibar, E. 2005. "Difference, Otherness, Exclusion." *Parallax* 11 (1): 19–34.

Banks, M. and A. Gingrich (eds). 2006. "Neo-Nationalism in Europé and Beyond." In *Neo-Nationalism in Europe and Beyond: Perspectives from Social Anthropology*, 1–26. Oxford: Berghahn Books.

Berg, Clarissa and P. Hervik. 2007. "Muhammad krisen. En politisk kamp i dansk journalistik." *AMID Working Paper Series* 62/2007, Aalborg: CoMID Publications.

Blaut, J. 1992. "The Theory of Cultural Racism." *Antipode* 24 (4): 289–99.

Boe, C. S. and P. Hervik. 2008. "Integration Through Insult." In *Transnational Media Events. The Mohammed Cartoons and the Imagined Clash of Civilizations*, edited by E. Eide, K. Risto, and A. Phillips, 213–34. Gothenburg: Nordicom.

Døving, C. A. 2007. "Medierne og 'den kollektive muslim'." *Politiken* (Feature article).

Elkjær, J. and A. Bertelsen. 2006. "Kulturkamp på kulturgangen." *Journalisten* 5, March 15. Accessed October 10, 2012. http://www.journalisten.dk/kulturkamp-pa-kulturgangen

Fairclough, N. 2006. *Language and Globalization*. London: Routledge.

Forsvaret. n.d. *Forsvarets Mission og Vision*. Accessed August 6, 2012. http://forsvaret.dk/FKO/Documents/FKO/Forsvarets_MVs.pdf

Giddens, A. 1998. *The Third Way. The Renewal of Social Democracy*. Cambridge: Polity.

Gingrich, A. 2006. "Nation, Status and Gender in Trouble? Exploring Some Contexts and Characteristics of Neo-Nationalism in Western Europe." In *Neo-Nationalism in Europe and Beyond: Perspectives from Social Anthropology*, edited by A. Gingrich and M. Banks, 29–49. Oxford: Berghahn Books.

Gingrich, A. and M. Banks (eds). 2006. *Neo-Nationalism in Europe and Beyond: Perspectives from Social Anthropology*. Oxford: Berghahn Books.

Gould, P. 1998. *The Unfinished Revolution: How the Modernisers Saved the Labour Party*. London: Abacus.

Gullestad, M. 2006. *Plausible Prejudice. Everyday Experiences and Social Images of Nation, Culture and Race*. Oslo: Universitetsforlaget.

Hannerz, U. 1999. "Världsbild, kultursyn, medborgarskap." In *Globalisering: Demokrati-utredningens forskarvolym*, Vol. 9, 365–83. Stockholm: Statens Offentliga Utredningar (SOU).

Hansen, H. F. 2005. "Evaluation in and of Public-Sector Reform: The Case of Denmark in a Nordic Perspective." *Scandinavian Political Studies* 28 (4): 323–47.

Hansen, L. 2002. "Sustaining Sovereignty: The Danish Approach to Europe." In *European Integration and National Identity. The Challenge of the Nordic States*, edited by L. Hansen and O. Wæver, 50–87. London: Routledge.

Hardis, A. and H. Mortensen. 2003. "Kulturkamp." *Weekendavisen*, January 17.

Hervik, P. 1999. *Den generende forskellighed. Danske svar på den stigende multikulturalisme*. Copenhagen: Hans Reitzels Forlag.

———. 2011. *The Annoying Difference. The Emergence of Danish Neonationalism, Neoracism, and Populism in the Post-1989 World*. New York: Berghahn Books.

———. 2012a. "The Danish Muhammad Cartoon Conflict." *Current Themes in IMER Research 13*, Malmö Institute for Studies of Migration, Diversity and Welfare (MIM): Malmö University.

———. 2012b. "Ending Tolerance as a Solution to Incompatibility: The Danish 'Crisis of Multiculturalism'." *European Journal of Cultural Studies* 15 (2): 211–25. (Theme issue edited by A. Lentin and G. Titley.)

Hervik, P. and M. Rytter. 2004. "Med ägteskab i focus." In *Ægtefællesammenføring i Danmark*, Udredning nr. 1, Chapter 6, 131–60. Copenhagen: Institute for Human Rights.

Hervik, P. and S. Boisen. 2013. "Danish Coverage of 22/7." *Nordic Journal of Migration Research* 3 (September): 179–186. (Theme issue edited by P. Hervik and S. Meret.)

Hjarvard, S. 2006. "Religion og Politik i Mediernes Offentlighed." In *Gudebilleder. Ytringsfrihed og Religion i en Globaliseret Verden*, edited by L. Christoffersen, 44–71. Copenhagen: Tiderne Skifter.

———. 2008. "The Mediatization of Religion: A Theory of the Media as Agents of Religious Change." In *Northern Lights: 2008 Yearbook of Film & Media Studies*. Bristol: Intellect Press.

Huntington, S. 1993. "The Clash of Civilizations?" *Foreign Affairs* 72 (3): 22–49.

———. 1996. *The Clash of Civilizations and the Remaking of World Order*. New York: Simon & Schuster.

Hvenegård-Lassen, K. 2002. *På lige fod*. PhD Diss. Department of Nordic Philology/Minority Studies, Copenhagen University, Copenhagen, Denmark.

Kavolis, V. 1977. "Moral Cultures and Moral Logics." *Sociological Analysis* 38 (4): 332–44.

Klausen, J. 2009. *The Cartoons That Shook the World*. Connecticut: Yale University Press.

Linde-Laursen, A. 2007. "Is Something Rotten in the State of Denmark? The Muhammad Cartoons and Danish Political Culture." *Contemporary Islam* 1 (3): 265–74.

Lykkeberg, R. 2008. *Kampen om sandhederne*. Copenhagen: Gyldendal.

Miles, R. 1993. *Racism After "Race Relations."* London: Routledge.

Mudde, C. 2007. *Populist Radical Right Parties in Europe*. Cambridge: Cambridge University Press.

Møller, B. and L. Togeby. 1999. *Oplevet diskrimination. En undersøgelse blandt etniske minoriteter*. Copenhagen: The Board for Ethnic Equality.

Nævnet for Etnisk Ligestilling (Board for Ethnic Equality). n.d. *Nævnet for etnisk Ligestillingshistorie, herunder arbejdet med begreber og indsatsområder*. Copenhagen: Board for Ethnic Equality.

Press, B. 2002. *Spin This! All the Ways We Don't Tell the Truth*. New York: Pocket Books.

Trågårdh, L. 2002. "Sweden and the EU: Welfare State Nationalism and the Spectre of 'Europe'." In *European Integration and National Identity. The Challenge of the Nordic States*, edited by L. Hansen and O. Wæver, 130–81. London: Routledge.

9

Becoming a Minority: Ethno-Manufacturing in The Netherlands*

Paul Mutsaers, Hans Siebers, and Arie de Ruijter

Introduction

Brubaker recently reviewed the scope of nationalist and ethno-political reactions to the current economic upheaval and observed that nationalism and politicized ethnicity are now endemic to modern polities and "chronically available form[s] of discourse, policy, and practice" (2011, 105). Theorizing about the various intersections of the economy, the nation state, political ethnicity, culture, class, race, and capitalism is nothing new, of course, and many perspectives are taken in contemporary social sciences and the humanities. Some focus on the role of ethnicity in the realization of surplus value on commodity markets and predominantly see it as a marketing principle or even a commodity in itself, as "ethnic populations" remake themselves in the image of the cooperation (Comaroff and Comaroff 2009). Others concentrate on the protection of the

* We owe our gratitude to Marjolein Dennissen for her effort to collect data for one of our research projects.

national economy and domestic goods and services in times of global capitalism. Others again work on the ethnic and racial segmentation of the labor market and of the working classes (e.g., Bonacich 1972) or on the race/class nexus in general (e.g., Gilroy 1987). And there are those who ground their work in the political economy of labor migration (cf. Castles and Kosack 1972; Miles 1984). We are far removed, in other words, from an abdication of the effort to understand the interrelation of the economy and various identity forms (e.g., ethnicities, national communities, religious enclaves, and the like). This is an important topic and for good reasons. The heart of progressive politics is to take seriously the inner connections between economic differences and—genuine or putative—ethnic, cultural, or racial differences (Michaels 2006).

Cultural issues must, thus, "be embedded within a wider framework of political and economic questions" (Siebers 2004, 301). In this chapter, we set ourselves a modest aim, namely to comprehend how matters of ethnicity, politics, and the economy interrelate in The Netherlands by looking at the direct impact of migrant-hostile politics on ethnic boundaries in the labor market and in educational settings. So we are going to show, briefly, that migrant-hostile statements by Dutch politicians trickle down, so to speak, to the work floor and fuel ethnic boundaries between colleagues and students. As such, we show that migrant-hostile politicians are complicit in turning such work and educational spaces into fertile breeding grounds of what we call "ethno-manufacturing"; the manufacturing of ethnicity out of raw materials (migrant-hostile scripts) into a dominant factor of social organization. We argue that separating these domains of analysis (i.e., the economy, politics, and culture/ethnicity) can be hazardous as it may contribute to the belief that if politicians, or other central actors, would stop engaging in "culturespeak," this will miraculously solve the troubles that cultural minorities experience (Hannerz 1999) in, say, a certain economic niche. Granted, discourse is powerful, but culturespeak (which, nowadays, basically boils down to speaking about "other" cultures in the negative) is not just floating. It is exactly becoming powerful because it has enduring effects and inclines toward institutional anchorage and will sediment in the economy if it is around long enough. Weber has already strongly argued in his time that "the belief in group affinity, regardless of whether it has any objective foundation, can have important consequences" (Weber et al. 1978, 389).

Ethnicity is not merely a belief in being part of an ethnic group or being different from other members of society. Weber's quote points to important consequences in terms of monopolistic closure (Jenkins 2008), that is, the monopolization of economic resources and opportunities (Wimmer 2013). These real consequences, thus, refer to the distribution of resources, such as jobs and career opportunities, giving ethnic in-group members an edge over those who are considered to belong to an ethnic out-group. These real consequences are easily overlooked by those who work from a radical constructivist paradigm. They stress that ethnicity/culture is "always" processual, situational, optional, fluid, and in flux (cf. Wimmer 2008, 2009). In its desire to ward off essentialism, the subtext of radical constructivist work is that individual choice, meaning-making, and fluidity "must" prevail even in cases of stable and solid boundaries; they transform situationalism from an epistemological stance into an ontological absolute. The epistemological openness to subjective interpretations, fluidity, and flux in such approaches is conflated with an obstinate belief that such interpretations "must" be fluid and constantly in flux. Such approaches discard any indication that such interpretations may be structured by very solid and fixed boundaries, imposed by or preserved in harsh economic realities. Ethnicity is, however, not merely "a cognitive scheme of little consequence to the life chances of individuals, or one individual 'identity choice' among many others" (Wimmer 2009, 253, emphasis original). Radical constructivism prevails in narrative approaches to ethnicity in the labor market (cf. Essers and Benschop 2009).

In this chapter, we will first argue that in a way there is an analogy between such radical constructivist thinking and Dutch assimilation politics, although the immediate remark is necessary that Dutch assimilation politics combines such thinking with its exact opposites: communitarianism and structural-functionalism. The argument is based on Bauman's book *Modernity and Ambivalence* (1991) in which he presented his pioneering work on the sociology of assimilation. He argues that the liberal call to minorities to assimilate is fraught with ambivalence and contradictions: "ethnic–religious–cultural strangers are... tempted to embrace the liberal vision of group emancipation (erasing of a collective stigma) as a reward for individual effort of self-improvement and self-transformation" (ibid., 71). But in doing so, a "conservative curse hangs over the liberal project" (ibid.), because assimilation programs request minorities as individuals to denounce communal loyalties only to replace them with a demand of (group-based) cultural conformity to the host society. The ambivalence Bauman (1991) refers to manifests itself in several ways, which we will show in the next section, for it to be important for an understanding of the current situation in The Netherlands, which is discussed in the same section. The third section will be a small intermezzo in which we explain our approach to ethnicity, by elaborating on the ethnic boundary paradigm and the emphasis it puts on the understanding of ethnicity as a political phenomenon. In the section that follows, we show that political statements affect ethnic relations in the labor market (both discursively and materially), despite the "construction of innocence" (Pierce 2003) that Dutch politicians easily hide behind. We are only able to deal in a tentative manner with the direct impact of political discourse on ethnic relations in Dutch institutions and argue that they require more elucidation. Suggestions for future research are given in our conclusions.

Assimilation and Ambivalence

One of the ambivalences of assimilation that Bauman (1991) gave studied attention has already been mentioned: The relation between individuals and communities is highly ambivalent and, therefore, confusing for minorities (as we will show later on, when we briefly discuss that they are sometimes complicit to their own "minorization"). Assimilation "[comes] in the disguise of benevolence" as it "[goes] down in history as a part of the liberal political program of the tolerant and enlightened stance" of the state (ibid., 107). However, although "cultural assimilation [is] an intrinsically individual task and activity, it [is] applied to the community as a whole" (ibid., 142). What's more, "assimilatory success [is] to be assessed and marked individually, but the stigma from which the successful assimilation [is] meant to emancipate [has] been assigned collectively, to the community as a whole" (ibid., 131). (This is, for instance, illustrated by a parliamentary assistant working for the True Fins, who recently proposed to force migrants to wear special identification badges on their sleeves, to make "policing significantly easier." Her proposal resembles the one by Dutch Integration Minister Rita Verdonk [2003–06] to oblige migrants to wear vignettes that symbolize their degree of distinction vis-à-vis society.) And finally, "assimilation [is] a bid on the part of one section of society to exercise a monopolistic right to provide authoritative and binding meaning for all" (Bauman 1991, 105), and it does that through ideas about cultural group belonging-ness endowed with a sort of popular structural-functionalism (Vertovec 2011). Focusing on The Netherlands, the latter implies that Dutch cul-ture is seen as a system, in which all values, cultural practices, and social institutions are part of an integrated whole, a cohesive system based on the necessary interdependence and equilibrium of its parts. In line with radical constructivist thinking, it is, thus, expected from minorities that they shed their cultural affiliations as individuals, only to confront them with group-based Dutch culture. This ambivalence has been translated in The Netherlands in a political program dubbed by Van Houdt et al. (2011) as neoliberal communitarianism.

Second, there is ambivalence in the way Dutch assimilation politics deals with the intersection of culture and economy. It ignores the effects of politics-induced culturalization of minorities on their socio-economic position in society (the "construction of innocence" referred to earlier), but continuously stresses that the under-representation of minorities in the economy is due to their own cultural flaws, imperfections, and their cultural "otherness." We, therefore, sympathize with Rath (1991) who called for a shift from a "minorities" paradigm to a "minorization" para-digm that not only looks at the culturalist argumentation undergirding such minorization but also at the subordinate positions of migrants in terms of distributions of (scarce) resources as its product, referred to earlier and further discussed in the fourth section.

Finally, there is ambivalence in the political representation of, and impact on, ethnicity and culture. It is generally argued in The Netherlands that politicians like Geert Wilders—who is the leader of the Dutch Freedom Party that won 24 of the 150 seats in Parliament in 2010 and maintained 15 of those seats after the 2012 elections—have a right to voice hostility against migrants since they would represent sentiments and views held by a considerable part of the Dutch electorate. In this argument, ethnic distinctions like the one between the majority popula-tion and migrants come first; they are subsequently expressed and rep-resented by politicians like Geert Wilders. Not only does this not square with the apparent fluidity of ethnicity and culture that is initially assumed in assimilation programs, it also ignores the agentic and creative power of ethno-politics. Ethnic categories and ethnic identities are treated as entities that would predate politics, as if they have an autonomous ontology that needs no further explanation. As Wimmer (2009) has shown, these notions are in line with the Herderian heritage of understanding ethnicity as something basically shaped by the particular cultural traits an ethnic group shares and distinguishes it from other ethnic groups, as something quasi-natural or rather primordial (Roosens 1989).

Migrant-Hostile Politics in The Netherlands

It may come as no surprise considering its role as an important colonial power (something which goes virtually undiscussed in contemporary Dutch debate on migration and integration; this should, in fact, not be a parenthetical remark, but we lack space to elaborate upon it in this text) that The Netherlands has known migration throughout its history. It only became an explicit issue in Dutch politics and media with the economic recession and de-industrialization in the 1980s and the mounting unemployment among migrants that followed. These were the days after decades of political construction of the Dutch welfare state. In this line, the Dutch government initially adopted a migrant-friendly position by opening doors for family migrants and refugees as well as by facilitating naturalization processes (Geuijen 2004). Admitted migrants could count on positive governmental action pursuing equal treatment and proportional representation (Entzinger 2003). Only those who lagged behind in terms of institutional participation were targeted by public attention and policy intervention (Rath 1991) aimed at improving this participation (Ministerie van Binnenlandse Zaken 1994). Legal obstacles to participation were removed, soft affirmative action legislation was launched, the government concluded contracts with large firms, and the SME branch organization pledged to take measures to increase the number of ethnic minorities in their labor forces.

Apart from these welfare-state-oriented policies, migrants also became "culturalized" within the framework of multiculturalism. Drawing on the concept of compartmentalized or a pillarized society—a concept used to manage socio-political and cultural differences in Dutch society until the 1960s in which society was split up in three or four pillars/communities (Catholic, Protestant, Socialist and, arguably, also Liberal) each having their own parties, sports clubs, schools, trade unions, churches, and so on—migrants were conceived of as the fifth pillar. They were framed in culturally essentialist terms (Grillo 2003), i.e., as people whose identities are derived from their cultural community membership. These cultural communities were basically understood in Herderian, i.e., in essentialist, static, and systemic terms. Government policies even invested in educational facilities to support migrants' "ethnic–cultural identities."

When the neoliberal agenda after the fall of the Berlin Wall became the leading political reality in The Netherlands of the 1990s—prescribing free markets, privatization, deregulation, and competition between workers—the launching of attacks against welfare-state-oriented policies toward migrants was just a matter of time. The initiative came from Frits Bolkestein, former leader of the right-wing liberal party, The People's Party for Freedom and Democracy (VVD), who came to dominate Dutch politics after 1992. He criticized such policies stating that minorities' "integration" was in a deplorable state (de Volkskrant, 12 September 1991). He voiced an emerging discontent in politics with migrants' isolation (Rath 1991) and their involvement in the so-called "bastard spheres of integration," such as crime and welfare dependency (Engbersen and Gabriëls 1995). In a populist vein, Bolkestein contended that a debate was going on among "ordinary people" who needed to be understood and voiced (Prins 2002). He claimed to speak his mind about the "truth" and the "facts," and considered such truth-speak "typically Dutch." These essentialist claims were followed by outright cultural fundamentalism (Stolcke 1995), claiming that Dutch cultural traditions are incompatible with those of nonwestern migrants (Ghorashi 2010). This notion of cultural incompatibility—and the subsequent call for monoculturalism—has been repeated in various forms by those who followed Bolkestein's lead after the turn of the century, e.g., people like Pim Fortuyn, Rita Verdonk (VVD), Ayaan Hirsi Ali (VVD), and Geert Wilders The Freedom Party (PVV), who came to produce an ever more insulting genre of political discourse. Pim Fortuyn called Islam a "backward culture" (de Volkskrant, 9 February 2002) and various offensive phrases entered the political scene, such as "Moroccan street scum" and "goat fuckers," i.e., Muslims, in the lingo of Theo van Gogh who joined Ayaan Hirsi Ali to produce a film called Submission, with Koran texts painted on a naked mutilated female body that supposedly legitimizes violence against women. Geert

Wilders talks about "skull rag taxes" (taxing headscarves), "hate palaces" (i.e., mosques), "the fascist book" (the Koran), etc. Rob Oudkerk, a social-democrat Amsterdam alderman and former MP coined the term "cunt Moroccans" (*kut Marokkanen*) to depict Moroccan youngsters involved in petty crime. This political discourse (Prins [2002] called it a "new realist" discourse) made it possible that migrant-hostile statements could become ever less circumspect.

Bolkestein and other leading migrant-hostile voices after him, thus, maintained the essentialist notion of migrants that had already taken root since the 1980s, and this continuation can partly explain their success (see also the widespread discontent among left-wing liberals about the ban on any "intercultural" critique imposed by cultural relativism; cf. Wikan 2002 for Norway). There are, however, a few important differences between the previous multiculturalism and the current monoculturalism.

First, the former framed relations between cultural communities in terms of cultural relativism, whereas the latter argues in favor of cultural incompatibility between these communities (cf. Stolcke 1995). In line with these cultural-fundamentalist ideas—that organize "cultures" spatially, each in their own place (8)—migration laws have been introduced that favor territorial closure. In the wake of the Alien Act of 2000, the country is becoming increasingly closed for asylum seekers. The number of asylum applications has significantly dropped from 52,600 in 1997 to 9,700 in 2007 (www.cbs.nl). Any drop in asylum applications and increase in "removals" or "deportations" is welcomed by the minister in charge. Recently, the government has legislated quotas to expel illegal foreigners that instruct the police to proactively track undocumented foreigners, regardless of the proved fact they are offenders. The police are instructed to use ethnic profiling, i.e., to focus their surveillance particularly on those who can be identified as foreigners. On a yearly basis, about 6,000 foreigners are detained without any trial or charge for an average of 76 days (De Nationale Ombudsman 2012), some in prisons in which their health is protractedly undermined (Zembla, January 20, 2012). International institutions like Human Rights Watch (Trouw, April 9, 2003), The Parliamentary Assembly of the Council of Europe (de Volkskrant, October 28, 2006) and The European Court of Human Rights (de Volkskrant, January 12, 2007) have recurrently denounced the Dutch government for systematically violating asylum seekers' human rights. Since 2006, the Integration Act Abroad (WIB) obliges specific groups of migrants to take a test in their home country to assess their knowledge of the Dutch language and customs, before applying for admission (cf. Suvarierol 2012). Human Rights Watch (2008) has denounced the Dutch government for systematically violating human rights with the enactment of WIB. Likewise, the European Court of Justice has reproved the new Dutch policies on immigration and integration (de Leeuw and van Wichelen 2012).

Second, monocultural (assimilation-) politics stress the importance of the individual responsibility of migrants. The Civic Integration Newcomers Act (*Wet Inburgering Nieuwkomers*) was issued in 1998 which obliges non-European Union newcomers to take a 12-month integration course, i.e., 600 hours of Dutch language training, civic education, and preparation for the Dutch labor market (Jopke 2007). Integration policies have become ever more coercive and have shifted attention from civic to cultural integration. Assessments focus on the appropriation of Dutch norms and values (Jopke 2007; Ministerie van VROM 2007a). Since 2006, migrants are obliged to pay for the courses in full and take "their own responsibility" to assimilate into Dutch culture. The same holds true for the WIB.

Finally, whereas multiculturalism was principally focused on the institutional participation of migrants (in education, the labor market, etc.), assimilation politics are endowed with a structural-functionalism (see Vertovec 2011) that assumes that if one part of the cultural system (seen as an assemblage of values, cultural practices, and social institutions) is "perceived to be vulnerable or expunged, the integrity of the entire system is considered to be in danger" (ibid., 245). Hence, the persistent worry about migrants' institutional "and" cultural participation. By this logic, the two are inextricably bound up with one another. Evidence abounds of the political belief in this connection. The 2003–06 Integration Minister Rita Verdonk repeatedly stated that migrants' problems in the labor market correlate with their "deviating" norms and values. The Rutte I government (2010–12) proposed to make citizens' rights on social security conditional upon talking the right language (Dutch) and wearing the right clothes (no burqas or veils) in job application interviews, aiming to reduce the number of ethnic minorities on benefit (NCR Handelsblad, January 29, 2012; SCP 2012). It is in this context that we must understand the communitarianist policies that have come to play an important role. In line with the call for a revival of "Dutch national awareness" (Paul Scheffer, NCR Handelsblad, January 29, 2000), the government has launched several initiatives to reinforce culture along nationalist lines, including the nationalist rewriting of official history textbooks and the official proclamation of a canon of Dutch history. Advised by the communitarianist writer Amitai Etzioni (2001), Prime Minister Jan Peter Balkenende (2002–10) made the revitalization of Dutch norms and values a key policy objective. Cultural fault lines are no longer accepted and migrants need to identify with what is typical to Dutch society, its rituals and key values (Ministerie van VROM 2007b, 14–17). Their assimilation into Dutch culture is symbolized in a naturalization ceremony, symbolizing the culturalization of citizenship (Verkaaik 2010).

In sum, there has been a shift in The Netherlands from multiculturalism (aiming at integration) to a monoculturalism (aiming at assimilation) that aims at migrants' institutional and cultural participation and blurs boundaries between institutional and cultural life to the point of dissolving. However, if we look at truth-speak data, the fact remains that after more than a decade of assimilation programs involving massive numbers of migrants, disparities in labor market participation between the "ethno-national majority" and "non-Western minorities" in The Netherlands persist, with unemployment figures (2001–11) fluctuating between 3 and 5 percent for the former and between 8 and 16 percent for the latter. Over these years, unemployment figures for "non-Western" migrants are on average four times higher than for non-migrants (CBS 2012), and discrimination in the labor market is endemic (Nievers and Andriessen 2010). Apparently, if societal participation was open to migrants provided they would assimilate culturally, these programs aiming at assimilation have not been able to deliver.

We argue that explanations can not only be sought in the wicked combination of radical constructivist thinking on the one hand (e.g., fluid perspectives on culture) and structural-functionalist thinking on the other (essentialist notions of culture as an integrated system), we must also focus on an unasked question: What is the impact of migrant-hostile discourses as embraced by Dutch politicians of various persuasions on ethnic relations and disparities in the workplace? And how do cultural fundamentalist and essentialist notions endure in the economy, that is, how do they become institutionally anchored in various institutions such as the labor market and our educational system? These are big questions that admit of no easy answers. Let us first say a few words about how we approach ethnicity, and then give some insight into the production or "manufacturing" of ethnic identities and closure under the aegis of Dutch ethno-politics, on the basis of various research projects carried out in large Dutch organizations, including the Dutch Tax Administration, the Dutch Ministry of Agriculture, the Dutch Police and a university of Applied Sciences.

Ethnic Boundaries

Already in the eighteenth century, Johann Gottfried von Herder portrayed ethnic groups as bounded entities, each with a specific culture, a dense network of solidarity, and a shared identity (Wimmer 2009). This view has informed much structural-functionalist work in anthropology and highlights the various cultural elements that are shared by a bounded ethnic community in a systemic, stable, and consistent way, and that differentiates the community from other ethnic or national communities. Weber's definition of ethnic groups as "human groups that entertain a subjective belief in their common descent" (1978, 389) constituted a rupture with this Herderian view. In his *Economy and Society*, Weber pointed out that the basic issue of ethnic groups is not their assumed shared culture. By contrast, it is the constructed "belief" of having a common descent that differentiates ethnic groups.

It was only years later that Herder's heritage would again be seriously contested, this time by Scandinavian anthropologists led by Fredrik Barth. They argued in favor of a focus on "the ethnic 'boundary' that defines the group, not the cultural stuff that it encloses" (Barth 1969, 15, emphasis original). Years later, Barth (2007, 10) commented:

> Contrary to the common-sense reifications of people's own discourses, and the rhetoric of ethnic activists as well as anthropology textbooks, ethnic identity is determined not by massive facts of shared culture and shared history, but instead in each case by a more limited set of criteria. It

can also be deeply affected if it is subject to the manipulations of political entrepreneurs.

Barth added to Weber's work that "the belief in common ancestry is likely to be a 'consequence' of collective political action rather than its 'cause'" (Jenkins 2008, 10, emphases original). He coined ethnicity as the outcome of political action, as a deeply political phenomenon.

Finally, and this is a repetition of earlier sections, ethnic boundary research not only needs to take on board political processes that incite ethnic boundary constructions, but also economic issues in terms of ethnic inequality in access to vital resources. Since ethnic boundary research induces an interest in political acts of boundary construction "and" in inequalities in resource distribution, we argue that taking a perspective from political economy will be fruitful to study ethnicity in the contemporary Dutch society. In short, we, thus, argue in favor of an approach to ethnicity in terms of ethnic boundary constructions that avoids the pitfalls of both Herderian structural-functionalism and radical constructivism. It focuses on how ethnic identity and ethnic exclusion or closure are produced as well as the political–economic conditions and outcomes of such ethno-manufacturing in terms of political discourses, power processes, and inequality in access to resources.

Ethno-manufacturing in Dutch Work and Educational Settings

Recent qualitative (e.g., Siebers 2009; Siebers and Dennissen 2012) and quantitative (Siebers 2010) studies have demonstrated that migrant-hostile discourses in Dutch media and politics directly fuel ethnic conflicts and closure in career developments in the Dutch tax administration and several other workplaces, putting ethnic minorities both at a discursive and material disadvantage. These discourses are, in other words, a direct producer of ethnic inequality in the labor market, and manufacture ethnicity into an important organizing principle in the social fabric. Through structural equation modeling, it is shown "that tensions among colleagues triggered by public events that express this discourse fuel the career insecurities of migrant employees in particular" and "have negative career consequences for them," measured by salary scales (Siebers 2010, 475). The dominant discourse on migrants and migration in Dutch politics has carelessly passed into everyday language in work settings.

The impact of dominant discourse on work relations involving employees with a Muslim and/or Moroccan background clearly surfaced in one of the projects we carried out (cf. Siebers and Dennissen 2012). One of our respondents, a female second generation migrant with a Moroccan background (24 years old) said:

> Every time I came to work in the afternoon I found a printed newspaper article put on the table—about Moroccans, about foreigners, about asylum seekers. Every time it had a negative message…. After two months my [majority—eds] colleague told me: "Yes, you cunt Moroccans ruin everything all the time over here." I had to think about this sentence for two days before it dawned on me. Did she really say that?… "You." Was I ruining everything? I do not even have the time to do so…. Then it was quiet for a month and then it came repeatedly: "You Moroccans… I am sorry to say, but those cunt Moroccans, terrible people, I don't mind if they get shot" (Interview 2011).

Nearly all our informants acknowledged that such events of ethnic tensions only refer to specific moments. They are incidents that express a pattern, but do not occur on a daily basis; rather, only when triggered by events in the media and politics. Ethnic boundaries are manufactured out of raw materials, i.e., migrant-hostile scripts provided by politicized media discourses, but with a lasting impact on feelings of insecurity of employees with a Muslim and Moroccan background, nourished over time by media input.

The passage quoted above is directly linked to the utterances of the Amsterdam alderman referred to earlier, who coined the term "cunt Moroccans." However, we also came across usages of gender-centric discourses on Islam as produced by Islam critics Geert Wilders and Ayaan Hirsi Ali (see the film *Submission* referred to earlier in the chapter). As a result, our female respondents are repeatedly confronted with questions from majority colleagues about their headscarf or about the role of their fathers and brothers who are portrayed as purveyors of arranged marriages (insinuating that Muslim women are oppressed by their brothers, husbands, and fathers). Several of our respondents told us that they decided to quit their job or abstain from asking for promotion due to these kinds of remarks and questions. Again, ethnic boundaries entail exclusion from resources.

Our respondents used a war-like language like having to "defend" themselves or to "fight off" the remarks by majority colleagues triggered by the dominant discourse in Dutch media and politics. This war-like language is readily retrievable from PVV (Geert Wilders's Freedom Party) sources, which features words such as *tuigdorpen* (re-education camps for "Moroccan street scum") and proposals to send urban commandos to events of social unrest involving Moroccan youngsters. Inspired by Geert Wilders's political allies, the Rotterdam city government has installed "city commandos" whose task it is to enter migrants' houses to make sure that they talk Dutch at home. Recently, after a loss of nine seats in the 2012 parliamentary elections, Geert Wilders thanked his outgoing MPs for fighting "side-by-side in the trenches for years," clearly invoking images of war and combat (PVV Newsletter, September 2012).

These hostile images directly fuel ethnic boundaries that are manufactured on the spot infused by such war-like political language. This is illustrated by a fragment from an interview with Meryem (all names of respondents presented here are pseudonyms), a woman with a Turkish background, who we interviewed in a research project in another Dutch public organization:

> I did very well [in the organization—eds].… I've been working here for 20 years and I managed pretty well to climb the ladder. I was on my way to the highest level. […] But all of a sudden everything changed. I wondered whether it had something to do with the political climate. Is it because of the new government [the PVV had recently come to support the government—eds]? Are people within this organization so easily manipulated by political pressure? Promotion plans were aborted and my superiors distanced themselves from me. Was I a threat? Did people become afraid of me? […] One of the things I'll never forget is that my superior told me "you and me, we have been enemies for centuries already." I soon realized that this was about Christianity and Islam. I am not a Muslim; I had never read the Koran. But then I bought one and read it, twice! I started reading about the prophet Mohammed. I wanted to. For nights I had been awake, crying, considering to "go back" to Turkey, where I was not even born. I am born in The Netherlands. (Field notes 2011)

188   Paul Mutsaers, Hans Siebers, and Arie de Ruijter

Before we had this conversation with Meryem, we only knew her from hearsay. This was in the heyday of her career, when her colleagues unanimously considered her a "high potential" with a promising career, which is exceptional for people with a migration background in this organization. But this changed around the same period her superior invoked a sort of Huntingtonian clash-of-civilizations thesis, often found in Geert Wilders' culture-clash discourse:

> To the cultural relativists, the Shariah-socialists, I would proudly say, "Our Western culture is superior to Islamic culture." Or to quote Wafa Sultan when she compared the Western culture with Islam: "It's not a clash of civilizations; it's a clash between barbarity and reason." (Speech of Geert Wilders in Copenhagen, June 15, 2009, retrieved from http://www.pvv.nl)

After a year on leave, Meryem was allowed to return to the organization, albeit to another location where she was assigned the role of team leader of a team that was soon to be dismantled due to cutbacks and reorganizations. Thus, her new assignment was a very low profile and ungrateful one. In short, Meryem's supervisors took over the political war-like discourse and revised her promotion plans drastically. As a result of such ethnic boundary drawing, Meryem herself became inspired by Islam and her Turkish background, inventing her own Muslim and Turkish identity due to such ethnic boundary constructions. Hers is a clear case of a "thickening" of culture due to ethnic boundary construction, not the other way around as a Herderian approach would have it.

It is also a clear case of migrants' complicity in their own minorization, so to speak. In basically all our labor market studies, we came across instances in which ethnic minorities tried to resist essentialization of their identities (by presenting themselves as professionals, for instance; i.e., by directing their identity work toward professionalism rather than ethnicity or culture), but often did not succeed. In fact, they would very often speak about themselves as "*allochtones*" (which is the word used in Dutch to denote non-western ethnic minorities), or about Turks or Moroccans in the sense of "this is how we do things." One particular case springs to mind: A Turkish–Dutch police officer is invited by his managers to give a course to his colleagues on honor killings. He decides to take an autobiographical approach and tells his co-workers how he had almost killed his sister-in-law to protect the honor of the family. The urge that he felt, he said, is ingrained in Turkish culture and is something that all Turks feel (see Mutsaers, forthcoming, for further information about this case of self-minoritization)

Ethnic boundaries are also found in Dutch educational settings. In a university for applied sciences, we asked both students and teachers to keep a diary for a week and write about their experiences with ethnic diversity in school. Some manifestations of migrant-hostility surfaced, including this one:

> I'm infinitely annoyed by the fact that our school is hundred percent pro-multiculturalism/Islam. Everywhere I look, I'm confronted with Islam. If not in the Hallal-corner in the canteen, then by the over-abundance of veiled girls in the hallways. I find such a way of female suppression disgusting. This school also propagates Islam by allowing an Islamic students association to distribute roses to students at the birthday of warlord Mohammed, without telling them that these roses have a religious/ideological connotation. Well, I've also been intimidated by guys with an Islamic persuasion, because I was wearing an Israel pin on my jacket. When telling this to security, I was asked to take off the pin. They rather capitulate than act against those who neglect the values that are lived by at this school, according to the statutes. In short, I am getting sick and tired of the pro-multicultural policy of this school. (Diary of a majority student, 2011)

Being an active PVV member, it is not surprising that the PVV discourse plays a central role for Christian, indicated by words like "capitulation," "warlord Mohammed," and "100 percent pro-Islam." In our interview with him, he frequently deployed the term "Islamization," dominant in Wilders' repertoire, referring to the school's "self-Islamization." His PVV-inspired discourse fuels ethnic conflicts with fellow students with a migration background. Exemplary is the following, shared with us by one of Christian's classmates (male first generation migrant from Morocco):

> He [Christian—eds] has a very strong opinion about Islam and Muslims in general. It's his right to think that way, I would say, but what disturbs me is that he gives expressions of it at random moments, often in the form of a "Hitler-like speech" [original in English—eds]. At a certain point I was walking away from the lecture-hall with some fellow students and then I heard him shouting "there goes Fouad with his disciples." (Diary of a minority student, 2011)

In the interview, Fouad said that he had never associated himself with Muslims or with Islam, that he attended Christian primary and secondary schools and preferred to see himself as an individual. Nonetheless, he was constantly framed by Christian and others as a member and representative of an Islamic group. Here, we have another instance of ethnic differences and cultural elements being invented on the spot to construct an ethnic boundary, inspired by dominant discourse in politics. In quoting Barth, Bauman (2000, 177) keenly observed that "borders do not acknowledge and register the already existing estrangement; they are drawn, as a rule, before the estrangement is brought about." These boundaries have serious consequences in terms of access to resources. Fouad told us that they impeded him in team work, an important aspect throughout the curriculum. Such experiences made him feel highly uncomfortable and urged him to distance himself from his fellow students.

Conclusions

We argue that the migrant-hostility (Siebers 2010) of which we have given some impressions here is gauged by its capacity to operate across a broad range of political opinion (cf. the recent contributions of the labor party to the criminalization of illegality) and is no longer conjunctural but structurally present in The Netherlands. Its discourse triggers a pattern of events occurring in interactions between migrants and non-migrants at work and in college. The boundaries that are drawn between them have serious consequences, not only emotionally but also in terms of access to vital resources such as jobs, career opportunities, and study success. Even for those who have to bear the brunt of these boundaries, they are difficult to escape from, and we have come across several cases in which a good deal of "self-minorization" is going on (which is also an important issue in Bauman 1991). We did not explicitly focus on the role of minority leaders in this self-minoritization, but we do not have indications that they play an important role in the experiences of migrants in the work and educational settings we have studied.

Ethnic boundaries (ethnic identity "and" ethnic exclusion) are, thus, manufactured under the influence of a dominant discourse on migrants and migration that has emerged in Dutch media and politics. This discourse provides both the raw materials and the design for this ethno-manufacturing between people in society. Its impact is visible in the culturalization of migrants that started in the 1980s in the framework of multiculturalism and has continued to the present day in a monocultural draft of cultural essentialism. The ideas colleagues and students have about migrants are framed in these Herderian (cf. Wimmer 2009) or popular structural-functionalist (Vertovec 2011) notions of migrants as members of cultural communities and bearers of ethnically specific norms and values they would bring to work or to school. This culturalist framing of migrants allows for the construction of innocence on the part of majority members and politicians (cf. Pierce 2003) from the 1980s onward: people are responsible for their own lives and if they would only abandon their own culture (the liquid or fluid conception of culture held by radical constructivists) and assimilate into the Dutch mainstream, the national heart could again beat as one and inequality would be something of the past. We have already pointed to the wickedness of this idea, in the sense that it combines highly liquid/fluid notions with highly rigid/essentialist notions of culture.

To explain and understand in more depth both the emergence of the migrant-hostile discourse and its consequences in terms of fueling ethno-manufacturing in relations between people in society, we argue for the need of a political–economic analysis of both their conditions and outcomes. Here, we need to link up with earlier political–economic work on ethnicity and race in the labor market that proliferated in the 1970s (e.g., Bonacich 1972; Castles and Kosack 1972) and 1980s (e.g., Shulman 1984; Williams 1987) and that points to the ethnic and racial segmentation of the labor market and the working classes. We would like to make three contributions to that literature. First, our approach points out we need not only to engage in macro analysis, but also in mezo- and micro analyses of how ethnicization processes work out in organizations and between colleagues and students. Second, earlier political–economic work on ethnicity in the labor market has typically taken the ontological status of ethnic groups for granted (Bonacich, for instance, talks about "antagonism between 'ethnic groups'," 1972, 547, emphasis added). We argue, though, that an analysis of ethnic exclusion from a perspective of political economy needs to explain the manufacturing of these ethnic groups and cleavages instead of taking them for granted. Third, we claim in line with this that we need to take seriously the role that a new generation of ethno-political entrepreneurs (i.e., migrant-hostile politicians of various political persuasions) plays in the erection of ethnic boundaries in the labor market, where they acquire enduring relevance in terms of economic disparities.

It deserves to be noted that we do not ask for a return to multiculturalism. We concur with Tripathy and Padmanabhan (this volume) that multicultural politics already developed the idea of "minority cultures" as finished products with ahistorical essences, an idea that served as a stepping stone for later monocultural drafts of "minority cultures." Both drafts are archaic and their truth claims to "culture" as a bounded entity are incredible in a Europe that is characterized by a "multiplication of experienced difference" (Siebers 2004) that is now best grasped by what Vertovec (2007) called "super-diversity." If we wish to respect such super-diversity, rather than impose a false order upon it (see again Bauman 1991), we need to move from substantive notions of inclusiveness (i.e., cultural definitions of equality that require cultural assimilation as its precondition) to formal definitions of equality (focusing on civic citizenship and legal protection against discrimination). Acquitting Geert Wilders when he is charged with hate speech is not the way to do this.

Bibliography

Barth, F. (ed.). 1969. "Introduction." In *Ethnic Groups and Boundaries. The Social Organisation of Cultural Difference*, 9–38. Long Grove, IL: Waveland Press.
———. 2007. "Overview: Sixty Years in Anthropology." *Annual Review of Anthropology* 36: 1–16.
Bauman, Z. 1991. *Modernity and Ambivalence*. Cambridge: Polity Press.
———. 2000. *Liquid Modernity*. Cambridge: Polity Press.
Bonacich, E. 1972. "A Theory of Ethnic Antagonism: The Split Labor Market." *American Sociological Review* 37 (5): 547–59.
Brubaker, R. 2011. "Economic Crisis, Nationalism, and Politicized Ethnicity." In *The Deepening Crisis. Governance Challenges After Neoliberalism*, edited by C. Calhoun and G. Derluguian, 93–108. New York: New York University Press.
Castles, S. and G. Kosack. 1972. "The Function of Labour Migration in Western European Capitalism." *New Left Review* 73 (May–June): 3–21.
CBS (Centraal Bureau voor de Statistiek). 2012. *Werkloosheid allochtonen in 2011 iets opgelopen*. Retrieved on September 5, 2012. www.cbs.nl
Comaroff, J. L. and J. Comaroff. 2009. *Ethnicity, Inc*. Chicago: University of Chicago Press.

de Leeuw, M. and S. van Wichelen. 2012. "Civilizing Migrants: Integration, Culture and Citizenship." *European Journal of Cultural Studies* 15 (2): 195–210.

Engbersen, G. and R. Gabriëls. 1995. *Sferen van Integratie. Naar een Gedifferentieerd Allochtonenbeleid.* Amsterdam: Boom.

Entzinger, H. 2003. "The Rise and Fall of Multiculturalism: The Case of The Netherlands." In *Towards Assimilation and Citizenship: Immigrants in Liberal Nation-States*, edited by C. Joppke and E. Morawska, 59–86. Houndmills, Basingstoke: Palgrave Macmillan.

Essers, C. and Y. Benschop. 2009. "Muslim Businesswomen Doing Boundary Work: The Negotiation of Islam, Gender, and Ethnicity Within Entrepreneurial Contexts." *Human Relations* 62 (3): 403–23.

Etzioni, A. 2001. *The Monochrome Society.* Princeton: Princeton University Press.

Geuijen, K. 2004. *De Asielcontroverse: Argumenteren over Mensenrechten en Nationale Belangen.* Proefschrift, Universiteit van Tilburg, Tilburg, The Netherlands.

Ghorashi, H. 2010. "From Absolute Invisibility to Extreme Visibility: Emancipation Trajectory of Migrant Women in The Netherlands." *Feminist Review* 94(1): 75–92.

Gilroy, P. 1987. *There Ain't No Black in the Union Jack.* Chicago: University of Chicago Press.

Grillo, R. D. 2003. "Cultural Essentialism and Cultural Anxiety." *Anthropological Theory* 3 (2): 157–73.

Hannerz, U. 1999. "Reflections on Varieties of Culturespeak." *European Journal of Cultural Studies* 2 (3): 393–407.

Human Rights Watch. 2008. "The Netherlands. Discrimination in the Name of Integration." May 15. Accessed September 5, 2012. http://www.hrw.org/en/node/82373/section/1

Jenkins, R. 2008. *Rethinking Ethnicity. Arguments and Explorations*, 2nd edn. Los Angeles: SAGE.

Jopke, C. 2007. "Beyond National Models: Civic Integration Policies for Immigrants in Western Europe." *West European Politics* 30 (1): 1–22.

Michaels, W. B. 2006. *The Trouble with Diversity. How We Learned to Love Identity and Ignore Inequality.* New York: Henry Holt.

Miles, R. 1984. "Marxism Versus the Sociology of 'Race Relations'?" *Ethnic and Racial Studies* 7 (2): 217–37.

Ministerie van Binnenlandse Zaken. 1994. *Integratiebeleid Etnische Minderheden: Contourennota.* Tweede Kamer, Vergaderjaar 1993–94, 23 684, 1–2. Den Haag: Ministerie van Binnenlandse Zaken.

Ministerie van Volkshuisvesting, Ruimtelijke Ordening en Milieu (VROM). 2007a. *Deltaplan Inburgering: Vaste Voet in Nederland.* Den Haag: Ministerie van VROM.

———. 2007b. *Integratie 2007–11: Zorg dat je Erbij Hoort!* Den Haag: Ministerie van VROM.

Mutsaers, P. forthcoming. "'All of Me'. Psychologizing Turkish–Dutch Police Officers in The Netherlands." *Anthropology of Work Review*.

Nationale Ombudsman. 2012. *Vreemdelingenbewaring. Strafregime of maatregel om uit te zetten*. Retrieved October 16, 2013. www.nationaleombudsman.nl

Nievers, E. and I. Andriessen. 2010. *Discriminatie niet-Westerse Migranten op de Arbeidsmarkt 2010*. Den Haag: Sociaal en Cultureel Planbureau.

Pierce, J. 2003. "'Racing for Innocence': Whiteness, Corporate Culture, and the Backlash Against Affirmative Action." *Qualitative Sociology* 26 (1): 53–70.

Prins, B. 2002. "The Nerve to Break Taboos: New Realism in the Dutch Discourse on Multiculturalism." *Journal of International Migration and Integration* 3 (3, 4): 363–79.

Rath, J. 1991. *Minorisering: De Sociale Constructie van "Etnische Minderheden"*. Amsterdam: SUA.

Roosens, E. 1989. *Creating Ethnicity: The Process of Ethnogenesis*. Newbury Park: SAGE.

SCP (Sociaal Cultureel Planbureau). 2012. *Verzorgd uit de Bijstand. De Rol van Gedrag, Uiterlijk en Taal bij de Re-integratie van Bijstandontvangers*.

Shulman, S. 1984. "Competition and Racial Discrimination: The Employment Effects of Reagan's Labor Market Policies." *Review of Radical Political Economics* 16 (4): 111–28.

Siebers, H. 2004. "The Management of Multiculturalism: Coming to Terms with the Multiplication of Experienced Difference." *International Journal of Multicultural Societies* 6 (2): 300–21.

———. 2009. "Struggles for Recognition. The Politics of Racioethnic Identity Among Dutch National Tax Administrators." *Scandinavian Journal of Management* 25 (1): 73–84.

———. 2010. "The Impact of Migrant-Hostile Discourses in the Media and Politics on Racioethnic Closure in Career Development in The Netherlands." *International Sociology* 25 (4): 475–500.

Siebers, H. and M. Dennissen. 2012. "'Traces of Hate': How the Dominant Migrant-Hostile Discourse in Dutch Media and Politics Influences Inter-Ethnic Relations Between Employees in Dutch Work Settings." Research Paper 31, Tilburg Papers in Culture Studies, Tilberg University, Tilberg, The Netherlands.

Stolcke, V. 1995. "Talking Culture: New Boundaries, New Rhetorics of Exclusion in Europe." *Current Anthropology* 36 (1): 1–24.

Suvarierol, S. 2012. "Nation-Freezing: Images of the Nation and the Migrant in Citizenship Packages." *Nations and Nationalism* 18 (2): 210–29.

Van Houdt, F., S. Suvavierol, and W. Schinkel. 2011. "Neoliberal Communitarian Citizenship: Current Trends Towards 'Earned Citizenship' in The United Kingdom, France, and The Netherlands." *International Sociology* 26 (3): 408–32.

Verkaaik, O. 2010. "The Cachet Dilemma: Ritual and Agency in New Dutch Nationalism." *American Ethnologist* 37 (1): 69–82.

Vertovec, S. 2007. "Super-Diversity and Its Implications." *Ethnic and Racial Studies* 30 (6): 1024–54.

———. 2011. "The Cultural Politics of Nation and Migration." *Annual Review of Anthropology* 40: 241–56.

Weber, M., G. Roth, and C. Wittich. 1978. *Economy and Society: An Outline of Interpretive Sociology.* Berkeley: University of California Press (First published in 1922).

Wikan, U. 2002. *Generous Betrayal. Politics of Culture in the New Europe.* Chicago: The University of Chicago Press.

Williams, R. M. 1987. "Capital, Competition, and Discrimination: A Reconsideration of Racial Earnings Inequality." *Review of Radical Political Economics* 19 (2): 1–15.

Wimmer, A. 2008. "The Making and Unmaking of Ethnic Boundaries: A Multilevel Process Theory." *American Journal of Sociology* 113 (4): 1–54.

———. 2009. "How to Study Ethnicity in Immigrant Societies. Herder's Heritage and the Boundary-Making Approach." *Sociological Theory* 27 (3): 244–70.

———. 2013. *Ethnic Boundary Making. Institutions, Networks, Power.* Oxford: Oxford University Press.

10

The Specter of Communalism and the Eugenic Solution to Britain's Immigration Problem

Gëzim Alpion

Introduction

Focusing on the nature of the intranational relations among "indigenous" British peoples and their attitudes toward the "colored"[1] workers who started arriving in Britain in the late 1940s, in this chapter I propose that Enoch Powell's speeches in the late 1960s reflected a "traditional" stance toward immigrants as well as a concern about the demographic changes which were taking place in parts of Britain, especially in England, from the mid-1950s.

Powell's rhetoric on immigration in general and especially his insistence that the numbers of Afro-Asian immigrants "are of the essence" (1969b, 37), I contend in this study, represent the last sustained effort in 20th century British politics to discuss this issue in the vein of the Enlightenment-inspired discourse that permeated 19th-century imperial attitudes toward non-Europeans, especially "colored people."

Powell stops short of approaching the "colored population" that had settled in Britain with the mindset of scientific racism. Nonetheless, the emphasis he puts on stopping completely and with immediate effect the net migration from the West Indies, India, and Pakistan, as well as simultaneously initiating the repatriation of the "colored people" who were already in the country, I argue in this chapter, indicate clearly that his devotion to Britain, especially his insistence to keep England white, marked the most aggressive as well as the last sustained public expression of xenophobia and white supremacism in British politics in the second half of the 20th century. Powell's nationalist and racist views as well as his eugenic solution to the immigration of colored people are explained both in the context of the time when they were made and the lasting impact that his classical education and German culture had on him.

The chapter also approaches the British elites' treatment of Powell in the context of the prevailing institutionalized dislike for so-called populist politics and populist politicians. I contend that Powell was not a populist politician although at times he employed the populist rhetoric especially to warn against "communalism." While Powell apparently intervened in the immigration debate partly to stem the apparent "ethnicization" of various constituencies of Great Britain, the reaction of the British establishment toward his views was also a "timely" intervention to curb the rise of "ethnic" nationalism in England at a time when Britain was moving from an Empire to a nation state.

The chapter finally assesses the impact of Powell's castigation by the officialdom on British politics and the immigration debate in Britain. I conclude that rather than continue shunning Powell as the bogeyman of British politics, policy makers and social scientists alike need to engage with and critique anew his controversial views on immigration especially at a time when, as a number of European leaders have recently claimed rather hastily, we are apparently witnessing the failure of "multiculturalism."[2]

The British Empire and Multiculturalism

Following the end of the Crimean War in 1856 and the suppression of the Indian Mutiny in 1858, Neill notes, "[t]he whole world was open to Western commerce.... The day of Europe had come" (1990, 273).

The period in question was favorable especially for the consolidation of British rule over India.

Throughout their presence in India, the British had tried not to interfere too much with Indian religions, cultures, costumes, and traditions. This "non-interference" policy was often compromised by the officials of the East India Company, which led to the decision of the British Crown taking direct control of India in 1858. In the same year, Queen Victoria issued a Proclamation through which she was eager to appease angry Indians and signal a new stage in their relationship with Britain:

> We disclaim alike the right and the desire to impose Our convictions on any of Our subjects. We declare it to be Our royal will and pleasure that none be in anywise favoured, none molested or disquieted by reason of their religious faith or observances, but that all shall alike enjoy the equal and impartial protection of the law…. And it is Our further will that, so far as may be, Our subjects, of whatever race or creed, be freely and impartially admitted to offices in Our service, the duties of which they may be qualified by their education, ability and integrity, duly to discharge. (Neill 1990, 274)

Queen Victoria's claim that institutionalized discrimination on any grounds would not be tolerated across the Empire was both incongruous and paradoxical because, like other colonial European powers, throughout the 19th century, Britain implemented a doctrine of racial superiority and preached the unfitness of the colonized Asian and African countries for self-governance.

On the other hand, Queen Victoria's 1858 message was a timely and well thought-out public relations gesture heralding, at least in theory, the dawn of a "new" legal era in India as well as in other British-controlled territories. The proclamation is perhaps the earliest official articulation of what, over a century later, would be known as "multiculturalism."

Between Myth and Reality

Queen Victoria's proclamation initiated the myth about Britain as a fair "mother country" that was committed to treat all its overseas subjects on an equal footing. Britain benefited from this carefully crafted public image especially when the British Empire needed its overseas "equal" subjects' commitment for the "common good." Hundreds and thousands of colonial soldiers enlisted in the British army during both World Wars. Many of them made enormous sacrifices in the name of "their" empire and the imagined "mother country" they heard so much about but never visited.

The first opportunity for many colonial soldiers to get to know their "mother country" came toward the end of the WW II. Throughout the war, a large number of them were stationed in Britain where they wanted to stay when the conflict came to an end in 1945. As many as 50 percent of West Indian servicemen, for instance, expressed the wish to settle in Britain.[3] Much to their surprise and disappointment, their requests were turned down.

To get back on her feet after the war, Britain needed manpower. The British political elite knew that the required workforce could be secured from the colonies but was apprehensive of the move to allow colored immigrants into the country, especially in large numbers. In the end, the more practical-minded participants in this "closed-door" debate had it their way and the first colored workers started arriving in Britain in the late 1940s.

An important moment in the history of postwar immigration in Britain is the docking of the freighter "Empire Windrush" in Southampton Harbour with 492 Jamaicans on board on June 22, 1948. For this contingent, as well as for the 125,000 West Indians immigrating to Britain throughout the 1950s, arriving in the "mother country" did not turn out to be the homecoming they had expected. The first generation of migrant hopefuls realized from the start that, no matter how much they were needed, Britain was neither prepared nor willing to treat them the same as the indigenous workforce, not only in employment but also in housing and education.

The unfair treatment that West Indian immigrants received in the "mother country" was to a large extent related to their physiognomy. The truth is that by then Britain had hardly treated white immigrants any better either. Behind the officially endorsed welcoming rhetoric about Britain's hospitality there is a less savory reality. Powell's claim in his Birmingham speech on April 20, 1968 that "[t]he Commonwealth immigrant came to Britain as a full citizen, to a country which knew no discrimination between one citizen and another" (1969b, 39) could hardly be further from the truth. Far from being the epitome of fairness, "Britain has an impeccable pedigree of racial and cultural intolerance of any new— and, therefore, fearsome—element in the population, dating back into the nineteenth century" (Smithies and Fiddick 1969, 55). In 1902, for instance, Conservative MP Major William Evans Gordon urged the House of Commons to put immigration urgently under control because his countrymen were "ruthlessly turned out to make room for foreign invaders" (Smithies and Fiddick 1969, 55). In this case, the "invaders" were Italians, Romanians, Russians, and Poles. To Gordon, the invasion was so serious that "[i]t is only a matter of time before the population becomes entirely foreign" (ibid.). The immigrants had allegedly turned everything upside down: rents were raised by 50–100 percent, schools were overcrowded with thousands of foreign children (ibid.), and the country was on the verge of moral collapse. Gordon warned that "[a]mong the thousands who came here there is a considerable proportion of bad characters" (ibid.). Britain was obviously swamped by alien criminals, gamblers, bandits, and prostitutes. Gordon foresaw that a storm was brewing, which "if it be allowed to burst, will have deplorable results" (ibid., 56).

After WW II, colored workers replaced European "aliens" as a threat to Britain's "indigenous" population. Some newspapers in the Midlands such as the *Birmingham Post*, *Evening Mail*, and *Sunday Mercury* published outbursts of local people and civic leaders well before Powell made his inflammatory speeches in the late 1960s. On September 25, 1959, for instance, the *Birmingham Evening Mail* published a tirade by Councilor Collett against "the coloured immigrant who comes in peace and humility and ends by being the arrogant boss." In Collett's view, colored men should not refuse doing menial jobs as that is all they are capable of doing. "Only good coloured immigrants," Collett concludes, "should be allowed to come here, good in morals and health, and they should be licensed so that their good behaviour and limitation is guaranteed."

The apocalyptic tone, pathos, and diction apparent in Gordon's speech and Collett's outburst make for uncanny precursors to Powell's vision of Britain as a country on the verge of collapse because of the impact of immigration.

The British and the "Inferior Other"

Throughout the empire, the British saw themselves as a nation with, to borrow a phrase from Max Weber, "a providential 'mission'" (1970, 176). The print media in particular played a crucial role in constructing the imperial British identity, starting and maintaining "an everyday plebi-scite" (Renan 1882), and forging Britishness in the shape of an "imag-ined political community" (Anderson 1983).

The British press constructed the "cohesion" and "superiority" of the British nation at the expense of the "fragmented nature" and "inferior-ity" of the subjugated nations and, to some extent, of any "backward" country, power and culture much along the lines of the antiquated "Greek-barbarian" racial imaginary polarity which was replaced in the 19th century with the "civilized-savage" dichotomy.[4]

Concentrating on magazines such as the *Gem* and *Magnet*, in his essay "Boys' Weeklies," George Orwell draws attention to media ste-reotyping and ridiculing of foreigners in the British press in the first half of the 20th century. In a tone echoing David Hume's condemna-tion in his 1748 essay "Of National Characters" of the tendency of "[t]he vulgar... to carry all 'national characters' to extremes" (Hume 1998, 113), Orwell observes that, notwithstanding occasional attempts to describe the natives as individual human beings, on the whole, the two magazines' basic assumptions are that "nothing ever changes, and foreigners are funny" (Orwell 1995, 178). For instance, in the *Gem* of 1939, Frenchmen are Froggies, Italians are Dagoes, and Americans are old-style stage Yankees.

While the tendency was to describe more or less any nation in deroga-tory terms, the worst stereotyping was reserved for nonwhite peoples. In addition to the press, throughout the 18th and 19th centuries, the "racist" discourse was generated also by scientists and philosophers. Notwithstanding his aversion for stereotyping mentioned earlier, in a footnote to the same essay, Hume states that he is "apt to suspect the negroes and in general all other species of men... to be naturally inferior to the whites"[5] (Eze 1997, 33). In an apparent attempt to exonerate Brit-ain's enslavement of colored people, Hume claims that his conclusion on the "inferiority" of the "negroes" is based on their "underachievement" in "our colonies" as well as "all over Europe" (ibid.).

Hume's views on the "species of men" who are "naturally inferior to the whites" should be seen in the context of the obsession with taxono-mies that characterized the Enlightenment, as well as of the sustained efforts to "legitimize" the exploitation of the "uncivilized" colonized peoples, especially the millions of Africans transported as slaves to the

New World. In this respect, Hume's infamous footnote on the "innate inferiority" of the slaves is a modern rephrasing of Aristotle's view that some people are more suited for manual labor and as such "destined" by nature to "serve others." Hume's and other Enlightenment philosophers' and men of science's obsession with skin color and their tendency to determine intelligence on the basis of physiognomy would inevitably turn "whiteness" and "blackness" into central categories to racial thinking in modern times. Hume's views on the "inferior" nonwhites illustrate, what Smith (2013) calls, "the curious paradox of Enlightenment thought, that the supposedly universal aspiration to liberty, equality and fraternity in fact only operated within a very circumscribed universe."

The British media played its part in stereotyping and misrepresenting nonwhite peoples also in the first half of the 20th century. In the *Gem* of 1939, Orwell notes, the Chinese are the 19th-century pantomime Chinamen, with saucer-shaped hats, pigtails and pidgin-English (Orwell 1995, 178), Indians are comic babus of the Punch tradition, and the "negro" is described as "comic" and "very faithful" (ibid., 179).

This kind of literature on foreigners, especially colored peoples, that the British had been exposed to for so long, would have a direct impact on their attitude toward the immigrants who started arriving in Britain from the late 1940s.

Powell, the Media, and Party Politics

In the wake of WW II, the British government did not have a clear policy in terms of how many foreign workers would be allowed to enter the country and regarding their dispersal around Britain. As a result, while certain areas witnessed a large influx of immigrants, others received few or none. According to Powell, out of over 600 parliamentary constituencies, less than 60 were badly affected (1969a, 19).

The failure of the parliament and the government to listen to the concerns of local councilors and Members of Parliament about this issue was one of the reasons why Powell felt he needed to turn immigration into a national issue in the late 1960s. He saw himself as a politician with a mission and the media as an indispensable tool with which to accomplish it.

Powell understood very well the media's role and power as an effective propaganda tool. This explains why he distributed copies of the Birmingham speech before he actually delivered it on April 20, 1968, and why he used uncorroborated "examples" of immigrants allegedly mistreating the indigenous population. Shortly after the speech, he told the *Daily Mail* that "the best way of getting listened to is to humanise your theme by talking about an individual" (Smithies and Fiddick 1969, 14). As a result of the unprecedented attention the local and national media paid to the "blockbuster," as the editor of the *News of the World* called the Birmingham speech, Powell finally succeeded in bringing national attention to immigration.

His inflamed rhetoric backfired on him, however. The British political class condemned his views and the most severe criticism came from his own party.

It has been suggested that Powell's controversial speeches on immigration in 1968 were not in keeping with his interest in this issue but a calculated publicity stunt to secure the leadership of the Conservative Party. Powell was an ambitious politician and if indeed he chose to use the immigration card to further his political career, he was neither the first nor would he be the last British politician to do so. Lewis argues that Powell was a victim of an ongoing power struggle in the Conservative Party:

> It was known, or at least said, in party circles that [Edward] Heath was hoping for an excuse to get rid of Powell, and that in this feeling he had most of the Shadow Cabinet with him. They had found his dissection of party policy proposals uncomfortable; and he was finding that Heath ignored his views or prevented him increasingly from putting them forward. (Lewis 1979, 107)

Heath apparently saw Powell as a contender for the leadership of the Conservative Party. By that time, Powell was already a scholar, a soldier, a philosopher, and a statesman with valuable experience in government and in opposition. If Heath wanted to rid himself of Powell, he was aware that he would need quite a strong reason to justify sacking him.

With his widely mediatized Birmingham speech, Powell could not have offered Heath a better reason to remove him from the Shadow Cabinet. Heath wasted no time in condemning Powell's rant against immigrants as being "racialist in tone, and liable to exacerbate racial tensions," a verdict which even the unrepentant Powell could hardly disagree with.

Heath was also annoyed because Powell apparently failed to consult with him over the Birmingham speech. As far as Heath was concerned, Powell had been "calculatedly disloyal" (Lewis 1979, 106), a charge which Powell strongly denied. In Powell's view, "[i]t was to the 'tone' of my speech that objection was taken" (1969c, 64).

Powell's outspokenness as well as the support he received from working class people and some sections of the media obviously made the British political and media elites feel uncomfortable and embarrassed. As Heffer puts it, Powell's detractors assailed him, among other things, "for his temerity in thinking that, at times, he knew better than the Conservative Party, and had a right to condemn its moral and intellectual failings" (1998, 960). This point was articulated very clearly by the BBC's David Frost during an interview. In a moment of frustration, Frost interrupts Powell saying:

> DF: You "underestimate" us. I feel a great sympathy for the people you talk about, make no mistake about that, but—and the people who've got a real problem now, but you—what you do is you "underestimate" us all so much. (Frost 1969, 113, emphasis added)

Frost accused Powell of "underestimating us" (ibid., 114) once more shortly afterward. Powell's opponents in politics and the media obviously felt that he had made them look as if they were out of touch with what people thought about the important issue of immigration.

Aversion to Populist Politics

Enoch Powell's falling out with Edward Heath and the criticism and condemnation he received from political allies and opponents as well as media and religious circles can be explained to some extent in the context of the British establishment's traditional "contempt" for so-called "populist politics" and "populist politicians" as well as in light of claims made by scholars on the power of the media to "manage" and "manipulate" rather than "express" the "public will."[6]

Political, economic, and intellectual elites in the West have a long tradition of disregard and dislike for democracy and the masses (Dewey 1987; Keane 2007; Bernstein 2010). This became more apparent when the industrial and graphic revolutions of the 18th and 19th centuries turned what was known as "rabble," "multitude," "mob," and "a Dark Continent beyond the understanding of the civilized elite" (Furedi 2005) into "mass."

Mass media, especially newspapers, have been traditionally seen by European politicians and intellectuals as a means through which populist leaders air the views of those "dirty people of no name," as the historian Claredon called the masses (cited in Carr 1971, 50).

Powell himself had strong reservations about the role of the media in democracy (1969b, 39). He was mainly concerned, however, about the behavior of politicians toward the masses. "[A]lmost everywhere," he argued on July 13, 1971, "a common assumption is silently shared... that the citizen cannot, must not, fix his own goals or choose his own good" as a result of "the normal assumption" that his aims "are set by the state" (Powell 1971b). In his view, "[w]e do not usually notice this partly because the modern state uses the vocabulary of individual liberty ('human rights,' etc.), just as the totalitarian state uses the terminology of democracy" (ibid.).

Referring to its traditional sidelining and disconnection from the public and inability "to understand what makes people tick," Furedi maintains that:

> the British political class assumes that the public suffers from irrational prejudice and is easily misled by xenophobic demagogues. This suspicion towards what may lurk beneath the soul of everyday society is deeply ingrained in the more leftist and liberal sections of the elite. It is paradoxical that this group, which continually denounces racism, does not recognize its own brand of contempt for those it deems morally inferior. It is worth recalling that the racial thinking first emerged in Europe among the elite that regarded the lower orders as both biologically and morally inferior to itself. (2005)

O'Neill detects "a barely concealed contempt for the voting masses" also in the "frenzy" against Robert Kilroy-Silk,[7] another controversial former British politician addressing the issue of immigration with hardly more sensitivity than Powell:

> The word that pops up most often in critiques of Kilroy-Silk is "populist"— he's a "media populist," accuses Nick Cohen; he has an "abrasive populist manner" says one commentator; he's a "dangerous populist" says another.

What they're really saying is that Kilroy-Silk is trying to appeal to the masses and, dumbasses that the masses are, they might just fall for it and give in to his "populist patter." As one contributor to a web discussion board wrote: "There is a disenfranchised proletariat rump whose opinions are informed by this sort of xenophobic, populist crap." (2005)

Powell's speeches, especially those on immigration, at times reveal signs of populism. This is seen in his use of the first personal pronoun "we," the references to anonymous individuals, and the claims about the high level of support he received.

Notwithstanding the populist elements of his rhetoric, Powell was not necessarily a populist politician. His "populist rhetoric" should be seen, among other things, in the context of his concern about the irresponsible way, in his view, language was used by the government and the media. There is a "danger," he wrote on July 13, 1971:

that we may fall prey to one of the most dangerous of political epidemics— that of metaphor.... It is my thesis that much of the language of our current debate is unconscious metaphor of the most dangerous kind: the confusion of the economic and the political. (1971b)

At this stage, Powell is mainly concerned about the government's handling of Britain's membership in the European Economic Community, an issue to which we will return shortly. Powell also believed that the dangerous "political epidemics of metaphor" is noticeable in the government's and the national media's interpretation of the concept of "compassion," mainly regarding housing (1968a), and especially the immigration issue. Powell was adamant that the British establishment was inclined not to call things by their name, a tendency which, on September 27, 1969, he defined as "a humbugging abuse of language... intended to deceive."

In addition to Powell's aversion for the "humbugging" diction with which he believed "politics is cursed," the directness of the controversial "populist rhetoric" he employed is also a reflection of his views regarding the obligation of elected politicians toward the "demos." This is a recurrent theme in Powell's speeches. He justifies recounting in the Birmingham speech a controversial conversation with a constituent by saying: "I do not have the right not to do so... I simply do not have the right to shrug my shoulders and think about something else" (Powell 1969b, 36). Powell also believed that "it is the duty of a politician to make and to declare his judgement" (1969c, 73).

On February 12, 1971, Powell advised an audience in France not to be misled by the British politicians speaking in favor of Britain joining the ECC. In his words, their "unanimity and show of confidence" is nothing more than the public stance that those "who speak officially are in duty bound to maintain" (1971a).

The key phrase in the above quote is "duty bound." Powell was aware of his obligation to the Conservative Party and the Shadow Cabinet when he gave the Birmingham speech. However, he apparently did not understand loyalty to the party as an ultimate goal. Nor did he seem to have perceived politics as an end to retain or come to power. He was critical of anyone, irrespective of party affiliation, who, in his view, avoided addressing important issues to serve their own interests. He found hypocritical the compassionate rhetoric of the then Labour Cabinet; Prime Minister Harold Wilson's purpose, Powell argued on September 27, 1969, is the enforcement upon the citizens by the use of the powers of government redistribution of income which they hoped would stand the Labour Government in good stead at the next election "in terms of votes". Three years earlier, Powell took a swipe at the Labour Government and his own party saying that it was "absolutely absurd to say that immigration either is not, or ought not to be, an issue" at the 1966 election (1966). It was because he was "duty bound," he emphasized in Eastbourne (1969c, 64), that he took up the theme of immigration again since his vilification for the Birmingham speech earlier in the year.

"The Numbers Are of the Essence"

Whenever Powell raised the issue of immigration, he would always mention that his main concern was the large number of immigrants. He stressed that "numbers are of the essence" especially in Birmingham (1969b, 37) and Eastbourne (1969c, 68). In 1968, he put the figure of the immigrants who were already in the country at "1.25 million" (ibid., 69), predicting that between 1983 and 1988 it would stand at "3.5 million" (Powell 1969b, 36), and between 2000 and 2002 it would vary between "3.5 millions" (Powell 1967), "4.25 million" (Powell 1969c, 73), and "5–7 million" (Powell 1969b, 36). In percentage terms, in 1968, Powell held that by the end of the 20th century immigrants in Britain would represent between "5 percent" (Powell 1967), "a little over 6 percent" (Powell 1969c, 73), nearly "one-eighth" (Frost 1969, 107), and even "approximately one-tenth of the whole population" (Powell 1969b, 36).

Following the Birmingham speech, Powell was often rebuked for his "unrealistic" figures. All the same, he maintained that the assumptions which produced the figures "are deliberately pitched low" (1969c, 73) and as such they were "neither random nor ill-considered" (ibid.). Regarding the claim that the number of immigrants in 1985 will be in the order of 3.5 millions, for instance, he was keen to stress that that was "the figure given to Parliament by the spokesman of the Registrar General's office" (Smithies and Fiddick 1969, 145).

The issue which still merits attention today about Powell's obsession with immigration statistics is not if they were accurate predictions—according to the 2001 Census, the ethnic minority population in the UK was 4.6 million, i.e., 7.9 percent of the country's total population—but that they refer almost exclusively to the "colored population" and the motives he had in referring to them ceaselessly.

Criminalizing Colored Immigrants

Powell divided colored immigrants into two main groups when he provided statistics about the alien population in Britain from the late 1940s onward: West Indians and Afro-Asians; in the latter, he included Indians, Pakistanis, and South Asians who came to Britain from Kenya in the late 1960s and early 1970s.

Powell was keen to highlight constantly that the number of so many colored people was allegedly causing a variety of problems ranging from putting pressure on local services to the complete transformation of certain areas. He wrote on February 16, 1967 that he lived in Wolverhampton within a stone's throw of streets which "went black" (Powell 1967).

Powell had a tendency to highlight primarily the unsocial and criminal behavior allegedly characterizing colored immigrants. He deliberately demonized and criminalized the colored population, especially the black immigrants, to blame them for the "exodus" of the indigenous population from formerly "white" areas. To illustrate the "plight" of the white people, Powell used information he claimed he had received from talking to his constituents and anonymous letters. What one can draw from these maliciously selected case studies is that colored people were a "menace" to all age groups of white people, especially the elderly. The reasons why Powell chose the case of an old lady, apparently the last white person in her street, who was allegedly mistreated by the "negroes," can hardly be missed. She had apparently turned into a prisoner in her own home and was being persecuted in her own country for which her family had made enormous sacrifices: "[s]he lost her husband and both her sons in the war" (1969b, 41).

In a speech, echoing previously mentioned sentiments expressed by the Conservative Member of Parliament in 1902 about the "bad character" of "a considerable proportion" of European immigrants, and the Birmingham Councilor's call in 1959 to license colored immigrants "so that their good behavior and limitation is guaranteed," in 1968, Powell stated:

> With the malefactors among our own people we have got to cope; they are our own responsibility and part of our own society. It is something totally different when the same or similar activities are perpetrated by strangers, and above all when they occur in the course of an increase in the numbers of those strangers and an extension of the areas which they occupy—an increase and an extension to which the victims perceive no end in sight. Surely only very clever people could fail to understand so simple a point. (1969c, 68)

Effective as the carefully selected examples of the "victimized" white individuals and their colored "tormentors" were, Powell was aware that a blanket victimization of all colored immigrants would do more harm than good to his smear campaign. He did manage, however, to find an "offence" with which, he hoped, he could charge all colored immigrants with: in his view, the overwhelming majority were communalists at heart.

The Specter of Communalism

By the late 1960s, Powell warned that most colored immigrants in Britain were disconnected from the rest of the indigenous population which, he argued, stemmed from "[t]he irregular pattern of population and living [that] grew up higgledy-piggledy in the early years of immigration"

(1967). He paid attention to the lack of integration especially in the Walsall speech on February 9, 1968. Referring to the policy of the Wolverhampton Corporation to ask immigrant workers "to decide which if any of the rules of their sect they will keep," he concluded:

> It will be the opposite to the equal treatment of all persons within the realm if employers are placed in the position of adjudicating upon the requirements of their employees' religion. The issue in this instance is not racial or religious discrimination: it is communalism. (1969a, 21–22)

Such "liberties," Powell argued in Birmingham, imply the elevation of the colored immigrants and their descendants into "a privileged or special class" (1969b, 39).

Powell argued that communalism was spreading in Britain mainly because of the strong inclination of the West Indian and Afro-Asian immigrants to live "in their own communities," speak "their own languages," and maintain "their native customs" (1969c, 71). He predicted on February 16, 1967 that the tendency was bound to worsen. In Birmingham the following year he warned about the consequences of this trend on the immigrants who are not keen on communalism *per se*, and the indigenous population:

> Now we are seeing the growth of positive forces acting against integration, of vested interests in the preservation and sharpening of racial and religious differences, with a view to the exercise of actual domination, first over fellow-immigrants and then over the rest of the population. (1969b, 42)

To make his argument more effective, Powell quotes from a speech by John Stonehouse, a Labour MP and government minister:

> The Sikh community's campaign to maintain customs inappropriate in Britain is much to be regretted.... To claim special communal rights (or should one say rites?) leads to a dangerous fragmentation within society. This communalism is a canker; whether practised by one colour or another it is to be strongly condemned. (ibid., 42–43)

Occasionally, Powell made some half-hearted remarks on the efforts everyone should make to ensure the integration of the colored population (1967). All the same, he is adamant that this can never be successfully achieved because, as he puts it on March 25, 1966, "there is really not one immigration problem, but two distinct and separate immigration problems. One is concerned with the immigrants who are here already. The other is concerned with control over entry to this country" (Powell 1966).

By this time, Powell held that the inflow and the outflow of colored immigrants could be balanced over a period of years by greatly reducing the rate of admission and encouraging "voluntary" return to whence they came (ibid.). Not for long. A year later, he wrote the size of the problem could be eliminated "by virtually terminating net immigration" (Powell 1967) and employing "aid, inducements and encouragements to immigrants to rejoin families in their country of origin or to return thither" (ibid.). From this moment onward, Powell saw repatriation as important an issue as the complete halt on net immigration. So much so that, on November 16, 1968, he suggested that the resettlement of the colored immigrants "ought to be, and it could be, organized now on the scale which the urgency of the situation demands, preferably under a special Ministry for Repatriation or other authority charged with concentrating on this task" (1969c, 77).

Although Powell was aware of the drastic nature of his proposal, he maintained that this was the only way to eventually protect Britain from the dangers of "communalism," the "colour problem," and "racial discrimination" (1966) which, he was keen to emphasize, are endemic in other countries, especially in India and the USA. "Communalism has been the curse of India," he wrote on February 9, 1968, "and we need to be able to recognize it when it rears its head here" (1969a, 21). If his proposal was not implemented, he warned, by the end of the 20th century Britain would face a color problem "similar in magnitude to that in the United States now" (ibid.).

Powell, the British Empire, and the UK

Powell took enormous pride in the British Empire and regretted its demise. With the empire gone, he saw the preservation of the United Kingdom as vital to Britain's survival as a state and raised his voice any time he believed the Union was in danger. Powell believed that from the 1950s onward Britain's dangers came from the US, the European Economic Community, and the presence of the colored population.

According to Heffer, Powell's "main, unresolved conflict with his opponents was the question of whether the British people wished to remain a nation" (1998, 959). I contend that, in Powell's view, his opponents also failed to grasp the detrimental impact the three aforementioned "threats" would have especially on the heart of the UK: England.

England's unique place among the nations of the British Isles was forged from the start of the second millennium. According to Bartlett (2001), in the Middle Ages, the British Isles exemplified the variety of a number of relationships: the degree of ethnic diversity, the degree of political centralization and unity, and the lack of direct connection between ethnic and political homogeneity. In early medieval Ireland and Wales, for instance, "a high degree of cultural unity coexisted with marked political fragmentation; in Scotland a unified kingdom emerged, formed of territories of great cultural and ethnic diversity" (ibid., 53). In England, however, the "relatively close match between the kingdom of England and the English" (ibid.) produced, what Davies calls, a "regnal and ethnic solidarity" (1994, 20). Having acknowledged that this situation generated different types of nationalism, Bartlett concludes that:

> England is a simpler case. A longish history of political unity under one dynasty, a common language, and the territorial integrity aided by an island location all created a "match between people and polity" that gave English nationalism an earlier, more continuous, and more apparently self-evident history than the nationalism of most other parts of Europe. (2001, 53)

Powell was aware that "the duration and natural evolution" (1971a) of English national identity become apparent only if they are seen in the context of "a thousand years of English history" (1969b, 36). Equally important, in this respect, is his firm belief in the unique role of the English parliament in forging English national identity. Although he referred often to "the British" Parliament, in his view, this institution was fundamentally an English establishment, thus, echoing the sentiments of the 19th-century British politician John Bright who in 1865 stated that "England is the Mother of Parliaments," a phrase which is often wrongly quoted as a reference to the British Parliament. "Take Parliament out of the history of England," Powell said in France on February 12, 1971, "and that history itself becomes meaningless" (1971a).

England's special status within Great Britain does not lessen the role and importance of the other three nations included in the union. Indeed, much of the success of the British Empire was down to the important role played by each of the four nations that together constructed the British identity.

On the whole, throughout the Imperial Era, this shared identity was not seen as a threat to the more immediate national identity. The English, Scots, Irish, and Welsh were not concerned with Britishness when they were in the UK. Their Britishness became more of a signifier, an indicator of who they collectively were, when they went overseas.

The collective British national identity had a strong appeal in the past, especially among the middle classes and the aristocracy, because, to quote Davenport (2005), "it was based on material interest. No doubt some identified with a mythical and backward-looking idea of 'Britishness', but essentially the British nation state was seen as the best guarantor of maintaining living standards."

During the time of the empire, as a result of the lack of Welsh institutions, different from the Scots and Irish, the Welsh would usually identify Britain with England, and see the English as epitomizing the "British." There were cases when even the Scots would equate Britain with England and the British with the English. This is particularly the case in the writings of two well-known 19th century Scottish authors, Thomas Carlyle (1841) and Samuel Smiles (1859), which abound in numerous references to England, the English, and the Englishman's character.

Different from the Scots, Welsh, and Irish, when Britain was an empire, the English would normally presume that, in their case, Britishness meant Englishness, something which was often reflected in the English newspapers and the political discourse. When the Conservative MP, mentioned earlier, demanded in 1902 that the government should no longer allow European immigrants to enter the country, what he was concerned about was not the detrimental effect immigration was allegedly having on Britain but on England. The victims he identified were not British but "English families" (Smithies and Fiddick 1969, 55). He was worried that, as a result of the foreigners, "an English working man" (ibid., 56) and not a British subject was apparently unable "to enjoy his day or rest" (ibid.).

The gradual loss of overseas influence and territories from the end of WW I and more rapidly in the wake of the WW II meant that Britain was changing from an imperial power to a nation state. The inevitable end of the empire was bound to bring to the surface, and with an increased urgency, the issue of the relationship of the four nations comprising Great Britain and, more importantly, the question of England's position and role in this uneasy union. The British monarchy and the British political elite were obviously interested in maintaining the *status quo* at home, which in the postwar years meant that Britain should outlive its rapidly eroding empire.

Notwithstanding the aforementioned personal motives of Powell's political opponents to sideline him, I contend that his swift vilification immediately after the Birmingham speech indicates that the British ruling elite was not prepared to tolerate his "racialist" views for two reasons. Like Powell, they were aware of Britain's benefits from having a multiethnic and multicultural society much earlier than when the heated immigration debate began in the late 1960s. On the other hand, unlike Powell, they apparently envisaged that his nationalistic rhetoric could lift the lid on long-standing nationalist antagonisms at home. The British establishment's determination to condemn Powell at a time when the Scots were debating their own future as a nation was probably one of its most important decisions after the WW II, a decision which, in hindsight, was perhaps paramount to the survival of the UK as a *state*.

Powell, the English Nationalist

Powell put the blame squarely on the government for the large number of colored immigrants in Britain. In his view, the root of the problem was the British Nationality Act 1948 which saw the creation of the status of "Citizen of the United Kingdom and Colonies" as the national citizenship of both the UK and its colonies. Powell "inveighed against" this Act "from the outset" (1969c, 70) and over the years tried hard "from inside and outside government" to urge legislation (ibid.), although without success. He was adamant that "[i]f Britain had provided herself in 1956... with what every nation under the sun possesses—a law defining its own people—what a world of anguish past and future would never have been!" (ibid.). On February 16, 1967, he castigated as "slow" and "timid" the decision of the government to act in the wake of "the rising flood of immigration which came on the post-election boom of 1960" (Powell 1967).

In Powell's view, the Commonwealth Immigrants Act 1962, which limited the right to migrate to the UK only to those issued with employment vouchers, finally made "our law like that of every other country on earth, in recognizing the difference between its own people and the rest" (Powell 1967). All the same, he maintained that the 1962 Act came very late.

In Eastbourne, Powell explained one of the main reasons why he was so critical of the way British governments had been handling the immigration of colored people from 1948:

> [U]ntil 1962, this country, alone of all the nations in the world, had no definition of its own people, so that for all purposes an Englishman born in Birmingham and a tribesman from the North-West Frontier were indistinguishable in the law of the United Kingdom. (1969c, 63)

In his speeches and articles on immigration in the late 1960s, Powell was often keen to emphasize that England was affected by immigration more than any other part of the UK, and in Eastbourne he even claimed that "it is virtually only England which is affected" ((ibid., 69). As a result of this concentration of colored immigrants, he argued, some areas in England, like his Wolverhampton constituency, "are already undergoing the total transformation to which there is no parallel in a thousand years of English history" (1969b, 36). He feared the worst was yet to come.

The "victims" in Powell's articles and speeches, mentioned earlier, are all English. The victimization of the English people, he stressed in Birmingham, came from the colored population and the government. He claims a constituent told him he would prefer to leave England with his three children if he could afford it mainly because he believed that "[i]n this country in fifteen or twenty years time the black man will have the whip-hand over the white man" (ibid.). In the same speech, Powell expressed his strong opposition to calls by politicians, media people, and religious leaders for legislation "against discrimination" (ibid., 39) because, in his view, the English people themselves have turned into "a persecuted minority" (ibid., 40).

In spite of his Welsh heritage and aforementioned commitment to the survival of the UK, Powell was essentially an English nationalist.[8] The nature of his devotion to England becomes clearer if seen in the context of the stages of his commitment to the British Empire, Britain, and England, and the order in which each of them in turn emerged as his main emotional attachment.

As mentioned earlier, Powell was proud of the British Empire and had an ambition to become Viceroy of India. He spoke emotionally about the might of the empire even in his old age (Shepherd 1996, 9). Britain replaced the empire in importance when he realized that the events in Europe in the mid-1930s would eventually lead to war. If until then Powell had seen "the nation in the framework of the British Empire," now Britain and the British nation became his main concern: "what mattered to me, more than anything that could happen to me personally was the outcome of that war that was to come for the existence of the nation" (Roth 1979, 24).

Even at that early stage, Powell saw the war as being a major threat especially to England; he had no doubt that "at stake was the freedom of England" (ibid.).

Notwithstanding Powell's early attachment to England, this part of Britain became his main concern when he articulated his fears about the long-term impact of the colored population in the late 1960s. Powell's stance as an English nationalist is better understood in the context of the impact that Germany, his "spiritual homeland" (Shepherd 1996, 25), and German culture, of which he "was to remain in uncritical awe" as a young man, had on him.

Powell believed that the only way for the British nation to survive was to follow the German model. As Walker Connor notes, prior to the outbreak of WW II, Germany was among the handful of states that clearly qualified as a nation state, which means that the "state" and the "nation" were indistinguishably linked in the popular perception. To the Germans, Germany "was something far more personal and profound than a territorial–political structure termed a state; it was an embodiment of the nation-idea and therefore an extension of self" (Connor 1994, 42).

Powell was opposed to Hitler and Nazism. Hitler's purge of his political rivals in the summer of 1934, Powell would recall later, left him "in a state of shock… shock which you experience when, around you, you see the debris of a beautiful building in which you have lived for a long time" (Roth 1970, 24). The event, Shepherd (1996, 28) contends, marked the disillusionment of Powell with German culture. The shock was strong enough to make Powell keen to enlist in the British army "from the first day that Britain goes to war" (Heffer 1998, 22).

Notwithstanding his aversion for Hitler, the German leader's propaganda about the "superiority" of the Aryan race as well as the disturbing views of some German philosophers like Kant (1950) and Hegel (1902) on the "inferiority" of colored people apparently made a lasting impact on the young Powell. After all, Powell "remained addicted to German culture" (Heffer 1998, 22) throughout his life. As he put it in 1966, the happiest and most glorious hours of his life as a scholar "have been with German books" (ibid., 28).

For someone who does not know much about German history, the fact that Powell gave the Birmingham speech on January 20 would hardly seem significant. Given that Powell was so immersed in German culture, however, his decision to deliver the most important speech of his career on the anniversary of Hitler's birthday seems more like a sinister choice than an unfortunate memory lapse. The final solution Powell devised in the late 1960s to virtually cleanse Britain, especially England, from the colored population shows clearly that he was a white supremacist. Powell was keen to use intimidating language and tactics and thinly veiled threats intended for colored immigrants who would not pack up and leave England. His prediction in Eastbourne that "the People of England will not endure it" (Powell 1969c, 73–74) amounts to an ominous call to arms to the English to resist "an invasion which the Government apparently approved and their fellow-citizens—elsewhere—viewed with complacency" (Powell 1967).

Finally, Powell's obsession to preserve the homogeneity of indigenous white population, his tendency to see the presence of colored people as a clear and present "menace" (ibid.) and a hidden "evil" (Powell 1969b, 35) that had to be tackled even in the knowledge that it could not be stopped completely (Powell 1969a, 19), and the apocalyptic vision that failure to act immediately is "like watching a nation busily engaged in heaping up its own funeral pyre" (1969b, 37) are unmistakable signs of the lasting impact of his classical education, especially of the views that a number of classicists at the start of the 20th century held on the fall of civilizations. One such classicist, Frank, wrote in his essay "Race Mixture in the Roman Empire": "what lay behind and constantly reacted upon all such causes of Rome's disintegration was, after all to considerable extent, the fact that the people who built Rome had given way to a different race" (1916, 705). Echoing Frank's views about the same issue, Duff (1928) saw "race-mixing" as a "threat" of contemporary immigration.

For someone like Powell who had studied and excelled in classics at King Edward's School, Birmingham, and at Trinity College, Cambridge, who had published scholarly articles on ancient civilizations from an early age, and who at 25 was appointed Professor of Greek at the University of Sydney, the presence in his articles and speeches on immigration of numerous references to the classical world, especially to ancient Greece and Rome, was unavoidable. The influence of this attachment to classics is apparent especially in the tone and diction of the Birmingham address, otherwise known as the "Rivers of Blood" speech. Toward the end of this speech, Powell uses an allusion to Virgil's *Aeneid* with the purpose of warning ominously of an apocalyptic future: "As I look forward, I am filled with foreboding. Like the Roman, I seem to see 'the River Tiber foaming with much blood'" (1969b, 43).

As mentioned earlier, Powell was fairly accurate in predicting in the late 1960s the numbers of immigrants in Britain by the end of the 20th century. Likewise, he was a little off the mark in his estimate of the size of immigrant population in England. The 2001 Census revealed that at the start of the 21st century in England the immigrant or immigrant-descended population made up 9 percent of the total population, whereas in Scotland and Wales only 2 percent, and in Northern Ireland less than 1 percent. Today, there are areas in England where the population is predominantly non-English.

Notwithstanding the figures, Powell's prophecies of social and racial conflicts between the indigenous population and the colored immigrants, indeed the large number of foreigners who have settled in the UK since the late 1960s, have not materialized. Even more significant is the fact that, in spite of ongoing concerns about the government's lack of a clear policy on immigration, the people of England and across the UK have not endorsed nor have they appropriated Powell's xenophobic and racist views.

Conclusion

Powell saw the presence of colored population as a "threat" to the "cohesion" of the English nation which, he believed, would eventually undermine the very existence of the UK as a state. He failed to see that in the wake of WW II immigration was an unstoppable phenomenon. The dismantling of the colonial system and the trend of globalization made inevitable demographic changes in the UK and other former colonial powers in Western Europe.

Powell was eager to emphasize in Eastbourne that from the 1950s "the people of Britain are faced with a *fait accompli*, that all sorts of excuses are invented and we are told in terms of arrogant moral superiority that we have got a 'multi-racial society' and had better like it" (1969c, 69). The problem in Britain's case, as well as in other former colonial powers, was that by the time their grip on the colonies slipped away, they were ill-prepared to treat fairly the immigrant force they needed to keep their economies going. It is hardly a coincidence that, apart from some halfhearted remarks, Powell did not mention the benefits of immigration to UK economy.

Powell's tendency to indiscriminately criminalize colored immigrants, to highlight their alleged innate communalism, and the reluctance to respect and appropriate new cultures were, and remain, deeply offensive and repulsive. Equally disturbing is his eugenic solution, a drastic measure which Britain's establishment had the farsightedness to condemn outright when he articulated it in the late 1960s. It is primarily for these reasons why, to this day, he remains the bogeyman of British politics. Among politicians, one must enjoy a near untouchable status, as was the case with Margaret Thatcher, to dare make a positive remark on Powell. A number of people in the public eye have been rebuked over the last few years for praising Powell's views on immigration.[9]

In the modern world, almost every society and country is multiracial, multicultural, multiethnic, multilinguistic, and multireligious. In this multilayered world, it is important that citizens preserve their identities and respect the identities of others as well as try to discover what, in spite of their differences, they share. This sharing is paramount for building and maintaining a cohesive society.

Only in a cohesive society can a spirit of togetherness be forged. This togetherness is possible if we do not see our native cultures as set in stone and incapable of dialogue and fusion. Powell did not even consider that such fusion is possible; he held that a colored immigrant does not "by being born in England become an Englishman" (1969c, 77).

All the same, all indications are that this togetherness, although "dismantled" (Bauman 2003, 119), is already in Britain and across the world. What are required are more coordinated efforts among politicians, community leaders, and social scientists to detect and promote it.

Notes and Bibliography

Notes

1. The terminology referring to the skin color of the immigrant population in Britain in this chapter reflects the lexicon employed by the media, Enoch Powell, and the authors of the publications consulted.
2. Some of the European leaders who have recently spoken about the failure of multiculturalism in their countries include former French president Nicolas Sarkozy, German Chancellor Angela Merkel, and British Prime Minister David Cameron.
3. For information on the West Indian servicemen's wish to remain in Britain at the end of WW II and the British government's plans to ship them home, see Pilkington (1990).
4. I have addressed the representation of foreigners in the British press in the article "Western Media and the European 'Other'—Images of Albania in the British Press," which is included in the collection of essays *Encounters with Civilizations: From Alexander the Great to Mother Teresa* (see Alpion 2011).
5. David Hume edited slightly the 1748 essay "Of National Characters" and its accompanying infamous footnote several times. The quotes from the 1748 footnote in this chapter are taken from the 1754 version which is believed to include the most important modifications. For the full 1754 version of the footnote, see Eze (1997, 33). For Hume's complete essay, see Hume (1998).
6. For the role of the media in managing rather than expressing the public will, see Hall (1986), Curran (2003), and Bernstein (2005).
7. Robert Kilroy-Silk is a former British politician and television presenter. His show *Kilroy* was canceled by the BBC in 2004 following the publication in the *Sunday Express* of his controversial article entitled "We Owe Arabs Nothing" on January 4 of that year. I have written about Kilroy-Silk's racist views in my article "Why Human Rights Must Never Just Be Selective," *The Birmingham Post*, January 31, 2004, 8.
8. By the time Enoch Powell was born in 1912, his family had been living in England for four generations.
9. For information on the criticism that some people in the public eye in Britain have received in recent years for praising Enoch Powell, see Furth (2009), and Prince (2009).

Bibliography

Alpion, Gëzim (ed.). 2011. "Western Media and the European 'Other'—Images of Albania in the British Press." In *Encounters with Civilizations: From Alexander the Great to Mother Teresa*, 117–51. New Brunswick, NJ: Transaction Publishers.

Anderson, B. 1983. *Imagined Communities: Reflections on the Origin and Spread of Nationalism*. London: Verso.

Bartlett, R. 2001. "Medieval and Modern Concepts of Race and Ethnicity." *Journal of Medieval and Early Modern Studies* 31 (1): 39–56.

Bauman, Z. 2003. *Liquid Love: On the Frailty of Human Bonds*. Cambridge: Polity Press.

Bernstein, R. J. 2005. *The Abuse of Evil: The Corruption of Politics and Religion Since 9/11*. Malden: Polity Press.

———. 2010. *The Pragmatic Turn*. Cambridge: Polity Press.

Carlyle, T. (1841) 1966. *On Heroes, Hero-Worship and the Heroic in History*, edited by C. Niemeyer. Lincoln: University of Nebraska Press.

Carr, E. H. 1971. *What Is History?* Harmondsworth: Penguin.

Connor, Walker. 1994. "A Nation Is a Nation, Is a State, Is an Ethnic Group, Is a…." In *Nationalism*, edited by J. Hutchinson and A. D. Smith, 36–46. Oxford: Oxford University Press.

Curran, J. 2003. *Media and Power*. London: Routledge.

Davenport, N. 2005. "The Trouble With Re-Branding Britain." *Spiked-Online*, August 12. Accessed August 14, 2005. http://www.spiked-online.com/Articles/0000000CACFB.htm

Davies, R. 1994. "The Peoples of Britain and Ireland, 1100–1400: I. Identities." *Transactions of the Royal Historical Society*, sixth series 4: 1–20.

Dewey, John. 1987. "Democracy is Radical." In *John Dewey: The Later Work, 1925–53, Vol. 2: 1935–1937*, edited by J. A. Boydston et al., 296–99. Carbondale: Sothern Illinois University Press.

Duff, A. M. 1928. *Freedmen in the Early Roman Empire*. Oxford: Clarendon Press.

Eze, E. C. (ed.). 1997. *Race and the Enlightenment: A Reader*. Oxford: Blackwell.

Frank, T. 1916. "Race Mixture in the Roman Empire." *The American Historical Review* 21 (4): 689–708.

Frost, David. 1969. "Frost on Friday, 3 January 1969." In *Enoch Powell on Immigration*, edited by B. Smithies and P. Fiddick, 95–129. London: Sphere.

Furedi, F. 2005. "None of Them Knows What We're Thinking." *Spiked-Online*, May 4. Accessed May 6, 2005. http://www.spiked-online.com/Articles/0000000CAAF2.htm

Furth, N. 2009. "Sarah Kennedy 'Spoken to' by BBC for Praising Enoch Powell During Radio 2 Show." *Mail Online*, July 19.

Hall, S. 1986. "Popular Culture and the State." In *Popular Culture and Social Relations*, edited by T. Bennett et al., 22–49. Milton Keynes: Open University Press.

Heffer, S. 1998. *Like the Roman: The Life of Enoch Powell*. London: Weidenfeld & Nicolson.

Hegel, G. W. F. 1902. *Lectures on the Philosophy of History*. London: G. Bell and Sons.

Hume, David. 1998. "Of National Character." In *D. Hume's Selected Essays*, edited by S. Copley and A. Edgar, 113–25. Oxford: Oxford University Press.

Kant, Immanuel. 1950. "On the Different Races of Man." In *This is Race: An Anthology Selected from the International Literature on the Races of Man*, edited by E. W. Count, 16–24. New York: Henry Schuman.

Keane, J. 2007. "The Twenty-First Century Enemies of Democracy." *Lecture, Sociology Seminar Series: 2007–08*, University of Birmingham, UK, November 13. Unpublished.

Lewis, R. 1979. *Enoch Powell: Principle in Politics*. London: Cassell.

Neill, S. 1990. *A History of Christian Missions*, 2nd edn, revised by O. Chadwick. London: Penguin.

O'Neill, B. 2005. "Why Waste Time Tanning Kilroy's Hide?" *Spiked-Online*, February 8. Accessed February 12, 2005. http://www.spiked-online.com/Articles/0000000CA8BA.htm

Orwell, George. 1995. "Boys' Weeklies." In *Writing Englishness: 1900–1950—An Introductory Sourcebook on National Identity*, edited by J. Giles and T. Middleton, 177–85. London: Routledge.

Pilkington, E. 1990. *Beyond the Mother Country: West Indians and the Notting Hill White Riots*. London: I. B. Tauris.

Powell, E. 1966. "Speech at Wolverhampton." March 25. Accessed October 20, 2013. http://enochpowell.net/fr-81.html

———. 1967. "Facing Up to Britain's Race Problem." *Daily Telegraph*, February 16. Accessed October 20, 2013. http://www.enochpowell.net/fr-82.html

———. 1968a. "Speech at Chippenham," May 11. Accessed October 20, 2013. http://www.enochpowell.net/fr-46.html

———. 1968b. "To the Preston Amounderness Round Table, Lytham St Annes," October 10. Accessed October 20, 2013. http://www.enochpowell.net/sd-05.html

———. 1969a. "Walsall Speech, 9 February 1968." In *Enoch Powell on Immigration*, edited by B. Smithies and P. Fiddick, 19–22. London: Sphere.

———. 1969b. "Birmingham Speech, 20 April 1968." In *Enoch Powell on Immigration*, edited by B. Smithies and P. Fiddick, 35–43. London: Sphere.

———. 1969c. "Eastbourne Speech, 16 November 1968." In *Enoch Powell on Immigration*, edited by B. Smithies and P. Fiddick, 63–77. London: Sphere.

———. 1971a. "To the *Association Des Chefs D'Enterprises Libres*, Lyons," February 12. Accessed October 20, 2013. http://www.enochpowell.net/sd-49.html

———. 1971b. "To the Monday Club, Painters' Hall, London", July 13. Accessed October 20, 2013. http://www.enochpowell.net/sd-50.html

Prince, R. 2009. "Daniel Hannan Risks Angering David Cameron by Praising Enoch Powell." *The Telegraph*, August 26.

Renan, E. 1882. *Qu'est-ce qu'une Nation?* (*What is a Nation?*), translated by I. M. Snyder. Paris: Calmann-Levy.

Roth, A. 1970. *Enoch Powell: Tory Tribune*. London: Macdonald.

Shepherd, R. 1996. *Enoch Powell*. London: Hutchinson.

Smiles, S. (1859) 2002. *Self-Help: With Illustrations of Character, Conduct, and Perseverance*, edited by P. W. Sinnema. Oxford: Oxford University Press.

Smith, J. E. H. 2013. "The Enlightenment's 'Race' Problem, and Ours." *The New York Times*, February 10. Accessed September 6, 2013. http://opinionator. blogs.nytimes.com/2013/02/10/why-has-race-survived/

Smithies, B. and P. Fiddick (eds). 1969. *Enoch Powell on Immigration*. London: Sphere.

Virgil. 2006. *The Aeneid*, translated by R. Fagles. London: Penguin.

Weber, Max. 1970. "The Nation." In *From Max Weber: Essays in Sociology*, edited and translated by H. H. Gerth and C. Wright Mills, 171–79. London: Routledge & Kegan Paul.

PART 3
The Indian Experience

11

Minority Question in India

Bishnu N. Mohapatra

Introduction

This chapter focuses on explicating the shifting contours of "minority question" in India. It tries to do this in the light of changing historical frames. Two things are kept at the forefront of this chapter. First, the "minority question" has been posed within a broader narrative of society and social change in India. This is informed by the belief that any discussion on "minorities" in isolation or without paying attention to the larger political and social system will be vacuous. Second, while discussing this theme, I have tried to forge a narrative that is deliberately open-ended and resistant to an artificial closure. Without this, I fear, the narrative can very well get frozen and the discourse of minorities gets reified.

In a constitutional democracy, minorities are expected to be the articulators of their problems, makers of their identity, and the protectors of their interests. It is also true that through their collective effort, they create their shared world that is experientially renewed from time to time. However, minorities, like many other identity groups, do not fully control the identity-making process. Nor is this process a monolith. The members of "majority" also play a significant role in this process. In some contexts, a constructed majority sees the minority group as a threat, as an entity that demands "unjustifiable" protection, and finally, one that complicates the project of nationalism. In other words, while constructing and fortifying its identity, the "majority" group constructs minority groups as its "other".

Historically speaking, the "Hindu nationalist" discourses in India display a great deal of ambiguities toward the religious minorities. In recent decades, their views on the "minority question" have become intensely majoritarian as well as exclusivist. Needless to say, the minorities' self-definitions and the Hindu-nationalist discourses stand opposed to each other. Understanding the contestation between the two is crucial for the comprehension of the "minority question" in India. At this point, let me introduce a couple of caveats. First, the "minority question" cannot and should not be understood within a rigid and binary grid of majority–minority[1] relation in India. The logic of constitutional democracy and competitive electoral politics often complicates this picture. Hence, it is important to recognize that several processes mediate the relationship between the two. Second, it is important to remember that discourses on minorities are necessarily layered and multifaceted for the simple reason that they are articulated and reproduced in varied locations and informed by conflicting interests and visions. It is important to recognize that the understanding of the "minority question" in India is not about capturing the pure particularism of minorities. Third, it is also vital to see how through the operation of government policies and "technologies" the category of "minority" is constituted, and how it changes over a period of time.

Section I

India's diversity is indeed proverbial. More than a billion people who live in the country speak about 4600 languages/dialects (including the 18 recognized in the eighth schedule of the Constitution[2]) belonging to 12 language families and 24 scripts. The country has nearly 2,800 ethnic communities and nearly 20,000 caste groups.[3] India houses all the major religions of the world. According to the 2001 Census of India,[4] nearly 80.5 percent Indians were Hindus, and Muslims, Christians, Sikhs, and Buddhists were 13.4 percent, 2.3 percent, 1.9 percent, and 0.8 percent of the total population, respectively. A cross-cutting of communities across a large territory is a significant feature of India's diversity. It is also worth remembering that these religious groups are not monoliths, they are internally diverse, and there are communities who tend to think of themselves as bearers of plural religious identities (Mayaram 1997; Nandy 1999).[5] It is within these complexities that one has to locate the majority–minority relations in India.

Let me at this point outline some of the contexts in which the problem of the "minority question" in India has been discussed in recent decades. The scholars of Indian democracy tend to agree that the last two decades of the 20th century witnessed a great deal of social churning in the country. A large number of people belonging to the marginal sections of the Indian society finally "arrived" to stake their claims and assert their rights in the polity.

The social churning, however, is only a part of the story. The rise of the "Hindu Right" during the later part of the last century is equally significant. The mobilization of Hindus around the issue of *Ramjanam-abhumi* (the birth place of Ram) and the eventual demolition of the Babri Masjid on December 6, 1992, in Ayodhya, shook the secular foundations of the Indian polity. Undoubtedly, with this, the relationship between the religious minorities (particularly the Muslims) and the Indian State hit its lowest point. Once again, the wreckage of the Babri Masjid brought forth the issue of the nature of Indian polity and State and, above all, the "idea of India" into the domain of fierce contestation. A variety of explanations are offered concerning this tragic event. The votaries of "Hindutva" interpret the event as a logical outcome of the state's policy of "minority appeasement" and consider it as the fallout of the postulates of Nehruvian secularism, which they claim to be inauthentic and pro-religious minorities. The secularists, on the other hand, tend to explain the event in terms of the growing communalization of the Indian society over a period of time. Some talk of the Indian state's eroding capacity to engage with the religious minorities that contributed to the worsening of communal situation in the country. It is true that notwithstanding the campaign of the Bharatiya Janata Party and other Hindu organizations such as the Rashtriya Swayamsevak Sangh, the Vishva Hindu Parishad, and the Bajarang Dal, a larger number of people disapproved the demolition of the masjid.[6]

The reactions of the Muslims to the demolition of Babri Masjid were predictable. Most of them were angry and dejected. The communal riots

in different cities that followed the demolition took the pathos and helplessness of the Muslims to a new intensity. The Indian Muslims found
themselves, as someone evocatively pointed out, "in a twilight terrain
where hope and despair live in uneasy truce."[7]

Despair arising out of communal violence was not something new to
the Indian Muslims. According to available data, during 1978–93, communal violence in India increased dramatically in comparison to the previous decade. After the partition of 1947, communal violence[8] subsided
till 1960; it rose once again, peaking in 1969, and then a substantial
decline between 1971–77. The number of districts affected by communal violence increased from 61 in 1961 to 250 in 1986–87 (Hasan 1988,
2469). Even the Christian minorities have expressed a deep sense of
insecurity as a result of increasing atrocities against them in recent years.[9]
Several reports on communal violence over the years have very clearly
established that these were not natural outcomes of India's diverse social
fabric. In many instances, the violence was shaped by prior planning,
political calculations, state apathy, and organized revenge. The anti-
Sikh violence in Delhi and other cities in the wake of Indira Gandhi's
assassination in 1984 and the anti-Muslim violence in Gujarat in 2002,
just to cite the most well known, can prove this quite well. The point I
am trying to make is that the increasing violence against the minorities
in recent decades has given the "minority question" an added urgency.
Once the feeling of insecurities increases in the minds of the minorities,
then the presence of secularism as a mere policy of intent or the existence of constitutional safeguards alone are not enough. In this context,
demands on the part of the minorities for the effective implementation of
the existing safeguards and for the protection of their lives and property
are of great value. No minority rights talk in India is or can ever be free
from such existential anxieties. And these anxieties often get embedded
in the complicated process of history and memory.

I have deliberately highlighted the issue of religious minorities in this
chapter, for I think it is politically salient today. Although the problem of
linguistic minorities emerges from time to time, it does not seem to have
the "pathological" edge that it once had during the first two decades after
independence. In a comparative sense, India's agony over religion and
religious identity continues to persist. Thus, from the religious minorities' point of view, the persisting anxieties continue to be informed both

by security and developmental deficits. The anxiety over physical security is an old one. But anxiety over "developmental deficits" emerged later and acquired a greater visibility in the last three decades or so. Though related, these anxieties are presented in two distinct registers or political idioms, but in different ways together they produce compelling "subjectivities" for minority groups. In turn, these "subjectivities" get enmeshed with public institutions and government policies, tactics, and technologies.

Minimally, a weak numerical position as well as socio-economic status remains central to the definition of a minority. But how weak this strength has to be and what is the appropriate level at which a group's status has to be seen are not easy to answer. For instance, if the Muslims can be defined as a minority group at the all-India level, it may not be so when we consider the province or local level as the relevant unit. For instance, the Muslims are not a minority in Jammu and Kashmir. According to the National Commission for Minorities Act, 1992, the minority status of a community is determined simply by the notification of the Central Government. Currently, the National Commission for Minorities' jurisdiction extends to five minority groups: Muslims, Christians, Sikhs, Buddhists, and Parsis. From a numerical vantage, one can consider Jains to be a minority group. But they have not been accorded that status of a minority at the National level. However, nine state governments within their territorial limits have recognized them as one (Ministry of Minority Affairs, Government of India 2007, 12). For the purpose of Article 30 of the Indian Constitution that allows minorities to establish and manage their religious institutions, the minority status is determined with reference to a state.[10] During the Constituent Assembly Debate, some of the Dalit members defined their status as a "political minority" whose defining feature was not their numerical disadvantage but their social and economic backwardness and caste injustices. Similarly, tribal groups never saw themselves as a minority in numerical terms but as a distinct people partly shaped by a history of injustices and exploitation by nontribal communities. In order to address the developmental deficits, the government of India has created a category called "minority-concentrated districts,"[11] a demographic grid that is contrasted with the rest of the national/administrative space. Two conclusions follow from this. First, although an important dimension, numerical weakness alone does not define a minority. Second, minority status is essentially fluid and it varies across level and time.

Section II

Community consciousness and mobilizations are creatures of history. But like most creatures of history, they are never fully under its control. On the basis of the existing historical scholarship, it is plausible to argue that the cultural or religious differences between communities per se did not determine their relationship; it is the selective utilization and dissemination of symbols in a given political context that made the inter-community relationship harmonious or conflict-ridden.

There is no doubt that colonial state for its own survival exploited the cultural/religious divisions, and through this process reified them. For instance, some argued that the granting of separate electorates to the Muslims in 1909, on the plea of a handful of elite Muslim leaders, was a clear example of colonial state's policy of counterpoise[12] to the Congress. But to suggest that it is the colonial state alone that created the divisions among communities would be an exaggeration. However, there are other ways in which the role of the colonial state and its varied practices toward the intercommunity relations can be understood. The argument here is that colonialism did not inaugurate the communal differences/conflict[13] in India, but through its interventions changed their trajectories and political possibilities.

As early as the 1880s, Syed Ahmad Khan raised the fear of Hindu majoritarianism in the context of the Colonial State's policy of introducing native representation at the local level. As time passed, the demands for special protection for the Muslims in the legislatures and various services of the colonial state gave rise to a "vocabulary of minorityism"[14] that survived even into the postcolonial period. As mentioned above, the separate electorate was provided for the Muslims in the Legislative Councils in the Act of 1909. Seven years later, the Congress and the Muslim League accepted the principle of separate representation. Subsequently, the Government of India Act of 1919 extended the separate electorate to other communities such as Sikhs, Christians, and some European groups. In the Government of India Act of 1935, this was further extended to include the depressed classes who had hitherto been a part of the Hindu majority. The application of this provision was somewhat diluted[15] at the intervention of Gandhi who strongly felt that the strategy of the colonial state was to further divide and weaken the process of national mobilization. The rise of collective demands from various religious and caste groups in the early part of the 20th century fitted quite well with the British perception of the Indian society as a country of discrete religious, caste, and other groups. It is within this context that "minority rights" as special provisions for minority groups emerged.

It is clear that the temporary acceptance of the "separate electorate" by the Congress was dictated by sheer political pragmatism rather than by any principled commitment to political safeguards for the minorities. This is not to say that there was no principled discussion on "minority safeguards" within the Congress. In the Congress resolution of December 28, 1927, assurance was given

> ...to the two great communities that their legitimate interests will be safeguarded in the legislatures and such representation of the communities should be secured for the present, and if desired, by the reservation of seats in joint electorates on the basis of population in every province and in the Central Legislature.[16] (Ansari 1996)

It further resolved that "in the future Constitution, liberty of conscience shall be guaranteed and no legislature, Central or Provincial, shall have power to make any laws interfering with liberty of conscience" (ibid., 96).

The Nehru Report of 1928—produced under the chairmanship of Motilal Nehru—and the Sapru Committee Report (1945) shaped, among other things, the future contour of the minority question in India. Largely "rights-based" and within a broader national vision, the reports provided for reserved seats in legislatures for minorities. The reports also spoke of the need for creating new institutions to safeguard minority rights. These reports, in a significant sense, can be read as a part of an ongoing debate on these issues not only within the Congress, but also between them, the colonial state, and the leaders of the Muslim League. Underlying the recommendations outlined in these reports, one can see the emergence of an agentic view of minorities, a political subjectivity partially trapped within the logic of colonial rule. Abul Kalam Azad echoed this in his famous Ramgarh address in 1940 when he spelt out the Congress's view that the minorities "should judge for themselves what safeguards are necessary for the protection of their rights and interests. The majority should not decide this."[17]

It is not difficult to imagine how an agentic idea of a minority (individual or community) can produce at its very heart a political ambiguity. If the minorities are free to choose their future, can they opt out of that very nation state that wishes to keep them as minorities? Will they be allowed to play a key role in forging a nationalist imaginary for the whole people? How can minority rights be embodied in the practice of governance? What remains in the domain of possible and how is that very domain structured? Once the Constitution-making process began, the inherited practices were seen in a new light, and the older terms such as representation, citizenship, and minority rights were subjected to new interpretations. It seems the old and repressed anxieties appeared in new intense forms.

Section III

While discussing minority rights, interpreters of the Constituent Assembly debates (1946–49) point toward a break, a disjuncture between the early and later drafts of the Indian Constitution. Before we discover the reasons underlying the emendations, one should view it at multiple levels: values, biases, and limits.

The Constituent Assembly of India was convened as a result of the Cabinet Mission Statement of May 16, 1946.[18] On December 13, four days after the Assembly began its session, Nehru moved a resolution outlining the general principles and philosophy that the Constitution should adhere to and reflect. The Constitution, according to him, would secure justice to all, equality of status, of opportunity, and before law to every citizen. In the new Constitution, "safeguards shall be provided for minorities, backward and tribal areas, and depressed and other backward classes."[19] After spelling out the general objectives on January 24, 1947, the Constituent Assembly went on to elect an Advisory Committee on the rights of citizens, minorities, and tribal communities and excluded areas under the chairmanship of Vallabhbhai Patel. Various communities[20] had had their representation in the Committee. In order to smoothen the Constitution-making process, the Advisory Committee had to appoint several subcommittees whose function was to look into the specific issues and themes. The Minority Sub-Committee comprising of 26 members started functioning under the guidance of Dr H. C. Mookherjee, representing the Christian community in the Assembly.

On April 17 and 18, the Minority Sub-Committee reflected on the issue of fundamental rights from the "point of view of minorities."[21]

The Sub-Committee's rejection of a "separate electorate" as a means of securing political safeguard was quite emphatic. Knowing the position of the Congress on separate electorate, this was not surprising. Similarly, the Committee's support for the reservation of seats (within the joint electorate system) in legislatures for the minority communities was equally overwhelming. It was also agreed that the reservation of seats would be for 10 years and it would be reconsidered at the end of this period. The Sub-Committee's recommendation of not having a statutory provision for the reservation of minorities in the Cabinet was decided by a slender margin. However, they agreed to have a convention similar to the one in the Government of India Act, 1935, which could provide for the representation of minorities in the Cabinet. The reservation of jobs in Public Services for different communities was a divisive issue too. Except for the Parsis and the Indian Christians, the reservation of jobs for the rest was accepted by a majority vote.

In his letter of August 8, 1947 to the President of the Constituent Assembly, Vallabhbhai Patel as the Chairman of the Advisory Committee on Minorities, Fundamental Rights, etc. outlined the provisions pertaining to minority rights to be included in the future Constitution of India.[22] On the issue of political safeguards, he reiterated the position of the Minority Sub-Committee. After debating on these issues on August 27 and 28, 1947, the entire report of the Advisory Committee was adopted by the Assembly. By about February 1948, the recommendations of the Advisory Committee were incorporated into the Draft Constitution. The provisions for the minorities were contained in Part XIV of this Draft.

In his letter of May 11, 1949 to the President of the Constituent Assembly, Sardar Patel wrote:

> Although the abolition of separate electorates had removed much of the poison from body politic, the reservation of seats for religious communities, it was felt, did lead to a certain degree of separatism and was to that extent contrary to the conception of secular democratic state.[23]

The debate that followed in the Assembly on this issue on May 25 and 26, 1949 saw a triumph of a "homogenizing nationalism." The language was so powerful that even the provision of "proportional representation" was also seen as divisive and impractical. Some even considered the proposal for "safeguards," "weightage," "protection," and "reservation" as undemocratic.[24] "India today is suffering," said Patel, "from want of blood. It is completely anemic. Unless you put blood into its veins, even if we quarrel about concessions or reservations, we will get nothing."[25] The discordant voices of a few who appealed to the Assembly to retain certain forms of political safeguards for the minorities naturally did not make any impact. The recommendations for political safeguards for religious minorities in terms of reservation of seats in legislature, affirmative action in public employment were soon dropped.

In the changed circumstances, Scheduled Castes (SCs) and Scheduled Tribes (STs) were separated from the religious minorities. Once again, plea for respecting the claims of the religious minorities was outvoted in the Assembly. There was very little debate on the issue and the undesirability of reservation of jobs for the religious minorities was almost taken for granted. In fact, in his speech referring to the Sikhs, Sardar Patel even portrayed the demand for reservation of jobs as an admission of a community's weakness and inferiority.[26] The provision for the appointment of a "minority officer" met with similar fate. Instead of a minority officer, the Assembly created the provision for a Special Officer only for the SCs and STs. Within the general rubric of "educational and cultural rights," protection of minority rights (both linguistic and religious) was envisaged in the Draft Constitution. However, during the course of the debate, the proposal that the children of the minorities should receive primary education, although agreed as a sound principle, was not incorporated in the Constitution as a right. Similarly, from the draft provision, "No minorities shall be denied admission to educational institution maintained by the state...," the term "minorities" was replaced by the term "citizen." Ambedkar thought that making it a universal principle was the best way to fight discrimination and to make the state more responsive to the fundamental right.[27]

It can be argued that in the atmosphere of hate and violence that followed the partition, the talk of right claims, particularly on the part of the minorities, tended to appear as divisive and particularistic. It is not surprising then that some members of the Constituent Assembly treated the problem of majority and minority as necessarily divisive and antinationalistic. For Dr P. S. Deshmukh, "There [was] no more monstrous word in the history of Indian politics than the word 'minority'."[28] Mr R. K. Sidhwa expressed similar sentiment when he stated: "I only, wish, Sir that the phrase 'minorities' should be wiped out from the history."[29]

A contextual reading of the debate shows that these extreme statements were uttered while discussing the issue of separate electorate for the minorities. A large segment of opinion in the Assembly, however, took the presence of majority and minority communities as an integral feature of the Indian society. For them, devising ways and means to reconcile the interests of majority and minority was the main challenge. Right from the beginning, separate electorate, as a political safeguard for the minority communities, was not a part of the Constitutional design. For the Congress nationalists, it was an intrinsic part of the colonial governance in India. Their revulsion toward it was not something new. Yet, against the backdrop of partition, hatred for separate electorate got stretched to any political safeguard for the religious minorities. Along with the provision of separate electorate, the proposals for the reservation of seats and proportional representation were also thrown out of the window. I am not suggesting that the reservation of seats in the legislature for the religious minorities was the most appropriate way of granting them political representation. Indeed, against the backdrop of intense communal conflict at the time of Independence, it might have encouraged fragmentation in the emerging political community in India. But the rejection of several other provisions such as reservation of jobs and the appointment of a special officer for the minorities was not entirely convincing. There was no doubt that the Constituent Assembly was fully and unequivocally committed to the values of nondiscrimination, of universal rights for the citizens, and of religious freedom. It also clearly demonstrated its dedication to the protection of cultural and linguistic diversities of the Indian society. But its commitment to grant special rights for the minorities (particularly the religious ones) was evidently ambivalent.

One can never fully explain this ambivalence, as many scholars do, by referring to the fact of partition and the communal violence of 1947. It is true that a significant majority of the Congress leaders saw the enactment of a regime of universal rights along with a set of individual and collective rights sufficient to protect the interest of the minorities (Jha 2008). In their view, minority representation in legislature and affirmative action in public services were not necessary. In fact, some saw the special representation as undermining the values of democracy, secularism, and universal citizenship. The conservative right-wing elements viewed mandatory presence of religious minorities in legislatures inimical to the project of nation building in India. Some saw the nationalist vocabulary as suffering from "a normative deficit" (Bajpai 2008) concerning group representation, and that accounts for the withdrawal of political representation for minorities recommended in the first draft of the Constitution.

To a suggestion that the issue of minority rights should be discussed after the process of partition is over and after having full information regarding the state of minorities in Pakistan, Ambedkar reacted that the rights of minorities should be "absolute rights."[30] One should not overinterpret this statement. In fact, there is enough evidence to suggest that the minority rights discourse was hardly unencumbered; it was dependent on so many things including the making of a "compact nation." It was seen either as transitory or as a must-fit into other concerns of the state and nation. Speaking on the issue of the withdrawal of reservation of seats in legislatures for the minorities, except the SCs, Nehru wrote:

> ...it was the right thing to do, not only from the point of view of pure nationalism, which it is, but also from the separate and individual viewpoint of each group, if you like, majority or minority.... Therefore, I think that doing away with this reservation business is not only a good thing in itself... it is a very good move for the nation and for the world. It shows that we are really sincere about this business of having secular democracy.[31]

It is easy to see how Nehru's argument oscillated between the registers of nationalism and democracy. Patel tilted more toward pragmatism. For him, the earlier concession of political safeguards was dictated by the objective of "easing the suspicions"[32] of the minority groups. Pandit Gobind Ballabh Pant's argument concerning the separate electorate was from the vantage point of democracy. For him, democracy requires a minimal sense of solidarity among different groups and a robust sense of citizenship for its effective functioning. The establishment of separate electorate destroys the solidarity and undermines the value of citizenship. According to him, "the success of democracy is to be measured by the amount of confidence that it generates in different sections of the community."[33] Special provisions for the minorities in the political domain, according to S. J. Jerome D'Souza,[34] were compatible with the values of democracy. He saw the minority communities as interest groups and the policy of reservation as a viable means of securing their representation in the legislatures.

During the long debate on minority rights, contending conceptions of democracy and nationalism were played out in an unequal manner. Some minorities felt that the safeguards would help them to play a better role in the emerging nation. Any strong demand for special treatment for the religious minorities met with suspicion. Those minority groups which refused to demand political and economic safeguards were appreciated. They became the "good" minorities. By implication, those who insisted on being treated separately were seen as "bad" minorities. One member in the Assembly even suggested that the minorities would be in a stronger position if they were to surrender the safeguards.[35]

A conventional reading of the debates highlights the way the Constitution incorporated the plural social order of India by recognizing specificities while providing a comprehensive regime of rights for every citizen of the country. Whether or not it embodied or reflected liberal values is still a matter of debate. My reading of the debate is different in the sense that I have tried to show the limits within which the discourse of minority rights was framed. I have also tried to point out the presence of some of the anxieties concerning minority rights, stemming partly out of the immediate historical experience, but to a large extent by the participants' ideas of nation building. What will happen to the national unity if the distinctiveness of the minorities is recognized (?) was the often-asked question. The preeminence of this question was almost taken for granted. Such anxieties have not disappeared from the political discourse in India.

Before I end this section, let me make a few cautionary remarks to clarify the arguments I have made. The project of nation making that shaped the discourse on minority rights during the early years of independence should not be confused with the project of nationalism propagated by the Hindu right. I do not suggest that the members of the Congress were articulating an exclusivist conception of nationalism on the floor of the Assembly. Nor am I arguing that the anxieties concerning the religious minorities were a product of their nationalism. My point is simply this: the well-meaning Congress leaders, including Nehru, sincerely believed that to acknowledge the communitarian sensibilities (the religious ones in particular) in politics would be to justify and entrench them. This fear, I have argued, circumscribed the trajectory of minority discourse to a considerable extent. But this fear or uneasiness was and still is very different from the ones articulated by the Hindu right in recent years. A cursory look at the debate in the Lok Sabha (The House of the People) on the issue of forming a National Minority Commission would prove my point. During the debate, the old fears and anxieties were invoked by those who were opposed to the creation of the Commission.

It is very clear that finally in the Constitution-making process the severance of religious minorities from Dalits and tribal communities was complete. Political representations and affirmative actions were seen as appropriate strategies (even though for a temporary period) to address social and educational backwardness and historical injustices only of the Dalits and the tribal communities. It took years before a religious minority—particularly a Muslim—emerged as a subject constituted by her/his socio-economic backwardness. This is not to say that in the initial decades after independence, the economic and educational status of Muslims was satisfactory. The argument is that the acknowledgment of "backwardness," to a large extent, was a function of minority groups emerging as targets of state policy and intervention. This is a significant shift to which I will turn now.

Section IV

Looking at the changes since the 1980s, one can argue that "minority question/rights" in India is getting more and more "governmentalized." This shift is, undoubtedly, neither sudden nor fully settled. The use of Foucault's idea of governmentality is deliberate. Focusing on momentous changes between the 16th and 18th centuries, Foucault wrote about the way in which State in Europe gradually got governmentalized. By which he meant the ways in which a "specific albeit complex form of power whose target was population, its principal form of knowledge political economy and its technical means apparatus of security" (Foucault 1991). He also pointed out the ways in which juridical sources and territorial grounding of power slowly made way for governmental technology and tactics.

To the extent a minority group is a part/segment of a "population" and, therefore, becomes a target of state policy, it is deeply imbricated within the power matrixes of the State. But this is not the only thing that is significant here. In fact, the exercise of power not only involves the state's intervention but also a process of self-disciplining of the population. In some sense, Foucault forced us to see the futility of reducing state and individual/community relations to pure juridical elements.

In an insightful article,[36] Chatterjee argues that a disjuncture between juridical sovereignty and governmental technology provides the site on which religious minorities attempt to assert their cultural rights in India. "It is because of a contestation on the ground of sovereignty," he suggests, "that the right is asserted against governmentality" (Chatterjee 2010, 229). I think the ground of sovereignty from the vantage point of the religious minorities remains acutely slippery, and their attitudes toward governmental power or tactics are not necessarily oppositional. For some years now, one of the central goals of the federal government is to enhance the welfare of religious minorities. With this in view, it has devised specific policies, but these are not necessarily claimed as rights by religious minorities. At the same time, language of autonomy and rights are invoked while the minority groups fight against the majoritarian tendencies within the state and society. Since the publication of Chatterjee's essay, the sway of governmental power vis-à-vis the religious minorities—more so with the Muslims—has intensified. As a target population of government policies, the state's engagement with them has increased. In turn, it has come to shape their political subjectivities.

The "governmentalization" of minority question was shaped by and constitutive of the knowledge produced largely under the auspices of the Indian state. As early as 1957, a committee instituted by the Congress highlighted three areas of concern for the minorities in India. First, it highlighted the feeling of discontent prevalent among the minority groups due to their poor representation in the service sector, at the center as well as in the provinces. The Committee also felt the necessity of giving adequate representation to the minorities, particularly in the lower-ranking jobs in military, the railways, and so on (Kabir 1968). Second, it noted that the minority groups felt discriminated against in connection with the distribution of state resources for trade, industry, and commerce. Finally, the Sub-Committee drew attention to the feeling of the minorities of not being adequately represented in various representative bodies of the state. The recommendations of the Sub-Committee were taken seriously by the central government. The Prime Minister wrote to the Chief Ministers to pay attention to the employment position of the minorities and report to him. However, these efforts were discontinued on the ground that any special provision with regard to employment for the minorities would entrench their minority identity and encourage fissiparous tendencies in the society (ibid., 46).

By the late 1970s, the minority question was very much present in the Indian political horizon. The *Janata* regime at the Center in 1977–78 articulated the need to have a re-look at the institutional and political sides of safeguards for religious minorities. However, when Indira Gandhi returned to power after the Janata interlude, she felt the need to address the minority disenchantment toward the Congress. In her letter of May 11, 1983, she wrote to all the members of the Council of Ministers and to all the Chief Ministers of the states outlining a broad policy statement regarding the minorities. Known in the administrative lingo as the "Prime Minister's '15-point programme on minorities'," it articulated various issues afflicting the minorities in India. It inevitably spoke about the ways in which communal riots could be prevented. It advised the state governments to "give special consideration to minorities"[37] while recruiting personnel into state bureaucracies. Nearly 23 years later, in a different political context, another Congress Prime Minister—Manmohan Singh—re-crafted the old "15-point programme for the welfare of minorities."[38] The new version of the program talks of providing equitable share for minorities in economic activities and employment through existing and new policies. It also proposes that 15 percent of the targets and outlays under various schemes should be earmarked for minorities. In a sense, these 15-point programs were a response to and a direct acknowledgment of economic and educational backwardness of the minority groups. Manmohan Singh's declaration gave the program a new developmental impetus and urged for new governmental tactics for addressing the marginality and development deficits of minorities.

Although for long, the marginality of certain religious minority communities was common sense, it was the Gopal Singh Committee Report of 1983 that gave it an empirical basis and a new kind of coherence. In its report on the minorities, it drew attention, among other things, to the educational backwardness of Muslims. On the basis of a survey, it highlighted the excessive dropout of Muslim children at the primary school level and their underrepresentation in the domains of higher and technical education.[39] The report also highlighted the underrepresentation of Muslims in different spheres of government employment. The underrepresentation of minorities in legislatures—once again particularly of the Muslims—was also a matter of great debate and concern. Till date, their representation in the Lok Sabha has never gone beyond 9.04 percent (Siddiqui 2000, 13). The representation of the Muslims in the decision-making bodies of the main political parties was equally dismal (Razzack and Gumber 2000, 14). The competitive and formal democracy's capacity to respond to the demands of the minorities was also evidently limited. At any rate, the desire to change their status from objects of electoral politics (vote banks) to subjects of political change is gradually occupying a central place within the minority discourse in the country. However, to view these political sensibilities as a pure reflection of an undifferentiated minority community would be mistaken.

By the time the Central Government instituted the Sachar Committee and the National Commission for Religious and Linguistic Minorities (also known as Ranganath Misra Commission), certain shifts were slowly discernible within the policy and political domains. Within the government circle, attempts were being made to better target population groups including the backward minorities for delivering welfare programs. Sachar Committee submitted its report in 2006 and Ranganath Commission in 2007. During this period, the visibility of the National Commission for Minorities also increased. The United Progressive Alliance created a Ministry of Minority Affairs at the central level to "ensure a more focused approach toward issues relating the minorities and facilitate the formulation of overall policy and planning, coordination, evaluation and review of the regulatory framework and development programs for the benefits of the minority communities."[40] The creation of the National Minorities Development and Finance Corporation (1994) and the National Commission for Minority Educational Institutions Act (2004) is part of a greater "governmentalization" of the minority question that I mentioned before.

I think the Sachar Committee and Ranganath Misra Commission reports can be read as an effort in guiding the minority question in new directions. Notwithstanding the empirical richness of these reports, the revelation of Muslims' socio-economic and educational backwardness was not something new. Years ago, the Gopal Singh report, as mentioned earlier, had delivered a similar conclusion. However, in a changed national scenario, findings of backwardness resonated in new ways among Muslim communities seized by majoritarian stereotypes and an intense psychosis caused by violence and discrimination. In some curious ways, the Sachar Committee report also contained possibilities of transforming the fact of developmental deficits into a larger democratic story. It was not surprising that young Muslims in different parts of the country raised the question as to why even after 56 years of constitutional democracy in India, equal citizenship in terms of certain basic human development is denied to so many of them. The report, quite predictably, did not give an answer to this fundamental question, but it created new occasions for reinterpreting old questions and revisiting past understandings.

Some argue that a focus on developmental deficits, rather than on identity-related questions, would create new contexts for civic–political rather than ethnic mobilization among the Muslim communities in India. No doubt in the past, excessive emphasis on identity issues, though legitimate, did not push their democratic agency very far. The majoritarian forces saw the interest articulation of religious minorities as a religious group through a lens of exclusivist nationalism. Even some well-meaning liberals fear that mobilization of secular interest through a religious grid may undermine the future of Indian democracy. Though analytically distinct, in some situations the opposition between "identity" concerns and "secular" interest cannot be sustained. But the tension between the two will remain for a foreseeable future.

At the heart of greater governmentalization of minority question (particularly involving religious minority) in India remains a tension. As targets of government policies, minority groups are bracketed within or treated as a part of the "socially and educationally backward classes."

But at the same time, they are not the same as Other Backward Classes recognized by the Indian Constitution. Therefore, they cannot be offered the same ameliorative policies like Other Backward Classes such as SCs and STs. As a matter of fact, they were excised from the larger body of "backward classes" at the making of the Constitution. It is their religious identity that complicates their status as a marginal group. Whether backward Muslims or impoverished minority groups can get reservation in employment and education (like SCs and STs) is no more discussed as a pragmatic policy question. It is deeply entangled with an embattled past that the policy makers find it difficult to expunge. As the minority question gets governmentalized in India, religious minority identity as a citizen is experienced as a split. As a target of government policy, her identity is viewed in relation to her backwardness. But even in experience of backwardness or marginality, her identity is circumscribed by her religious difference. It is difficult to imagine that in near future this split can be reconciled.

Notes and Bibliography

Notes

1. Here my objective is not to deny the usefulness of the categories of majority and minority. Indeed, these categories are and will remain useful within democratic theory. As an empirical or descriptive idea, the existence of these categories is undeniable in most societies. But the question is: what are the substantive contents that go into the making of these categories? Their permanence (of course, in a relative sense), and the recognizable and enduring boundaries also provide coherence to these categories. I am of the view that the "minority question" in India cannot be adequately understood within a dyadic grid of majority and minority. This is what seems to be implied, although indirectly, in Rajeev Bhargava's distinction between the "majority–minority syndrome" and "majority–minority framework." See Bhargava (1999).
2. The Constitution of India (1995 edition), Eighth Schedule, 326.
3. Quoted in Nandy (1998, 54). See also Singh, K. S. and The Anthropological Survey of India. 1994.
4. The Census of India 2001. Although the 2011 Census enumeration is complete, by the time I was finalizing the paper the religious profile of India was not ready.

5. The Anthropological Survey of India's *People of India* suggests that nearly 15 percent of communities in India occupy a zone of intermediate identities. It is also pointed out that 64.2 percent of all communities of India are bilingual. Quoted in Mayaram (1998).
6. Opinion polls suggested that only 22.7 percent of the Indian electorate found the demolition justified. Against this, 38.1 percent termed it as unjustified. See Mitra and Singh (1999).
7. Statement of Mohd. Zeyalul Haque quoted in Hasan (1996, 177).
8. Varshney (1997). See also Nandy (1999).
9. *Lok Sabha Debate* on Atrocities on Linguistic and Religious Minorities in the country on August 17 and 18, 2000. Mostly, the discussion veered around the attacks on the Christians and the churches in several parts of India.
10. The judgment of the Supreme Court of India in *T. M. A. Pai Foundation and Others v. the State of Karnataka and Others* (2002), in Ranganath Misra Commission Report, 2007.
11. Ministry of Minority Affairs, Government of India (2012).
12. For an early academic articulation of the counterpoise argument, see Krishna (1939).
13. See Bayly (1985).
14. See "Introduction" in Hasan (2001).
15. Instead of the conventional separate electorate model, a new strategy of representation was devised for the "depressed classes." This new model involved two stages. All the members registered in the general electoral roll in a constituency reserved for the Depressed Classes formed an Electoral College that will elect a panel of four candidates belonging to their class. In the second stage, one out of this panel elected by the Electoral College was elected by the general electorate. This model was a product of the Poona Pact agreed between Gandhi and Ambedkar.
16. Resolution passed on December 28, 1927 by the Indian National Congress at its 42nd session held in Madras, quoted in Ansari (1996). The "two great communities" mentioned in the Resolution referred to the Muslims and the Depressed Classes.
17. "An Extract from Presidential Address of Maulana Abul Kalam Azad—Ramgarh, December 1940" in Hasan (2001, 61).
18. Even on a limited franchise, the Constituent Assembly was meant to represent various interests and communities. Out of 296 members to be elected from the Provinces of the British India, the community-wise break-up was the following: Hindus: 163, Muslims: 80, Parsis: 3, Anglo-Indians: 3, Indian Christians: 6, Sikhs: 4, Schedule Castes: 31, and Backward Tribes: 6.
19. CAD, Vol. 1, 59.
20. Communities such as the Muslims, the Hindus, the Depressed Classes or the Scheduled Castes, the Sikhs, the Indian Christians, Parsis, Anglo-Indians, and the tribal and excluded areas were represented in the Advisory Committee.

21. "Letter from Dr H. C. Mookherjee to the Chairman, Advisory Committee on Fundamental Rights, Minorities, etc. 19 April, 1947," in Ansari (1996, 240).
22. "Letter from Vallabhbhai Patel to the President of the Constituent Assembly of India, 8 August 1947," CAD, Vol. V, 243–47.
23. "Letter from Sardar Vallabhbhai Patel to the President of the Constituent Assembly of India, 11 May 1949," CAD, Vol. VIII, 311.
24. "Speech of Sardar Sochet Singh, 26 May 1949," CAD, Vol. VIII, 340.
25. CAD, Vol. VIII, 354.
26. "Speech of Sardar Patel, 14 October 1949," CAD, Vol. X, 248.
27. "Speech of Ambedkar, 8 December, 1948," CAD, Vol. VII, 923.
28. "Speech of Dr. P. S. Deshmukh, 27 August 1947," CAD, Vol. V, 201.
29. "Speech of Mr. R. K. Sidhwa, 27 August 1947," CAD, Vol. V, 209.
30. "Statement of Ambedkar, 1 May 1947," CAD, Vol. II, 507–08.
31. "Statement of Jawaharlal Nehru, 26 May 1949," CAD, Vol. VIII, 330–32. Also see, Gopal (1988).
32. "Statement of Vallabhbhai Patel, 26 May 1949," CAD, Vol. VIII, 352.
33. "Statement of Govind Ballabh Pant, 27 August, 1947," CAD, Vol. V, 222–23.
34. "Statement of S. J. Jerome D'Souza, 27 August 1947," CAD, Vol. V, 231–32.
35. "Statement of B. A. Mandloi, 6 November, 1948," CAD, Vol. VII, 272.
36. See Chatterjee (1994); I have used the essay here from this volume.
37. "Prime Minister's Fifteen-Point Programme on Minorities, 1983," in Ansari (1996), 488.
38. Annual Report 2011–12, Ministry of Minority Affairs (www.minorityaffairs. gov.in), executive summary. The program was announced in June 2006.
39. "The Final Report on Minorities of India" by the Gopal Singh Committee, June 14, 1983, see chapter IV. This Committee was set up by the Home Ministry to look into the condition of Scheduled Castes, Scheduled Tribes, and minorities of the country.
40. Ministry of Minority Affairs (www.minorityaffairs.gov.in), see the section about the Ministry.

Bibliography

Ahmad, Imtiaz, Partha S. Ghosh, and Helmut Reifeld (eds). 2000. *Pluralism and Equality: Values in Indian Society and Politics*. New Delhi: SAGE.

Alam, Javed. 2000. "A Minority Moves into Another Millennium." In *India's Another Millennium*, edited by Romila Thapar. Delhi: Viking.

———. 2008. "The Contemporary Muslim Situation in India: A Long-Term View." *Economic and Political Weekly*, January 12–18.

Ansari, Iqbal A. 1996. *Readings on Minorities: Perspectives and Documents, Vol. 2*, 95. Delhi: Institute Of Objective Studies.

Baird, Robert D. 1978. "Religion and the Legitimation of Nehru's Concept of the Secular State." In *Religion and the Legitimation of Power in South Asia*, edited by B. L. Smith. Leiden: E. J. Brill.

Bajpai, Rochana. 2000. "Constituent Assembly Debates and Minority Rights." *Economic and Political Weekly*, May 27.

———. 2008. "Minority Representation and the Making of the Indian Constitution." In *Politics and Ethics of the Indian Constitution*, edited by Rajeev Bhargava. Delhi: Oxford University Press.

Basu, Amrita and Atul Kohli (eds). 1998. *Community Conflicts and the State in India*. Delhi: Oxford University Press.

Baumeister, Andrea. 2000. *Liberalism and the "Politics of Difference."* Edinburgh: Edinburgh University Press.

Bayly, C. A. 1985. "The Pre-History of 'Communalism'? Religious Conflict in India 1700–1800." *Modern Asian Studies* 19 (2): 177–203.

Beaglehole, J. H. 1967. "The Indian Christians—A Study of a Minority." *Modern Asian Studies* 1 (1): 59–80.

Bhargava, Rajeev (ed.). 1998. *Secularism and Its Critics*. Delhi: Oxford University Press.

———. 1999. "Should We Abandon the Majority–Minority Framework?" In *Minority Identity and the Nation-State*, edited by D. L. Seth and Gurpreet Mahajan. Delhi: Oxford University Press.

———. 2008. *Politics and Ethics of the Indian Constitution*. Delhi: Oxford University Press.

Bhargava, Rajeev, Amiya Kumar Bagchi, and R. Sudarshan (eds). 1999. *Multiculturalism, Liberalism and Democracy*. Delhi: Oxford University Press.

Bilgrami, Akeel. 1992. "What is a Muslim? Fundamental Commitment and Cultural Identity." *Economic and Political Weekly*, May 16–23.

Bose, Sugata and Ayesha Jalal (eds). 1999. *Nationalism, Democracy and Development: State and Politics in India*. Delhi: Oxford University Press.

Brass, Paul. 1991. *Ethnicity and Nationalism: Theory and Comparison*. New Delhi: SAGE.

Burchell, Graham, Colin Gordon, and Peter Miller (eds). 1991. *The Foucault Effect*. London: Harvester Wheatsheaf.

Carens, Joseph H. 2000. *Culture, Citizenship, and Community: A Contextual Exploration of Justice as Evenhandedness*. Oxford: Oxford University Press.

Chandhoke, Neera. 1999. *Beyond Secularism: The Rights of Religious Minorities*. Delhi: Oxford University Press.

Chatterjee, Partha. 1994. "Secularism and Toleration." *Economic and Political Weekly*, Vol. 29, No. 28, July 9. [2010; reprint. *Empire and Nation: Selected Essays*. New York: Columbia University Press.]

———. 1995. *The Nation and Its Fragments*. Delhi: Oxford University Press.

———. 2010 *Empire and Nation: Selected Essays*. New York: Columbia University Press.

Chatterji, Joya. 1998. "The Bengali Muslim: A Contradiction in Terms? An Overview of the Debate on Bengali Muslim Identity." In *Islam Communities and the Nation*, edited by Mushirul Hasan. Delhi: Manohar.

Das, Veena (ed.). 1992. "Introduction." In *Mirrors of Violence: Communities, Riots and Survivors in South Asia.* Delhi: Oxford University Press.

———. 1995. *Critical Events: An Anthropological Perspective on Contemporary India.* Delhi: Oxford University Press.

Engineer, Asghar Ali. 1991. *Communal Riots in Post-Independent India,* 2nd edn. Hyderabad: Sangam Books.

Fernandes, Walter. 1999. "Attacks on Minorities and a National Debate on Conversions." *Economic and Political Weekly,* January 16–23.

Foucault, Michael. 1991. "Governmentality." In *The Foucault Effect,* edited by Graham Burchell, Colin Gordon, and Peter Miller. London: Harvester WheatSheaf.

Frankel, Francine R., Zoya Hasan, Rajeev Bhargava, and Balveer Arora (eds). 2000. *Transforming India: Social and Political Dynamics of Democracy.* Delhi: Oxford University Press.

Galanter, Marc. 1984. *Competing Equalities: Law and the Backward Classes in India.* Delhi: Oxford University Press.

Gopal, S. 1988. "Nehru and Minorities." *Economic and Political Weekly,* Special Article, November.

Gupta, Raghuraj. 1985. "Changing Role and Status of the Muslim Minority in India: A Point of View." *Journal Institute of Muslim Minority Affairs* 5: 181–202.

Hansen, Thomas Blom. 1999. *The Saffron Wave: Democracy and Hindu Nationalism in Modern India.* Delhi: Oxford University Press.

———. 2000a. "Governance and Myths of State in Mumbai." In *The Everyday State and Society in Modern India,* edited by C. J. Fuller and Veronique Benei, 255–72. New Delhi: Social Science Press.

———. 2000b. "Predicaments of Secularism: Muslim Identities and Politics in Mumbai." *Journal Royal Anthropological Institute* 6.

Hardgrave, Robert L., Jr. 1993. "India: The Dilemmas of Diversity." *Journal of Democracy* 4 (4): 54–68.

Hasan, Mushirul. 1979. *Nationalism and Communal Politics in India.* Delhi: Manohar.

———. 1988. "In Search of Integration and Identity: Indian Muslims Since Independence." *Economic and Political Weekly,* Special Article.

———. 1996. "Minority Identity and its Discontents: Ayodhya and Its Aftermath." In *Religion, Religiosity and Communalism,* edited by Praful Bidwai, Harbans Mukhia and Achin Vanaik. Delhi: Manohar.

———. 1997. *Legacy of a Divided Nation: India's Muslims Since Independence.* Delhi: Oxford University Press.

———. (ed.). 2001. *India's Partition: Process, Strategy and Mobilization,* reprint edn. Delhi: Oxford University Press.

Hasan, Zoya. 1998. *Quest for Power: Oppositional Movements in Uttar Pradesh.* Delhi: Oxford University Press.

Jayal, Niraja Gopal. 1999. *Democracy and the State: Welfare, Secularism and Development in Contemporary India.* Delhi: Oxford University Press.

Jha, Shefali. 2008. "Rights Versus Representation: Defending Minority Interests in the Constituent Assembly." In *Politics and Ethics of the Indian Constitution*, edited by Rajeev Bhargava. Delhi: Oxford University Press.

Kabir, Humayun. 1968. *Minorities in a Democracy*. Calcutta: Firma K. L. Mukhopadhyay.

Khalidi, Omar. 1993. "Muslims in Indian Political Process: Group Goals and Alternative Strategies." *Economic and Political Weekly*, January 2–9.

Khilnani, Sunil. 1997. *The Idea of India*. London: Hamish Hamilton.

Kothari, Rajni. 1988. *State Against Democracy: In Search for Humane Governance*. Delhi: Ajanta Publications.

Krishna, K. B. 1939. *The Problem of Minorities or Communal Representation in India*. London: George Allen and Unwin.

Krishna, Sankaran. 2000. *Postcolonial Insecurities: India, Sri Lanka, and the Question of Nationhood*. Delhi: Oxford University Press.

Kymlicka, Will. 1995. *Multicultural Citizenship: A Liberal Theory of Minority Rights*. Oxford: Clarendon Press.

———. (ed.). 1995. *The Rights of Minority Culture*. Oxford: Oxford University Press.

Kymlicka, Will and Wayne Norman (eds). 2000. *Citizenship in Diverse Societies*. Oxford: Oxford University Press.

Larson, Gerald James. 1997. *India's Agony over Religion*. Delhi: Oxford University Press.

Lijphart, Arend. 1996. "The Puzzle of Indian Democracy: A Consociational Interpretation." *American Political Science Review* 90 (2): 258–68.

Madan, T. N. 1993. "Whither Indian Secularism?" *Modern Asian Studies* 27 (3): 667–97.

Mahajan, Gurupreet. 1998. *Identities and Rights: Aspects of Liberal Democracy in India*. Delhi: Oxford University Press.

Mahmood, Tahir. 1997. *Minorities Commissions: Raison d'etre, Role and Responsibilities*. New Delhi: National Commission for Minorities.

———. 2001. *Minorities Commission: Minor Role in Major Affairs*. Delhi: Pharos Media & Publishing.

Massey, James. 1999. *Minorities in a Democracy: The Indian Experience*. Delhi: Manohar.

Mayaram, Shail. 1997. *Resisting Regimes: Myth and Memory in a Muslim Community*. Delhi: Oxford University Press.

———. 1998. "Rethinking Meo Identity: Cultural Faultline, Syncretism, Hybridity or Liminality." In *Islam: Communities and the Nation*, edited by Mushirul Hasan. Delhi: Manohar.

Metcalf, Barbara D. 1995. "Too Little and Too Much: Reflections on Muslims in the History of India." *The Journal of Asian Studies* 54 (4): 951–67.

Ministry of Minority Affairs, Government of India. 2007. *Report of the National Commission for Religious and Linguistic Minorities* (*Ranganath Misra Commission Report*), 12. www.minorityaffairs.gov.in

Ministry of Minority Affairs, Government of India. 2012. *Annual Report 2011–12*. www.minorityaffairs.gov.in.

Misra, Salil. 2001. *A Narrative of Communal Politics: Uttar Pradesh, 1937–39*. Delhi: SAGE.

Mitra, Subrata K. and V. B. Singh. 1999. *Democracy and Social Change in India*, 145–46. New Delhi: SAGE.

Mohapatra, Bishnu N. 2001. *"Democracy and the Claims of Diversity: Interrogating the Indian Experience."* Paper presented at the Conference on Dialogue on Democracy and Pluralism in South Asia, Delhi, March.

Nandy, Ashis. 1988. "The Politics of Secularism and the Recovery of Religious Tolerance." *Alternatives* 13 (3): 177–94.

———. 1998. "Pluralism as the Politics of Cultural Diversity in India." In *Making a Difference*, edited by Rukmini Sekhar. SPIC MACAY.

———. 1999. "Coping with the Politics of Faiths and Cultures: Between Secular State and Ecumenical Traditions in India." In *Ethnic Futures: The State and Identity Politics in Asia*, edited by J. Pfaff-Czarnecka, Darini Rajasingham-Senanayake, Ashis Nandy, and Edmund Terence Gomez. New Delhi: SAGE.

Nandy, Ashis, Sikha Trivedy, Shail Mayaram, and Achyut Yagnik. 1995. *Creating a Nationality: The Ramjanmabhumi Movement and the Fear of the Self*. Delhi: Oxford University Press.

Pettit, Philip. 2000. "Minority Claims Under Two Conceptions of Democracy." In *Political Theory and the Rights of Indigenous Peoples*, edited by Duncan Ivison, Paul Patton, and Will Sanders. Cambridge: Cambridge University Press.

Razzack, Azra and Anil Gumber. 2000. *Differentials in Human Development: A Case for Empowerment of Muslims in India*. New Delhi: National Council of Applied Economic Research.

Seth, D. L. and Gurpreet Mahajan (eds). 1999. *Minority Identities and the Nation-State*. Delhi: Oxford University Press.

Shaikh, Farzana. 2001. "Muslims and Political Representation in Colonial India." In *India's Partition: Process, Strategy and Mobilization*, edited by Mushirul Hasan. Delhi: Oxford University Press (sixth impression).

Shakir, Moin. 1980 (February). "Electoral Participation of Minorities and Indian Political System." *Economic and Political Weekly*, Annual Article, Vol. XV, nos 5, 6, and 7.

Siddiqui, M. K. (ed.). 2000. "Muslim in Free India." In *Differentials in Human Development: A Case for Empowerment of Muslims in India*, edited by Azra Razzack and Anil Gumber, 13. Delhi: National Council of Applied Economic Research.

Singh, K. S. and The Anthropological Survey of India. 1994. *People of India*, Vol. 1, Vol. VIII (1996). Delhi: Oxford University Press.

Smith, Donald Eugene. 1963. *India as a Secular State*. Princeton, NJ: Princeton University Press.

Tully, James. 1995. *Strange Multiplicity: Constitutionalism in an Age of Diversity*. Cambridge: Cambridge University Press.

Upahdyaya, Prakash Chandra. 1992. "The Politics of Indian Secularism." *Modern Asian Studies* 26 (4): 815–53.

Varshney, Ashutosh. 1993. "Contested Meanings: Hindu Nationalism, India's National Identity, and the Politics of Anxiety." *Daedalus*, July.

———. 1997. "Hindu–Muslim Riots 1960–1993: The National Picture (Mimeo)." In *Structure or Civic Life and Communal Violence: Hindus and Muslims in India.*

Wadhwa, Kamlesh Kumar. 1975. *Minority Safeguards in India.* Delhi: Thompson (India).

Weiner, Myron. 1997. "India's Minorities: Who Are They? What Do They Want?" In *State and Politics in India*, edited by Partha Chatterjee. Delhi: Oxford University Press.

Wright, Theodore, Jr. 1966. "The Effectiveness of Muslim Representation in India." In *South Asian Politics and Religion*, edited by Donald E. Smith. Princeton, NJ: Princeton University Press.

———. 1997. "A New Demand for Muslim Reservations in India." *Asian Survey* xxxvii (9): 852–58.

Documents and Primary Sources

Annual Reports of the Minorities Commission, 1978–91.

Census of India, 1991. 2001

Commissioner of Linguistic Minorities Reports (Relevant years).

Constitutional Proposals of The Sapru Committee, 1945.

Constituent Assembly Debates, Vols. I–XII.

Dr Gopal Singh Panel Report on Minorities, June 14, 1983.

Jawaharlal Nehru: Letters to Chief Ministers (1947–64), Vols. 1–5.

Laws of State Minorities Commissions and Boards (National Commission for Minorities Publication), 1998.

Lok Sabha Debates (Relevant years).

Minorities India (Newsletter of National Commission for Minorities), 1997–98.

People of India: An Introduction, (ed. K. S. Singh), Anthropological Survey of India, 1992.

Readings on Minorities: Perspectives and Documents (two vols.) Ed. Iqbal A. Ansari, Delhi, Institute of Objective Studies, 1996.

The National Commission for Minorities Act 1992.

India Human Development Report, Abusaleh Shariff (National Council of Applied Economic Research), 1999.

The Constitution of India (As modified up to the 1 January 1995).

Ministry of Minority Affairs, Government of India, www.minorityaffairs.gov.in

12

The Politics of Hurt Religious Feelings: The Minority as Emotional Subject in India

Mohamed Mehdi

Introduction

When we attribute an emotion to a political community, we do not usually mean that each member of the group is subject to the same emotion, or that the group's emotion is a mere aggregate of the feelings of individuals. We speak as though the group itself, in some mysterious sense, experiences pain or anger. Thus, in a political discourse often dominated by liberal assumptions about the individual as the primary unit of politics, the politics of emotion is a rare case in which we speak about collectivities as subjects in their own right, and not as mere collections of individual subjectivities. This subtle transition to speaking about the multitude as a subject of feeling, however, is often accomplished through an uncritical naturalizing or essentializing that ignores the normative force that emotions have for members of a group. Learning to belong to a group means learning to feel (or not to feel) in a particular way. Affective bonds develop and sustain solidarity across class, nation, and gender as we develop the expectation of knowing how others feel. The collective cultivation of political emotion can potentially be nurtured from the ground up and through a variety of means, including, for example, song, literary narrative, theater, and ritual. What we learn through these processes is not just how to feel or belong; rather, we redefine and re-shape our ethical orientation toward the world and develop methods for communicating this to others.

This process can be contrasted with the way in which a particular group emotion, that is, hurt religious feelings, has recently come to dominate the politico-religious life of Muslims in India. Religious feelings are a legal category in India, accompanied by an institutional framework that provides for their recognition, mediation, and negotiation. Instead of the development of multiple, varied, and nuanced connections between feeling, history, ritual, and text as suggested above, we find religious communities making prominent claims to the very same emotion, that of outraged hurt. The claim of hurt feelings is almost unreflective: it does not admit of modulation in accordance with proportion of hurt or seriousness of harm, and it is made with an ardor that often drowns out more subtle ways in which people feel. It enforces a moment of choice where one either sides with those who accept the offense on the grounds of freedom or right, and those who cannot abide by it. It teaches us how to belong, but only by teaching us to feel in ways that forego the epistemic potential of collective emotional life. Thus, a tension between religious feeling and emancipatory politics emerges, not because of the raw naturalness of emotion, but rather because of the way in which legal and political institutions constrain and direct the development of collective subjects of political and religious emotion.

While the emotions of groups are often understood as reactions rooted in nature or embedded in cultural essences, legal remedies for hurt religious feelings have played a powerful role in shaping the emotional dimensions of what it means to be a religious minority in India. The self-representation of both minority and majority groups as emotional subjects to be recognized by the state has brought a shared nexus of feelings to the fore of religious life, hurt feelings flanked by anger and outrage. This particular dynamic is relevant to broader questions about the politics of emotion in democratic societies. When we analyze the ways in which institutions of the state provide the framework for the emergence of emotional categories for citizens that in turn generate certain complexes of affect, attitude, and practice, it becomes increasingly difficult to imagine ways in which religious feelings can play a part in an emancipatory politics that challenges those very institutional structures. If, as Ahmed has argued, affects function in sticky ways, not only tying people together, but also binding values, ideas, and objects, then the work of unsticking, when called for, will not be easy (Ahmed 2004, 2010). This suggests that a progressive politics of emotion will require a lot of unlearning and the discovery of resources to aid in this process.

Much of this chapter will focus on the ways that the politics of hurt feelings have been important to the construction of the political identity of Indian Muslims. This has not just involved the many consequences of adopting the performance of outrage in response to public speech. For despite the many cases that continue to arise of Muslims responding collectively to perceived insults against Islam, the politics of hurt feelings has, at the same time, been effectively co-opted by reactionary majoritarian groups. Muslims have come to occupy a dual role, both as the subject and as the cause of hurt and outrage. In contrast with this process, we can, without positing an authentic Muslim subject of emotion, think of the great diversity of collective performances of emotion, religious feeling, that occur at some distance from the state to suggest some of the resources that may be available to question the affective connections that have been forged by the politics of hurt feelings.

The Politics of Hurt Feelings

Let me begin with a more general discussion of the idea of hurt feelings as a political category. The politics of hurt feelings is primarily concerned with representation. When peoples' feelings are hurt, then, it is often as a result of words or images. These can be words or images that directly offend, as a result of what they say or show, or also words that offend indirectly, not because of the content itself, but because of a particular reference that the content can suggest when used in a particular environment. But hurt feelings can also result from a sense of being left out, having not been given due consideration. And this can result not only from words or images but also from policy decisions. In many cases, these two kinds of sources of hurt feelings, misrepresentation and lack of consideration, are closely linked. One of the reasons why symbols can be used in ways that hurt is not so much the content of the symbolism, as I mentioned above, but what their historical connotations might be. In these kinds of cases, there is an indeterminacy about the meaning of the symbol; "It could mean many things," it is asked, "so why is it being interpreted in a way that is offensive?" Perhaps, the point is rather that the offense results from a lack of consideration that is evident when a symbol is used whose meaning is contested and, for some, painful. "You should have known better," as a phrase, is one way of suggesting this lack of consideration.

When it comes to the politics of hurt feelings, then, there seem to be two primary kinds of claims involved: one concerned with representation through speech and symbolic imagery, and the other concerned with due consideration. Both of these are ultimately related to respect and inclusion as ideals, which is why political claims made on the basis of hurt feelings have some purchase in a pluralist framework. In national contexts where claims for just inclusion have been important to minority political movements, the politics of hurt feelings is useful in the wake of reforms where the inclusion of minority groups as equals has already been accepted in principle. At this stage, claims regarding hurt feelings are advanced as a way of establishing that the principle has not been adequately put into practice, when publicly acceptable discourse does not reflect the aspiration to equal respect.

There are significant ways in which the politics of hurt feelings contribute to social and political movements. On a pedagogical and epistemic level, it can demand the official acceptance of stories, of the experience of historical pain, as elements in a larger narrative that cannot be suppressed. We learn that it is appropriate to feel hurt when these stories are denied or their symbolic representatives are misused or unacknowledged. In this vein, hurt feelings play a role in the reclamation of dignity, where we recognize that regularly obscured lines of psychic self-defense, which rule out certain kinds of names and symbols, can be openly defended. In making this defense, we develop a sense of history and of our connection to it. Further, the politics of hurt feelings has allowed for the cultivation of a sense of solidarity and connectedness between and among peoples who develop a shared understanding of a common source of collective pain. This has been accompanied by public and popular negotiations, critiques, and debates about the meanings of symbols and words that take place in a variety of forums. This process highlights the understanding that issues of inclusion and equality cannot be treated merely through legal and policy mechanisms. The politics of hurt feelings seeks to hold others accountable for what they say and how they say it. While many see this as a form of policing of thought and speech, in some ways this is precisely because the politics of hurt feelings, in this context, seeks to show where the personal and political meet.

It is interesting, though, that in recent years, some of the most vocal uses of the politics of hurt feelings in the West have involved claims being made by reactionary groups. One example was the proposed building of a Muslim community center in Manhattan, New York in the general vicinity of the attacks of September 11, 2001. Some groups claimed that this was an affront to their feelings, that it was a deliberate attempt to exploit and deepen the pain of the attacks. The claim made was not explicitly legal in nature, in that it did not point to any law that had been violated. The opposition to the building did nonetheless seek to argue that the municipality did not take into account the feelings of the majority precisely because, in its claims to equality, it was too sensitive to the demands for inclusion of a minority group. As we will see, a similar dynamic is apparent in the Indian politics of hurt feelings. This co-opting move is indicative of the thinning out of the emotion of hurt feelings, its detachment from other sources of pain related to historic and systemic injustices, and its connection to symbolic representation, outrage, and pride. In the Indian context, this connection has been facilitated by institutional and legal instruments.

Indian Law and Religious Feelings

The politics of collective hurt feelings in India has a very different origin than the progressive politics of minority rights. The entry of hurt feelings into Indian political discourse begins with the positing of a particular kind of feeling: religious feeling.[1] Section 295A of the Indian Penal Code states,

> Whoever, with deliberate and malicious intention of outraging the religious feelings of any class of His Majesty's subjects, by words, either spoken or written, or by visible representations insults or attempts to insult the religion or

the religious beliefs of that class, shall be punished with imprisonment of either description for a term which may extend to two years, or with fine, or with both.[2]

Unlike the original Section 295 of the 1860 Code, which specifically prohibits insulting a religion by defiling or damaging a place of worship or religious objects, Section 295A singles out religious feelings for protection. The aim is not to protect feelings in order to prevent the pain of insult, but rather to prevent violence and social unrest resulting from hurt religious feelings. It does not seek to protect communities from oppression or exclusion that might be enforced by derogatory public representations. It does not identify only vulnerable communities for protection, but rather the feelings of any religious community.

The phrase "religious feelings" might, in another context, bring to mind awe, wonder, or mystical love. Yet, in the context of Indian law, it refers to the sensibilities we have as members of a group: sensibilities that can easily be offended if that group is intentionally subjected to insulting words or images. "Religious feelings" refers to the feelings we have of identification with a religion and the beliefs associated with that religion. They are not seen as the result of experience, or of a process of development or cultivation. Rather, they are treated as a given: members of a religious group share feelings of identification with the religion and its beliefs—even if they do not actually hold those beliefs as individuals and even if they do not understand them.

The addition of Section 295A to the Indian Penal Code occurred in 1927 after the response to the publication of a tract called *Rangeela Rasool* ("Colorful Prophet," literally, but with connotations of sensuality and abandon), and which presented the story of the Prophet of Islam as that of a sensuous womanizer whose legacy can best be understood through his marriages.[3] The pamphlet was published by a Hindu publisher, Rampal of Lahore. It was associated with the Arya Samaj, and gained the attention of Gandhi who addressed it in a *Young India* article of 1924.[4] The initial Urdu publication met with outraged responses and public protest. But as the case wound its way through three levels of the courts, the initial conviction being followed by one unsuccessful appeal and then finally a successful appeal in the High Court, the publication gained greater notoriety. The outrage following the High Court's acquittal was much greater than that following the initial publication, and it finally led to the murder of the publisher.

The courts initially convicted the publisher on the grounds of incitement of religious hatred or enmity and undermining religious harmony, under Section 153A. This was finally overturned by the High Court on the specific grounds that satirizing a dead religious leader does not constitute promoting hatred against the current members of a community.[5] The central question for the judge was not one of protecting freedom of speech. Rather, he recommended that there should be an additional section of law passed to cover such cases in the future. In his recommendation, he explicitly refers to religious feelings. The case as it was presented to him, he seems to have held, was indeed offensive, but not on the grounds that the law considers offensive: it did not promote enmity between communities in any direct sense. The offense or hurt felt by Muslims, their emotional reaction, was not relevant in proving that the words were intended to promote enmity against Muslims. From this process emerged Section 295A which emphasized the intent to hurt the religious feelings of a group as punishable.

A high-profile case in the pre-independence period involving Section 295A just a few years after it was passed was the banning of the *Angare* anthology. This was put out by future members of the Progressive Writers Association who were themselves from Muslim families but who offered a radical critique of religion, especially regarding the treatment of women, in the form of a collection of short stories.[6] There are a couple of points about the reaction to its publication that are worth noting in contrast to the case of *Rangeela Rasool*. First of all, though there was no question here of communal strife, since the authors were also identified as Muslim, the publication nonetheless received an intense amount of public critique within official circles and from the establishment press. Second, the question of free speech was explicitly raised during the controversy in opposition to the call for proscription. This was apparent in the response to the ban written by Mahmuduzaffar and published in Allahabad's *Leader* in April 1933. He states, "[The authors] stand for the right of free criticism and free expression in all matters of the highest importance to the human race in general and the Indian people in particular" (Mahmud 1996, 450–51). The defenders of *Rangeela Rasool* were Arya Samaj members who cited vengeance for public lectures that mocked Swami Dayananda as their motivation. Their method was to offer a lampoon of the life of Prophet Muhammad. In contrast, *Angare* was a collection of stories written by progressive writers from Muslim families, engaged in a critique not of iconic figures, but of oppressive social practices prevalent in their own community. In siding with the conservative establishment, the government and large sections of the media could then cite, in support of decisive action for banning the collection, the negative effect on the feelings of the Muslim community through these attacks on their practices, and the potential for disorder and violence to arise.

The third and final iconic case I will mention is from a more recent period, and will be much better known by most: the case of M. F. Husain and the relentless pressure, legal and extra-legal, that was raised against him by forces of the Hindu right, national parties as well as local organizations. The works at the center of these attacks, beginning in 1996,[7] first included nude depictions of deities and came to include his painting *Bharatmata* or Mother India, which depicts a nude female figure superimposed on the shape of India's map. Some of the complaints against Husain were made under the category of obscenity. But a common legal charge concerned the hurt sentiments of Hindus.[8] Those charges which were considered by the courts were dismissed.[9] But the popular outrage, violent attacks, and threats took a serious and frightening toll and forced the artist to leave India. Even after Husain's adoption of Qatari citizenship and permanent departure from India had become a mark of shame for the country and the government and courts were calling for his return, Bharatiya Janata Party leader S. S. Ahluwalia said, "The fact remained that no one had the right to hurt the sentiments of any community in the name of freedom of expression" (*The Hindu* 2010). In addition to the legal charges, though, the defense of hurt sentiments prompted a whole range of actions, many of which did not take direct aim at Husain himself, but at exhibitions of his work, plays about his life, and television programs.[10] The extreme violence, which ranged from the vandalizing of galleries displaying Husain's work to the burning of effigies created an atmosphere of intimidation which neither the courts nor the efforts of secularist groups were able to effectively counter.

In looking at these three important cases, we see a telling progression. In the first, we have the mobilization of collective expressions of outrage and anger against what is perceived as an insulting representation of an important symbol by members of another community. This response is taken up as a predictable or even natural reaction that calls for a legal remedy, the protection of the feelings of religious groups against intentional harm. The neutral framing means that the law should apply to all religious groups, suggesting that hurt religious feelings are of the same nature for different communities and lead to similar outcomes.

With this move, the state emphasizes a thin notion of religious feelings, feelings which do not belong to adherents of any particular religion, but to all who feel emotionally invested in their religious community and its beliefs. It is implied in this process that religious feelings, unlike other feelings, are relevant for state protection because when they are hurt they lead to outbreaks of violence. The logic might be further held to suggest that Indians in particular have religious feelings that are easily hurt, and that this pain is regularly, almost naturally, the cause of social unrest and violence. To enshrine this in criminal law, rather than in social policies, for example, suggests that this is an abiding feature of Indian religious life.[11]

The impact of Section 295A, further, was not only to highlight the idea of hurt religious feelings, but, further, to introduce the notion of these feelings as belonging to a class of people, rather than to individuals. This, in turn, points toward public words and images, speech that circulates, as the sort that can be offensive in the particular way suggested by the section of law. It is not a surprise, then, that in the *Angare* case, freedom of speech is brought into direct and open conflict with the aim of avoiding religious conflict and social disorder through the protection of the feelings of a particular religious community. In encouraging claims on the behalf of a religious group whose feelings have been intentionally hurt, Section 295A provides a legal mechanism that curtails progressive speech that is critical of religious practices, even when that speech originates from within the community. The law, thus, allows the identification of a community with the feelings of outrage that some members lay claim to. Political speech must as a result be moderated to respect the feelings of religious groups that are seen as arising naturally and predictably and that tend toward violent expression. At the same time, this allows the state to appear as a fair defender of the sentiments and sensibilities of religious communities, especially minority religious communities. The state, through its application of 295A, identifies the outrage voiced in the name of conservative Muslims and their sympathizers as representative of Muslim religious feelings, and privileges them over the feelings of the oppressed and marginalized characters, many of them women, in the stories collected in *Angare*, and of their progressive sympathizers.

In the third case, six decades later, the dynamics are again different. The religious feelings at play now are not those of the minority community but rather the feelings of Hindus as represented by Hindu nationalists. The offender, the cause of hurt, is a Muslim who, in the name of freedom of speech, his accusers say, is devising ways of hurting Hindus by misrepresenting their deities and their nation while pretending to create art. Even in the absence of a conviction, Husain was made to pay a heavy price, as were his defenders. And more than this, the law provided a platform from which the nationalist Hindu groups could, first, aggressively assert the importance of their feelings, second, adopt the posture of the aggrieved whose psychic wounds have become unbearable, and third, paint Muslims back into the corner as not the aggrieved but the aggressors, the cause of hurt, who hide behind secular values to denigrate the beliefs, values, and feelings of Hindus. This rhetorical opportunity was more important than any conviction could have been. In fact, a conviction would have brought into question the central premise that the secular state is biased toward minorities while ignoring the rights of the majority. The position of the aggrieved, of the hurt collective emotional subject, is, thus, competitively sought out, for there is power in feeling pain, the strength of knowing oneself through the forceful construction and defense of particular norms and lines that cannot be crossed and the corresponding demand for their recognition by others.

Feeling Hurt and Being Muslim

As we have seen, the legal and extra-legal negotiations of hurt religious feelings have had a particular salience for Muslims. Indeed, though the legal category of hurt religious feelings is framed in neutral language, it has had an unusual role in shaping what it means to be a Muslim in contemporary India. On the one hand, Muslims have been constructed as those whose feelings are protected, a vulnerable emotional subject of hurt feeling. On the other hand, there is the implicit recognition of danger, the eruption of hurt into anger and violence, which must be forestalled through legal remedy for the offense. This points to the fact that Muslims are, at the same time, considered a source of pain, the offenders rather than the offended. The deployment of the politics of hurt feelings depends on adopting this dual position of the offended as well as the potentially offensive, a violent threat that is beyond reason and requires legal containment.

This ambivalent position is apparent in, for example, the recent statement by the Majlis-E-Ittehadul Muslimeen[12] leader and Member of Parliament Assaduddin Owaisi, in response to protests against the YouTube video mocking the Prophet Muhammad, *Innocence of the Muslims*.[13] Owaisi commented that,

> We have told the community, we have requested them that, yes, all of us are pained and hurt, but the best way of showing our pain and anger is not to allow our emotions to take over. Fortunately the people at large have understood the message given by our *ulemas*, our scholars, our political leaders. (Asia News Monitor 2012)

Political and religious leaders have, thus, taken on the role of spokesmen for this murky but volatile entity of the religious feelings of Muslims, while at the same time having to reassure others that they are working to keep these feelings in check, to prevent them from erupting or "taking over," in Owaisi's words.[14] Muslims are, thus, sent the message that belonging to the community involves feeling pained by certain representations, and, further, that this is a pain that should be laced with anger. For the leaders, it provides the opportunity to be a broker with the state, to present the hurt purportedly felt by Muslims and the leaders' ability to check its transformation into violence as bargaining chips for power and recognition. In this role, the political leadership is vested in maintaining and often encouraging the extra-legal expressions of hurt and outrage by community members as a purportedly natural response to hurtful triggers.

The proximity of hurt feelings to anger is evident from the fact that they can only be verified or made public through collective displays of outrage. What is said to feel like pain for the offended must look like anger to the offenders and to the state that must then act or be put on warning. The public display of anger can also be gratifying for the protesters; it not only reinforces affective ties within the group, but is also a momentary glimpse of power when others feel compelled to apologize (Chakrabarty 2005).

But pain and hurt feelings could be taken up differently, for collective pain and hurt can just as well call for being assuaged rather than avenged, and they can give rise to movements for healing. They can be taken up as challenges for exercising the religious values of forgiveness and mercy, or for affirming one's faith in the face of attacks. This is particularly so when the attacks do not consist in the murder of innocents, as Muslims have experienced repeatedly at the hands of the Indian state, but rather in negative representations of cherished icons.[15] This points to the fact that the politics of hurt feelings, despite the emotive language in which it is couched, is centered on contestations for power.[16] The very character of participating in collective hurt of this nature precludes a contemplative or introspective response from which a complex and sustained ethical investigation can be initiated. The normative force of identifying with the putatively pre-political feelings one should have as a Muslim, thus, shapes the experience of feeling hurt within the contours of concepts motivated by the legal mechanisms of the state.

The reliance on legal remedies to respond to claims of offended religious sentiment has also placed Muslims in an ambivalent relation to free speech as a legal right. Often, this has concerned the speech of writers who are, at least by name and birth, themselves Muslim, as in the *Angare* case, but also more recently with Salman Rushdie and Taslima Nasreen. The Indian State has, in the name of protecting the religious feelings of Muslims, not hesitated to ban materials that could be deemed offensive. It was among the first nations to ban Rushdie's *Satanic Verses*, for example, and was also among the first to block access to the *Innocence of the Muslims* video on YouTube in September 2012. When Taslima Nasreen came under fire from the Muslim religious establishment, state and central governments pressured her to leave the country, as she eventually did after her attempts to remove offending passages from her book and to apologize for hurting religious sentiments were deemed insufficient (Riaz 2008). When Muslim groups complained that their feelings were outraged by the 2009 publication of an article in the *Statesman* by Johann Hari titled "Why Should I Respect These Oppressive Religions?" in which he cites the marriage of Muhammad to Aisha when she was nine years old, the editor and publisher were promptly detained before being released on bail (BBC 2009).

This creates a situation, first, in which in order to honor the feelings which are held to be constitutive of their identity, Muslims must become complicit with a state whose repression can often be turned against them, thus, placing them in tension with an emancipatory politics.[17] Whatever progressive potential there is in learning to critique a history of misrepresentation through the identification of offending symbols, and, in the best case, relating this to other aspects of economic and political exclusion, is, thus, conceptually hobbled.

Second, the appeal to hurt feelings has led to the cultivation of a particular skill in reading symbols and texts for the offensiveness they bear. This involves paying close attention to imagery and symbolism in a manner that is finely honed in the age of digital mass communication. Indeed, it is a skill in reading without reading, where the hurt comes to reside in the very being of the symbol, the text, or in the person of the purveyor, Rushdie or Nasreen, for example. We can, again, imagine an alternative approach, where the pain remains a felt experience with causes beyond the trigger. This would allow for an investigation of the source of the psychic hurt, and an engagement with the offending words or images to place them in a proportionate relation to other injustices. However, the political discourse of hurt religious sentiments calls for an approach to owning the pain where we make it our own precisely by projecting it onto a symbol or a person, and, thus, develop our own repertoire of interchangeable offending figures and sacred lines, all affectively equal, for the purpose of our collective emotional mobilization.

Third, the habit of reading the public sphere for offensive speech and images has flattened the terrain of discourse about religion, obliterating distinctions between what speech should and should not be taken seriously. When it is the expression of religious feeling that is privileged, the particular nature of the trigger is not as important as the effect it becomes identified with. This has meant that individuals or groups who otherwise lack political influence can impact religious politics by producing crude digital materials as provocation. One prominent recent example is the aforementioned YouTube video. In other cases, Muslim groups have themselves circulated digital materials with the aim of manufacturing an angry response. In 2012, the agitations in Mumbai in response to anti-Muslim violence in Burma targeted the media for its perceived failure to report the extent of the atrocities. This perception of media bias was based in a belief that genocide was being concealed, and the "evidence" being relied on by the protesters consisted in faked videos and pictures shared through social media (Saeed 2012). The other side of the media-savvy policing of offensive speech and imagery, then, is an uncritical rendering of all speech as equally worthy of emotional response. As the opportunities for offense thus proliferate, the responsibilities of Muslims on the one hand to be hurt and of the state on the other to be account-able for the defense of legally posited religious feeling become almost unmanageable and take on an oversized presence in the political produc-tion of Muslims as a minority.

The idea of hurt religious feelings has become ubiquitous in Indian minority politics beyond the legal level, playing multiple roles.[18] For the state, it provides a justification for repressive policies and for gratifying electoral vote banks; for religious leaders, it provides a source of power both within the community and vis-à-vis the state. For the media and for the public, it provides an occasion for dwelling in controversy, and revisiting simplistic debates about violence, free speech, and the mean-ings of symbols. For the multitude, it can offer a sense of togetherness and empowerment, however brief. For Muslims, it has become one of the ways in which a collective identity is felt, teaching us what it means to be Muslim. The various registers of outrage weave a thread of political continuity among Muslims nationally and internationally where there are otherwise many communities separated by class, language, beliefs, practices, and history. Participating in the political rituals of denouncing hurtful speech and symbols creates a shared emotional identity across differences, but also a shared sense of what is inviolable. It might seem that we begin with a sense of community and purely religious and sacred protected symbols and beliefs, and that these form the basis for the col-lective experience of hurt religious feelings to which the state must then respond. But if we see the very notion of collective hurt religious feelings as a legal and political construct that has shaped public discourse and emotional experience, then, we must pay attention to the way in which it comes to exert a normative force in motivating our sense of who we are. The collective expression of hurt feelings in response to symbolic representations is one of the central ways in which Muslims have been given a political voice. And, thus, learning to feel hurt in the right way, in response to the right objects, has played an increasingly dominant role in shaping Muslim identity.

When we step back for a moment and remember what it is like to have our feelings personally hurt, we might remember that it can be a lonely, isolating experience rather than one that binds people together. Feeling hurt makes one feel vulnerable, and we often want to hide this from others, and so attempt to mask our emotional pain. The politics of hurt feelings, perhaps rightly, rejects this internalizing aspect. However, in the context of Indian politics, this rejection has had less to do with publicizing the hidden traumas of injustice and more to do with adopting the posture of injured pride. Humiliation has become the focus. In the case of the Hindu right, it is always a question of having salt rubbed into wounds that are already felt to be there; the sense of pride, confirmed through its injury, becomes a mark of belonging. The hurt is most fundamentally linked not to the content of the speech, but to the fact of its being said. It is not the content that must be retracted or punished, but rather the will to say it.[19]

The affective connection of hurt with wounded pride, and with the desire for competitive advantage in the realm of public discourse, inhibits the epistemic potential of feeling hurt,[20] and it masks the systemic injustices that underlie the struggles for recognition of minority groups. The thinning out of the experience of hurt feelings facilitates a reflexive appeal for legitimacy to the state, for its recognition of the felt humiliation, and this is played out on a flattened terrain of interchangeable figures and triggers. This is what has allowed reactionary groups to effectively deploy the politics of hurt feelings in their production of religious and political community. While I have suggested that the law has played a foundational role in this process, it may be that the politics of hurt feelings has come full circle to shape the way legal judgments are made. As John Dayal, president of the All India Christian Council remarked following the Supreme Court's judgment on the use of the Babri Masjid site in Ayodhya, "The courts are not ruling on points of law but on the feelings and faith of people, which gives the majority community an extraordinary power in a multi-cultural nation such as India and can have serious implications in other disputes of this nature."[21]

Conclusion: The Tenth of Muharram

A few years ago, I attended the tenth of Muharram procession in the Old City of Hyderabad. During the day, we witnessed the procession itself, led by a venerable elephant carrying the *alam* (battle standard or flag representing the flag of Imam Husain at the Battle of Karbala), representing Prophet Muhammad's grandsons. The Hyderabad procession, *Bibi ka Alam* (traditional title of the Muharram procession in Hyderabad), is several centuries old. It had been inaugurated during the Qutb Shahi reign and continues to this day as one of the largest processions in South Asia. Among the many thousands who were present, Shi'a, Sunni, and non-Muslims, those who stole the show were the young men whose stamina as vigorous mourners withstood the heat and their self-inflicted wounds.

But it was possible to wonder if this was indeed grief. The machismo of the young men seemed just as likely an explanation for the exuberance on display in this public act of mourning. It was not just the vigor of the *maatam* (the activity of mourning, in Muharram this involves wailing and self-flagellation) that gave this impression, but the raised replicas of swords that greeted the emergence of the flags and battle standards. But the emotional tenor had tilted drastically by the evening. At the *sham-e-ghariban* (evening ritual held on the tenth of Muharram that takes place in a graveyard to mourn the dead), which I witnessed with my uncle, the late Urdu poet Mazhar Mehdi, people gathered in graveyards and wept. They wept not only for the residents of the cemetery but for the dead of Karbala. Later in the night, we found ourselves in the lanes of Darulshifa, where makeshift public address systems had been set up from block to block, and in the darkness it was impossible to move as every inch of the streets was occupied by seated mourners. As they listened to the amplified *nauhas* (story that describes the martyrdom of Imam Husain) and *marsiya* (poem that is recited or sung in mourning and remembrance of the martyrdom at Karbala), they wailed in grief, cried loudly and, in a way, privately. Each person seemed to be wrapped up in their own pain though they shared a public space and a reason for their pain.

During the procession, I saw several young men who wore T-shirts that read "Muharram is a movement against terrorism." The immediate meaning of this was not clear to me. Perhaps, the idea was that by mourning the massacre of the Prophet's descendants we show solidarity with victims of terrorist violence, that we oppose the killing of innocents. I learned only much later that the T-shirts were provided by the group Husseini Youths, who seek to couple their devotion to Shi'a principles with a concern for social justice and the rights of Muslims across the globe. They produced other T-shirts as well, including one bearing an icon representing Mahatma Gandhi with a quote in which he extols the sacrifice of Imam Husain.

I end this chapter with this story because it reminds us of the bewildering complexity of religious feelings, hurt feelings, that is dumbed down by the legalistic concepts that dominate our current political context. It also provides a small glimpse of some of the resources that could be engaged with in remaking the connections between religion, emotion, knowledge, history, and politics. In contrast with the affective and epistemic thinness of the politics of hurt feelings, it suggests that intensity of religious feeling, understood more broadly, need not be opposed to political and ethical thinking. And, finally, in contrast with the one-size-fits-all nature of the politics of hurt religious feelings that fosters competition for state recognition, the religious feelings that have more substantial affective roots within particular beliefs, practices, and histories can, in fact, be a more fruitful basis for conversation and exchange between communities. There are, of course, many similar examples we could point to that suggest that religious feelings are not a given property of a group; rather, they are learned and passed on and also transformed in performance, conversation, and texts. The politics of hurt feelings, on the other hand, has served to reinforce the problematic view that religious emotion consists in natural and inescapable reactions of anger and outrage rooted in a sense of inviolable identification with a set of shared fundamental beliefs. It is this political, affective, and epistemic complex that will have to be unstuck.

Notes and Bibliography

Notes

1. The 1860 code includes references to hurt religious feelings in Section 298, which focuses on attacks on individuals based on religion. See http://www. indiankanoon.org/doc/1569253/. Section 295A, instituted in 1927, is the first to refer to the religious feelings of a class.
2. Available at http://www.vakilno1.com/bareacts/indianpenalcode/S295A. htm
3. Thursby (1975) provides a detailed discussion of the case. There appears to be some confusion over the authorship of the pamphlet, with Pandit Chamupati, as cited by Thursby, or Prashad Prataab suggested in Sarwar (2012). The Hindi version names Chamupati as author. The name of the author was not revealed during the legal proceedings against the publisher. Sarwar traces the ancestry of Pakistan's anti-blasphemy laws (295B and 295C) to this affair.
4. See *Collected Works of Mahatma Gandhi*, Vol. 28, 173, his "Notes" from *Young India*, June 19, 1924, where he says, "I have asked myself what the motive possibly could be in writing or printing such a book except to inflame passions."
5. I follow Thursby's account here (op. cit.). A different interpretation of the ruling is presented in Sorabji (1994).
6. See Mahmud (1996). The article provides a helpful summary of the case as well as excerpts and translations from the responses of different publications at the time.
7. See *The Statesman*, October 8, 1996, "Mumbai Police Register Case Against Husain."
8. See, e.g., *The Hindustan Times*, February 13, 2006, "PIL filed against M. F. Husain."
9. See, e.g., *The Hindu*, May 9, 2008, "Husain Deserves to Be Home and Painting, Says Court."
10. See, e.g., the site of the reactionary group Hindu *Janajagruti Samiti*, which has an entire section devoted to their campaign against M. F. Husain at http://www.hindujagruti.org/news/6787.html.
11. See, e.g., Sorabji, op. cit., for an uncritical acceptance of this view.
12. The MIM is a political party in Hyderabad with a large constituency among the Muslims of the Old City.
13. This video created a worldwide wave of protests in the autumn of 2012 because of its portrayal of Muhammad as a sex-crazed and foolish man. In some ways, it is an interesting parallel to the case of *Rangeela Rasool* discussed above.
14. The MIM leader's comments in 2012 are in stark contrast to his vitriolic response in 2007 when he whole-heartedly endorsed the physical assault

on the Bangladeshi author Taslima Nasreen at the Press Club in Hyderabad. See Riaz (2008).

15. In this context, we can also think of using satire to counter media represen-tations, as was the case in the #Muslim Rage trend that arose on Twitter in response to news coverage of the response to *Innocence of the Muslims*.

16. This point is well developed in Riaz, op. cit.

17. See Riaz, op. cit., for an account of the practical effects of this tension in dividing opposition to the Nandigram SEZ.

18. Actual legal cases under Section 295A have continued to proliferate in trou-bling ways. Just this year, at least two cases have been initiated by Christian groups. One is against Sanal Edamaruku, an outspoken atheist, for expos-ing a leaking pipe as the cause of the miraculous tears of blood of a statue of the Virgin Mary. The other is against the makers of the film *Kya Super Kool Hain Hum* for a scene in which a Christian priest is shown conducting a marriage ceremony between two dogs.

19. This is a key difference from the notion of blasphemy, which is targeted by the cousins of Section 295A found in Pakistani law. Where blasphemy, as a concept, locates offense in the content of the speech, the notion of hurt religious feelings leads us to focus on the hurtful intentions of speech. The fact that someone would want to say it, and get away with it, is what is, in the final analysis, deemed to be offensive. Thus, while anti-blasphemy laws purport to protect the honor of the religion, the focus of hurt religious feel-ings is on the injured pride of the believers.

20. One important example from the Indian context of attempting to develop this potential, which has its own difficulties, can be found in Gandhian in-spired movements. Gandhi's *Hind Swaraj* can be read as a pedagogical tract in which the character of the Editor attempts to co-opt the wounded pride of the Reader toward a more morally, politically, and epistemically power-ful emotional response to imperial rule. The hurt of the imperial subject is taken as a starting point for developing a fuller conception of self-rule.

21. See *The Hindu* (2010). Compare this to the statement in a Shiv Sena edito-rial from the same period regarding a police case about noise limits on the *Dussehra* (is an important Hindu estival) procession. Asking why mosques are allowed to blare the *azaan* (Muslim call to prayer), the editorial says, "We also know the law. Nobody should teach us law. Law should respect our feelings, then we will respect law" (PTI, October 20, 2010). I am grate-ful to Anil Persaud for bringing this to my attention.

Bibliography

Ahmed, Sara. 2004. *The Cultural Politics of Emotions*. Edinburgh: Edinburgh University Press.

———. 2010 "Happy Objects." In *The Affect Theory Reader*, edited by Melissa Gregg and Gregory J. Seigworth. Durham: Duke University Press.

Asia News Monitor. 2012. "Anti-Islam Film Protests Muted Among India's Muslims." September 25.

BBC. 2009. "Pair Held for 'Offending Islam'." February 12.

Chakrabarty, Dipesh. 2005. "'In the Name of Politics': Sovereignty, Democracy and the Multitude in India." *Economic and Political Weekly*, July 23.

Hindustan Times. 2006. "PIL Filed Against M. F. Husain." February 13.

Mahmud, Shabana. 1996. "*Angare* and the Founding of the Progressive Writers' Association." *Modern Asian Studies* 30 (2). 447—67.

Riaz, Ali. 2008. "Constructing Outraged Communities and State Responses: The Taslima Nasreen Saga in 1994 and 2007 (2)." *South Asia Multidisciplinary Academic Journal* 2.

Saeed, Yousuf. 2012. "How to Start a Riot out of Facebook." Accessed November 3, 2012. http://kafila.org/2012/08/13/how-to-start-a-riot-out-of-facebook-yousuf-saeed/

Sarwar, Bina. 2012. "Malicious Intent." *New Humanist*, November 6. Accessed November 10, 2012. http://www.scribd.com/doc/102544895/rangeela-ra-sool-pdf (in Hindi).

Sorabji, Soli. 1994. "Freedom of Expression and Censorship: Some Aspects of the Indian Experience." *Northern Ireland Legal Quarterly* 45: 327.

The Hindu. 2008. "Husain deserves to be home and painting, says Court." May 9.

———. 2010 "M. F. Husain Welcome to Return Home: Centre." February 26.

———. 2010. "Indian Muslim, Christian Groups Flay Court Verdict on Religious Site." October 2.

The Statesman. 1996. "Mumbai Police Register Case Against Husain." October 8.

Thursby, Gene. 1975. *Hindu–Muslim Relations in British India.* Leiden: Brill (ff. 40).

13

The Indian State and the Minority's Right to Culture

Malavika Menon

The Indian State has been both explicit and reticent when discussing its minorities. While community-based identities were discerned in colonial times, it was the Indian State that sought to institutionalize them into categories. Yet, despite this categorization, it shied away from granting them a political status, resorting instead to recognizing them as cultural categories. Also, a significant omission on the part of the Indian State at the stage of Constitution making was the ambiguity in defining a minority. While it identified certain communities as belonging to minorities, the discussions did not result in the definition of what constitutes a minority. This was evidently left to the courts to decide as and when the question arose.

It is in this context that the present chapter is significant as it examines the relationship the Indian State shares with its minorities through the prism of a particular right assigned by the Constitution: Article 30 that guarantees to religion- and language-based minorities the right to establish and administer educational institutions of their choice. However, this right was arrived at after lengthy deliberations in the Constituent Assembly and subsequently dealt with by the judicial courts in independent India.

Like any other phenomenon or category, that of the minority in India too has to be examined within a context, a predominant idea within which the idea of minority is dominant, significant, and serves as a yardstick. A secular democracy provides for this context. Increasingly, the treatment of minorities has served as a yardstick to examine the success of how democratic a polity is. In India, minorities have been closely linked to the idea of the secular, to the value of secularism, and to the efficacy of secularism as State practice. Thus, a discussion on minorities in India would be incomplete without invoking the idea of secularism. Secularism in determining religion–state relations inadvertently finds place in a discussion on minorities in India, in particular the religion- or culture-based minorities.

Many ideas have been invoked and theorized to understand secularism in India. The ideas of nondiscrimination (Mahajan 2002) and principled distance[1] serve as useful analytical tools to examine the minority question in relation to the cultural and educational rights of minorities. Not only were these reflected in the Constituent Assembly Debates, but in the judgments of the Supreme Court as well.

While minorities, in the way we understand them today, did not exist in colonial India, one would err in omitting attempts by the British to articulate in some manner the plurality that existed in India. Thus, for instance, the Census of 1931 included a category of "Minor Religions" or of "Brahmanic," i.e., those Hindus not belonging to the Arya Samaj, Brahmo Samaj, Adi-Hindus, Adi-Dravidas, etc. The Census also recognized the converts in the provinces of Bihar, Orissa, Central Province (CP), and Berar where Jains and Buddhists returned themselves as Hindus.

The beginning, perhaps, of a statist construction of minorities or of delineating communities into categories for preferential treatment can be traced to the Communal Award of 1931 that identified Muslims, Europeans, Sikhs, Indian Christians, and Anglo-Indians as eligible for separate electorates. While drafting the Constitution in 1946–49, it was this arrangement that was claimed as an entitlement by the Sikhs and the Muslims, and it was this very claim to political entitlements that was diluted in the event of partition, rendering "Cultural and Educational Rights," i.e., Articles 29 and 30 as significant to rights of minorities. Before the chapter discusses the idea of minorities and their rights in the Constituent Assembly, let me make a cursory note of the broad framework within which cultural diversity and religion operate in the West and in India, and what questions it has raised in the scholarship.

Minorities and Their Rights

At the outset, this chapter marked out a secular democracy as central to the study of minorities. This is so for the following reasons: The nature of plural societies, constituted by many groups possessing distinct lineages, cultures, religious practices, languages et al., has been a characteristic feature of most societies. However, while most societies are plural, not all of them operate within a democratic state. In plural societies, the freedom to observe and practice one's religion or way of life depended to a large extent on the consent of the dominant group. Theorists have argued that in such societies, dominance was expressed through political and symbolic terms (Mahajan 2002). The advent of democracy altered the situation. A democratic polity was associated with the institutional-ization of erstwhile claims that took the form of rights and entitlements by the State. This led to a questioning of the premise of plural societies which operated on the twin principles of consent by the dominant and an absence of dissent by smaller groups.

Second, addressing issues of discrimination and nondiscrimination becomes a crucial marker for the success of a liberal democracy. Liberal democracies, therefore, sought to counter discrimination and achieve equality for all. The magnitude of this can be understood best by examin-ing the minority question. Especially in the West, it was the minority—the immigrant, the indigenous, or the self-governing entities—that sought to challenge established norms which existed in these countries. It was this minority that inaugurated diversity in political and cultural terms. The minority question also challenged established norms within these states and brought to the fore the perpetuation of cultural discrimina-tion. Hence, democracy, while it ensured a degree of legal equality to groups, failed to address cultural discrimination that led to a feel-ing of alienation among a section of the body politic. Discrimination was practiced in many ways such as denial of full political rights to groups not belonging to the dominant culture or to those who chose to practice their way of life, resulting in second-class citizenship. This subterranean condition gained prominence in the 20th century with the influx of migrants in the West. They constituted individuals and groups who had traversed territories to avail of employment opportunities during the postwar economic boom, attaining the status of guest workers in Europe. While membership to the political community of the immigrant state was implausible, the migrants did seek the right to practice their ways of life, of attire, language, traditional education, religious instruction, etc. Eventually, this made it imperative for the host countries to make way for a multicultural approach.[2]

While religious minorities and their cultural practices played a significant role in Western European countries, in Canada, the minority question had serious political repercussions, as they were not immigrants, but members belonging to former self-governing territories incorporated by conquest. This resulted in the creation of national minorities who chose to retain their distinctiveness vis-à-vis the larger body politic (Kymlicka 1995, 13). It is here that multiculturalism found its roots by linking cultural diversity to equality among cultural communities, and highlighting continued discrimination even after formal legal rights had been granted (Mahajan 2002). It also highlighted the inadequacy of the principle of "equality of all" interpreted as one of sameness.[3]

Third, the idea of nondiscrimination in religious matters is crucial to examining the secular aspect of Indian democracy. Minorities, especially religion-based minorities and, more recently, caste-based minorities, have determined the nature and purpose of secularism in India. Cultural diversity in India, at least as articulated by the State, has been predominantly a religion-based discourse. Whether in the practice of religious neutrality by the British or divided sovereignties based on religious antagonisms, religious identities have fueled passions and posed a challenge to State institutions.

While questions of the secular–religious dichotomy arise in many sites, one can broadly categorize them into situations of intense communalism on one hand and state intervention in domains considered largely religious and community-oriented on the other. Minority groups form a part of both. Therefore, cultural diversity in India has been articulated by the Hindu Nationalist Movement, a right-wing ideological platform that uses the principle of "equality of all" to justify its dominance and preaches assimilation of other minor cultures/religions. Here, the minority is constructed as the alien and antagonistic other. This finds expression in their ideology and practice of politics.

Scholarship that has emerged in the field of politics and sociology has reflected on this communal aspect as much as it has reflected on religion. When examined in the backdrop of communalism, secularism has met with proclamations of its demise in the Indian State (Nandy 1985). The minority question has been central to this discourse, as to be secular, a polity needs to be inclusive; it needs to secularize, and while acknowledging the regressive tendency of some aspects of ascriptive identities, it has to nonetheless preserve culture-based value systems that are considered essential to their (minorities) development. Hence, the Indian State has attempted twin processes of accommodation and negotiation. In direct political terms, i.e., of party politics, the state has failed its minorities on more than one occasion, and politics in India has had its predicaments with the secular ideal that forms an intrinsic part of the Indian ethos. It is perhaps this quality of the secular that our nationalist leaders abided by and, hence, it remained undefined, finding a mention in the Preamble to the Indian Constitution two decades into independence.

In India, the quotidian question has been how to preserve religious ways of life while maintaining independent spheres of influence of state and religion. This idea of keeping the two separate was how secularism emerged in the West. However, the Western idea of the secular did not actively protect minorities. Instead, it separated the sacred and the temporal, clearly demarcating the functions of the State to the latter and absolving itself of any responsibility to minor cultures, or religion for that matter.

In India, the practice of religious neutrality by the British was compromised on more than one occasion by compulsions of state patronage associated traditionally with the ruler in matters of endowments for religious purposes, supervising religious festivals, administering affairs of the temples and mosques, and missionary work, to name a few. While it was clear that the postcolonial Indian State would not follow an established religion, it was impossible to deny religious liberties as constituting citizenship rights.

Thus, unlike the West, the Indian State conceived a nation where minorities were not treated as distinct entities. This was because in India

minority groups were not immigrants, but had been part of the subconti-
nent for centuries. Some like Sikhism were sects that had developed into
distinct religious entities. Hence, minorities were considered a part of
the State, though entitled to some safeguards vis-à-vis the majority that
had the potential to dominate. It is to avoid this subtle assimilation that
the Constitution has certain rights that address specific cultural markers
relating to minority communities. Besides that, the Constitution contains
a host of rights that legitimize the practice of religion.[4]

Rights of Minorities in the Making

In India, the general principle guiding the rights of minorities was that
they served as safeguards and as a means of the preservation of culture.
Under colonial rule, one can discern the few attempts to articulate the
plurality that existed in India. While rights per se were not extended
to any group, safeguards for certain sections of the population were an
important feature of the Government of India Act 1935; the Communal
Award identified certain communities as eligible for separate electorates,
seats were given to Marathas in Bombay, and special constituencies were
reserved for the Depressed Classes. This was a significant landmark as it
was for the first time that definite communities or groups were marked
out as deserving special treatment. Safeguards were also extended by giving in to claims for representation in the public services. Starting 1925,
the Government of India initiated the policy of reserving a certain percentage of direct appointments to government service for the redress of
communal inequities. In particular, this policy was adopted to secure
increased representation for Muslims in the public services.

Deliberations specific to the rights of minorities in the Constituent
Assembly were guided by the nationalist vision that took shape during
colonial times.[5] The beginnings of the construction of minorities perhaps
was reflected in the composition of the Constituent Assembly, following
the recommendations of the Cabinet Mission that recognized three communities in India—General, Muslim, and Sikh, with the "General" category including all communities that were not Muslim or Sikh. Smaller
minorities that were likely to lose out on population basis were to be given
full representation upon all matters of special interest to minorities.

A further categorization included "major minorities" such as Hindu minorities in Muslim provinces and Muslim minorities in Hindu provinces, the Sikhs in Punjab and the Depressed Classes who had a considerable representation in the provinces. Smaller minorities like Indian Christians, Anglo-Indians, and tribal representatives were to be taken care of by constituting an Advisory Committee within the Constituent Assembly that would look into issues such as fundamental rights, clauses regarding minority protection, and proposals for the administration of tribal and excluded areas. Thus, minorities were identified at the very first stage of drafting the Constitution.

A perusal of the debates in the Constituent Assembly reflects the lack of unanimity in constituting a minority. While communities were identified as minorities, why they were chosen as minorities and not others was an issue that was left unaddressed.

However, no efforts were spared to explain at length the nature of minorities as fixed entities and the scope of their rights. Thus, K. T. Shah's "Note on Fundamental Rights" gave an overview of the idea of a minority group and defined the parameters of their rights within a secular state. He said,

> Rights of Minorities are taken as an important aspect of the Rights of Man. The term "minorities" in this connection refers not to political minorities but to those fixed and unchanging entities, distinguished by religion or nationality, culture or language, which made small groups in the midst of larger populations. They have fundamental differences regarding the ways of life which demand special safeguards and protection with reference to those items which they prize specially, namely religion, culture or language. (Rao 1967)

He further states,

> ...Rights of minorities are obligations of majorities, that they shall cultivate toleration and equal regard for the ways of life, thought or worship of their sister communities however much they may differ from them, or safeguards for minorities rather than positive privileges for the latter. (ibid.)

The Constituent Assembly was convened from August 1946 to November 1949 and its proceedings were not independent of the influence of external factors.[6] The provisions envisaged for the minority groups in 1947 were different from the rights that were finally granted to the minorities once partition became a certainty. As indicated by the division recommended by the Cabinet Mission and as argued by some scholars, the basis for granting minority status to a group was not so much its numerical status as the disadvantage suffered by it vis-à-vis the rest of the population. Given this, the Assembly identified three kinds of minorities—religious minorities, backward castes, and tribes (Bajpai 2000). The nature of safeguards differed from the consideration of both political and cultural safeguards to the assigning of merely cultural safe-guards by 1949—a direct result of partition that occurred along religious lines. Many of these trends will be reflected in the following sections.

A Short Note on Procedure

Soon after the Assembly was constituted in January 1947, Govind Ballabh Pant moved a resolution for the setting up of an Advisory Committee on Fundamental Rights, Minorities and Tribal and Excluded and Partially Excluded Areas. The Muslim League was conspicuous by its absence in these crucial proceedings, as it was, when the Sub-Committee on Minori-ties was appointed in February 1947 and chaired by H. C. Mookherjee—a Christian leader from Bengal.[7] The Sub-Committee decided to circulate a questionnaire to get an idea of the kind of demands that were to be taken into account while deciding the rights of minorities. The question-naire included queries on the nature of political, economic, and cultural safeguards for minorities at the Central and Provincial levels, a suitable mechanism to oversee the functioning of these rights, and, last but not least, the time period till which this recognition should be given and under what circumstances these rights should be withdrawn.

Following the circulation of this questionnaire, representations were received by Ambedkar and Jagjivan Ram (Depressed Classes), by Ujjal Singh and Harnam Singh (Sikhs), and by Parsis and Anglo-Indians. Both Jagjivan Ram and Khandekar demanded that the Scheduled Castes (SCs) being equal to the Muslims in terms of population should be given simi-lar representation in the reservation of seats in the legislatures, minis-tries, public services, and the judiciary. Suggestions for safeguards for SCs were also forwarded by the All India Adi-Hindu Depressed Classes Association. The Sikhs demanded special educational facilities and reservations in public services similar to those for the SCs and Scheduled Tribes (STs), reservation for the backward classes within their religion, namely Mazhabis, Ramdasias, and Kabirpanthis, and the reservation of seats in the Central legislature and Central Cabinet.[8] The Anglo-Indians demanded a fundamental right to receive education in English. For this, they demanded that English schools run by them continue receiving grants from the state with an increase in the share of such grants.

The Parsis and Christians did not make specific demands. Homi Mody conceded that Parsis should receive treatment at least equal to that given to one of the smaller minorities. A demand for protection of language was forwarded by R. N. Brahma from Assam for the tribal people, as well as those who had settled in the plains—to protect their own dialects and forms of religion and worship, besides reservations in the legislature and public services.

The Sub-Committee in its subsequent meetings decided against separate electorates to the legislature. Reservation for Anglo-Indians and Parsis was deferred for consideration by the Advisory Committee, as was the representation of Sikhs, given the uncertain situation in East Punjab. Reservations in the public services were extended to the SCs, Muslims, Anglo-Indians, and plain tribes.

Rajkumari Amrit Kaur was against any kind of rights or privileges for minorities, whether religion-, caste-, or gender-based. K. T. Shah, while noting the growth of religious minorities, opined that safeguards for minorities would have to protect the religion and culture of communities without creating divisions such as the one created by separate electorates. The rights of minorities were not the obligation of the majority alone, but rather the guarantees of the entire community.[9]

However, as mentioned before, crucial changes took place by the time the Assembly's work was drawing to a close in the latter half of 1949. From accepting elections to Central and Provincial legislatures on the basis of joint electorates, the Constituent Assembly's Drafting Committee withdrew special privileges for religious minorities, i.e., reservation of seats in the legislature and representation in public services. Special safeguards were guaranteed only for the backward and depressed sections such as the SCs and STs—a decision accepted by the Assembly in May 1949.

Cultural rights, however, were retained, and, perhaps, it is for this reason that the right to establish and administer educational institutions by religion- and language-based minorities' gains precedence. They were not meant to compensate the withdrawal of the political safeguards, but were regarded as a middle path to secure minority interests that did not swing to the extremes of having political safeguards in the form of separate representation, and nevertheless protected the groups against majoritarian tendencies (K. M. Munshi).

While the focus of the debate regarding cultural rights of minorities was on the feasibility of religious instruction in community-based schools that received state aid, the issue was resolved by inserting a conscience clause[10] that forbade the minority-administered school from imposing religious instruction on those wards who did not wish to receive such instruction.[11] This was to ensure that the principle of nondiscrimination guided both minorities and non-minorities, and safeguards for the former did not trespass the rights of non-minorities.

While discussions on what the right to culture would constitute do not have a direct bearing on this chapter, the following statement by B. R. Ambedkar demonstrates how the members attempted to conceptualize the term. Clarifying the meaning of the term "minority" as adopted by the Drafting Committee, Ambedkar stated,

> On reading the paragraph contained in the original fundamental rights it will be noticed that the term "minority" was used therein not in the technical sense of the word minority as we have been accustomed to use it for the purposes of certain political safeguards, such as representation in the legislatures, services and so on. The word is used not merely to indicate the minority in the technical sense of the word; it is also used to cover minorities which are not minorities in the technical sense, but which are nonetheless minorities in the cultural and linguistic sense. For instance, for the purposes of this (Draft) Article 23, if a certain number of people from Madras came and settled in Bombay for certain purposes, they would be, although not a minority in the technical sense, cultural minorities. Similarly, if Maharashtrians settled in Bengal, they may not be minorities in the technical sense; they would be cultural and linguistic minorities in Bengal. That is the reason why we dropped the word "minority" because we felt that the word might be interpreted in the narrow sense of the term.

> ...Another thing which has to be borne in mind regarding (Draft) Article 23 is that it does not impose any obligation or burden upon the State. It does not say that, when for instance the Madras people come to Bombay the Bombay government shall be required by law to finance any project of giving education either in Tamil language or any other language. The only limitation that is imposed by (Draft) Article 23 is that if there is a cultural

minority which wants to preserve its language, script and culture, the State shall not by law impose upon it any other culture which may be either local or otherwise. Therefore, this article really is to be read in a much wider sense and does not apply only to what I call the technical minorities as we use it in our Constitution. (Constituent Assembly Debates, Vol. VII)

There was also apprehension regarding whether denominations were to be included. Regarding the scope of the beneficiaries, there was an opinion that including sects would only blur and fragment the recipients of these rights. There was also a strong possibility of recognizing sects within the majority Hindu religion itself. Moreover, the pervasiveness of such sects would mean that any number of groups would constitute a minority at a particular place or time.[12]

Therefore, one can gather from the debates that the members, while acknowledging the fluidity of the nature of minorities in India, sought to negotiate with the groups for a coherent entity which could benefit from the rights given by Articles 29 and 30 of the Constitution.[13] While the pervasiveness of minorities was a cause for concern, it was its religious appeal that preoccupied the minds of those discussing cultural rights.

Adjudicating Rights of Minorities: Negotiating Claims

Such being the nature of debates, the Constituent Assembly members gave the ultimate responsibility for arbitration regarding these rights to the judicial courts in India. While drafting the Constitution, the concern was to ensure the State does not in any way endorse one religion over another, even on the pretext of protecting minorities. Such was the Assembly's preoccupation with the matter that they chose not to spell out "religious and linguistic groups" that fall within the scope of Article 30. Perhaps, it was implied in the course of the debates that the right belonged to the Christian, Muslim, Anglo-Indian, Sikh, and Parsi communities as it was in the interest of their claims to continue with traditional forms of education and the right to culture was interpreted in this manner.

In independent India, the responsibility of defining the scope and intent of the right to culture rests with the courts under writ jurisdiction. This chapter will touch upon select cases as an instance of the Court's intervention in shaping minority rights in India. It may be mentioned here that the chapter will be drawing from cases of the Supreme Court only.

Broadly, the questions that have come before the Court in relation to minority educational institutions have been regarding the right of establishment and administration. While the terms "to establish and administer" may appear to be fairly simple at the outset, they carry with them a number of interpretations. For instance, it is in the course of interpreting the right to "administer educational institutions of their choice" that the Court has raised issues regarding the establishment of the institution by a minority. In this context, the Re Kerala Education Bill[14] has been slated as a significant landmark in the short history of jurisprudence when studying minority rights, as it brought to the fore a significant anomaly in the interpretation of the minority question in India, i.e., how to determine a minority.

Arising from a situation where a national minority,[15] i.e., the Christian community, formed a state majority in Kerala, the crucial question of the "unit as per which the minority is to be determined" was the highlight of this case.[16] More than 40 years later, the question was revived in the T. M. A. Pai case.[17] In both cases, the Court interpreted the minority to be determined according to the State. It was this logic of determining the minority state-wise that the Supreme Court used to evade the petition of the Jain community to be notified as a national minority.[18] It is for this reason that the Jain community, while it has been a denied minority status at the national level, is given minority status in states of Himachal Pradesh, Jharkhand, Madhya Pradesh, Maharashtra, Uttar Pradesh (UP), and Uttarakhand. In a recent development early this year in January 2014, the Union Government accorded the Jain community a minority status.

Furthermore, the Court has chosen to interpret the right to establish and administer differently. Hence, for instance, if one were to compare the judgment of the Supreme Court in the Kerala Education Bill and the Azeez Basha case, 1967, which examined the minority status of the Aligarh Muslim University (AMU), one observes that the Court has, in the former, read the right to establish and administer minority educational institutions separately. This, according to the court, was to allow pre-Constitutional educational institutions to enjoy the safeguards provided by Article 30. Thus, in the Kerala Education Bill, it held that it is not imperative that the right to administer has to be read conjunctively with the right of establishment. However, the Court took a contrary view in the Azeez Basha case, where it questioned the setting up of the AMU by the Muslim community. In this case, the court held that the rights to establish and administer had to be read together. It then sought to depart from its earlier precedent set in the Kerala Education Bill regarding pre-Constitution educational institutions and proceeded to state that the AMU, known originally as the Muhammedan Anglo-Oriental (MAO) College, though set up by the Muslim community, could not be interpreted as being "established" by them as it was under the 1920 Act, and enjoys its current status. The Court held, "The Act may have been passed as a result of the efforts of the Muslim minority, but that does not mean that the University, when it came into being under the Act of 1920 was established by the Muslim minority." The Court argued that the institutions established by the Muslim minority were the MAO College, the Muslim University Association, and the Muslim University Foundation Committee, and these three institutions approached the government to bring into existence a university, the degrees of which would be recognized by the government. Thus, AMU was neither established nor administered by the Muslim community, as it came into being and was administered by the statutory bodies created under the Act of 1920 (*S. Azeez Basha and Another v. Union of India*, 1967, SCR(1) 833).

In the St. Stephen's case, the court conceded that the educational institution was established by the Christian minority and henceforth recognized the autonomy of the college to follow its own procedure for admissions. However, it read Articles 29(2) and 30(1) together, stating that the former was a "special right" which would prevail over the general right guaranteed to minorities under Article 30(1). The court held that in the case of an educational institution receiving grants from the State as was the case with St. Stephen's, Article 29(2) will prevail and a "sprinkling of outsiders" was admissible. However, the court held that this neither violated the right of the institution under Article 30 nor did it imply that the institution had shed its minority character (*St. Stephen's College v. The University of Delhi*, 1991).

Furthermore, the Court made an exception in declaring the Arya Samaj to be a minority belonging to the Hindu religious minority in the State of Punjab and upheld its right to seek protection of Article 30(1).[19] In doing so, once again the Court read Articles 29 and 30 together, stating that being "a section of citizens having a distinct language, script...," they could be understood as being a minority. In its judgment, it maintained that the autonomy of the Arya Samaj was not curbed by the provisions of the Guru Nanak University Act 1969, making compulsory the study of Punjabi and teachings of Guru Nanak (*D.A.V. College v. the State of Punjab*, 1971). Yet, in the *Ahmedabad St. Xaviers College Society and Another v. the State of Gujarat*, 1974, the Court held that Articles 29 and 30 were mutually exclusive and that if the latter is made an extension of the right under Article 29(1), then the fundamental rights of minorities will be taken away. Hence, the court held that Article 30 cannot be "whittled down" by reading it along with Article 29(1).

However, in *Brahmo Samaj Education Society and others v. State of West Bengal and others*, 2004, the Court chose not to determine the minority or denominational status of the Brahmo Samaj, relying instead on Article 26(a) which stated that "every religious denomination or any section thereof can establish and maintain educational institutions," subject to public order, morality, and health.[20] This has been the stand of the court in the case of the Jain minority, where in the cause of secularism, the court warned against conferring a minority status upon communities. It said:

> The Minorities Commission instead of encouraging claims from different communities for being added to a list of notified minorities under the Act, should suggest ways and means to help create social conditions where the list of notified minorities is gradually reduced and done away with altogether.... Differential treatment to linguistic minorities based on language within the State is understandable, but if the same concept for minorities on the basis of religion is encouraged, the whole country will further face division on the basis of religious diversities. (*Bal Patil and Another v. Union of India and others*, 2005)

While the court has been fairly consistent in adjudicating a principle of reasonable restrictions or regulations when exercising the right to "administer educational institutions of their choice," in the Islamic Academy case, it held that unaided minority educational institutions—which, in its previous judgments, the court ruled could enjoy complete autonomy in determining who they wished to admit—were now to enjoy such autonomy only up to the level of undergraduate education. However, different considerations came into play for educational institutions, including technical and professional institutions at the level of graduation and postgraduation. It held that imparting education was primarily a function of the State and it is only because the state could not bear the burden of public education that private institutions emerged to fill the gap. On this pretext, the State took upon itself the responsibility of regulating these institutions, as the right under Article 30 was not absolute and subject to regulation to ensure there was no profiteering or capitation fee, and that members from backward classes also found a place within these institutions (*Islamic Academy of Education and Another v. the State of Karnataka and others*, 2003).

Conclusion

In the recent past, a Constitutional amendment inserted Clause 5 to Article 15 of Part III of the Constitution on Fundamental Rights[21] making it mandatory for all educational institutions—including private educational institutions, whether aided or unaided by the state—to admit students from the backward classes, as well as SCs and STs. However, educational institutions under Article 30 were exempt from this responsibility of affirmative action.

The Supreme Court addressed the above issue in *Ashok Kumar Thakur v. Union of India and others*, 2008, wherein the crucial question of whether the exclusion of minority educational institutions from the ambit of Article 15(5) was in violation of Article 14 arose. The Supreme Court, however, did not consider the matter in great detail and ruled,

> The exclusion by itself is not severable from the rest of the provisions. This plea is not tenable because the minority institutions have been given a separate treatment in view of Article 30 of the Constitution. The exemption of minority educational institutions has been allowed to conform to Article 15(5) with the mandate of Article 30 of the Constitution....

The preceding sections demonstrated how the State approached the minority question. However, what we hear at present are voices of discontent from some quarters of the minority communities regarding the inadequacy of the rights provided to them. While progressive voices seek redress from within existing institutions and structures, there has been a strong lobby for reservations within existing religious minorities.

These claims have gained legitimacy with the findings of government-sponsored projects like the Sachar Committee Report and the Ranganath Mishra Commission Report that project the Muslim community, in particular, as backward in comparison to other communities. The Ranganath Mishra Report endorses reservations for backward sections among religious minorities.

The demand for reservations itself is not a new one: the Sikh community, for instance, sought reservation for backwards amongst them, namely, the Mazhabis, Ramdasias, and Kabirpanthis, in public services and special educational facilities similar to that given to SCs and STs. Moreover, some states like Andhra Pradesh, Kerala, and Karnataka have recognized backwards within the Muslim and Christian communities as being entitled to reservations. The demand for reservations by Muslims at the national level began in the 1990s, and the National Movement for Muslim Reservation has sought reservations not as Muslims but as a backward, deprived class.

Yet, the idea of perpetuating minorities is a concern for a progressive society. While reservations were considered important by the members of the Constituent Assembly, at no point did they envision the extension of reservation beyond the initial 10-year period. The same was true for the grants given to the Anglo-Indian community. Reservations, unlike safeguards, were not meant to be permanent. Perhaps, it is for this reason that the cultural right to minorities did not entail a provision for reservation. It served as a robust enabling clause, ensuring that educational institutions managed by minorities faced no discrimination by the State. Neither did the courts allow the right to acquire leviathan-like qualities, curbing the autonomy of the educational institutions with regulations as and when state support was sought.

A perusal of the minority certificates issued annually by the National Commission for Minority Educational Institutions established in 2005, reveal a significant increase in the number of educational institutions headed by minority communities. A perusal of the number of minority certificates issued annually in the past eight years shows a significant increase in the number of educational institutions headed by minority communities. The State of Kerala tops the list with over 3,500 certificates issued since 2005, followed by the State of UP with over 1,500 certificates issued. Yet, despite this marked increase, one cannot help but ponder how the growing use of this right has served the larger interests of the minority communities. While Article 30 was meant to be a safeguard, it has over the years, with the support of the State, become a means for the minorities to practice citizenship. While the members of the Constituent Assembly would have wanted this, the exemptions enjoyed by them have repercussions for minorities other than those based on religion and language and, hence, reflect on India's secular democracy.

Notes and Bibliography

Notes

1. The idea of principled distance legitimizes State involvement in religion in a manner that facilitates the enjoyment of cultural goods by the citizens. Political secularism is not a simple division of the sacred and the secular, but a way of regulating relations between the two to promote values within a liberal democratic polity.

2. For instance, the Swann Report of 1955 recognized the need for multicultural education in State-run schools, thereby exposing students to religious pluralism in Britain. Schools worked closely with local religious leaders, including Muslims, to ensure the content of religious education took into consideration the religious background of the school pupils.

3. The contention against the notion of sameness as represented in the idea of universal citizenship was challenged as being difference-blind. Young articulated this in her critique of liberal equality, stating that universal citizenship had failed to redress issues of inequality and injustice and hence differentiated citizenship representing the plurality of values was imperative (1989).

4. Articles 25–28 in Part III of the Constitution contain a host of rights that guarantee freedom of religion, ranging from the right to practice and propagate religion, to administer religious endowments, mandate religious instruction, etc.

5. The Karachi session of the Indian National Congress seriously considered safeguards for minority populations; the importance of religious liberty and cultural autonomy were recognized in the Nehru Report of 1928—with both Motilal Nehru and Tej Bahadur Sapru rejecting separate electorates in favor of the right to culture, while Jawaharlal Nehru in his Objectives Resolution stated that in the future Constitution of India, "adequate safeguards shall be provided for minorities, backward and tribal areas and depressed and other backward classes."

6. The irony, so to speak, of the fixedness of the minority category was reflected in Ambedkar's appointment to the Constituent Assembly on a Muslim League ticket. This demonstrated a sense of solidarity and common apprehension, felt equally by the two largest minorities in India at the time vis-à-vis Swaraj demanded by the dominant upper-caste Hindu nationalists.

7. Separate subcommittees were formed for the tribal areas of Assam and for tribals in plain areas outside Assam. They were the Northeast Frontier (Assam) Tribal and Excluded Areas, and the Excluded and Partially Excluded Areas (other than Assam).

8. The Sikhs also proposed the division of the Punjab province into two sub-provinces—Northwest and Southeast Punjab, each with its own legislature and cabinet. Common affairs were to be dealt with in a joint legislature with Sikh representation equivalent to Muslim representation in the Central legislature. Post partition, the nature of demands altered from political representation to the recognition of language, script and culture, and equal status of Sikh backward classes to Hindu SCs, etc.

9. K. M. Munshi invoked the idea of a secular state in the recognition of a religious community:

> This minority right is intended to prevent majority controlled legislatures from favouring their own community to the exclusion of other communities. The question, therefore, is whether it is suggested that the State should be at liberty to endow school for minorities? Then it will come to this that the minority will be a favoured section of the public. This destroys the very basis of fundamental rights.

10. The conscience clause was recommended by the Indian Education Commission of 1882. Though not implemented by the British Government, it was adopted first by the United Provinces to forbid compulsory instruction in Christian schools in 1920.

11. Draft Clause 16 read, "No person attending any school maintained or receiving aid out of public funds shall be compelled to take part in the religious instruction that may be given in the school or to attend religious worship held in the school or in premises attached thereto." Constituent Assembly Debates (CAD), Vol. V. This has been incorporated as Article 28 in the Indian Constitution.

12. K. Santhanam said,

> In our country, even in the same religion, there are a number of denominations.... In a particular area, a particular Hindu denomination may be in a majority—we don't want Saivaite to give Saivite instruction; the Vaishnavites to give Vaishnavite instruction, the Lingayats.... We do not want to give even the slightest loophole for such controversies.

13. These articles find mention under "Cultural and Educational Rights," containing the following provisions:
Article 29: Protection of Interests of Minorities:

(1) Any section of the citizens residing in the territory of India or any part thereof having a distinct language, script, or culture of its own shall have the right to conserve the same.

(2) No citizen shall be denied admission into any educational institution maintained by the State or receiving aid out of State funds on grounds only of religion, race, caste, language, or any one of them.

Article 30: Rights of Minorities to Establish and Administer Educational Institutions:

(1) All minorities, whether based on religion or language, shall have the right to establish and administer educational institutions of their choice.

(2) The State shall not, in granting aid to educational institutions, discriminate against any educational institution on the ground that it is under the management of a minority, whether based on religion or language.

14. The term "Re" in the title of the case refers to the Reference made by the President under Article 143(1) of the Indian Constitution.

15. The term is currently used to indicate the status assigned to the Christians, Muslims, Parsis, Sikhs, and Buddhists as the religious minorities of India, based on the Official Gazette, 1993. Most recently, the Jain community has been accorded minority status in January 2014.

16. The counsel on behalf of the State of Kerala stated,

It is easy to say that a minority community means a community which is numerically less than 50 percent; but then the question is 50 percent of what? Is it 50 percent of the entire population of India or 50 percent of the population of a State forming a part of the Union? (Re Kerala Education Bill, 1957, SC 182).

17. ...In order to determine the existence of a religious or linguistic minority in relation to Article 30, what is to be the unit, the State or the country as a whole?.... The opening words of Article 30(1) make it clear that religious and linguistic minorities have been put on par, insofar as that article is concerned. Therefore, whatever the unit—whether a State or the whole of India—for determining a linguistic minority, it would be the same unit in relation to a religious minority. (*T. M. A. Pai Foundation v. State of Karnataka*, 2002, SC 481).

18. ...Henceforth, before the Central Government takes a decision on claims of Jains as a "minority" under the National Commission for Minorities Act, the identification has to be done on a State basis. The power of the Central government has to be exercised not merely on the advice and recommendation of the Commission, but on consideration of the social, cultural and religious conditions of the Jain community in each state. (*Bal Patil and Another v. Union of India and others*, 2005, SC 464).

19. The Court noted, "It is undisputed, and it was also conceded by the State of Punjab that the Hindus of Punjab are a religious minority in the State though

they may not be so in relation to the entire country" (*D. A. V. College v. State of Punjab and others*, 1971, SC 638).

20.   ...Every religious denomination or any section thereof can establish and maintain educational institutions under Article 26(A) of the Constitution subject to public order, morality, and health. Reading Articles 19(1) (G) and 26(A) together, the petitioners have a right to establish and manage educational institutions and hence we do not think it necessary to decide the issue of minority/denominational status of Brahmo Samaj. (*Brahmo Samaj Education Society and others v. State of West Bengal and others*, 2004, SC 36).

21.   Article 15(5) states:

> [N]othing in this Article or in sub clause (G) of Clause (1) of Article 19 shall prevent the state from making any special provision, by law, for the advancement of any socially and educationally backward classes of citizens or for the Scheduled Castes or Scheduled Tribes in so far as such special provisions relate to their admission to the educational institutions including private educational institutions, whether aided or unaided by the State, other than the minority educational institutions referred to in Clause (1) of Article 30.

Bibliography

Bajpai, Rochana. 2000. "Constituent Assembly Debates and Minority Rights." *Economic and Political Weekly* 35 (21–22): 1837–45.

Bhargava, Rajeev (ed.). 1998. "What is Secularism for?" In *Secularism and Its Critics*, 486–542. New Delhi: Oxford University Press.

Census of India. 1931. General Reports, 1. Microfilm, New Delhi: NMML.

Chandhoke, Neera. 1999. *Beyond Secularism: The Right of Religious Minorities*. New Delhi: Oxford University Press.

Chatterjee, Partha. 1998. "Secularism and Tolerance." In *Secularism and Its Critics*, edited by Rajeev Bhargava, 345–79. New Delhi: Oxford University Press.

Constituent Assembly Debates. 1949. New Delhi: Lok Sabha Secretariat.

Kymlicka, Will. 1995. *Multicultural Citizenship: A Liberal Theory of Minority Rights*. Oxford: Clarendon Press.

Mahajan, Gurpreet. 2002. "Secularism as Religious Non-Discrimination: The Universal and the Particular in the Indian Context." *India Review* 1 (1): 31–51.

Nandy, Ashis. 1985. "An Anti-Secularist Manifesto." *Seminar* 314: 1–12.

Parekh, Bhikhu. 1999. "Common Citizenship in a Multicultural Society." *Round Table* 351: 449–60.

Rao, B. Shiva. 1967. *The Framing of India's Constitution: Select Documents*, Vol. 2. New Delhi: Universal Law Publishing.

Young, Iris Marion. 1989. "Polity and Group Difference: A Critique of the Ideal of Universal Citizenship." *Ethics* 99 (2): 250–74.

14

Waqf and Urban Space: Production of Minority Identity in Hyderabad's Old City

Shireen Mirza

"Discourse about space" is "discourse of space," Henri Lefebvre observed, while reflecting on space as a heuristic category. Studying spatiality, since Lefebvre's influential theory has meant thinking about space as a construct that influences and is influenced by materiality, action, ideology and imaginary worlds. Preceding this, space was seen from the perspective of urban planning as one that acts as a container of events and material objects. By virtue of emphasizing the relationality between space and other entities such as time, matter, social action, ideas, and representation, Lefebvrian notions of space have had serious implications in studying social relations.

Extending this notion of space as ontologically related to the social, this chapter seeks to think about the production and experience of a minority imaginary as distinct and a segregated category in the naming of certain properties as Muslim *Waqf*[1] lands in the case of Hyderabad's old city. Minority imaginaries, as described in this chapter, are constructed on spatial categories in that properties notified as Muslim *Waqf* not only seem to occupy space by marking an area as distinctly Muslim but are also situated in space effecting identity and experience.

Space comes to be perceived and conceived as belonging to a minority Muslim community associated with a particular form of worship, belief, and identity. Not only do state policies perceive of particular neighborhoods as "minority electoral bases," particular spaces are also perceived as "Muslim areas" against which other identities of civic, secular, developed, global, nonghetto are constructed. More importantly, inhabitants of these "Muslim areas" experience these spaces as those that can be identified with, their aesthetics, symbolism, historical, and cultural familiarity providing a sense of security and mode of identification in an otherwise alienating urban terrain. Through this the primacy of religious identity over other forms of social identification is experienced, religion becoming a powerful base of personal identification and collective representation.

Visually prominentand dramatically distinct, the Shi'as form a diverse sect among the Muslims. Their small numbers amongst the dominant Sunnis tend to make them endogamous and live in close proximity to each other. More importantly, the community gathers for public ritual performances of mourning and flagellation that infuse urban space with Islamic iconography, black flags, ornately carved standards, eulogies that play in public space, and blood that is shed by commemorators in a spectacular display of mourning called *matham*. Live links also connect the community in the Middle East, South Asia, and the West via a sacred geography that extends between Iran, Karbala in Iraq, and Damascus in Syria. Material artifacts related to the charismatic religio-political leaders or the *Imams* are consecrated as people undertake pilgrimages to birthplaces and cemeteries of Imams, bringing about mobility as well as transposing and vernacularizing images of this sacred geography.

The creation of a distinct Shi'a quarter in Hyderabad's old city is at one level built around structures that replicate this sacred geography, such as spaces for commemorating the battle of Karbala known as *'ashurkhana* in South India or *Imambadha* in the North. The Shi'a neighborhoods in Hyderabad's old city can be seen to have grown around *'ashurkhana* properties which house standards or *alams* that symbolically represent the Prophet's grandson's martyred army in Karbala. The Shi'as as well as people from other communities visit these spaces of commemoration, for it is believed that on making contact with the symbolic standard, the martyred Imams mediate in the lives of those who seek intercession. Further, Muharram congregations that commemorate the martyrdom are held in this quarter through the year, although the topography of the urban space is entirely transformed during the two months of Muharram and Safar when urban space is infused with Islamic iconography and spectacular ritual display.

The Shi'as casually refer to this quadrant as "our (*apna*) area," in a manner of implying the sense of familiarity with the neighborhood and its people, the security they seem to derive from it, and the mine-ness expressed through signs of urban religiosity in standards installed on roofs of houses as well as sites of ritual commemorations such as *dargahs* and *'ashurkhanas* that populate every lane. Some of these public *'ashurkhana* properties are open to crowds of devotees who visit these complexes in times of crisis, as part of family traditions and practices of everyday life.

Srinivas's (2004) work on festivity and the making of civic space in Bangalore is a reminder of the embodied relation to space. What she calls "landscapes of urban memory" using the *Karaga* festival in Bangalore is an account of the genesis of civic space constituted through ritual performance calling into being a mnemonic relation to space when people gather every year for the procession (ibid.). Similarly, public flagellation and the drawing of one's blood using sharp instruments such as blades, chains, and knives is, at one level, a re-enactment of the battle of Karbala that renews a spiritual connection between the commemorator and the Imam martyred in Iraq in 680 A.D. At another level, this embodied memory is also linked to the local history of Muslim rule that patronized public Shi'a practices. Objects, words, images, sounds, smells, and tastes that represent personal and collective pasts through individual and social acts of remembering forge attachments to space expressed through memory.

This sense of spatial attachment and collective identity through space is evident in Hyderabad's old city—where mannerisms, styles of clothing, accents, and food cultures associated with Muslim-ness are seen as being imbedded within the space. In relation to this, the old city seems to be defined as a separate area from the rest of the city, for its inhabitants and others. Although, the sense of distinctiveness partially derives from being a historic center of the city, contemporary neoliberal-led development that ensured lack of amenities such as broad roads, sanitation, and connectivity bypass and segregate the old city as the rest of the city steadfastly heads toward achieving global status.

Different identities get leveled out, including ethnic, linguistic, caste, gender, sexual, as well as denominational ones such as Sunni, Shi'a, Bohra, Khoja, under the umbrella category of minority. Primarily, the idea of a minority is posited in opposition to the numerically stronger Hindu majority, an equally homogenizing category. In substance, the basis of categorizing people and their practices is part of discursive processes in which religion is seen as a domain that is associated with the sacred as well as with personal belief known to exclusively bind a group. Religion-based group identities such as Hindu, Muslim, Sikh, and Christian are canopied under the term minority or majority. Other modes of belonging, injustices, and marginal conditions under which individuals and communities may live, while bearing religious affiliations, then are subsumed under these categories. And yet, the idea of a minority community did not always exist in the form we know it today in that political discourse did not categorize people into groups based on practices termed as "religion."

Like the fields of gender, communalism (Pandey 1992), and sexuality (Bose and Bhattacharyya 2007) unpacked in some recent research exploring the historical and social conditions that have constituted the matrix in which ideas take root, religion and minority can be seen as colonially mediated categories that are socially constructed (Hacking 1999). Religion as a category is constructed by relating, practices associated with the sacred or other-worldly states, to identities personal in their manifestations, that are considered as part of the same experience. This idea of a religious minority as a segregated category is forged in opposition to the urban sphere or a domain constituted as the public through rational critical discourse as well as notions of civil society—as an arena of organization and practice that is located outside the state and is separate from the realm of family, faith, and market.

Any participation in political discourse or forms of urban presence takes place from the predefined terms ascribed to it. And yet, despite the constructed nature of a religious minority in relation to the dominant majority, the idea of a Muslim minority is also experientially authorized. The experience of being and becoming a minority then is a lived everyday truth, evidenced by the burgeoning Dalit and Muslim slums in growing cities with increasing levels of poverty, lack of access to education, and employment, as well as amenities in comparison to the rest of the city. Therefore, while reflecting on the constructed nature of becoming minority that aims to critique the frozenness, segregation, and uniformity of minority discourse attempted in this chapter, it is important to bear in mind the discrimination faced on the one hand, and the sense of distinctiveness, comfort, agency, and identification on the other that makes the category of a minority one that is experientially authorized.

This is particularly in the context of Hindu right agendas seeking to disentitle minorities or making shrill demands for integration under the ruse of secularism rendering their forms of belief and practice suspicious. Further, the rhetoric constructs the Muslim as the outsider whose patriotic loyalties are questionable and for whom religious authority and belonging to the Islamic brotherhood (*ummah*) holds more salience than structures of the nation state. Within this rubric of right-wing discourses, the process of becoming a minority is attributed to what is constructed as its being with piety at its core. Conforming to Islamic tradition and through it identifying with the distant lands of Arabia, in the case of the Sunnis as well as with Iran and Iraq in the case of the Shi'as, is seen as the essence of being a minority.

Emphasizing the constructed nature of becoming a minority is a reminder that modes of belonging to a larger Islamic geography as well as forms of piety enacted predate the nation state as a construct—as can be seen in the local recreation of a sacred geography in the case of Shi'as of Hyderabad's old city. This is not to explain away the popular experience of religiosity, as often left liberal discourses tend to do in response to the allegation of piety above other loyalties leveled against minorities. The popular realm of religious experience is distinctly expressed by minorities, which can be seen as much a source of strength and identity as a collective strategy of survival which needs to be taken seriously and explored immanently.

In keeping with this, the idea of a Muslim minority can be seen enabling a distinct identity expressed through belonging to the space of the old city, where bodily acts of remembering through ritual performance revert to a past history. For the Shi'a quadrant of the old city draws from the deeply entrenched historically dominant public culture of Shi'ism that perhaps provides its inhabitants with a familiar terrain to navigate their livelihoods as outside options often close in. This local culture has deep historical routes in state patronage by the Indo-Persian Qutub Shahi dynasty (1512–1687) that imagined Hyderabad city as an extension of Iran and declared Shi'ism as state religion. Further, a dominant Shi'a public culture established during this time gained popularity as part of the local courtly culture within the predominantly Sunni Asif Jahi dynasty (1724–1948), notwithstanding a brief interval during the Mughal emperor Aurangzeb's rule. The popular dominant Shi'a public culture in Hyderabad was displaced after Indian independence, already hollowed by years of association as a Princely State during the British Raj. After independence, patronage of these Shi'a public practices was devolved to a host of *Waqf* bodies, which are managed and controlled by the erstwhile nobility with participation from the diasporic Iranian–Hyderabadi Twelver community.

Alluding to this local history, the chapter describes the inventory of the institution of *Waqf* after the forced accession of the Princely State of Hyderabad into the territories of the Indian Union from 1948 onwards. Furthermore, it explores socio-legal developments that transformed age-old public structures built by the local Muslim kings to what came to be known as "Muslim *Waqf*" properties in postcolonial India, by examining legal debates around religious endowments instituted by the erstwhile kings of the Princely State to maintain these properties. The primary aim of the chapter, then, is to explore the idea of minority produced in discourse, mapped onto urban space, which is in turn influenced by the colonial and postcolonial understanding of what is majority, minority culture, religion, and society. The chapter, therefore, attempts to relate this socio-legal process to the production of urban space, in which the idea of a minority coproduces a distinct Muslim quarter in the historic old city of Hyderabad around these contested *Waqf* properties.

Production of Shi'a Quadrant in Hyderabad's Old City

Hyderabad's old city was originally the site where the Indo-Iranian Shi'a King of Golconda Mohammed Quli Qutub Shah founded the city nearly four centuries ago in 1589 on the southern bank of the River Musi when the adjoining fortress town of Golconda became overpopulated. Today, it is considered as the decrepit and crime-prone district of Hyderabad, the capital of Andhra Pradesh State and the sixth largest city of India, with a population of around 2,545,000 in 1981 (Yagnik 1984). The growth of Hyderabad city has diversified into what could be clubbed as four different parts based on different models of development.

The part of the city on the southern bank of River Musi, the original "walled" city of Hyderabad when it was founded, is now referred to as the "old city," with a high concentration of Muslims. For compared to the Muslim percentage of the entire State of Andhra Pradesh, which is about 8 percent, in Hyderabad city itself (excluding Secunderabad and its districts) the Muslim population is about 43 percent according to the 1971 Census. Further, in 18 out of 50 municipal constituencies in the old city, the Muslim population is above 50 percent. In six of these, the population is above 70 percent (ibid.). This is perhaps the reason the old city is often referred to as a "Muslim ghetto" that is commonly suspected of "breeding" "terrorism" and violence. As a pocket that has a high density of Muslim population, this area votes for the local Muslim All India Majlis-e-Ittehadul Muslimeen[2] political party that has been winning state elections since 1984. This includes constituencies of Charminar and Yakutpura comprising of Shi'a neighborhoods of Daru Shifa, Noorkhan Bazaar, Dabeerpura, Purani Haveli, and Chatta Bazaar who also vote for the local Sunni party.

The second part of Hyderabad city is the original cantonment area of the British that held their barracks, markets, and churches to the North of River Musi, which developed into present-day Secunderabad. The separation of the old city from Secunderabad was a process that began in the early 20th-century with the division between what came to be known as the "native" areas or *mulki* areas from the British cantonment area of Secunderabad and nonmulki areas, consisting of foreigners recruited from British India as well as the native Telugu populace (Leonard 1978). The third part of the city could be seen as comprising the Qutub Shahi Golconda fort area and the military lands of the Indian army that is merging with the rest of the expanding metropolis of Hyderabad. Further west from here is the newly developed township which, due to its high-quality infrastructure, is called HiTec city or Cyberabad and includes areas of Madhapur, Kondapur, Gachibowli, and Uppal and could be seen to constitute a separate fourth part of the city.

In itself, the old city was settled along community lines, in which community trade of settlers acted as a nucleus for further settlement. This includes, for instance, separate quadrants occupied by the Arabs and Marathas in the southeastern part of the quadrant, the Arabs in the locality of Barkas (local pronunciation of barracks), while the Marathas settled in Shah Ali Banda and Brahmin Wadi (now Gowlipura) localities bordering the palace of the notable Prime Minister Sir Kishen Pershad Bahadur. A dramatic demographic change within the old city took place after the Police Action in 1948 in which the Indian army, as part of a military operation named "Operation Polo," forced the accession of the Princely State that resulted in massive killings of rural and urban Muslims.

The profile of the social group inhabiting the old city transformed as a result of episodes of violence, trailing the Hindu–Muslim polarization that followed the Police Action. Naidu's study profiles changes within the old city in the transitory years of independence, the decade between 1941 and 1951. She describes a mass exodus of population, especially of Muslims who constituted 73 percent of the total population, which according to her, from 69 percent in 1951, shrank to about 55 percent in 1961. On the other hand, the Hindu immigration into the old city increased from 25 percent to 45 percent. With the exodus of Muslims during 1951–61, she describes, there was an influx of Hindus into certain parts of the old city. With the falling prices of land and buildings, the Hindus, more confident of the future, took advantage of this factor and invested (Naidu 1990, 27). The proportion of Hindu immigrants in the old city during 1951–61 was 56 percent of the total immigrants and their proportion in the population increased from 21 percent to 40 percent during the decade (ibid.).

The Shi'as, many of whom held high posts under the Nizams and occupied the Northeast quadrant, fled either to Pakistan, the North of India, or sold their mansions in the old city and moved to newer areas. According to Naidu, the Shi'as seem to have almost disappeared from the census map, and from 1951–61, the Shi'a population of the old city decreased from 22 percent to 6 percent, and by 1980s constituted, in her estimate, only 4 percent of the entire population. Simultaneously, the rural Muslim poor were either confronted with massive killings, looting, and rape during the Police Action or rising unemployment moved in entire groups to parts of the old city. These migrants tended to live in clusters in a neighborhood of their social community, where visible signs of Muslim influence and culture were left over from the time of the Nizam (Naidu 1990, 27).

Areas predominated by Muslims, following demographic changes, were re-read as Muslim areas, marked as they were by the presence of historic mosques, and 'ashurkhanas following the demographic change that sought to territorialize space. For when the local 'ashurkhanas were built in the newly founded Hyderabad city (now referring primarily to the old city) by the erstwhile Muslim kings, they were public institutions for which resources were granted from the central treasury or the *Sarf-i-Khas* from the provision of land allotted for private expenditure. This meant they were spaces that were inherent to the city and were not seen as religiously defined Muslim spaces, given their use by other communities. Also, at the time of construction, the chief functionary or the trustee or the caretaker (*mutawalli*) belonged to any community—Sunni, Shi'a, or Hindu—and was appointed for its maintenance, and the post was hereditary resulting in the descendants almost inheriting the property (Reddy 1984). Further, these were spaces related to the well-being of the city and its inhabitants, which ensured safety from floods, drought, famine, fatal diseases, etc.

The royal house for commemoration (*Badshahi 'ashurkhana*), for instance, was built soon after the foundation of the new city was laid in 1591 by Sultan Muhammad Quli Qutub Shah V in 1596, with Persian enamel work. The king appointed the family of the current trustee Mir Nawazish Ali Khan to maintain and administer the property as well as to oversee the rituals performed in its precincts. Standards were installed and later, wooden columns were built during the reign of Mir Nizam Ali Khan Bahadur, Asaf Jah II. The king also conferred feudal lands (*jagir*) yielding revenue of ₹12,000 for the expenses, which was extended by ₹2,000 by Sikandar Jan Bahadur, Asaf Jah III.

Likewise, the *Bibi ka alam 'ashurkhana* located in Yakutpura in the Shi'a quadrant of the old city is a complex dedicated to the standard of the daughter of the Prophet—Fatima Zehra. The standard is believed to contain a plank of wood on which Imam Ali is suppose to have given the final ablutions to his wife Bibi Fatima, and was brought to Golconda from Karbala during the time of Abdullah Qutub Shah (1625–72) and paraded in Muharram processions since the genesis of the city. The efficacy of the standard is believed to derive from the relics it contains, and its aura from the authenticity it represents dating back to the Qutub Shahi period, although the 'ashurkhana complex itself was built by the Sunni fifth Nizam and renovated by the last Nizam in 1925. Further, six pocket diamonds are suspended from the standard, offered by the fifth Nizam. At the same time, it is believed that the standard had protected the city and its inhabitants from an incident of floods when water receded from the city on the prayers of its inhabitants. As decreed by the fifth Nizam, a grant from the Sarf-i-Khas funds was instituted for the Sunni caretaker family of the property, whose current heir Mir Aliuddin Arif holds the position.

At a later date, the Azakhana-e-Zehra 'ashurkhana was constructed by the seventh and last Nizam in the Shi'a neighborhood of Daru Shifa, with the involvement of prominent Shi'a nobles of the time. The 'ashurkhana complex was dedicated to the Nizam's mother, built in the vicinity of her palace, King Koti. The standards installed in the complex are made of an alloy of five metals (or panchrasi), under the instructions of the Nizam, in Qutub Shahi designs by craftsmen of Hyderabad, and are studded with precious stones engraved with verses of the Quran. The property is owned by the family trust of the Nizam's Shi'a descendants who administer the property to date.

Taken together, these three complexes came to make up what I am referring to as the Shi'a quarter of the old city, extending from Daru Shifa to Yakutpura and Dewan Devdi. While this quarter was always associated with a public Shi'a culture, the segregated, distinct religious identity attending it is a more recent process. In particular, the violence that accompanied the Police Action contributed to homogenizing the population residing in this quarter, although it cannot be claimed that a single community occupies it. For one, there are different communities amongst the Shi'as who live in separate areas within the quarter, such as the Iranians in Irani Galli near their Darbar-e-Hussaini 'ashurkhana, and Twelver Khojas in Purani Haveli near their Baitul Qayam 'ashurkhana. Further, the resident population is also not entirely Shi'a, since a uniformly homogeneous population in a South Asian urban context is not plausible. There is, however, a predominance of Shi'a households unlike in any other part of the city. More importantly, the Shi'as explicitly identify with the area as an old historic and, therefore, authentic ritual center that can collectively be claimed as their own through ritual and memory.

Collective acts of remembering make possible identification with a sacred geography via a mediating history that localized this sacred geography. Ritual modes of remembering, therefore, mnemonically relate to the erstwhile Princely State as a culturally familiar territory, which can be seen in the adherence to the same route, format, and traditions followed in the Bibi ka alam procession as was the case during the Princely State when it was a state procession. The route of the procession has not altered—it begins at the Bibi ka alam 'ashurkhana (in Yakutpura), crosses the Yakutpura historic gate (*darwaza*), moves to Charminar, then to Daru Shifa where it halts at *Azakhana-e-Zehra* 'ashurkhana, and ends at Chaderghat. This historic route acts as a spatial strategy of symbolically marking the place through which a public identity is asserted using physical space. The route of the procession then acts as a spatial narrative of carving out space that came to be associated epistemologically with minority as an exclusive religious category.

Satish Deshpande explores the idea of "spatial strategy" as a narrative of structuring and producing social space, through Foucault's concept of heterotopias or a reflection of a utopia or abstract space onto real space. Tracing spatial strategies in the idea of Savarkar's Hindutva as a sacred geography or Nehruvian nation-space as shaped by an economic geography, he defines the idea of a spatial strategy as linking ideological, abstract, and imaged spaces to concrete physical space:

> A spatial strategy not only unfolds *in* space, it is also *about* space—its appropriation, deployment, and control. Such strategies are among those designed to support and maintain relations of power or of resistance. Considered as ideologies, spatial strategies can be seen as articulating the physical–material and mental imaginative aspects of social space. In short, successful spatial strategies are able to link, in a durable and ideologically credible way, abstract (imagined) spaces to concrete (physical) places. (Deshpande 1998, 23, emphases original)

Further, Deshpande explores this relationship between imagined space and concrete physical space in order to understand spatial strategies employed by the Hindutva movement in successfully transforming particular places into heterotopias. He delineates three kinds of spatial strategies, that is, those centered on-site where a particular site is (re) constructed as unique and bearing a singular essence, such as Ayodhya as a site of essence as *the* birthplace of Ram; those neighborhoods where the everyday embeddedness of a locality is privileged for mobilization or campaign often resulting in violence; and finally, in pilgrimage routes and procession which is a synergistic fusion of both the site- and neighborhood-based strategies.

In the case of Hyderabad's old city, its urban space is produced through ritual routes, much like Deshpande's third spatial strategy. The public performance of ritual processions further becomes a metaphor for asserting community identity and spatial control. Public processions like the Ganesh, Bonalu, and *Pankha*, for instance, led to Hindu–Muslim riots during election campaigns in 1983, 1984, and 1985 that added to the identification of an area with a particular community. In particular, the Charminar area of the old city became an urban arena for community contestations, where, prior to 1976, the state assembly constituencies included Hyderabad's old city with a strong Muslim majority of voters, and the All India Muslim Majlis Party (AIMIM) represented the seats.

In the late 1970s, Naidu describes, under the aegis of the Ganesh Utsav Samiti, Hindu nationalist organizations such as the Vishwa Hindu Parishad, the Hindu Raksha Samiti, the Rashtriya Swayam Sevak, activists, and local businessmen came together to orchestrate a large-scale centralized Ganesh procession which comprised of 151 subprocessions. These subprocessions were rerouted to join around Charminar to form one mammoth procession that proceeded through Muslim-dominated areas in the center of the city to the Husain Sagar Lake, renamed Vinayak Sagar for the day. In the same year, the Bonalu procession, taken out by lower-caste Hindu women in worship of incarnations of Kali in July, began to take a route similar to the large Ganesh procession, which involved 35 subsidiary processions (Deshpande 1998). The very first Bonalu procession that used the new route sparked off a major Hindu–Muslim riot in 1981, as it passed through the Muslim Golconda neighborhood. Responding to public Hindu mobilization, the AIMIM began its own new *Pankha* procession after Hindu nationalist politicians reorganized the Ganesh festival in 1978. The *Pankha* procession takes place three days before the Ganesh festival and travels through several Hindu bazaars in a winding route to and from a Muslim shrine in the old city. Political leaders then address this procession, like the Ganesh festival, once it reaches its terminus. In 1983, the *Pankha* procession sparked off a riot when processionists allegedly desecrated a Ganesh idol in the Moazamjahi market.

The next section further explores this idea of the epistemic production of religion as a separate and distinct category through the process of reimagining ʻ*ashurkhana* properties as spaces associated with the religious practices of an exclusive community within a postcolonial legal discourse. It looks at the implications of designating these properties as Muslim *Waqf* properties, seeing this as a trope to understand the process of becoming a minority as an epistemic discourse.

Waqf Properties and Production of the Minority Identity

The ʻ*ashurkhana* properties in Hyderabad's old city pose a distinct problem of classification as Muslim *Waqf* properties in the context of Indian legal discourse. Being historically public spaces built by the local kings who instituted hereditary posts belonging to members of different communities, and being used by different communities for ritual enactment, contentions of ownership and classification of these properties arise under, firstly, Muslim *Waqf* properties and, secondly, Sunni or Shiʻa *Waqf*. Exploring these contentions acts as a kind of lens to understand the production of a religious minority identity as a recent construct as well as a result of various postcolonial processes.

These processes stem from the principle of legal pluralism maintained as the foundation of the British colonial state in India, wherein a fundamental distinction was drawn between state law and personal law. Colonial subjects were guaranteed that their respective community's scriptures would provide the basis for personal law, which would fall outside the jurisdiction of the colonial state (Beverley 2011, 159). This meant that the Raj and later the Indian state would define the scope of the "religious" or the "personal" domain, fixing the boundary between personal and state law (ibid.). Further, this also reified the division between "public law and personal law" and developed a system that entailed "a whole range of special exceptions and statutes that divided the legal domain along the lines of race and religion" (ibid.).

In the days of the Princely State of Hyderabad, all endowments—Muslim, Hindu, and Christian—were administered by the state-controlled ecclesiastic department (*mahkama-e-umoor-e-madhhabi*) under the regulation of Hyderabad endowment of 1939. The department was headed by the Director (*Nazim Umoor-e-Mazhabi*), assisted by four directors—one of whom was meant exclusively for non-Muslim affairs (Ahmed 1997, 43). After the fall of the Princely State, the Muslim *Waqf* Board was constituted under the *Waqf* Act, 1954, under the governorship of the Nizam (as *Rajpramukh*). According to the *Waqf* Act, 1954, Muslim institutions managed by the erstwhile kings would fall under the Muslim *Waqf* Board, which would act as a caretaker (mutawalli) on behalf of the Government. Properties belonging to the Princely State considered heritage such as mosques, 'ashurkhanas, and *dargahs* fell under the jurisdiction of the Muslim *Waqf*, except the Mecca Masjid and the Public Garden mosque. The heritage properties were then separated from the endowment department and handed over to the Muslim *Waqf* Board.

In the case of the Badshahi 'ashurkhana, for instance, the 'ashurkhana was declared as a protected monument by the Department of Archaeology. After the accession of the Princely State of Hyderabad and the transformation of the endowment department to *Waqf* committee, the 'ashurkhana came under the Muslim *Waqf* Board headed by the Nizam, who rented out parts of the premises for generating income for the 'ashurkhana, which has recently been contested by its present trustee. The squatters were evicted from the property, as per the direction of the Andhra Pradesh High Court, as recently as 2007.

Consequent to the reorganization of states, divided on the basis of language, new states of Andhra Pradesh, Maharashtra, and Karnataka were formed. As a result of the reorganization, some of the districts of erstwhile Hyderabad State were excluded from the jurisdiction of the Hyderabad Muslim *Waqf* Board, while new areas from the British dominions, including the Andhra Districts, were now part of the new State of Andhra Pradesh. For this reason, the earlier-constituted Hyderabad Muslim *Waqf* Board under the Nizam was dissolved. A new *Waqf* Board under the provisions of the Central *Waqfs* Act, 1954 came into existence, known as the Andhra Pradesh *Waqf* Board, with jurisdiction over the State of Andhra Pradesh.

'*Ashurkhana* properties associated with the Princely State were, how-ever, maintained by the Nizam not as *Waqf* properties but by allocating corpus of funds within trusts created by him, including the H. E. H. Nizam trust, the Azakhana Zehra Trust, the H. E. H. Nizam's Supple-mental Religious Endowment Trust, and the H. E. H. Nizam's Religious Endowment. Funds invested in these trusts were made from the Nizam's personal *Sarf-i-Khas* funds.

The "H. E. H. Nizam's Religious Endowment Trust" was created on November 2, 1950 with a corpus fund of ₹2,220 thousand, with one of the objectives being the upkeep of sacred buildings constructed in the lifetime of the Nizam, such as mosques (masjid), '*ashurkhanas*, and tombs (*maqbaras*). In particular, it included "the annual expenditure during the mourning period of Muharram and Safar and also during other religious months, when different kinds of ceremonies, religious discourses, are performed, including the religious offerings to the sacred shrines at Ajmer and Gulbarga" (Supreme Court Judgment 1965). In addition, an exclusive Azakhana Zehra Trust was created on March 29, 1951 for the upkeep of Muharram practices taking place at the '*ashur-khana Azakhana-e-Zehra*. As stipulated by the trust deed, the trust was created for the maintenance of the '*ashurkhana*, the poor-feeding house (*niazkhana*) attached to it, and the hospital (*shafakhana*) near it. The trust was endowed with ₹200,000, as well as another sum of ₹150,000, as investment in government bonds for the management, upkeep, and maintenance of the three buildings. Along with this, a further sum of ₹4,500 as well as a sum of ₹5,000 was set aside as an annual offering to cover the expenses of the annual ceremonies to be performed at the '*ashurkhana* during Muharram, such as reinstating standards, conduct-ing congregations, and sponsoring food for the attendants (High Court of Andhra Pradesh 1971). Likewise, on June 14, 1954, through the trust deed between the Nizam and the trustees Nawab Zain Yar Jung and a few others, a trust called "H. E. H. Nizam's Charitable Trust" was founded for general purposes of charity, including the relief of the poor in the State of Hyderabad, maintenance of religious institutions, and for the advance-ment of education without distinction of religion, caste, or creed. The trust deed specified its purpose of maintaining religious institutions without any restrictions toward any religions. This trust today manages the Bibi ka alam '*ashurkhana*, renovated by the Nizam with the advice of

Nawab Zain Yar Jung, and sanctions funds for its maintenance as well as awards a title (*jagir*) for the maintenance of the attendants.

And yet, despite the intention of the creator of the trust, if one looks at the legal discourse surrounding these trusts, it remains ambiguous if these properties can be classified as *Waqf* properties. In other words, it becomes ambiguous if a property could be declared as being under the purview of a Muslim *Waqf* if a Hindu can traditionally manage, own, or create a *Waqf* or if non-Muslims participate in Muslim religious rites. Notwithstanding this, legally, it is also established that

> ...once it is established that '*ashurkhana* is a place where *Peerlu* [Telugu for standards] are kept and where the tenth day of Moharam Festival is celebrated, it becomes clear that the suit property is an endowment for a religious purpose and constitutes a *Waqf* within the meaning of the *Waqf* Act. (Andhra Pradesh High Court 1977)

These contentions are raised in the litigations against the above-mentioned trusts created by the Nizam. For instance, in a case titled *Zain Yar Jung v. Director of Endowments*, 1962, the Supreme Court of India adjudicated that the endowment contracted between the Nizam and the trustees including Nawab Zain Yar Jung through the trust deed executed on June 14, 1954 was a public trust under English laws. The reason for categorizing the endowment as a trust as opposed to a *Waqf* was the distinction being made between a Muslim *Waqf* as a religious endowment under the *Waqf* Act, 1934 and a public charitable trust created since the endowment agreement includes benefits for non-Muslims. This was because the court viewed the endowment providing support for non-Muslim as not valid under Muslim law. This, it felt, transgresses the limits prescribed by the requirement of a valid *Waqf*, and it vested the title in the trustees and gave them absolute discretion to use the property and its income for any of the charitable purposes specified in the document (Supreme Court of India 1962). In doing so, the court invoked the intention of the Nizam as evident in the trust deed, in that non-Muslims as trustees were appointed, which it saw as indicative of the fact that the Nizam did not intend to create a *Waqf* but instead intended to create a trust. The court reasoned that the nonconfinement to any caste, religion, or creed belonged to the idea of public charity as opposed to an exclusive religion that the idea of *Waqf* property is based on.

The difficulty of relating historic public properties to a postcolonial legal discourse that defines a community or a minority based on demarcated notions of religion as a private or sacred domain produces further problems of classification as Sunni or Shi'a *Waqf* properties within the definition of a Muslim *Waqf* property. As seen in the case of *Andhra Pradesh State Waqf Board v. All India Shi'a Conference*; Syed Hassan Pasha and Askar Nawaz Jung, President of All India Shi'a Conference, filed a suit on behalf of the Shi'a Andhra Pradesh branch of the All India Shi'a Conference. The contending parties in this case were the Sunni Andhra Pradesh *Waqf* Board, along with the Muslim *Waqf* Board and individual succession claims by mutawallis in the Districts of Krishna and Guntur.

The All India Shi'a Conference submitted in their petition that all institutions and property relating to Muharram should fall under Shi'a *Waqf* and that they are wrongly classified as Sunni *Waqf* in the list published by the Andhra Pradesh *Waqf* Board. Further, they submitted that such property is not Sunni in origin since this property is connected with Muharram practices, which, they claimed, pertains exclusively to the Shi'a faith.

On the other side, in their appeal in the Supreme Court, the Andhra Pradesh *Waqf* Board contended that property relating to Muharram did not belong to Shi'as. They stressed that the Shi'as were not exclusively connected with the Muharram festival, since Sunnis also observe Muharram in their own way. Their suit included 32 various mutawallis from different parts of Andhra Pradesh who traditionally managed 'ashurkhana properties associated with Muharram. These properties were notified as Sunni *Waqf* as per the survey conducted by the *Waqf* Board. Of the 32 mutawallis, only two contended, since it did not matter to them if the property was to be declared as a Shi'a or a Sunni *Waqf*.

In response to this, the Supreme Court declared that all properties relating to Muharram belong to the Shi'a *Waqf* except in exceptional circumstances, such as in the case of the 32 mutawallis who were neither Shi'a nor Sunni (Supreme Court of India 2000). The Supreme Court then impugned the judgment of the High Court and remitted the matter to receive additional evidence, oral or documentary, on the question of whether each of these institutions is Shi'a or Sunni *Waqf* property.

The discursive effects of a postcolonial legal imagination can be seen in these contentions over the historic 'ashurkhana properties that produce the idea of a separate religious minority. 'Ashurkhana properties that were traditionally owned and used by different communities belie the neat legal categorization of Muslim Waqf properties, being based on the idea of a Waqf as a homogeneous, private, religiously defined identity. This production of minority identity as a religious identity can be seen to translate spatially, where space becomes increasingly defined through religious institutions associated with a familiar cultural and historical terrain, becoming identity markers and local symbols that underpin community belonging.

How does a unified Muslim identity synonymous with the category of religion get constructed in opposition to a normalized secular identity? This question is explored through the designation of historical properties as Muslim waqf institutions in Hyderabad's old city. In doing so, the chapter complicates the overused and undifferentiated category of the 'minority', by discussing the formation of a segregated Muslim quarter, associated with the Muslim subgroup of the Shi'as, who differ in their belief of divinely ordained community leadership embodied in the battle of Karbala that took place in 680 A.D. in present-day Iraq.

Conclusion

This chapter has looked at the re-inscription of historic 'ashurkhana properties from public, state-regulated properties in the Princely State of Hyderabad to Muslim Waqf properties defined as personal law that produced a separate domain of religion in the postcolonial imagination. It has, in particular, looked at three 'ashurkhanas that spatially mark the Shi'a quadrant of Hyderabad's old city built by the erstwhile rulers of the state—the Badshahi 'ashurkhana, Bibi ka alam 'ashurkhana, and Azakhana-e-Zehra 'ashurkhana. Legal contestations around the nature of these 'ashurkhana properties as Telugu, Sunni, or Shi'a Waqf properties, as well as the nature of public trusts instituted by the Nizam, discursively associate these complexes with a homogeneous, private, religious identity. This is despite the continued use of these spaces by different communities and the multiplicity of their ownership, since the appointed caretakers were selected on a hereditary basis by the erstwhile kings who traditionally belonged to different communities.

This discursive shift in the postcolonial imagination that deciphers *'ashurkhana* properties and the ritual practices performed in these spaces as belonging to a demarcated category of religion associated with an exclusive community, it argues, has produced the idea of the minority. This has spatial implications in that the historic *'ashurkhana* properties become defining spatial markers in constructing a Shi'a quadrant of the old city that has increasingly become homogeneous in its population. Further, this demarcation of a separate category of religion as private minority identity can be seen in the increasing segregation of the old city from the expanding metropolis, delinking it from the various social, political, and cultural connotations previously associated with it. And yet, the production of a discursive or spatial minority as a homogeneous and religiously defined category does not occlude the experience of being a minority. There is a real, everyday dimension to the constructed nature of being and becoming a minority that is relevant to its disentitled status. The production of segregation based on religious categories may perhaps be one of the contributing factors that has clearly alienated minorities from structures and processes that make up the nation state. This is evident in the increasing role of ritual, memory, and nostalgia as place-making strategies adopted by minorities to claim an active presence in contemporary India.

Notes and Bibliography

Notes

1. Gregory Kozlowski writing on Muslim Endowments and society in British India describes,

   > *Waqf* and its plural form, *awqāf*, are derived from the Arabic root verb, *waqafa*, which has the basic meaning of "to stop" or "to hold." When the word is employed in a legal sense with regard to a piece of land or a building, it signifies that henceforth that "property" is "stopped." In theory, it can never again change hands by inheritance, sale or seizure. (Kozlowski 1985, 1)

2. The AIMIM is a popular Muslim political party in Hyderabad, established by Nawab Bahadur Yar Jung. It began as a federation of Muslim religious heads in 1827 under the Majlis Ittehadul Bainul Muslimeen, formed to unite and help various Muslim sects and protect their social, economic, and educational interests. After the infamous 1938 Dhoolpet riots and the perceived militant demands of the Arya Samaj, Hindu Mahasabha, and State Congress, it transformed into a political party—the "All India Majlis Ittehadul Muslimeen." Bahadur Jar Jung was succeeded by Qasim Razwi, an advocate, till 1957. Before his departure to Pakistan, he nominated Abdul Wahed Owasi as its President, after which it came to be called the "All India Majlis Ittehadul Muslimeen." The AIMIM retained its Hyderabad seat in the Lok Sabha elections of 2004, which has been held by the AIMIM since 1984.

Bibliography

Ahmed, H. 1997. *Strategies to Develop Waqf Administration in India.* Hyderabad: Islamic Research and Training Institute Islamic Development Bank.

Beverley, E. L. 2011. "Property, Authority and Personal Law: *Waqf* in Colonial South Asia." *South Asia Research* 31 (2): 155–82.

Bose, B. and S. Bhattacharyya (eds). 2007. *The Phobic and the Erotic: The Politics of Sexualities in Contemporary India.* King's Lynn: Seagull Books.

Deshpande, S. 1998. "Hegemonic Spatial Strategies: The Nation-Space and Hindu Communalism in Twentieth-Century India." *Public Culture* 10 (2): 249–83.

Hacking, I. 1999. *The Social Construction of What.* Cambridge, MA: Harvard University Press.

Kozlowski, G. C. 1985. *Muslim Endowments and Society in British India.* Cambridge: Cambridge University Press.

Leonard, Karen. 1978. "Hyderabad: The Mulki–Non-Mulki Conflict." In *People, Princes and Paramount Power*, edited by R. Jeffrey, 88. Delhi: Oxford University Press.

Naidu, R. 1990. *Old Cities, New Predicaments: A Study of Hyderabad.* New Delhi: SAGE.

Pandey, G. 1992. *The Construction of Communalism in Colonial North India.* Oxford: Oxford University Press.

Rao, N. R. and S. Abdul Thaha. 2012. "Muslims of Hyderabad—Landlocked in the Walled City." In *Muslims in Indian Cities: Trajectories of Marginalisation*, edited by L. Gayer and C. Jaffrelot, 189–213. New Delhi: HarperCollins.

Reddy, R. S. 1984. *Hindu and Muslim Religious Institutions, Andhra Desa, 1300–1600.* Madras: New Era.

Srinivas, S. 2004. *Landscapes of Urban Memory.* Minneapolis: University of Minnesota Press.

Yagnik, A. 1984. *Communal Riots in Hyderabad—What the People Say.* Ahmedabad: SETU Centre for Social Knowledge & Action.

Court Cases

The A. P. State Wakf Board Hyderabad v. All India Shia Conference (Branch) A.P. &
Ors. C.A. No. 1805 of 1989. 2-3 2000. http://www.manupatrainternational.
in/supremecourt/1980-2000/sc2000/1030s000640.htm, last accessed on August
24, 2010.

H. E. H. Nizams Religious Endowment Trust. v. CIT, (SC). ITR 582. 26-10-1965.
http://www.manupatrainternational.in/supremecourt/1950-1979/sc1965/
s650128.htm, last accessed on August 24, 2010.

High Court Of Andhra Pradesh Commissioner of Wealth-Tax v. H. E. H. The Nizam's
Supplemental and Religious Endowment Trust. 89 ITR 80 (AP). 26-11-1971.
http://www.courtjudgments.org/h-e-h-nizams-religious-endowment-trust-
hyderabad-vs-commissioner-of-income-tax-andhra-pradeshhyderabad,   last
accessed on August 24, 2010.

Nawab Zain Yar Jung and Others v. The Director of Endowments and Others. D 1976
SC1569 (58). 09-04-1962. http://www.courtjudgments.org/nawab-zain-yar-
jung-and-others-vs-the-director-of-endowments-and-others/, last accessed
on August 24, 2010.

Andhra High Court V.V.V.R.K. Yachandra Bahadur v. The Andhra Pradesh Wakf
Board. AIR 1978 AP 156. July 15, 1977.

15

The Fragmented Minor: Tamil Identity and the Politics of Authenticity

Anjana Raghavan

The production of identity almost always requires an oppositional narrative. Framed against the creation of a major or minor other, it often draws on the legitimacy of an alternative history, using origin myths and cosmogonies which run parallel to, and are often more "original" than and clearly separated from the Other. The veracity of "authenticity," thus, becomes crucial to the very basis of an identity. This chapter primarily deals with the theoretical and ideological construction and production of "minor-ness" both as a category and an identity marker. In keeping with this main thrust, I examine mythologized imaginaries and origin narratives of Tamil identity and the intersections of race, ethnicity, religion, and gender wherever they emerge. I do not, therefore, engage with "minority politics" in the popular political understanding of the phrase particularly in the Indian context. Is the production of the minor, as the Deleuzian and Bakhtinian framings suggest, a dialogic one? Or is it, in fact, suggestive of an impasse—an unbreakable silence or an unspeakable language as Agamben (1999, 2002, 2005) and Kristeva (1982) suggest? As is often the case, there are no clear answers, and this chapter only seeks to better understand the context and create a space to articulate these issues through the selective exploration of Tamil identity narratives by both their creators as well as their dissenters.

Introduction

The production and politics of the minor have been vastly theorized by many scholars, and this chapter draws on some of those theorized images to both problematize and form a backdrop against which narratives of minor-ness may be examined. Many things may be implied by "minor-ness"; statistics, history, myth, oppression, and violence all constitute the minor. I intentionally avoid defining what I mean by "minor-ness" precisely because it is one of the questions that this chapter is founded on, and because the minor is too often interpellated by the major for neat definitions to be provided.

This chapter primarily deals with the theoretical and ideological construction and production of minor-ness both as a category and an identity marker. In keeping with this main thrust, I examine mythologized imaginaries and origin narratives of Tamil identity and the intersections of race, ethnicity, religion, and gender wherever they emerge. I do not, therefore, engage with "minority politics" in the popular political understanding of the phrase, particularly in the Indian context.

Does the creation of an alternative historical, racial, and cultural pedagogy produce the kind of revolutionary disruption that has been theorized by Deleuze and Guattari (1986, 2004), Agamben (1999, 2002, 2005), Kristeva (1982), Bakhtin (1984), and others, or is it a more complex phenomenon? The Bakhtinian emphasis on dialogue sets up an interesting premise within which to understand the production of the minor. Is the Tamilian a dialogic minor? More to the point, does the "Tamil devotee," to use Ramaswamy's (1997) coinage, want to be dialogic in the articulation of his/her minor-ness? The crux of these questions connects to the larger imagination of what minor identity and discourse ultimately consist of.

The first section of the chapter lays out some of the theoretical understandings of "minor-ness" as shown in the works of Deleuze and Guattari (1986, 2004), Agamben (1999, 2002, 2005), Bakhtin (1984), Bataille (1985), and Kristeva (1982). The understanding of the minor here ranges from the revolutionary to the unspeakable, and it is within this canvas that the Tamil narrative of minor-ness as such is explored. The second section explores Tamil language and religion as seen in the works of scholars like Ramaswamy (1997, 2004), Vaitheespara (2009, 2012), and others to understand the constructions of being Tamil. Tamil

Caivism (alternative to Saivism) as seen in Vaitheespara's work plays an important role in understanding how non-Brahminical *Saivism* informed the logic of Dravidian identity at large. The third section conflates these identity formations through language, mythologized history, and religion into what became known as the overtly political Dravidian movement headed by E. V. Ramasamy Naicker (Periyar) which then went on to create the political foundations of Tamil Nadu's political parties—the *Dravida Munnetra Kazhagam* (DMK) and the AIADMK (All India Anna Dravida Munnetra Kazhagam)—which remain the reigning parties of the present. I use the writings and ideas of these political figures selectively and only in relation to the production of minor-ness in Tamil identity and how it engages with notions of nationalism, colonialism, and "authentic" or "original" belonging. It is outside the scope and aim of this chapter to engage with the specific politics, policies, and ideologies of these politicians in relation to Tamil as well as Indian politics at large, or to fully problematize their relationships with caste and class politics in contemporary Tamil Nadu.

The final section returns to the questions of negotiating minor-ness and articulates the multiplicity of "being" minor that extend well beyond the theoretical understandings of minor-ness that we explore in the first section.

The Tamil case is evoked here for its nuanced narrative of becoming minor rather than as a linear or historical narrative. While there is plenty of work on Tamil politics, culture, and identity in disciplines of history, political science, anthropology, literature, and subaltern and postcolonial studies, which inform the foundations of this chapter, I attempt a more theoretical and epistemological intervention into how the minor is imagined and produced using Tamil-ness to illustrate the adequacies and inadequacies of existing theorizations of minor-ness.

The "Minor" Subject: Theoretical Constructions

I want to begin with some preliminary theoretical explorations of the other/minor/outside/marginal/reject body. Dipping in and out of several minor imaginings, Balibar (2005) in "Difference, Otherness,

Exclusion" writes of interior otherness and otherness as an imaginary. He asks,

> Does imaginary mean that the other is a pure fiction, a pure projection of the Western mind upon "Orientals" who can't help it, who are left outside of the picture that is supposed to picture them or is it the case that within this imaginary frame an actual encounter does take place, conflicted to be sure, but also in a sense "real," which would imply that the "real others" also somehow contribute to the construction of the idea of Otherness, albeit in a "subaltern" place, but which can involve irreducible difference? (Balibar 2005, 30)

I quote him at some length here because Balibar is asking an extremely pertinent question of otherness and its very constitution. The shared production of the "other" by the "insider" and the "outsider" makes exclusion even more uncomfortable than it already is. The self as the "other's other," thus, questions the process of identity creation as a narrative of opposition. It rather suggests that the creation of the self itself is a fundamentally oppositional process, needing the other as much as the other needs it. The production of the margin is, thus, interpellated with the center and vice versa, and the minor is constitutive of as well as constituted by the major.

Radhakrishnan (2007) in his volume of collected essays discusses this complexity of subject multiplicity at length in several of his papers. The deconstruction of dominant identities and the insurrection of subaltern identities is an extremely complicated dynamic that requires much careful exploration. Warning against the problems of binary historiographies, he writes that programmatically associating the minority with virtue and moral outrage as well as the majority with tyranny is a dangerous oversimplification and must be geopolitically and regionally contextualized. This is not at all to suggest that the minor invariably associates "itself" with moral uprightness, but rather that subaltern histories have had imposed upon them both from the "inside and the outside" the onus to create and produce a total and complete "other" history. That is to say, the major–minor dynamic itself seems to require these authentic, coherent, and complete narratives. The question of where subjugated and minor knowledge speak "from" also becomes crucial here. Are they located within major hegemonic discourses engaging, as it were, in a kind of self-abjection? Or are they located outside—in a "disinterested space that functions at a 'panoptic' remove from its object of criticism?"

(Radhakrishnan 2007, 33). It seems that this question of location is crucial to the minor articulation. Do subaltern subject positions "need" to be linked to the dominant hegemony, or is their very subalternity constituted by their refusal to validate the mainstream? In other words, if the "other" is forced into a certain "grand alterity... which is nothing 'other' than the ruling ideology in an antithetical or 'reverse narcissistic' contemplation of itself" (ibid.), is it truly the "other"?

In order to explore this complexity, I now turn to Deleuze and Guattari's (2004) conception of otherness and minority in their work on the Body without Organs (BwO) and their work on Kafka as a "minor" figure in Literature, along with the "other" in the work of Agamben (1999, 2002, 2005), Kristeva (1982), Bakhtin (1984), and Bataille (1985). In Deleuze and Guattari's conception, the BwO is a revolutionary body. Defying hierarchies and entirely constructed of flows, the BwO constantly walks the potentially fatal line between the inside and the outside. The Deleuzian principle of disruption, violence, and dislocation is central to this tightrope-walking. One must reach for the outside, but not without any perception of that outside. This is essentially the fear of a BwO. By its own volatility, it runs the risk of emptying itself, of self-destruction. The "system," then, is a necessary evil. It exists to be negated, just as speech exists for the unspeakable, only so it can be negated. The minor, in their work on Kafka too, is such a figure. Always embarking on a "line of flight," the minor always "escapes" the center, albeit in a zigzag and nonlinear fashion. The Bakhtinian grotesque is a similarly liminal body—always on the fringes, despicable, and unspeakable, it escapes the system in carnivalesque revelry and laughter, as it does in Bataillean excess. There is a certain glory in this kind of escape which is at once fantastic, lurid, and dangerous. In slight contrast, Agamben's *Homo Sacer* and the Kristevan abject are framed more in Balibar's terms of "other" as the loathing of the self. The homo sacer and the abject are always inarticulable, outside language, outside morality, defying by their presence alone. For them, the "line of flight" exists in their unspeakability, rather than in carnival.

In broad, ambiguous strokes then, we can see the distinctions between these different imaginings of minor-ness. The body of the homo sacer and the abject thus presented and represented is, without a doubt, extremely fragile and, in a sense, dangerous. It resembles the empty body, the "schizo" body that Deleuze and Guattari warn against in

A Thousand Plateaus. An empty body produces nothing, desires nothing. Agamben's Musselman desires only to survive, but that is not desire in either Bataille's sense of the term, or indeed, Deleuze's. Kristeva's abject sits, albeit uncomfortably, somewhere in-between where the abject *is* desire: unspeakable, but still desire. Abject desire challenges and revolutionizes by its very existence, taunting and teasing the center without actually speaking or being spoken to. When Agamben recounts the stories of "men" who used to be Muselmann—the abject—what is difficult to fathom is how exactly this process of being *der muselmanner* "ends," as it were. For if the "witness," the "survivor," tells only the shadow of a story, and indeed, often feels compelled to do so, he/she is still separate from the Muselmann. The survivor speaks *of* the Muselmann, because the Muselmann is unspeakable. He has no purpose nor aim but to survive, and the testimonies tell the readers that the Muselmann cared nothing for life in the sense of being human or retaining humanity. The accounts tell of desperate snatches for extra helpings of food, a complete destruction of their "self," the blank vacancy, and the revulsion they caused to those around them. As Agamben writes, "...the Muselmann, [is] the 'complete witness,' making it forever impossible to distinguish between man and non-man" (2002, 47). Ultimately, in some sense, the Muselmann is "imagined," because we are incapable of comprehending homo sacer in his/her "reality."

Similarly, Kristeva, in her theorizing of the abject, sees the abject as that which is deeply feared and loathed by the self.

> Abjection, according to Kristeva, is the ultimate ambiguity. It is that space where meaning, identity, system, all collapse. It is always excluded, banished, but in its banishment never stops challenging the "inside." The abject has no regard for boundaries and positions. It is neither moral nor amoral for both these stances can be legitimated and celebrated in their own ways within the existing normative frameworks. Abjection is outside of the very meaning of morality. (Raghavan and Tripathy, forthcoming)

Spat out in terrified revulsion and rejection, speakability or acknowledgment of the abject will be an acknowledgment of an abnegated self, which the self feels compelled to protect itself against. The BwO, however, as we have seen, has the potential to be the revolutionary. The minor has the potential to be truly free. This is the notion that underpins the transgressive rebel, the laughing grotesque body of excess and "minoritarianism," as Deleuze and Guattari envision it in their work concerning Kafka: "Desire is a mixture, a blend to such a degree that bureaucratic or fascist pieces are still or already caught up in revolutionary agitation" (Deleuze and Guattari 1986, 60). In keeping with the idea that nothing is ever stable and all courses are tangential, Deleuze and Guattari suggest that "justice" is itself desire and not "law." Indeed, as Agamben also suggests, law is the death of desire. Fear of being punished is far more "effective" than the actual punishment. Exploring the revolutionary potential of the BwO, the "becoming animal" or "the rebel" is a significant endeavor as Deleuze, Bataille, and Bakhtin envision it. The rejection of a "major"–"minor" divide, to escape that category entirely, is what Deleuze and Guattari suggest in their "becoming animal." It is not cowardice, nor is it any sort of imitation "of the father" in Freudian terms that the "becoming animal" resorts to, but an alternative experience, a line of flight, an escape which is not open to the homo sacer or the abject body. The "becoming animal" is free from form, given expression, and signifiers. It is free to exist. The minor writer in Deleuze and Guattari's work is completely "outside." They see this position as creating the possibility of forging the means for another community, consciousness, and sensibility.

Bakhtin's grotesque body is similarly a becoming body. He writes of the importance of openings, penetrable surfaces, in the body— the mouth, anus, bowels, genitals, etc. The grotesque body is utterly unconcerned with "smooth" surfaces. Understood in the context of a major–minor binary, this is an extremely significant point. The grotesque body is cosmic and timeless, unlike the "new" body which is closed, clean, and complete. There are no protrusions, bulges, or growths in this body, delineating it very clearly from what is *not* part of it. The grotesque body, like the BwO and minor, is always connected to other things; it can always escape and is part of the carnival—a time outside time. It speaks in many tongues, existing in a heteroglossia. The transgressive element, carnivalesque laughter, which mocks its own death, avoids the finality of it.

> A grotesque-word matrix drags the messy body into territory previously occupied by disembodied, hierarchical word systems. It spreads obscenities throughout learned talk, and degrades language in order to transform abstract thought into something more material, concrete, and widely shareable. (Morson and Emerson 1990, 438)

The imagery of the grotesque is such that by its very existence and its appalling candor, it breaks the fragile walls that keep structures and norms. For Bakhtin, the place of the "other" is clearly important. The "other" holds knowledge of the self, a "surplus of vision" that is inaccessible to the self. "[M]ere negation… can never produce a meaningful word" (Morson and Emerson 1990, 42), i.e., an "anti" stance does not necessarily lead to the creation of anything. There is little meaning in confrontation by itself or violence by itself. There is no point in empathetic "understanding" of the "other" because it is not dialogic and, hence, fruitless. According to Bakhtin, "any culture contains meanings that it itself does not know, that it itself has not realised; they are there, but as a potential" (ibid., 55). This resonates with both Deleuze and Guattari's notion of "becoming" and Bataille's focus on desire. The existence of an "outside" creates the potential for dialogue. The multiplicitous understandings of the "minor" body either as existing outside comprehension and articulation, forever outside, or as a challenging construct, constantly jettisoning the narrative of the major by opposing it outright as in Bakhtin's grotesque body, or as a careful negotiation between minor-ness and major-ness as in the BwO, provide some insight into the complex nature of what being minor constitutes. The following section which examines some narratives of Tamil identity through the lens of the minor illustrates both the importance and the shortfalls of the theoretical understandings discussed above.

Being Tamil: Religion, Language, and Minor-ness

It seems clear from the above discussion, brief though it is, that the production of otherness is a constant becoming, ranging from ecstatic to abject ways of exclusion. I now turn to examining some of these modes of producing otherness and the fantastic varieties of the other within a seemingly singular articulation of identity. The site of this examination is the formation of Tamil-ness within different discourses of identity production. I use "Tamil-ness" in its most flexible form, not following a strict chronology but rather looking at sections of different religious, political, and cultural genealogies that have emerged since the 18th century. Drawing on a variety of sources, this discussion is not meant to be an accurate historical account but rather an exploration of narratives of Tamil-ness in order to understand the polyphonic nature of otherness and minor-ness as it dissects every realm from religion, language, history, literature, politics, and everyday performances of identity.

Ramaswamy's (2004) work on the labors of loss and the imaginary of Lemuria as well as her book on Tamil devotion, what she terms "*tamilparru*," provides a very useful and engaging way into the complexities of identity production. Ramaswamy sees catastrophe and the fabulous as intimately tied to loss. The imagining of a "lost" civilization which is irretrievable forms a crucial part of what constitutes the Dravidian and Tamil identity. Early colonial anthropology and archaeology were very absorbed with the idea of the Lemurian continent. A prehistoric African–Asian landmass, it was the subject of great debate amongst colonial scholars which ultimately formed the "scientific" basis of Lemuria which came to be known as *Kumari Natu* or *Kumarik-Kantam* in the Tamil imaginary. Lemuria came to be seen as the ancestral homeland of the Tamil people, lost forever to the ocean, by J. Nallasami Pillai in the year 1898, followed by many other Tamil scholars, foremost among them Maraimalai Adigal, the famous Tamil Saivaite, as well as V. R. Nedunchezhian, one-time State Education Minister of Tamil Nadu. The creation of this civilizational origin myth was ratified and rationalized and most likely inspired, as mentioned earlier, by colonial discourse. Indeed, as we shall see, colonial discourse is central to the imaginings of Tamil identity.

The Lemurian continent offered the perfect link between Tamil and Dravidian as separate from India, especially linguistically. As Ramaswamy correctly points out, "for a large majority, Dravidian is always already Tamil" (ibid., 103). The renaming of Lemuria to Kumarik-kantam was very significant, notes Ramaswamy, because of the European and theosophists' allusions to Lemuria as home of the primeval bestial and savage man—the not-wholly-human. This understanding of Lemuria naturally had to be amended in light of Lemuria becoming the Tamil civilizational homeland. The etymology of the name Kumarik-kantam (*kumari* meaning virgin and *kantam* meaning continent) is indicative of the pristine motherland—young, fertile, virginal, pure, and immortal. It was also considered a land of gender egalitarianism where queens reigned supreme. The legend of Kanyakumari, the southernmost point in Tamil Nadu and of India, is also associated with a fiercely virginal and chaste Goddess who wins over *Siva*, the Tamil/Hindu ascetic God, through her penance. Her eternal virginity grants her the power to vanquish demons, clearly associating virginity with power which, as we shall later see, became strongly associated with the Tamil language. This interplay of the virgin woman, power, loss, and consequent descent into decadence forms a very important theme that repeats itself in different ways through very discrete articulations of Tamil identity. The strong influence of the virgin woman attacked and wounded by the Aryan, vedic north—sorrowful and usurped but never actually sullied—is also significant. The creation of the Tamil homeland or *Tamilakam*, as Ramaswamy points out, was closely associated with *Tayakam* or motherliness. Tamil becomes not only the first civilization and the origin of all humanity, but also the first language: primordial, but not primitive. The celebration of modernity and progress in the ancient Tamil civilization and the sense of glory "already achieved" are indicative of a strong need to establish cultural and civilizational primacy over all "others." The motif of loss that is littered through Ramaswamy's book is also crucial to the formation of Tamil-ness. The loss of literature, culture, and entire kingdoms to the "cruel ocean" makes the nature of the grief fantastic and irretrievable and the assertion of identity as "minor" in a certain sense, but deriving its power and glory from a primordial, originary space. This civilizational imaginary would soon give rise to the formation of an oppositional narrative, identifying the Aryan, vedic north as the enemy, its appropriation of Dravidian religion and culture, and the creation of a racial–ethnic and linguistic "other," which will be dealt with in the following sections. The production of a civilizational imaginary—not simply ethnic, racial, or cultural—is a radical construction of otherness. In some senses, we could see this as a Deleuzian "line of flight," but rather than invalidating the mainstream by disengaging, this production of otherness supersedes any claim of majority by declaring itself a primal civilization, that which is the beginning of beginnings, encompassing all strains of major and minor.

We now move on to a more specific discussion following the journey of how Tamil came to be identified as a language, ethnicity, and religion, all in one. I use once again Ramaswamy's (1997) work, *Passions of the Tongue*, in conversation with the work of Vaitheespara (2009, 2012) and Pandian (2007, 2009) as leads. In *Passions of the Tongue*, one sees the unmistakable creation and emergence of what Ramaswamy calls *parru* or devotion to Tamil. Also, interesting is the conflation of Tamil Saivism or *Saiva Siddhanta* and Tamil in the 20th century, severely critiqued and opposed by its more orthodox adherents. Having acquired civilizational authority, the usurped identity now progresses to other legitimizations. Ramaswamy observes that prior to the 19th century, Tamil was strongly linked to religion; this was to slowly transform itself into a far more "secular" link, though not necessarily by discarding religion, as Vaitheespara has argued, but by transforming and radicalizing the foundational distinctions that it created between Tamil and non-Tamil, Dravidian, and Aryan, finally binarizing into "non-Brahmin" and "Brahmin."

Vaitheespara's insightful paper on how religion has been re-inscribed as nation points to the many slippages and overlaps that constitute the beginnings of the political demand for a Tamil identity. Critiquing existing scholarship on the Dravidian movement and Tamil identity, he argues that Neo-Saivism, a movement that is featured but marginalized in most work on Dravidian/Tamil identity, is actually foundational to it. He sees the separation of the religio-cultural from the material as too absolute, and believes that to use the ideology of rational secularism, as present in colonialism, to explain the Dravidian movement is actually inaccurate. To extend this argument then, it is inaccurate to imagine the Tamil revolutionary minor as rooted purely in the secular rationalism that E. V. R. Periyar propounded, which then became constitutive of the Tamil "non-Brahmin" identity. Rather, we must acknowledge and unravel the multiple narratives of minor-ness as expressed through religion, language, and cosmologies or specific communities. Vaitheespara writes that the strain of Saivism which most significantly affected the political articulation of Tamil separatism and "non-Brahmin" identity is Neo-Saivism. It conflated the *Saivaite* tradition and theology with Tamil nationalism, and re-historicized the Tamil past through a re-configuration of Tamil as a language and its literary achievements.

Interestingly, we see that this recasting of Saivism into Neo-Saivism was far from docile, owing to its uncomfortable alliance with the Empire and Christian doctrine. Neo-Saivism's orthodox critics saw colonial and Christian missionary literature as the foremost wedge that drove itself between Tamils and non-Tamils and "non-Brahmins" and "Brahmins," creating a virulent and fanatical Tamil nationalism which was more pro-English than it was pro-Saivaite. Ramaswamy also notes that Neo-Saivism was engaged in a project of divinizing Tamil through non-Aryan, pure Tamil subjects. There is a strong reformist and purifying tendency in Neo-Saivism which uses the rhetoric of colonialism to rid Tamil culture of its "irrational" practices, blood sacrifices, etc., thus, reversing the common perception of southern culture as barbaric or primitive. Once again, we see the tendency of the Tamil minor subversion to link itself to a major narrative although overtly negating it. Vaitheespara's work suggests that the orthodox Saivaites were not at all anti-caste, and by implication that this radicalization by returning to the "true" Tamil past advocated by the Neo-Saivaites is actually not a return to the past at all. Rather, it is a clear articulation of modernity and reformation, further strengthened by the influence of English and Western philosophy on Neo-Saivaite saints. They were attempting to create an umbrella of Saivism that could be synonymous with Tamil nationalism and unite all non-Brahmins under a singular identity. It is also here that the Brahmin emerges as a clear enemy of the Tamil Saivaite, and by extension, Tamil culture and identity, by sullying the hitherto "pure" Tamil with the influence of the impure usurper, Sanskrit. "The ascendancy of Neo-Saivaite ideology was crucial to re-crafting and re-inscribing Tamil-ness as essentially non-Brahmin" (Vaitheespara 2012, 19). Orthodox critics though, as Vaitheespara points out, were convinced that this marriage of colonial writing using selective Indian scholarship was a destructive hybrid and an epistemic rupture that was out to invalidate local scholarship. More (2009) in his work also saw the agenda of Christian missionaries as favoring this rift between Brahmins and non-Brahmins for ease of disseminating Christian doctrine and religious conversion. He also saw the writings of Max Muller and Annie Besant, readily supported by Brahmins since it was entirely to their benefit, as creating this divide. It is important to note at this point that the point of dwelling on these accounts is not a truth claim but rather to understand the fractured and complex nature of what we now understand as Tamilian/Dravidian.

To return to Vaitheespara's argument, orthodox Saivaites considered Neo-Saivaites to be inauthentic posers who were trying to link Saivism and Tamil to their own partisan ends. This made Neo-Saivaites equal to "Periyarists" who, though self-proclaimed atheists, wanted temples to use Tamil hymns instead of Sanskrit. Critics saw this as a divisive move to isolate Tamil Hindus from other Indian Hindus. Thus, we see that the Neo-Saivaites themselves took a radical break from Saivism that Vaitheespara argues laid the foundations for the ideological basis and critical practice that was to form Periyar's Self-Respect Movement. The fissures within Tamil Saivism that were so instrumental in forging the non-Brahmin Tamil identity indicate that the focus of the Saivaite, non-Brahmin Tamil is unique in the sense that even though it challenges Aryan-Sanskritic and Brahminical hegemony, it does so not by resorting to the discourse of marginalization, but rather through the reconstruction of a grand mythological and civilizational history and mythology. Neo-Saivism explicitly reclaims Siva, one of the Hindu pantheon's major deities, as an "originally" Tamil God. By implication then, the northern, vedic Gods such as *Rama* or *Krishna* have been imposed upon the more ancient South and are not true to Tamil Saivism. Siva, in fact, as Ramaswamy and others note, is believed to have "given" the Dravidian people the divine and classical language of Tamil and to have presided over the first gathering or *Cankam*, celebrating Tamil language and culture. This narrative of separatism and exclusivity is clearly locked into a belief of an "original" major, the Tamils who were duped and manipulated by the usurping and devious minor, the Aryans.

It is also interesting to note that nowhere in the narratives do we see a militaristic defeat of the Tamils. As Pandian (2007) and others note in their work, Maraimalai Adigal, one of the best known proponents of Tamil Saivism, locked it into the caste identity of the *Vellalas*,[1] seeing them as the original model upper caste. They were glorified as agriculturalists, warriors, and scholars—benevolent feudal lords, who shared their goodness with all. According to Adigal, it was the Aryans who ingratiated themselves into Tamil society, pretending to pay obeisance to the Vellala community, all the while conniving and sowing the seeds of discord by way of caste distinctions, thus, facilitating a divisive and ideological victory over the glorious Tamils. While Adigal was against the caste system in principle, his solidarity with the Vellala community of which he was a part is all too obvious. We see here a complex network of fealties, both toward the "original" rulers, the Tamils, further narrowed down to Vellala Tamils, along with a clear opposition toward the Aryan who is represented by the Tamil Brahmin—a carrier and propagator of Sanskrit, but more importantly a figure of deceit, who worsted Tamil glory and subjugated it to his own selfish ends.

We will turn briefly to the ideas of Pandithar Iyothee Thoss, as discussed by Pandian (2007), Geetha and Rajadurai (2008), and others, to reiterate this idea of a radical break through religion and the originary construction of Tamil primacy. He belonged to the *Parayar* community which was classified as a "low" scavenging caste. It is important to note that Thoss saw the Parayars as superior to other scavenger castes and located Tamil supremacy within Buddhism. Dravidians in this narrative were originally Buddhist and usurped by Aryan fire worshipers once again through deceit and not militaristic conquest. Thoss's rehistoricization is very different from Adigal's in that he identified Buddhist priests to be the "original" Brahmins, replete with the sacred thread which they donned upon attaining enlightenment. In fact, all Brahmin customs and rituals today are corrupted appropriations of Buddhist practices, and Brahmins themselves were conduits and supporters of the Aryans. Thoss termed the authentic Buddhist Brahmins *Yathartha* Brahmins and the traitorous usurpers as *Vesha* Brahmins and said that a person "...to be a real Brahmin, he had to disown the practices that marked him as a 'Brahmin' in colonial Tamil Nadu" (Pandian 2007, 121).

In the ideas of both Adigal and Thoss, we see a high premium being placed on compassion and kindness and a distinct anti-Brahmin stance. It is difficult to term their radicalism as anti-caste given the nepotism for their own castes, unless we consider the Vellalas and Parayars to be part of the marginal fringe, which is in itself problematic, of course, considering that they belong to very different economic and cultural milieus. However, opposed against the Brahminical Other, the capitalized, single Other, as Radhakrishnan explains, we could understand it as a discourse of minor assertion. Both Adigal and Thoss delve deep into Tamil literature in order to substantiate many of their ideas; they also use or re-appropriate the Brahminical focus on purity, cleanliness, and in some cases even vegetarianism in order to create the proto or original Brahmin, the moral Brahmin, who is yet decidedly *not* Brahmin. In a sense, these discourses mock and jettison the very authenticity of the major by creating a disruptive history, a Deleuzian escape. Even though they use the figure of the major to ratify this history, the appropriation is both unique and challenging, both in terms of claiming Siva as an original Tamil God as well as in Buddhism, alluding to the violent history of Buddhism and Jainism in Tamil Nadu's own history. It involves an internal recreation of structures that absorbs western and enlightenment scholarship in a distinctly nonwestern way, making the line of flight distinctly non-linear.

Another important articulation of minor-ness in Tamil identity occurs through the production and divinization of the Tamil language. This discussion, however, has been excluded for purposes of brevity.[2]

Dravidian Tamil-ness: The Politics of "Self"-Respect

The complicity between reimaginations of Tamil identity and colonial structures of hierarchy provides an interesting entry point into the final discussion of this essay which uses some broad readings of the Dravidian movement and its articulation of Tamil-ness which has come to shape the politics of the state today. There has been a good amount, though not enough, of scholarship on the Dravidian movement by several British scholars as well as contemporary Indian ones.

Given that the entire history of the movement, from its inception as the Justice Party to its fragmentation into the DMK and AIDMK is both vast and complex, I focus on selective aspects which deal directly with the articulation of Tamil identity and its efforts toward the creation of a unified non-Brahmin bloc as opposed to the Brahminical Other. Before I unpack the specificities of identity formation, it is important to understand the broad chronological and political spread of the Dravidian movement. The emergence of the non-Brahmin as a significant category arose with the South Indian Liberation Front (SILF) in 1916, subsequently renamed the Justice Party. The Justice Party was one of the earliest articulations of a non-Brahmin identity with the publishing of the non-Brahmin manifesto, but as we shall soon discover, their political agenda was far more complicated and murky. It was in 1926, with the emergence of E. V. Ramasamy Naicker (E. V. Periyar) that the political and cultural articulation of Tamil-ness radically metamorphosed. The Self-Respect Movement, a social reform movement spearheaded by Naicker, gained great momentum over the next two decades, culminating in the formation of the Dravida Kazhagam (DK, Dravidian Association) in

1944. Shortly after, in 1949 came the formation of the factional party DMK (Dravidian Advancement Association) headed by C. N. Annadurai, who was Naicker's strongest Lieutenant.

After Anna's death in 1969, the leadership of the DMK passed to Mu. Karunanidhi, who still heads the party today, and in 1977 came the next major rift, the formation of the AIADMK under the leadership of M. G. Ramachandran (henceforth referred to as MGR), an extremely popular movie star and ardent supporter of the DMK until the break. Though a *Malayalee*[3] by birth, MGR was famous for playing the Tamil/Dravidian hero in films scripted both by Anna and Karunanidhi. On his demise, the baton passed to J. Jayalalitha, also a former movie star and a Brahmin woman. Due to constraints of time and space, this essay will not examine the present-day politics of the DMK and AIADMK, but it is important to note that the travails of Tamil-ness from SILF to DMK and AIADMK are vast, and the very foundations upon which many of these identity claims have been based have been rendered redundant owing to the all-too-familiar machinations of power and the gradual decline of radical-ism and internal critique (Geetha and Rajadurai 1992, 1993, 2008). As Radhakrishnan notes both succinctly and eloquently, "solidarity without critique is either a strait jacket or an empty Shibboleth" (2007, 225).

The Justice Party was, thus, the real beginning of a non-Brahmin articulation, challenging Brahminical and colonial collusions as well as criticizing non-Brahmins for their complacency. As Pandian notes in many of his writings, the Justice Party materialized the hitherto spiritual supremacy of the Brahmins and brought the crucial issues of economic resource distribution, access to education, etc. to the fore. It demanded a utilitarian, functional, and rational perspective that was not based on either supremacy of an inherent "mind and spirit" assigned by birth. The Justice Party was also clearly antinational, in the sense that it supported British rule inasmuch as it equalized caste and creed in a way that it considered Brahmins incapable of, i.e., Brahmins were incapable of disin-terested rule. This remains the common description of the Justice Party, noting important pioneers such as Nair, Theogaraya Chetty among oth-ers, along with the criticisms that it was ultimately not radical enough and was too self-interested, often preserving class distinctions.

More (2009), in his work, criticizes the adoption of imperial classi-fications of Brahmin, non-Brahmin, and "Untouchable" by the political parties of the time. He also notes that non-Brahmin, at this point, did not refer to Dravidian or Tamil and that Dravidian for Tamilians indicated a pan-South Indian, non-Brahmin identity, while to people from Kerala, Karnataka, and Andhra Pradesh, Dravidian was clearly Tamil. This semantic variance in the basic understanding of what constitutes Dravidian also indicates the complexities that would later enter into the claim to secession and a separate Dravida Nadu. This difference in understanding could also explain why the Justice Party saw the leadership of several non-Tamil figures in its time. What is interesting, however, is More's argument that though the non-Brahmin leadership of the Justice Party was pan-South Indian, the Brahminical "other" was essentially Tamil. In fact, there is a clear articulation of how Telugu[4] Brahmins themselves resented Tamil Brahmins. He documents in great detail the Telugu control and nepotism exercised by rich Telugu land owners who, while opposed to Tamil Brahmins who wielded significant political influence, were not really concerned with the Tamil cause. In fact, the Justice Party eventually recanted on its anti-Brahmin stance, much to the chagrin of political heavyweights including Naicker, and opened its membership and leadership to Brahmins. This brief insight into the Justice Party already indicates a highly fissured and varied understanding of the various categories associated with Tamil-ness, the Brahmin, and the non-Brahmin.

E. V. Ramasamy Naicker would soon change this, providing a far more unanimous and homogenizing rhetoric that would advocate the formation of a pan-non-Brahmin identity that was against religion/Hinduism, Aryans, Brahmins, caste, the Vedas, Sanskrit, Hindi, the Congress, and the pan-Indian nation as envisioned by the Indian National Movement. Hinduism was identified as the creator of caste, Aryans/Brahmins were seen as perpetrators of it, and it was, therefore, essential to eradicate the entire system. A virulent rationalist and atheist, Naicker ridiculed every aspect of Hinduism, particularly the scriptures and mythology. In fact, his critique of Hindu mythology—the Mahabharata, Ramayana, etc.—is reminiscent of early Christian missionary critiques of Hinduism in that the criticism in highly literal, superfluous, and judged on the basis of "reality." The other significant critique is based in morality. The vast perceived prevalence of sexuality, "perverse" sexuality, bestiality, infidelity, and even homosexuality in Hinduism rendered it unfit as a religion that was meant to guide people onto the "right" path (Veeramani 2005, 603). Naicker saw Hinduism as irrational and wasteful, while he considered Christianity and Islam relatively more "rational" and conducive to progress. His atheism is virulently anti-Hindu but relatively tolerant to Islam, Christianity, and Buddhism—although he did criticize the Indian version of Christianity, accusing it of being as discriminatory and casteist as Hinduism itself. Naicker's rhetoric tended to be more circumstantial and fluid, adopting different, and sometimes even contradictory, stances where required—a kind of strategic essentialism on the basis of necessity. His ideology was primarily influenced by Enlightenment, rationalism, and Russian socialism. Indeed, many of his arguments resonate with orthodox Marxism.

While Naicker had great regard for Tamil as a language and did see the Dravidian people as an older, separate race, he criticized any claims to authentic or divine Tamil. A utilitarian to the core, he saw language as a vehicle for both communication and progress, articulating his preference for Tamil in the language of "logic" and "functionalism." It is also significant to note that he saw the Brahmins' claim to Tamil as illegitimate and false. Citing Sanskrit as a bigoted language for possessing words such as *jati* (caste), *pathi vratha* (a devoted, chaste wife), *kanniga dhanam* (dowry), he argued that Tamil did not possess any equivalents of the same. In the same vein, however, he soundly criticized Tamil for possessing only the female words for widow and unfaithful woman, and added the male counterparts to the same. His internationalism extended to praising much of the West for its rationalism, colonialism, and socialism. In fact, there is little criticism of hierarchical structures other than caste created by Hinduism in his translated works: "...basing himself in rationalism, Ramasamy engaged in with Hinduism as a unified field of false beliefs" (Pandian 2007, 197). As Pandian suggests, Naicker saw the very flexibility of Hinduism as a suppressive Brahminical strategy which ostensibly coopted the opposition to caste citing various stories of "non-Brahmin" saints such as the *Alwars* and *Nayanmars* as well as those of "non-Brahmin," lower-caste and non-Hindu devotees, all of whom were accepted into the fold of Hinduism to create the illusion of benevolence.

Naicker, as Pandian states in his book, wanted to create a historic bloc of "Brahmin"-opposed interests and this included gender, labor, regional identity, language, and culture. Thus, we see the creation of the grand

and singular Other being reified and locked in oppositional narratives with multiple subject positions which, in their own turn, have been reified into a narrative of homogeneity. It is significant to note here that Pandian refers to Naicker's supporters as "converts" to his cause (Pandian 2007, 212) suggesting a certain millenarian zeal in this atheistic/rationalist movement. The fact of Naicker's radicalism and explosive disavowal of existing caste hierarchies along with his capacity for self-reflection and critique, especially when it came to the severe oppression and violence displayed against the "adi-Dravidars"/Dalits by Dravidian "upper" castes is undeniable. His criticism of the nation state and the impossibility of a "singular" Indian identity is also a crucial contribution to the articulation of subalternity. The centrality of orthodox Marxism, Enlightenment rationalism, and second-wave and Marxist feminist discourses are, of course, subject to the same criticisms that they have received in every other context in which these ideologies have been used. What is more significant, though, is that the absolute binarization of power and powerlessness is combined with the absence of any real engagement with the production of power and power structures. This creating of absolute binaries did not last very long, as the DK soon saw the split into the DMK headed by Annadurai, ironically after Naicker married a woman 40 years younger than him, eliciting severe moral criticism from many of his supporters.

We see the watering down of Naicker's radicalism very clearly as parties emerged out of what was a strictly social reform movement. We cannot tackle the vast movement of the DMK, AIDMK, and other fragmentations in this essay, but we will very briefly, in passing, consider some of the major changes that occurred with the rise of C. N. Annadurai and Mu. Karunanidhi as political leaders in the Tamil scene as displayed in their writing. Anna began as a vociferous supporter of the secessionist demand for Dravida Nadu, which was eventually withdrawn in light of "national interests" and replaced with a demand for federal powers. The fiercely atheistic stance that Naicker took was dropped in no uncertain terms when Anna articulated his "one family, one God" sentiments. He also focused on the language and is well known, like Karunanidhi, for his literary contributions to Tamil. Even more fervent than Naicker about what he termed "Hindi imperialism," he saw the Aryan–Dravidian divide as utterly irreconcilable and vociferously critiqued the idea of a monolithic nation. Anna also mitigated and calibrated the party's anti-"Brahmin" rhetoric and supported "Brahmin" and "non-Brahmin" concord as part of his political strategizing. Anna also drew connections between Bengal and Tamil Nadu, both culturally and intellectually, owing to Bengal's own anti-Hindi, regional nationalism. This is something we do not come across in E. V. R Naicker's own views, and it provides an interesting change in the cartographic imaginary of what constitutes "the North." We also see a distinct distancing from the radical feminism of E. V. R. Naicker from here on. Mu. Karunanidhi, in his literary work, often feminized Tamil and took it back to the older Tamil devotee-like articulations of Tamilparru. So it was that Mu. Karunanidhi, who took over DMK leadership in the 1970s and continues to hold it even today, moved even further away from Naicker's ideology.

The reason we have so cursorily glanced at post-E. V. R Naicker is simply to show the drastic changes both in ideology and politics, as well as the change in attitude toward Tamil-ness. The utilitarian functionalism that was so characteristic of Naicker's support for Tamil language and culture reframed itself into a discourse closer to the older assertions of Tamil nationalism, albeit without the radical edge. In both Annadurai's and Karunanidhi's time, we see a burgeoning of vociferous political propaganda through a film which would soon be immortalized by MGR, the leader of the AIDMK party. It was also in their time (1970) that the official invocation song *Tamilttay Vaalttu* was declared to be sung at all Government organizations, schools, and colleges, along with the renaming of Madras to Chennai. The "visible" markers of Tamil-ness were in place, but only in the shadow of severely diminished ideological markers.

Conclusion

In their articles on Neo-Brahminism and Dravidian Politics, Geetha and Rajadurai (1991, 1992, 1993, 1995) critique the present political system vociferously. They comment strongly on the "backward" castes as being repressive and hierarchical in a completely Brahminical mould. They describe backward caste casteism as a refracted ideology while Brahminism is the informing logic, the "origin" of the hegemonic power.

While the history of caste in India supports this view in many ways, it still remains both a linear and simplistic way of explaining the vagaries and machinations of power. If we consider the Nietzschean-influenced Foucauldian and Deleuzian understanding of power, we see that it is not only far more complex, but also that power is ultimately self-perpetuating and has multiple origins and trajectories of production that are then reified and internalized into subjects and "docile" bodies. To view the "Brahmin" and "non–Brahmin" as homogeneous, opposing categories which do not consider the fluidity of power is to engage in a certain kind of reductionism. Although scholars like Pandian, Geetha, and Rajadurai critique present-day non-Brahmin politics especially in reference to the Dalit condition and the problems within a homogenized non-Brahmin bloc where the Dalit is homo sacer par excellence, there is still a Brahminically inherited sense of hierarchy, as emphasized in the leadership of the AIADMK by a Brahmin woman, J. Jayalalitha, which negates the production of power and hegemonic constructions within "non-Brahminical" spaces, making them smooth moral spaces, creating an oversimplified discourse around subalternity. The minor here, then, is not really a carnivalesque or nomadic minor, capable of all sorts of fantastic lines of flight. His/her transgression is limited to the prescribed regulations on "how" to be a minor. The revolutionary potential of the minor, then, is a restricted one in the sense that the revolution is inscribed both within the singular "minor" identity and *against* a singular major one. There is no sense of the multiplicity of minor-ness in this kind of a discourse and, consequently, very little room for dialogue. While it must be noted that E. V. R Naicker was always open to dialogue and debate, albeit from a morally impregnable standpoint, much of the politics that followed was not so. In fact, in many ways, Naicker was himself a revolutionary minor, advocating fluidity and change and transgressing almost every hierarchical order that he came across. His unique oratorical ability and capacity for self-deprecatory humor makes him a carnivalesque figure, but the grotesque body, the real minor always defies reification. The minor can never be *a* movement, she is always many movements, resisting the violence of categorization. This did not happen with Naicker for obvious reasons, not least of which is his strident articulation of being a staunch utopian, with an ideal that was homogenizing and monolithic in many important ways.

I want to conclude with some thoughts from Anandhi's (2011) review of a Dalit-authored, semi-autobiographical book, *Sedal*. A story of a young woman who belongs to an untouchable performing community, Anandhi's reading offers a remarkably nuanced understanding of all the multiple possibilities that "being" a Dalit woman could mean. She teases out the complexities of caste positions and politics, particularly where she describes a fleeting moment of equal subservience experienced by the village Brahmin and *Sedal* to the rich *Vellala* landlord. Later on, we see the ultimate emasculation and disempowering of the rich upper-caste landlord who expresses his desire for *Sedal* but is rejected by her. Anandhi also writes of *Sedal*'s own prejudices, such as her refusal to accept certain kinds of food from a caste lower than hers, which confirm the nature of subalternity and minority. As Deleuze and Guattari note elsewhere in their work on Kafka, minor Literature does not necessarily spring from a new language. It is rather the creation of an autonomous and radical space *within* the major language. Anandhi also notes that many of the tragedies in Dalit lives are arbitrary, and beyond their control. There is no grand narrative of causality in this narrative of tragedy, and *Sedal*'s life is one of agency and assertion through a series of random chances. Born as a *Devadasi* and performer, we see that the very same agency that allows *Sedal* to be transgressive and envied by "respectable" women also serves to delegitimize and cripple her. As Anandhi correctly points out, power is often produced as well as limited by the same circumstances. The revolutionary, grotesque, nomadic, and abject are, thus, different facets of the minor. One cannot really exist without the other. To be able to escape in a "line of flight" that is transgressive, revolutionary, and joyous all at once, one must still pay the price of abjection and being grotesque, loathed, and expelled. In the course of this exploration it has also become clear that there can be no such thing as the "real" or "authentic" minor. Minor-ness defies any kind of reification and can disrupt major narratives *from* anywhere at any time. Just as the non-Brahmin cannot be identified as *the* minor, the Dalit too cannot own that identity, and the same applies to homogenizing categories of major-ness. What Anandhi's observations show us is that this particular production of literature is willing to acknowledge those multiplicities of subject positions. The story of *Sedal* reminds us that the minor does not always choose this abjection—it is often thrust upon her. To return to the beginning then, what *is* the minor? Is she a revolutionary, a glorious hero, a reject, a mouth sewed shut? I hope the discussions and arguments presented in this chapter, disparate though they may seem, uniformly suggest that the minor can be all, none, or even some, of these. The production of minor-ness lies in its fluidity and capacity to spread through the cracks. The story of minor *revolutions* is about allowing the abject back into the realm of the self, or at least begin a dialogue with it, to try to speak with the woman who has no language and to acknowledge that there are ways of speaking that no language understands.

Notes and Bibliography

Notes

1. *Vellala*: A relatively affluent non-Brahmin caste in Tamil Nadu.
2. Ramaswamy (1997), in her work, discusses the deification and divinization of the Tamil language, and traces the production of the Tamil devotee who sacrifices and martyrs himself for the cause of Tamil. The notions of chastity, femininity, and motherhood are closely intertwined with this divinization. Rangaswamy (2004) writes of the creation of the Dravidian martyr/hero and how his sacrifice of life is deified and becomes a marker of "Tamil-ness," making death the ultimate language.
3. *Malayalee* is the term for a person hailing from Kerala, a South Indian state.
4. *Telugu* is the term for person hailing from Andhra Pradesh, a South Indian state.

Bibliography

Agamben, G. 1999. *Remnants of Auschwitz: The Witness and the Archive.* New York: Zone Books.

———. 2002. *Remnants of Auschwitz: The Witness and the Archive.* Zone Books.

———. 2005. *State of Exception.* Chicago: University of Chicago Press.

Anandhi, S. 2011. "Beyond the Coherence of Identities: A Reading of *Sedal.*" *Economic and Political Weekly* XLVI (42): 27.

Bakhtin, M. 1984. *Rabelais and His World.* Translated from Russian by H. Iswolsky. Bloomington: Indiana University Press.

Balibar, E. 2005. "Difference, Otherness, Exclusion." *Parallax* 11 (1): 19–34.

Bataille, G. 1985. *Visions of Excess: Selected Writings, 1927–1939.* Translated from French by A. Stoekl. Minneapolis: University of Minnesota Press.

Bharathiar University. 2009. *Reflections: Essays and Speeches.* New Delhi: Macmillan India.

Benjamin, W. 1996. "Critique of Violence." In *Walter Benjamin: Selected Writings, Vol. 1: 1913–1926*, edited by M. P. Bullock and M. W. Jennigs. Harvard: Harvard University Press.

Chatterjee P. 2004. *The Politics of the Governed: Reflections on Popular Politics in Most of the World*. New Delhi: Permanent Black.

Cheran R. 1992. "Cultural Politics of Tamil Nationalism." *South Asia Bulletin* XII (1): 42.

Deleuze, G. and F. Guattari. 1986. *Kafka: Toward a Minor Literature*. Translated from French by D. Polan. Minneapolis: University of Minnesota Press.

———. 2004. *A Thousand Plateaus*, 2nd edn. London: The Continuum Publishing Company.

Foucault, M. 1980. *Power/Knowledge: Selected Interviews and Other Writings 1972–1977*, edited by C. Gordon. New York: Pantheon Books.

———. 2002. *The Order of Things: An Archaeology of the Human Sciences*. London: Routledge.

Geetha, V. and S. V. Rajadurai. 1991. "Dravidian Politics: End of an Era." *Economic and Political Weekly*, June 29: 1591.

———1992. "'Off With Their Heads': Suppression of Dissent in Tamil Nadu." *Economic and Political Weekly*, June 6: 1184.

———. 1993. "Neo Brahminism: An Intentional Fallacy?." *Economic and Political Weekly*. January 16–23: 129.

———. 1995. "One Hundred Years of Brahminitude: Arrival of Annie Besant." *Economic and Political Weekly*. July 15: 1768.

———. 2008. *Towards a Non-Brahmin Millennium: From Iyothee Thass to Periyar*, 2nd edn. Calcutta: Samya.

Hardgrave, R. L. Jr. 1964–65. "The DMK and the Politics of Tamil Nationalism." *Pacific Affairs* 37 (4): 396.

Karthikeyan, D., S. Rajangam, and H. Gorringe. 2012. "Dalit Political Imagination and Replication in Contemporary Tamil Nadu." *Economic and Political Weekly* XLVII (36): 30.

Kristeva, J. 1982. *Powers of Horror: An Essay on Abjection*. Translated from French by L. Roudiez. New York: Columbia University Press.

More, J. B. P. 2009. *Rise and Fall of the "Dravidian" Justice Party, 1916–1946*. Kerala: Kannur Institute for Research in Social Sciences and Humanities.

Morson, G. S. and C. Emerson (eds). 1990. *Mikhail Bakhtin: Creation of a Prosaics*. Stanford: Stanford University Press.

Nietzsche, F. 2008. *The Complete Works of Friedrich Nietzsche*, edited by O. Levy. Gadow Press.

Pandian, M. S. S. 2007. *Brahmin and Non Brahmin: Genealogies of the Tamil Political Present*. New Delhi: Permanent Black.

———. 2009. "Nation Impossible." *Economic and Political Weekly* XLIV (10): 65.

Radhakrishnan, R. 2007. *Between Identity and Location: The Cultural Politics of Theory*. New Delhi: Orient Longman.

Ram, K. 1995. "Rationalism, Cultural Nationalism and the Reform of Body Politics: Minority Intellectuals of the Tamil Catholic Community." *Contributions to Indian Sociology* 29(1–2): 291–318.

Ramaswamy, S. 1997. *Passions of the Tongue: Language Devotion in Tamil India 1891–1970.* California: University of California Press.

———. 2004. *The Lost Land of Lemuria: Fabulos Geographies, Catastrophic Histories.* California: University of California Press.

Rangaswamy, N. 2004. "Making a Dravidian Hero: The Body and Identity Politics in the Dravidian Movement." In *Confronting the Body: The Politics of Physicality in Colonial and Post-Colonial India*, edited by S. Sen and J. H. Mills. London: Anthem Press.

Subramanian, N. 2005. "The Political Formation of Cultures: The South Asian Experience." *Economic and Political Weekly*, August 27: 3821.

Tripathy and Raghavan. forthcoming. *Corporeal Cosmopolitanism: The "Right" of Desire.*

Veeramani, K. (ed.). 2005. *Collected Works of Periyar E. V. R*, 3rd edn. Chennai: The Periyar Self-Respect Propaganda Institution.

Venkatachalam, M. S. and M. Natarajan (eds). 2005. *Arignar Anna's Essays, Editorials, Epistles and Satires.* Chennai: Tamil Arasi Publications.

Vaitheespara, R. 2009. "Maraimalai Atigal and the Genealogy of the Tamilian Creed." *Economic and Political Weekly* XLIV (14): 45.

———. 2012. "Reinscribing Religion as Nation: Navenar Caivar (Modern Saivaites) and the Dravidian Movement." *South Asia: A Journal of South Asian Studies.* DOI: 10.1080/00856401: 702.

About the Editors and Contributors

Editors

Jyotirmaya Tripathy is Associate Professor in the Department of Humanities and Social Sciences, Indian Institute of Technology, Madras, India. His broad area of interest is cultural studies, particularly in the questions of identity and representation. He has published in these areas in journals like *Social Semiotics, Development in Practice, Journal of Developing Societies, International Journal of Cultural Studies, Journal of Third World Studies*, etc.

Sudarsan Padmanabhan received his PhD from University of South Florida and worked at Kenyon College, Ohio, USA, before joining the Department of Humanities and Social Sciences, Indian Institute of Technology, Madras in 2007. He specializes in social and political philosophy, and Indian philosophy and culture. His research interest lies in the confluence of law, democracy, and ethics in the public sphere. He has published in these domains in various journals and edited volumes including the *Routledge Handbook of Cosmopolitanism Studies*.

Contributors

Apostolos Agnantopoulos is a research associate at the Centre for International Studies, Dublin City University. After completing a PhD from the University of Birmingham, he taught as a lecturer at the University of

Westminster and Dublin City University. His research interests lie in the field of Greek foreign policy, the Cyprus conflict, EU external relations, and Europeanization.

Gëzim Alpion holds a bachelor's degree from Cairo University and a PhD from Durham University, UK. He is currently lecturer in Sociology at the University of Birmingham in England. He is considered "the most authoritative English language author" on Mother Teresa. His most well-known study to date is *Mother Teresa: Saint or Celebrity?* (2007).

Lajwanti Chatani is a professor in political theory at the Maharaja Sayajirao University of Baroda, and a convener of the Forum on Contemporary Theory, Vadodara, India. She is joint editor of the *Journal of Contemporary Thought*. She has edited a special issue of the journal (Vol. 27, Summer 2008) on "Revisiting the Political." She has also contributed to curriculum development and course materials pertaining to political theory at the Indira Gandhi National Open University and the National Council of Educational Research and Training, New Delhi.

Barbara Franz (PhD, Syracuse University) is a professor of political science. Her research interests juxtapose the phenomenon of mass migrations and refugee movements and what they mean for the stability of nations, the increasing potential of culture clashes within societies, and the root causes of migration movements. Her book *Uprooted and Unwanted: Bosnian Refugees in Austria and the United States* (2005) focuses on the experience of Bosnian refugees, especially women, in two host countries with vastly different settlement and social welfare policies. Her articles have appeared in journals such as *New Political Science, Journal of Ethnic and Migration Studies, European Journal of Women Studies, Feminist Review, AWR Bulletin*, etc.

Abdoulaye Gueye is professor of sociology at the University of Ottawa. He is the author of *Les Africains Africains en France*, African Intellectuals in France (2001) and *Aux Negres de France la Patrie non Reconnaissance*, To the Negroes of France the Ungrateful Motherland (2010). He has also (co)edited several books and journal issues. His work on blackness in the French context has appeared in several journals including *The Du

Bois Review, Comparative Studies of South Asia, Africa and the Middle East, and *French Cultural Studies.* In 2009, he was Fellow at the W. E. B. Du Bois Institute at Harvard University.

Peter Hervik holds a PhD in Social Anthropology from the University of Copenhagen, and is currently a professor at the Centre for the Study of Migration and Diversity (CoMID) at Aalborg University. Hervik has conducted research among the Yucatec Maya of Mexico and in Denmark on issues of identity, categorization, neoracism, neonationalism, ethnicity, multiculturalism, tolerance, and the news media. Besides teaching at the University of Copenhagen, Hervik has taught at the department of social anthropology, University of Oslo, minority studies, University of Copenhagen, International Migration and Ethnic Relations (IMER), and Malmö University, and recently completed six months as a visiting professor at Hitotsubashi University, Tokyo.

Mohamed Mehdi is associate professor of philosophy at Oakton Community College, near Chicago, USA. He received his PhD in philosophy from McGill University in 2008. His interests are in ancient political philosophy and in the political thought of 20th-century anti-colonial movements, particularly in India. He has also written and presented on the relevance of the humanities in higher education today, on the role of emotion in political action, and on Muslim identity in the West after the "War on Terror."

Malavika Menon is currently a researcher at the Jawaharlal Nehru Memorial Fund, New Delhi. She is pursuing her PhD in the study of minority educational institutions in India, from the Centre for Political Studies, Jawaharlal Nehru University. She undertook a review of the organizer for her MPhil, attempting to understand ideas of nationalism and secularism as reflected in the text.

Shireen Mirza is an Assistant Professor at the department of humanities and social sciences, Indian Institute of Technology, Madras. After completing her PhD from the Department of Anthropology and Sociology at the School of Oriental and African Studies, she carried out her postdoctoral research as part of the TISS–Max Planck "Urban Aspirations" project. Her research interests lie in areas of social anthropology of religion and identity, urbanization, and development, and globalization and modernity.

Bishnu N. Mohapatra is a professor at Azim Premji University, Bangalore, India. He has taught politics at the Centre for Political Studies at Jawaharlal Nehru University and University of Delhi, India, and has held visiting faculty positions at the University of Kyoto, Japan, and the National University of Singapore. He headed the governance portfolio of the Ford Foundation's South Asia office at New Delhi from 2002 to 2010. He is also a well-known Indian poet who writes in Oriya.

Ulf Mörkenstam is associate professor of political science at Stockholm University. His main fields of research are political theory and Swedish political history. In political theory, he has especially focused upon the normative debate on minority rights. He has written extensively on Swedish Sámi politics, and migration policy.

Paul Mutsaers is working as a PhD candidate at the Tilburg School of Humanities, Tilburg University (The Netherlands), and at the Police Academy of The Netherlands. He is working on a dissertation about ethnic diversity among the Dutch police.

Anjana Raghavan is a final year doctoral scholar in the department of humanities and social sciences, Indian Institute of Technology, Madras. She has a master's degree in cultural studies from Goldsmiths College, University of London, with a focus on gender and sexuality. Her research interests include the politics of corporeality, affect, and belonging, as well as re-imagining solidarities in the margins, particularly in South Asia.

Arie de Ruijter is professor of social sciences at Tilburg University. His research interests include issues of social cohesion, organization culture, and development cooperation. He is the dean of the Tilburg School of Humanities, chair of the National Commission for Development Cooperation, and director of the Centre for Global Citizenship (Amsterdam).

Hans Siebers is associate professor at the Tilburg School of Humanities, Tilburg University, The Netherlands. His research focus is on ethnic identity, ethnic relations, and ethnic inequality in work and education settings. His main quest is to discover the factors and processes that fuel the erection of ethnic boundaries in such settings, using both ethnographic and quantitative research strategies. He is also program director of the international Master Management of Cultural Diversity.

Sherrill Stroschein is a senior lecturer (associate professor) at University College London, where she directs the program in democracy and comparative politics. She was previously at Ohio University and the Harvard Academy for international and area studies. Her research examines the politics of ethnicity in democracies with mixed populations.

Index